H. H. Wilson

The Vishnu Purana - a System of Hindu Mythology and Tradition

Translated from the Original Sanskrit

H. H. Wilson

The Vishnu Purana - a System of Hindu Mythology and Tradition
Translated from the Original Sanskrit

ISBN/EAN: 9783741182761

Manufactured in Europe, USA, Canada, Australia, Japa

Cover: Foto ©ninafisch / pixelio.de

Manufactured and distributed by brebook publishing software
(www.brebook.com)

H. H. Wilson

The Vishnu Purana - a System of Hindu Mythology and Tradition

THE

VISHŃU PURÁŃA:

A SYSTEM

OF

HINDU MYTHOLOGY AND TRADITION.

TRANSLATED

FROM THE ORIGINAL SANSKRIT,

AND

ILLUSTRATED BY NOTES

DERIVED CHIEFLY FROM OTHER PURÁŃAS.

BY THE LATE

H. H. WILSON, M.A., F.R.S.,

BODEN PROFESSOR OF SANSKRIT IN THE UNIVERSITY OF OXFORD,
ETC., ETC.

EDITED BY

FITZEDWARD HALL.

VOL. III.

LONDON:

TRÜBNER & CO., 60, PATERNOSTER ROW.

1866.

VISHŃU PURÁŃA.

BOOK III.

CHAPTER I.

Account of the several Manus and Manwantaras. Swárochisha, the second Manu: the divinities, the Indra, the seven Ŕishis, of his period, and his sons. Similar details of Auttami, Támasa, Raivata, Chákshusha, and Vaivaswata. The forms of Vishńu, as the preserver, in each Manwantara. The meaning of Vishńu.

MAITREYA.—The disposition of the earth and of the ocean, and the system of the sun and the planets, the creation of the gods and the rest, the origin of the Ŕishis, the generation of the four castes, the production of brute creatures, and the narratives of Dhruva and Prahláda, have been fully related by thee, my venerable preceptor. I am now desirous to hear from you the series of all the Manwantaras, as well as an account of those who preside over the respective periods, with Śakra, the king of the gods, at their head.

PARÁŚARA.—I will repeat to you, Maitreya, in their order, the different Manwantaras,—those which are past, and those which are to come.

The first Manu was Swáyambhuva; then came Swárochisha; then, Auttami;* then, Támasa; then, Raivata;

* Some of my MSS. have Uttama. See note 2 at p. 5, *infra*.

then, Chákshusha: these six Manus have passed away. The Manu who presides over the seventh Manwantara, which is the present (period), is Vaivaswata, the son of the Sun.*

The period of Swáyambhuva Manu, in the beginning of the Kalpa,† has already been described by me, together with the gods, Ŕishis, (and other personages) who then flourished.[1] I will now, therefore, enumerate the presiding gods, Ŕishis, and sons of the Manu, in the Manwantara of Swárochisha.[2] The deities of this period (or the second Manwantara) were the classes

[1] The gods were said to be the Yámas (Vol. I., p. 109); the Ŕishis were Marichi, Angiras, &c. (Vol. I., p. 110, note 2); and the sons were Priyavrata and Uttánapáda (Vol. I., pp. 107, 108). The Váyu adds, to the Yamas, the Ajitas, who share with the former, it observes, sacrificial offerings. The Matsya, Padma, Brahma Puráńas, and Hari Vańśa,‡ substitute, for the sons, the grandsons, of Swáyambhuva, — Agnidhra and the rest (Vol. II., pp 101, 102).

[2] This Manu, according to the legend of his birth in the Márkańdeya Puráńa,§ was the son of Swarochis, so named from the splendour of his appearance, when born, and who was the son of the nymph Varúthini, by the Gandharva Kali.|| The text, in another place, makes him a son of Priyavrata.¶

* Compare the *Laws of the Mánavas*, I., 61, 62.

† The present Kalpa, the Váráha, from *varáha*, 'boar'. See Vol. I., pp. 58, 59.

‡ *Sl.* 415.

§ Chapter LXIII.

|| I find Kála.

¶ See p. 11, note ‡, *infra*. According to the *Bhágavata-puráńa*, VIII., I., 19, Swárochisha was son of Agni.

called Párávatas and Tushitas;[1]* and the king of the gods was the mighty Vipaśchit.† The seven Ŕishis[2]

[1] The Váyu gives the names of the individuals of these two classes, consisting, each, of twelve. It furnishes, also, the nomenclature of all the classes of divinities, and of the sons of the Manus, in each Manwantara. According to the same authority, the Tushitas were the sons of Kratu:‡ the Bhágavata calls them the sons of Tushitá by Vedaśiras.§ The divinities of each period are, according to the Váyu, those to whom offerings of the Soma juice and the like are presented collectively.

[2] The Váyu describes the Ŕishis of each Manwantara as the sons, or, in some cases, the descendants, in a direct line, of the seven sages, Atri, Angiras, Bhŕigu, Kaśyapa, Pulaha, Pulastya, and Vasishtha: with some inconsistency; for Kaśyapa, at least, did not appear, himself, until the seventh Manwantara. In the present series,‖ Úrja is the son of Vasishtha; Stambha springs from Kaśyapa; Práńa, from Bhŕigu; Ŕishabha descends from Angiras; Dattoli is the son of Pulastya; Niśchara springs from Atri; and Arvarívat is the son of Pulaha. The Brahma Puráńa and Hari Vaḿśa¶ have a rather different list, or, Aurva, Stambha, Kaśyapa,

* We read, Vol. II., p. 27, after an enumeration of twelve names: "These, who, in the Chákshusha Manwantara, were the gods called Tushitas, were called the twelve Ádityas, in the Manwantara of Vaivaswata." But our text, as now appears, places the Tushitas in the second Manwantara, not in the sixth: see p. 19, *infra*. Nor, according to the *Váyu-puráńa*, were they Vishńu, Śakra, &c.

† The *Bhágavata-puráńa*, VIII., I., 20, gives Rochana as the Indra of the second Manwantara or Patriarchate.

‡ Tushitá, according to the same authority, was their mother, as in our text, p. 17, *infra*.

§ So, rather, the *Bhágavata* appears to imply: VIII., I., 21.

‖ Professor Wilson seems to have followed, here, his own MSS. of the *Váyu-puráńa*, exclusively; and they must differ greatly from those to which I, after him, have access. Instead of Úrja occurs, in these MSS., what looks like a corruption of Turya or Úrva; for Práńa, Dróńa; for Dattoli, Dattátri; for Niśchara, Niśchala; and, for Arvarívat, Dhávat.

¶ *Śl.* 417.

were Urja, Stambha,* Práńa, Dattoli,† Ŕishabha, Niś-

Práńa, Bŕihaspati, Chyavana, and Dattoli:‡ but the origin of part of this difference is nothing more than an imperfect quotation from the Váyu Puráńa; the two first, Aurva and Stambha, being specified as the son of Vasishtha and the descendant of Kaśyapa, and then the parentage of the rest being omitted: to complete the seven, therefore, Kaśyapa becomes one of them. Some other errors of this nature occur in these two works, and from the same cause,—a blundering citation§ of the Váyu, which is named as their authority:

एते महर्षयस्तात वायुप्रोक्ता महात्मनः ।

A curious peculiarity, also, occurs in these mistakes. They are confined to the first eight Manwantaras. The Brahma Puráńa omits all details of the last six; and the Hari Vaḿśa inserts them fully and correctly, agreeably to the authority of the Váyu. It looks, therefore, as if the compiler of the Hari Vaḿśa had followed the Brahma, as far as it went, right or wrong, but had had recourse to the original Váyu Puráńa, when the Brahma failed him. Dattoli is sometimes written Dattoni and Dattotri; and the latter appears to have been the case with the copy of the Hari Vaḿśa employed by M. Langlois, who makes one of the Ŕishis of this Manwantara, "le pénitent Atri." He is not without countenance in some such reading; for the Padma Puráńa changes the name to Dattátreya, no doubt suggested by Datta-atri. Dattátreya, however, is the son of Atri; whilst the Váyu calls the person of the text the son of Pulastya. There can be no doubt,

* Stambha is an equally common reading in my MSS.

† So read three of my MSS. Variants are Dattoni, Dattori, Dattobhi, Dattokti, Dantoli, Dantobhi, and Dambholi. See, further, Vol. I., p. 154, note ‡.

‡ In MSS. of the *Brahma-puráńa* I find Stamba and Dattoni. The Calcutta edition of the *Harivaḿśa* has Stambo, Káśyapa, and Dattoni.

§ In *Ll.* 418.

|| Vol. I., p. 38.

chara,* and Arvarivat;† and Chaitra, Kimpurusha, and others were the Manu's sons.[1]

In the third period, or Manwantara of Auttami,[2] Su-

therefore, of the correct reading; for the son of Pulastya is Dattoli.‡ (Vol. I., p. 154.)

[1] The Váyu agrees with the text in these names, adding seven§ others. The Bhágavata has a different series.|| The Padma has four other names: Nabha, Nabhasya, Prasriti, Bhavana. The Brahma has ten names, including two of these, and several of the names of the Rishis of the tenth Manwantara. The Matsya has the four names of the Padma for the sons of the Manu, and gives seven others, Havindhra, Sukrita, Múrti, Apas, Jyotis, Aya, Smrita (the names of the Brahma), as the seven Prajápatis of this period, and sons of Vasishtha. The sons of Vasishtha, however, belong to the third Manwantara, and bear different appellations. There is, no doubt, some blundering, here, in all the books except the Váyu and those which agree with it.

[2] The name occurs Auttami, Auttama, and Uttama. The Bhágavata¶ and Váyu agree with our text (p. 11, *infra*), in making him a descendant from Priyavrata. The Márkańdeya calls him the son of Uttama,** the son of Uttánapáda;†† and this appears to be the correct genealogy, both from our text and the Bhágavata.‡‡

* One MS. gives Nischira.

† The much more frequent lection known to me is Urvarivat.

‡ There is, I incline to think, room for very grave doubt as to both these points. See note † in p. 4, *supra*.

§ I do not count so many; and those that I find are very corruptly written.

|| At VIII., I., 20, it says there were seven, but names only Urja and Stambha. Burnouf melts these two names into one.

¶ It calls him Priyavrata's son: VIII., I., 23.

** LXXII., 39. Auttama is the grandson's name, in the *Márkańdeya-puráńa*.

†† LXXIX., 3. Suruchi is there said to be Uttama's mother. For the same parentage, see Vol. I., p. 159, of the present work.

‡‡ Not from the *Bhágavata*, certainly. See note ¶, in this page. As to our text, see note ‡ at p. 11, *infra*.

śánti* was the Indra, the king of the gods: the orders of whom were the Sudhámans,† Satyas, Śivas, Pradarśanas,‡ and Vaśavartins;[1] § each of the five orders consisting of twelve (divinities). The seven sons of Vasishṭha were the seven Ṛishis;[2] and Aja,‖ Paraśu,¶

[1] The Brahma and Hari Vaṁśa** have, in place of these, the Bhánus; but the Váyu and Márkaṇḍeya†† concur with the text.‡‡

[2] All the authorities agree in this; but the Brahma and Hari Vaṁśa§§ appear to furnish a different series, also; or even a third, according to the French translation:‖‖ 'Dans le troisième Manwantara parurent, comme Saptarchis, les fils de Vasichṭha, de son nom appelés *Vâsichṭhas*, les fils d'Hiraṅyagarbha, et les illustres enfans d'Oûrdja. The text is:

वसिष्ठपुत्राः सप्तासन्वासिष्ठा इति विश्रुताः ।
हिरण्यगर्भस्य सुता वौर्जा¶¶ नाम सुतेजसः ॥

The meaning of which is: "There were (in the first Manwantara) seven celebrated sons of Vasishṭha, who (in the third Manwantara) were sons of Brahmá (i. e., Ṛishis), the illustrious posterity

* Satyajit, according to the *Bhágavata-puráṇa*, VIII., I., 24.

† Five MSS. have Swadhámans.

‡ Pratardanas represents the reading of two MSS.

§ Three MSS. exhibit Vaṁsavartins. Professor Wilson put "Vasavartis".

‖ In three MSS. Prajas occurs.

¶ A single MS. reads Parabhu.

** *Śl.* 625.

†† In my three MSS. I find Pratardanas, as in the Calcutta edition, instead of Pradarśanas. The Calcutta edition, at variance with my copies, has Swadhámans, for Sudhámans.

‡‡ The *Bhágavata-puráṇa*, VIII., I., 24, names the Satyas, Vedaśrutas, and Bhadras. Also see note * at p. 17, *infra*.

§§ *Śl.* 429.

‖‖ Vol. I., p. 38.

¶¶ The Calcutta edition reads ऊर्जा.

Divya, and others were the sons of the Manu.[1]

The Surúpas,* Haris, Satyas, and Sudhís[2] † were the classes of gods, each comprising twenty-seven, in the period of Támasa, (the fourth Manu).[3] Śibi‡ was the

---

of Úrjá. We have already seen that Úrjá was the wife of Vasishṭha, by whom she had seven sons, Rajas," &c. (see Vol. I., p. 155), in the Swáyambhuva Manwantara; and these were born again, as the Ṛishis of the third period. The names of these persons, according to the Matsya and Padma, are, however, very different from those of the sons of Vasishṭha given in Vol. I., p. 155, or, Kaukuṅḍihi, Kuruṅḍi, Dálbhya, Śankha, Praváhita, Mita, and Sammita.§

[1] The Váyu adds ten other names to those of the text. The Brahma gives ten altogether different. The Bhágavata|| and Padma have, each, a separate nomenclature.

[2] Of these the Brahma and Hari Vaṁśa¶ notice only the Satyas; the Matsya and Padma have only Sádhyas. The Váyu, Bhágavata,** Kúrma, and Márkaṅḍeya†† agree with the text.

[3] He is the son of Priyavrata, according to the text,‡‡ the Váyu, &c. The Márkaṅḍeya§§ has a legend of his birth by a doe;

---

* One MS. has Swarúpas. † Swadhís is the reading of one MS.

‡ Śikhi is, in my MSS., almost as common a lection. And herewith agrees the *Márkaṅḍeya-puráṇa*, LXXIV., 58. Triśikha is the name in the *Bhágavata-puráṇa*, VIII., 1., 26.

§ I have put Dálbhya for "Dalaya", on manuscript authority. The *Bhágavata-puráṇa*, VIII., 1., 24, names only Pramada, out of the seven; and he is not of the family as detailed in IV., 1., 41, 42. See Vol. I., p. 155, note 3.

|| VIII., 1., 23: Pavana, Sṛinjaya, Yajnahotra, and others unnamed.

¶ *Śl.* 427.

** I find—VIII., 1., 28, 29—the Satyakas, Haris, Víras, and Vaidhṛitis.

†† LXXIV., 57.

‡‡ See p. 11, note ‡, *infra*; also, p. 17, text and notes ‡ and §.

§§ Chapter LXXIV.

Indra, also designated by his performance of a hundred sacrifices, (or named Śatakratu*). The seven Ŕishis were Jyotirdhámán, Přithu, Kávya, Chaitra, Agni, Vanaka,† and Pívara.[1] The sons of Támasa were the mighty kings Nara, Khyáti, Śántahaya,‡ Jánujangha, and others.[2]

---

and, from his being begotten in dark tempestuous weather (तमस्), he derives his name.§

[1] Severally, according to the Váyu, the progeny of Bhŕigu, Kaśyapa, Angiras, Pulastya, Atri, Vasishtha, and Pulaha. There is considerable variety in some of the names. Thus, the Matsya has Kavi, Přithu, Agni, Akapi, Kapi, Jalpa,‖ Dhímat. The Hari Vaḿśa¶ has Kávya, Přithu, Agni, Jahnu, Dhátri,** Kapívat, Akapívat. For the two last the Váyu reads Gátra and Vanapítha. The son of Pulaha is in his place (Vol. I., p. 155, note 1),—Arvarívat or Vanakapívat. Gátra is amongst the sons of Vasishtha (Vol. I., p. 155). The Váyu is, therefore, probably, most correct, although our text, in regard to these two denominations, admits of no doubt:†† चरिर्वनकस्तथा पीवरश्च ।‡‡

[2] The Váyu, &c. agree with the text; the Váyu naming eleven. The Brahma, Matsya, and Padma have a series of ten names, Sutapas, Tapomúla, &c., of which seven are the Ŕishis of the twelfth Manwantara.§§

---

* This parenthesis was supplied by the Translator.

† Five of my MSS. read Varada. Two of my MSS. of the *Márkańdeya-puráńa* have Vanaka; the third, Varuńa. The Calcutta edition, LXXIV., 59, gives Valaka.

‡ In one MS. is Śántibaya; and, in one, Śántiharya.

§ The *Bhágavata-puráńa*, VIII., 1., 27, represents him as brother of Uttama.

‖ Corrected from the printer's "Salpa".   ¶ *Śl.* 426.

** The Calcutta edition has Janya and Dhámen.

†† See, however, note † in this page.

‡‡ The *Bhágavata-puráńa*, VIII., 1., 28, names Jyotirdhámán only.

§§ Agreeably to the *Bhágavata-puráńa*, VIII., 1., 27, they were ten in number, of whom it specifies Přithu, Khyáti, Nara, and Ketu.

In the fifth interval, the Manu was Raivata;[1] the Indra was Vibhu; the classes of gods, consisting of fourteen each, were the Amitábhas, Abhútarajasas,* Vaikuńthas, and Sumedhasas;[2]† the seven Rishis were

---

[1] Raivata, as well as his three predecessors, is regarded, usually, as a descendant of Priyavrata.‡ The Márkańdeya§ has a long legend of his birth, as the son of King Durgama by the nymph Revatí, sprung from the constellation Revatí, whom Ritavách, a Muni, caused to fall from heaven. Her radiance became a lake on Mount Kumuda, thence called Raivataka; and from it appeared the damsel, who was brought up by Pramucha Muni. Upon the marriage of Revatí, the Muni, at her request, restored the asterism to its place in the skies.

[2] The Brahma inserts, of these, only the Abhútarajasas, with

---

* Two MSS. have Ábhútaramas; two, Ábhútarayas; both which words look very like depravations of the reading in all my other copies, to-wit, Ábhútarajas. The ordinary reading of the line containing this term is:

अमिताभाभूतरयो वैकुण्ठाः सुमेधसः ।

That the first two names must be taken as welded into a compound embodying Ábhútarajas is attempted to be shown in note ‖ to the next page. See, further, note ¶, p. 17, *infra*. And hence the "Abhútarajasas" — *i. e.*, Abhútarajasas — of Professor Wilson may be open to correction, as regards its first syllable. Moreover, on the assumption that his MSS. were like mine, he has substituted the longer ending of the word for the shorter. See Vol. II., p. 101, note *; and p. 107, note ‡.

The Sanskrit scholar will have noticed, that, other considerations permitting, the line just quoted might yield Bhútarajas. The reading, unquestionably, of the *Bhágavata-puráńa*, VIII., V., 3, omits the vowel at the beginning. It is Bhútarayas; and it involves a corruption, I take it, as to its y, such as we have in Ábhútarayas. The *Márkańdeya-puráńa*, LXXV., 71, has, in my three MSS., Ábhútanayas or Bhútanayas, which, as could be shown, may easily have grown out of Ábhútarajas. The Calcutta edition exhibits Bhúpatis!

† In the singular, Sumedhas. Three MSS agree in reading Susumedhases.

‡ The *Bhágavata-puráńa*, VIII., V., 2, calls him uterine brother of Támasa. And see p. 11, note ‡, *infra*.

§ Chapter LXXV.

Hiraṅyaroman, Vedaśrí,* Urdhwabáhu, Vedabáhu,† Sudháman,‡ Parjanya, and Mahámuni.[1]§ The sons of

---

the remark, that 'they were of like nature (with their name):'

देवाश्चाभूतरजसस्तथाप्रकृतयः स्मृताः ।

i. e., they were exempt from the quality of passion. M. Langlois,¶ in rendering the parallel passage of the Hari Vaṁśa,** has confounded the epithet and the subject: 'dont les dieux furent les Pracŕitis, dépourvus de colère et de passion.' He is, also, at a loss what to do with the terms Páriplava and Raibhya, in the following passage, पारिप्लवाश्च रैभ्याश्च,†† asking: 'Qu'est-ce que Páriplava? qu'est-ce que Rébhya?' If he had had the commentary at hand, these questions would have been unnecessary: they are there said to be two classes of divinities: पारिप्लवो रैभ्यश्च देवतागणविशेषौ ।‡‡

[1] There is less variety in these names than usual.§§ Vedabáhu

---

* Devaśri, according to a single MS.

† In three MSS., Devabáhu.

‡ Two MSS. have Swadháman.

§ The *Bhágavata-puráńa*, VIII., V., 3, says that they were, with others, Hiraṅyaroman, Vedaśiras, and Úrdhwabáhu.

‖ The Sanskrit allows us to take the word as Ábhútarajases; meaning, perhaps, 'endowed with activity — *rajas* — as far as that possessed by the Bhútas.' See Vol. I., p. 83; and Vol. II., p. 74, note 2.

The *Váyu-puráńa* speaks of the Amŕitábhas and Ábhútarajas:

अमृताभाभूतरजा विकुण्ठाः सुसुमेधसः ।

For, just below this, it has the line:

इत्येतानीह नामानि चाभूतरजसं विदुः ।

On now comparing note * in the last page with note ¶, at p. 17, *infra*, it will be seen, that the gods under discussion were characterised by their possession, not want, of activity. In the latter passage here referred to, all Professor Wilson's MSS., including those now at Oxford, have, like my own, संभूतो राजसैः, or else संभूतो मानसैः.

¶ Vol. I, p. 39.

** *Śl.* 432:

देवाश्चाभूतरजसस्तथा प्रकृतयोऽपरे ।

†† *Śl.* 432.

‡‡ Of the gods of the fifth Manwantara the *Bhágavata-puráńa*, VIII., V., 3, 4, particularises the Bhútarayas and Vaikuńt́has only. See note * in the preceding page.

§§ See the *Márkańd́eya-puráńa*, LXXV., 73, 74.

Raivata were Balabandhu, Susambhávya,* Satyaka, and other valiant kings.†

These four Manus, Swárochisha, Auttami,‡ Támasa, and Raivata, were, all, descended from Priyavrata, who, in consequence of propitiating Vishńu by his devotions,§ obtained these rulers of the Manwantaras for his posterity.

Chákshusha was the Manu of the sixth period,[1] in

---

is read Devabáhu; Sudháman, Satyanetra; and Mahámuni, Muni, Yajus, Vásishtha, and Yadudhra. According to the Váyu, those of the text are, respectively, of the lineage of Angiras, Bhrigu, Vasishtha, Pulastya, Atri, Pulaha, and Kaśyapa. There is considerable variety in the names of the Manu's sons.

[1] Chákshusha, according to the best authorities, descended from Dhruva (see Vol. I., p. 177): but the Márkańdeya has a legend of his birth as the son of a Kshattriya named Anamitra; of his being exchanged, at his birth, for the son of Viśránta Rája, and being brought up, by the prince, as his own; of his revealing the business, when a man, and propitiating Brahmá by his devotions, in consequence of which, he became a Manu. In his former birth, he was born from the eye of Brahmá, whence his name, from Chakshus, 'the eye.'||

---

* Sambhávya is the reading of five MSS.; Susambhávya, that of one.

† Only Arjuna and Balivindhya are named in the *Bhágavata-puráńa*, VIII., V., 2.

‡ Uttama, as before, is here a variant. The *Vishńu-puráńa* is at odds with itself, if it here derives Auttami from Priyavrata,—not from Uttánapáda. See Vol. I. p. 159: also, p. 5, note ¶; p. 7, note ||; p. 8, note §; p. 9, note ‡, *supra*.

"Descended from Priyavrata" translates प्रियव्रतान्वयाः; and "for his posterity", आत्मवंशजान्. We may render: "one in lineage with Priyavrata"; but hardly, considering the context, "as his kindred", instead of "for his posterity". Uttánapáda and Priyavrata were brothers.

§ *Tapas*, 'austerity'.

|| Compare the *Bhágavata-puráńa*, VIII., V., 7.

which the Indra was Manojava:* the five classes of gods† were the Ádyas,‡ Prastútas,§ Bhavyas, Príthugas,‖ and the magnanimous Lekhas, eight of each:[1]¶ Sumedhas, Virajas, Havishmat, Uttama, Madhu,** Abhináman,†† and Sahishńu were the seven sages.[2] The kings of the earth, the sons of Chákshusha, were the

---

[1] The authorities agree as to the number, but differ as to the names; reading, for Ádyas, Áryas and Ápyas;‡‡ for Prastútas, Prabhútas and Prasútas; for Príthugas, Príthukas and Príthusas; and, which is a more wide deviation, Ribhus for Bhavyas. M. Langlois§§ omits the Prasútas, and inserts Divaukasas; but the latter, meaning 'divinities,' is only an epithet. The Hari Vaṁśa ‖‖ has:

आद्याः प्रसूता भव्याः पृथुगाश्च दिवौकसः । ¶¶
लेखा नाम महाराज पञ्च देवगणाः स्मृताः ॥

The comment adds: दिवौकस इति सर्वेषां विशेषणम् ।

[2] The Váyu reads Sudháman,*** for the first name; Unnata, for Uttama; and Abhimána, for Abhináman.††† The latter occurs

---

* Mantradruma: *Bhágavata-puráńa*, VIII., V., 8.

† See note * at p. 8, *supra*.

‡ One MS. has Áryas.

§ This reading is in none of my MSS. Two have Prasrítas; all the rest, Prasútas.

‖ Three MSS. have Píthagas.

¶ See p. 3, note [1], *supra*.

** Maru is in one MS.

†† Every one of my MSS. has Atináman.

‡‡ The *Bhágavata-puráńa* names the Ápyas only, of all the gods of this Patriarchate.

§§ Vol. I., p. 30.

‖‖ *Sl.* 437.

¶¶ The Calcutta edition has आप्याः, प्रभूताः, and पृथुकाः.

*** And so does the *Harivaṁśa*, *śl.* 435.

††† The *Márkańdeya-puráńa*, LXXVI., 54, has, in one of my three MSS., Unnata, as against Uttama in the other two; and so has the Calcutta edition, with which they all concur in reading Atináman.

powerful Uru,* Puru,† Śatadyumna, and others.:

The Manu of the present period is the wise lord of obsequies,§ the illustrious offspring of the Sun. The deities are the Ádityas, Vasus, and Rudras:¶ their sovereign is Purandara. Vasishṭha, Kaśyapa, Atri, Jamadagni, Gautama, Viśwámitra, and Bharadwája are the seven Ṛishis; and the nine pious sons of Vaivaswata Manu are the kings** Ikshwáku, Nabhaga,†† Dhṛishṭa,‡‡ Saryáti,§§ Narishyanta, Nábhanidishṭa,||||

---

also Abhinámin (Matsya) and Atináman (Hari Vaṁśa¶¶). The latter

---

* Here—as in Vol. I., p. 177—I have corrected the Translator's "Uru".

† Para is the worthless reading of two MSS.; and as many have Púru, the ancient form of the name. See Vol. I., p. 177, note †.

‡ Those named in the *Bhágavata-puráṇa*, VIII., V., 7, are Puru, Purusha, and Sudyumna.

§ Śráddhadeva; often taken as a proper name. Vaivaswata is intended. See p. 2, *supra*.

|| See Vol. II., p. 27, for their names.

¶ Add 'etc.' And see p. 15, note ‡, *infra*.

** See Book IV., Chapters I.–V., where I return to these kings.

†† Three MSS. have Nábhaga. As will be seen further on, this king should seem to bear another name, that of Nṛiga, which word several of my copies give here, as the reading.

‡‡ In two MSS., Dhṛishṭu; in one, Vishṇu; the former of which lections is of no account

§§ Here I correct the "Sanyati" of the original edition. Half my MSS. have Saryáti.

|||| Not one of my MSS. has this reading. Six—like two of Professor Wilson's, now at Oxford—give Nábhága and Dishṭa; two, Nábhága and Arishṭa; one, Nábhaga and Dishṭa; one, Nabhága and Dishṭa; one, Nábha and Dishṭa, &c. Moreover, it is shown, in the next page, that at least one of the commentators understands two kings to be here spoken of. And there is strong ground for believing that herein he is right.

Professor Wilson's choice of name—to which there is nothing, in any of the MSS. he used, nearer than नाभगो दिष्टः, occurring in one of them must have been suggested by the Nábhánedishṭha of the *Ṛigveda* and other ancient writings, to whom he refers in a note to Book IV., Chapter I.

¶¶ *Śl.* 436.

Karúsha, Príshadhra, and the celebrated Vasumat.[1]*

The unequalled energy of Vishńu, combining with

---

reads,† no doubt incorrectly, Bhrigu, Nabha, and Vivaswat, for Uttama, Madhu, and Havishmat.‡

The sons of Chákshusha are enumerated in Vol. I., p. 177.

[1] There is no great variety of nomenclature in this Manwantara. The Váyu adds, to the deities, the Sádhyas, Viśwas, Ma-

---

* The text is as follows:

करूषश्च पृषध्रश्च वसुमाँल्लोकविश्रुतः ।

On this it is remarked, in one of the commentaries, the other being silent:

वसुमाँल्लोकविश्रुत इति विशेषणद्वयं पृषध्रस्यैव । वसुमान्धैर्यवान् । गोवधपापे जातेऽपि लोभाभावाल्लोकविश्रुतः सर्वसंगपरित्यागेन मुक्तिप्राप्तेः । तथा सति नव पुत्रा महाबला इति वचनमुपपन्नं भवति ।

That is to say, the "Vasumat" of the text is an epithet of Príshadhra, denoting 'fortitudinous'.

It is thus evident how the commentator here makes out the exact tale of nine kings.

Discordantly, the *Bhágavata-puráńa*, VIII., XIII., 2, 3, has Ikshwáku, Nabhaga, Dhŕishńa, Śaryáti, Narishyanta, Nábhága, Dishńa, Karúsha, Príshadhra, and Vasumat,—ten, as it distinctly states. Reference will be made, in the sequel, to IX., I., 12. See, for nine sons of Vaivaswata, the *Márkańdeya-puráńa*, LXXIX., 11, 12.

At present, it need only be added, that the *Váyu-puráńa*, professing to name but nine sons of the reigning Manu, makes Prámśu the last, and says nothing of Vasumat as one of his brothers. Later Puráńas than the *Váyu* have manipulated its statements with a very free hand. For instance, the first line of the stanza in which it speaks of the sixth and seventh of Vaivaswata's Rishis, served, pretty certainly, as the type of the quotation given above; and hence the creation, there, of Vasumat. This stanza is thus expressed:

षष्ठो पृषध्रपुत्रस्तु वसुमाँल्लोकविश्रुतः ।

वत्सारः काश्यपश्चैव सप्तमो साधुसंमताः ॥

Of the two commentaries adduced in my annotations, that which I have hitherto designated as the smaller becomes, here at the beginning of Book III., considerably the ampler. From this point, not to mislead, I shall, till further notice, distinguish it as B; the other being called A.

† *Śl.* 435.

‡ Havishmat and Viraka, and these only, are spoken of in the *Bhágavata-puráńa*, VIII., V., 8.

the quality of goodness, and effecting the preservation of created things, presides over all the Manwantaras, in the form of a divinity.* Of a portion of that divinity Yajna was born, in the Swáyambhuva Manwantara,

---

ruts, and gods sprung from Bhrigu and Angiras.† The Bhágavata‡ adds the Ribhus;§ and most include the two Aświns, as a class. Of the Maruts, however, the Hari Vanśa remarks, that they are born in every Manwantara, seven times seven (or forty-nine); that, in each Manwantara, four times seven (or twenty-eight) obtain emancipation, but their places are filled up by persons reborn in that character. So the commentator explains the passages

मन्वन्तरेषु सर्वेषु प्राग्देवं सप्तसप्तकाः ।‖

and

मन्वन्तरे व्यतिक्रान्ते चत्वारः सप्तका गणाः ।¶

सप्तसप्तका एकोनपञ्चाशन्मरुतो देवाः प्रतिमन्वन्तरे भवन्ति । Commentary. तेषां मध्ये चत्वारः सप्तका अष्टाविंशति मरुतः । Commentary. It may be suspected, however, that these passages have been derived from the simple statement of the Matsya, that, in all the Manwantaras, classes of Ŕishis appear by seven and seven, and, having established a code of law and morality, depart to felicity:

मन्वन्तरेषु सर्वेषु सप्त सप्त महर्षयः ।
कृत्वा धर्मव्यवस्थानं प्रयान्ति परमं पदम् ॥

The Váyu has a rather different list of the seven Ŕishis:** or, Vasumat, the son of Vasishtha; Vatsára, descended from Kaśyapa;

---

* विष्णुशक्तिरनौपम्या सत्त्वोद्रिक्ता स्थितौ स्थिता ।
मन्वन्तरेष्वशेषेषु देवत्वेनाधितिष्ठति ॥

† With this enumeration corresponds that in the *Márk.-pur.*, LXXIX., 1.

‡ At VIII., XIII., 4, it adds, to the Ádityas, Vasus, and Rudras, the Viśwe devas, Maruts, Aświns, and Ŕibhus

§ For these gods, see Professor Wilson's Translation of the *Ŕigveda*, Vol. I., p. 46, note a.

‖ Śl. 441. ¶ Śl. 445.

** In this order: Viśwámitra, Jamadagni, Bharadwája, Śaradwat, Atri, Vasumat, Vatsára.

the will-begotten progeny of Akúti.[1]* When the Swá-

Viśwámitra, the son of Gádhi, and of the Kuśika race; Jamadagni, son of Kuru,† of the race of Bhṛigu; Bharadwája, son of Bṛihaspati; Śaradwat, son of Gotama,‡ of the family of Utathya;§ and Brahmakośa or Atri, descended from Brahmá.|| All the other authorities agree with our text.

[1] The nominal¶ father being the patriarch Ruchi. (See Vol. I., p. 108.)

* अंशेन तस्य जज्ञेऽसौ यज्ञः स्वायम्भुवेऽन्तरे।
आकूत्यां मानसो देव उत्पन्नः प्रथमेऽन्तरे॥

On this the two commentaries remark: तस्य विष्णोरंशेन स्वायम्भुवमन्वन्तरे। आकूत्यां मातरि यज्ञसंज्ञ उत्पन्नो यज्ञो बभूविवान्। यद्वा। प्रथमेऽन्तरेऽवसरे ब्रह्मणो मानसो य उत्पन्नो रुचिसकाशात्पितुर्यज्ञ इति।

According to this, "From a portion of him Yajna was born, in the Swáyambhuva Manwantara, of Ákúti; *or*, in this first Manwantara, *Yajna was born from Ruchi*, a god will-begotten *of Brahmá*." Hence the term *mánasa* must be taken to allude to Ruchi, Ákúti's husband, born from Brahmá in the first epoch of the Swáyambhuva Patriarchate. *Mánasa* cannot be applied to the child of a virgin. Males, not females, had will-begotten offspring.

† I find Ūru; also, Kuśa. See Book IV., Chapter VII.

‡ Corrected from "Gautama". This, importing 'son of Gotama', is Śaradwat's patronymic. See Book IV., Chapter XIX.

§ Corrected from "Utathya". In Vol. I., p. 153, note 2, I have amended "Uttathya".

In Professor Wilson's Translation of the *Ṛigveda*, Vol. II., p. 63, appears "Uchatthya" – *recte*, Uchathya – as father of Dirghatamas; and it is added, in a note: "The reading of the Puráńas is, invariably, Uttathya." "Utatthya" occurs *ibid.*, p. 83, note 6. These spellings, which I have never met with, must be incorrect; as the etymology – *uchatha*, 'praise' – of the Vaidik form of the name, Uchathya, clearly evinces.

These and suchlike minutiæ are not purposeless, seeing that the great Sanskrit Dictionary of Messrs. Boehtlingk and Roth inserts so copiously, as variants, transformations of proper names which owe their existence to mere inadvertence, but the reality or unreality of which cannot be judged of in the absence of manuscripts.

|| *Swáyambhuva*, in the original. ¶ But see note * in this page.

rochisha Manwantara had arrived, that divine (Yajna) was born as Ajita, along with the Tushita gods, the sons of Tushitá. In the third Manwantara,* Tushita† was again born of Satyá, as Satya, along with the class of deities so denominated. In the next period, Satya became Hari,‡ along with the Haris, the children of Harí.§ The excellent Hari was again born, in the Raivata Manwantara, of Sambhúti,|| as Mánasa, along with the gods called Abhútarajasas.¶ In the next period, Vishńu** was born of Vikuńthí,†† as Vaikuńtha, along

* Bhagavat then appeared as Satyasena, along with the Satyavratas, according to the *Bhágavata-puráńa*, VIII., I., 25.

† Here a name of Vishńu.

‡ Son of Hariśí and Harimedhas, says the *Bhágavata-puráńa*, VIII., I., 30.

§ The original has the locative हर्यायां, which supposes Haryá for the nominative.

|| Bhagavat manifested himself as Ajita, son of Vairaja and Sambhúti, in the time of the sixth Manu, Chákshusha, according to the *Bhágavata-puráńa*, VIII., V., 9. We read, in this page, that Vishńu appeared as Ajita, in the age of Swárochisha. His epiphany then was as Vibhu, son of Vedaśiras and Tushitá, declares the *Bhágavata-puráńa*, VIII., I., 21.

¶ All my MSS.—except that four of them have मानसैः for राजसैः—concur in reading:

रैवते ऽप्यन्तरे देवः संभूत्यां मानसो ऽभवत् ।
संभूतो राजसैः सार्धं देवैर्देववरो हरिः ॥

'In the Raivata *patriarchal* period, again, Hari, best of gods, was born, of Sambhúti, as the divine Mánasa,—originating with the deities *called* Rajasas'.

Mánasa is no inappropriate name for a deity associated with the Rajasas. We appear to have, in it, *mánasam*—the same as *manas*—with the change of termination required to express male personification. See Vol. I., p. 35, note *.

Sambhúti had a son Paurńamása. See Vol. I., p. 153. Also see the note immediately preceding this, and note ', at p. 10, *supra*.

** In the original, Purushottama.

†† We must read Vikuńthá. The Sanskrit presents the locative case as विकुण्ठायाम्.

Vikuńthá's husband was Śubhra, alleges the *Bhágavata-puráńa*, VIII., III.

with the deities called Vaikuńthas.* In the present Manwantara, Vishńu was again born as Vámana, the son of Kaśyapa by Aditi.† With three paces‡ he subdued the worlds, and gave them, freed from all embarrassment, to Purandara.[1] These are the seven persons

---

[1] There is no further account of this incarnation in the Vishńu Puráńa. Fuller details occur in the Bhágavata, Kúrma, Matsya,

V., 4. But, according to that authority, Vikuńtha appeared in the fifth Patriarchate, not, as here, in the sixth.

* That these gods appeared under Raivata, not under Chákshusha, we read in p. 9, *supra*.

† Hence, Vámana was brother of the Ádityas and Tushitas. See Vol II., p. 27. Also see p. 3, note *, *supra*. He is called the last-born of the Ádityas, in the *Bhágavata-puráńa*, VIII., XIII., 6.

‡ On the three strides of Vishńu, by reason of which he is called Trivikrama, see Professor Wilson's Translation of the *Ŕigveda*, Vol. I., Introduction, p. xxxiv.; and Vol. IV., p. 17, note: also, *Original Sanskrit Texts*, Part II., pp. 187 and 214–216; Part IV., Chapter II., especially pp. 54–58, and pp. 118, 119.

Dr Muir, in his *Mataparíkshá*, Part I.,—p. 105 of the Sanskrit, p. 16 of the English,—and twice in pages, just referred to, of his *Texts*, has quoted and translated a curious relevant passage from Durga Áchárya on Yáska's *Nirukta*. It is subjoined, together with Dr. Muir's latest version of it:

विष्णुरादित्यः। कथमिति। यत आह त्रेधा निदधे पदं निधत्ते पदं निधानं पदैः। क्व तावत्। पृथिव्यामन्तरिक्षे दिवीति शाकपूणिः। पार्थिवोऽग्निर्भूत्वा पृथिव्यां यत्किंचिदस्ति तद्विक्रमते तदधितिष्ठति। अन्तरिक्षे वैद्युतात्मना। दिवि सूर्यात्मना। यदुक्तम्। तमू अकृण्वन्त्रेधा भुवे कमिति। समारोहणे उदयगिरावुद्यन्पदमेकं निधत्ते। विष्णुपदे मध्यंदिनेऽन्तरिक्षे। गयशिरस्यस्तंगिरावित्यौर्णवाभ आचार्यो मन्यते।

"Vishńu is the sun [Áditya]. How so? Because [the hymn] says: 'In three places he planted his step'; i. e., plants his step, [makes] a planting with his steps. Where, then, is this done? 'On the earth, in the firmament, and in the sky', according to Śákapúńi. Becoming terrestrial fire, he strides over, abides in, whatever there is on earth; in the shape of lightning, in the firmament; and in the form of the sun,

by whom, in the several Manwantaras, created beings have been protected. Because this whole world has been pervaded by the energy of the deity, he is entitled Vishńu, from the root Viś, 'to enter', or 'pervade'; for all the gods, the Manus, the seven Rishis, the sons of the Manus, the Indras the sovereigns of the gods, all are but the impersonated might* of Vishńu.[1]

---

and Vámana Puráńas. The first of these (Book VIII., Chapters 15—23) relates the penance and sacrifices of Bali, son of Virochana, by which he had overcome Indra and the gods, and obtained supreme dominion over the three spheres. Vishńu, at the request of the deities, was born as a dwarf, Vámana, the son of Aditi by Kaśyapa; who, applying to Bali for alms, was promised, by the prince, whatever he might demand, notwithstanding Śukra, the preceptor of the Daityas, apprised him whom he had to deal with. The dwarf demanded as much space as he could step over at three steps, and, upon the assent of Bali, enlarged himself to such dimensions as to stride over the three worlds. Being worshipped, however, by Bali and his ancestor Prahláda, he conceded to them the sovereignty of Pátála.

[1] See the same etymology in Vol. I., p. 4, note 2.

---

in the sky. As it is said (in the R. V., X., 88, 10): 'They made him to become threefold'. Aurńavábha Áchárya thinks [the meaning is] this: 'He plants one foot on the '*samárohańa*' (place of rising), when mounting over the hill of ascension; [another], on the '*vishńupada*', the meridian sky; [a third], on the '*gayaśiras*', the hill of setting''.

* *Vibhútayah*, 'potencies'.

CHAPTER II.

Of the seven future Manus and Manwantaras. Story of Sanjná and Chháyá, wives of the Sun. Sávarńi, son of Chháyá, the eighth Manu. His successors, with the divinities, &c. of their respective periods. Appearance of Vishńu in each of the four Yugas.

MAITREYA.—You have recapitulated to me, most excellent Brahman, the particulars of the past Manwantaras. Now give me some account of those which are to come.

PARÁŚARA.—Sanjná, the daughter of Viśwakarman, was the wife of the Sun, and bore him three children, the Manu (Vaivaswata), Yama, and the goddess Yamí (or the Yamuná river). Unable to endure the fervours of her lord, Sanjná gave him Chháyá,[1] as his handmaid, and repaired to the forests, to practise devout exercises.* The Sun, supposing Chháyá to be his wife

[1] That is, her shadow, or image. It also means 'shade.' The Bhágavata,† however, makes both Sanjná and Chháyá daughters of Viśwakarman. According to the Matsya, Vivaswat, the son of Kaśyapa and Aditi, had three wives: Rájní, the daughter of Raivata, by whom he had Revanta; Prabhá, by whom he had Prabháta; and, by Sanjná, the daughter of Twashírí, the Manu, and Yama, and Yamuná. The story then proceeds much as in the text.

* "Devout exercises" renders *tapas*.

† VIII., XIII., 8. In the next stanza it adds, that some give the Sun a third wife, Vadavá. The commentator, Śridhara, identifies her, nevertheless, with Sanjná, who is said—VI., VI., 38—to have been transformed into a mare—*vadavá*.

Sanjná, begot, by her, three other children, Śanaiśchara (Saturn), another Manu (Sávarṇi*), and a daughter, Tapatí (the Taptee river). Chháyá, upon one occasion, being offended with Yama,[1] the son of Sanjná, denounced an imprecation upon him, and, thereby, revealed to Yama, and to the Sun, that she was not, in truth, Sanjná, the mother of the former.† Being further informed, by Chháyá, that his wife had gone to the wilderness, the Sun beheld her, by the eye of meditation,‡ engaged in austerities, in the figure of a mare, (in the region of Uttara Kuru §). Metamorphosing himself into a horse, he rejoined his wife, and begot three other children,—the two Aświns || and Revanta,—and then brought Sanjná back to his own dwelling. To diminish his intensity, Viśwakarman placed the luminary on his lathe, to grind off some of his effulgence, and, in this manner, reduced it an eighth: for more

---

[1] Yama, provoked at her partiality for her own children, abused Chháyá, and lifted up his foot, to kick her. She cursed him to have his leg affected with sores and worms: but his father bestowed upon him a cock, to eat the worms and remove the discharge; and Yama, afterwards propitiating Mahádeva, obtained the rank of Lokapála, and sovereign of Tartarus.¶

---

* Not named, here, in the original.

† छायासंज्ञा ददौ शापं यमाय कुपिता यदा ।
तदान्येयमसौ बुद्धिरित्यासीद्यमसूर्ययोः ॥

‡ *Samádhi.*

§ This parenthesis, as usual, is supplied by the Translator.

|| See Professor Wilson's Translation of the *Ṛigveda*, Vol. I., Introduction, pp. xxxv., xxxvi., and p. 8, note a; also, Vol. II., Introduction, p. viii.

¶ See the *Márkaṇḍeya-puráṇa*, Chapter LXXVII.

than that was inseparable.[1] The parts of the divine Vaishńava splendour, residing in the sun, that were filed off by Viśwakarman, fell, blazing, down upon the earth; and the artist constructed of them the discus of Vishńu, the trident of Śiva,* the weapon[2] of the god of wealth,† the lance of Kárttikeya,‡ and the weapons of the other gods: all these Viśwakarman fabricated from the superfluous rays of the sun.[3]

The son of Chháyá, who was called, also, a Manu, was denominated Sávarńi,[4]§ from being of the same caste (Savarńa) as his elder brother, (the Manu Vai-

[1] The Matsya says, he trimmed the Sun everywhere except in the feet, the extent of which he could not discern. Consequently, in pictures, or images, the feet of the Sun must never be delineated, under pain of leprosy, &c.

[2] The term is Śibiká, which properly means 'a litter'. The commentator calls it Astra, 'a weapon'.||

[3] This legend is told, with some variations of no great importance, in the Matsya, Márkańdeya, and Padma Puráńas (Swarga Khańda), in the Bhágavata, and Hari Vaḿśa,¶ &c.

[4] The Márkańdeya,** whilst it admits Sávarńi to be the son of the Sun, has a legend of his former birth, in the Swárochisha Manwantara, as Suratha Rája, who became a Manu by having then propitiated Devi. It was to him that the Durgá Máhátmya†† or Chańdi, the popular narrative of Durgá's triumphs over various demons, was narrated.

* Substituted, by the Translator, for Rudra.

† This is to translate Dhanada, one of the names of Kubera.

‡ The original has Guha.

§ Sávarńa is a variant.

|| So both the commentators call it.

¶ Chapter IX.

** Chapter LXXXI.

†† Or *Devi-máhátmya*.

vaswata). He presides over the ensuing, or eighth, Manwantara,* the particulars of which, and the following, I will now relate. In the period in which Sávarńi shall be the Manu, the classes of the gods will be the Sutapas, Amitábhas, and Mukhyas; twenty-one† of each. The seven Ŕishis will be Díptimat, Gálava, Ráma,‡ Kŕipa,§ Drauńi,‖ my son Vyása¶ (will be the sixth); and the seventh will be Ŕishyaśŕinga.[1] The Indra will be Bali, the sinless son of Virochana, who, through the favour of Vishńu, is, actually, sovereign

---

[1] The Váyu has Jámadagnya (or Paraśuráma), of the Kuśika race; Gálava, of that of Bhŕigu;** Dwaipáyana (or Vyása), of the family of Vasishtha; Kŕipa, the son of Śaradwat; Díptimat, descended from Atri; Ŕishyaśŕinga, from Kaśyapa; and Aśwatthámán, the son of Drońa, of the Bháradwája family. The Matsya and Padma have Satánanda, in place of Díptimat.

---

* Called Sávarńika or Sávarńaka, in the Sanskrit.

† My MSS. say 'twenty'; since they read:

तेषां गणस्तु देवानामेकैको विंशकः स्मृतः ।

And both the commentaries observe: विंशकः । विंशतिसंख्याकाः । The *Váyu-puráńa*, too, has twenty; and so the *Márkańdeya-puráńa*, LXXX., 5.

‡ Otherwise known as Paraśuráma.

§ Drońa's brother-in-law.

‖ *I. e.*, son of Drońa; namely, Aśwatthámán. See Book IV., Chapter XIX. Three of my MSS. have Drauńi, as has the printed *Márkańdeya-puráńa*, LXXX., 4. This form sins against grammar.

¶ Distinguished as Bádaráyańa.

** My MSS. here differ from the text, in reading:

कौशिको गालवश्चैव जामदग्न्यश्च भार्गवः ।

That is to say, Gálava was a Kauśika, and Jámadagnya, a Bhárgava. See pp. 14—16, note 1; and p. 16, note †, *supra*. Also see Professor Max Müller's *History of Ancient Sanskrit Literature*, p. 380; and p. 416, note 1.

of part of Pátála.* The royal progeny of Sávarńi will be Virajas, Arvarívat,† Nirmoha,‡ and others.§

The ninth Manu will be Daksha-sávarńi.[1] ‖ The Páras,¶ Maríchigarbhas, and Sudharmans will be the

---

[1] The four following Sávarńis are described, in the Váyu, as the mind-engendered sons of a daughter of Daksha, named either Suvratá (Váyu) or Priyá (Brahma), by himself and the three gods, Brahmá, Dharma, and Rudra, to whom he presented her on Mount Meru; whence they are called also Meru-sávarńis. They are termed Sávarńis, from their being of one family or caste:

यस्मात्सवर्णास्तेषां वै ब्रह्मादीनां कुमारकाः ।
सवर्णा मनवस्तेषां सवर्णत्वं च तेषु तत् ॥

According to the same authority, followed by the Hari Vaṁśa,** it appears that this Manu is also called Rohita. Most of the details of this and the following Manwantaras are omitted in the Matsya, Brahma, Padma, and Márkańdeya†† Puráńas. The Bhágavata‡‡ and Kúrma give the same as our text; and the Váyu, which agrees very nearly with it,§§ is followed, in most

---

* विष्णुप्रसादादनघः पातालान्तरगोचरः ।
विरोचनसुतस्तेषां बलिरिन्द्रो भविष्यति ॥

† The "Arvarivas" of the former edition was an oversight. Variants which I find are Urvarivat, Urvarívat, and Arvaríyat.

‡ Two of my MSS. have Nirmoka; one, Nirmogha.

§ According to the *Bhágavata-puráńa*, VIII., XIII., 11, 12, the gods will be the Sutapas, Virajas, and Amńitaprabhas; and among the sons of Sávarńi will be Nirmoka and Virajaska.

‖ All my MSS. have Dakshasávarńa. The ninth Manu will be son of Varuńa, according to the *Bhágavata-puráńa*, VIII., XIII., 18.

¶ Three MSS. give Paras.

** *Sl.* 468.

†† This Puráńa should here be omitted, as it contains a full exhibition of the details referred to. See its chapters XCIV. and C.

‡‡ It will be seen, from my notes, that its agreement with our text is not of the closest.

§§ If my five MSS. are to be trusted, it deviates therefrom very widely. I have recorded only a few specimens of these deviations.

three classes of divinities; each consisting of twelve: their powerful chief will be the Indra Adbhuta. Savana, Dyutimat, Bhavya,* Vasu, Medhádhriti,† Jyotishmat, and Satya will be the seven Rishis. Dhritaketu,‡ Diptiketu,§ Panchahasta, Nirámaya,|| Prithuśrava,¶ and others, will be the sons of the Manu.**

In the tenth Manwantara, the Manu will be Brahmasávarńi:†† the gods will be the Sudhámans, Viruddhas,‡‡ and Śatasankhyas: the Indra will be the mighty Sánti:§§

---

respects, by the Hari Vamśa. The Matsya and Padma are peculiar in their series and nomenclature of the Manus themselves: calling the ninth, Rauchya; tenth, Bhautya; eleventh, Meru-sávarńi, son of Brahmá; twelfth, Rita; thirteenth, Ritadháman; and fourteenth, Viśwaksena. The Bhágavata calls the two last Manus Deva-sávarńi and Indra-sávarńi.

---

* Of three MSS. the reading is Havya; and one has Sabya.

† Professor Wilson had "Medhatithi", which I find nowhere. Two of my MSS. have Medhámriti, a bad lection for what all the rest give, the name in the text.

‡ In a single MS. is Dhritiketu.

§ The former edition had "Driptiketu", for which I find no authority. A plurality of my MSS. read, like the *Váyu-puráńa*, as above; while five have Diptaketu; and two, Dásaketu.

|| It seems very likely that we here have *nirámaya*, 'free from disease', as an epithet of Panchahasta. In the *Váyu-puráńa*, it qualifies, in the plural, names preceding it.

¶ The *Váyu-puráńa* reads Prithuśravas.

** Of the sons of this Manu the *Bhágavata-puráńa*, VIII., XIII., 18, names only Bhútaketu and Diptaketu.

†† He is called Brahmasávarńa, also, as in the original of the end of this paragraph:

ब्रह्मसावर्णपुत्रास्तु रक्षिष्यन्ति वसुंधराम् ।

He will be son of Upaśloka, according to the *Bhágavata-puráńa*, VIII., XIII., 21.

‡‡ One MS. gives Viśuddhas.

§§ Śambhu: *Bhágavata-puráńa*, VIII., XIII., 22.

the Rishis will be Havishmat, Sukriti, Satya,* Apámmúrti, Nábhága, Apratimaujas, and Satyaketu:† and the ten sons of the Manu will be Sukshetra, Uttamaujas, Harisheńa,‡ and others.

In the eleventh Manwantara, the Manu will be Dharma-sávarńi:§ the principal classes of gods will be the Vihangamas, Kámagamas,|| and Nirmáńaratis,¶ each thirty in number;[1] of whom Vrisha** will be the Indra: the Rishis will be Niśchara, Agnitejas, Vapushmat, Vishńu,†† Áruńi,‡‡ Havishmat, and Anagha:§§

---

[1] Hence the Váyu identifies||| the first with days; the second, with nights; and the third, with hours.¶¶

---

* Four of my MSS. have Sabya; and two others have corruptions of it.

† Saptaketu appears in three MSS.

‡ Four MSS. have Bhúrisheńa; and this is the reading of the *Váyu-puráńa*, and of the *Bhágavata-puráńa*, VIII., XIII., 21.

§ In the original we have the elongated form, Dharmasávarńika.

|| In the *Váyu-puráńa*, Kámajas (or Vihangamas) and Manojavas.

¶ The *Váyu-puráńa*, by twice beginning a line with this word, proves that we are not to read Anirmáńaratis, 'of measureless enjoyment'; for the original – which, by the by, in none of my MSS. has -निर्माणरत° – might, otherwise, be taken to combine the names of the second and third classes of gods into a compound, thus:

विहंगमाः कामगमानिर्माणरतयस्तथा ।

Two copies have Nirváńaruchis, like the *Bhágavata-puráńa*, VIII., XIII., 26.

** Vaidhrita: *Bhágavata-puráńa*, VIII., XIII., 26.

†† One MS. has Vrishńi; one, Dhriti.

‡‡ Four MSS. exhibit Váruńi, the lection of the *Váyu-puráńa*. The reading of the *Bhágavata-puráńa*, VIII., XIII., 26, is Aruńa.

§§ Anaya, in three of my MSS.

||| I find a different adjustment of these identifications; but my MSS. differ, perhaps, from those used by Professor Wilson.

¶¶ *Muhúrta*.

the kings of the earth, and sons of the Manu, will be Sarvaga,* Sarvadharman, Devánîka, and others.

In the twelfth Manwantara, the son of Rudra, Sávarńi,† will be the Manu: Ŕitadhámant‡ will be the Indra: and the Haritas, Lohitas,§ Sumanasas, and Sukarmans|| will be the classes of gods, each comprising fifteen. Tapaswin, Sutapas, Tapomúrti, Taporati, Tapodhŕiti, Tapodyuti,¶ and Tapodhana will be the Ŕishis:** and Devavat, Upadeva, Devaśreshťha, and others, will be the Manu's sons, and mighty monarchs (on the earth).

In the thirteenth Mauwantara, the Manu will be Rauchya:[1]†† the classes of gods, thirty-three in each,

[1] The son of the Prajápati Ruchi (Váyu, &c.), by the nymph Mánini,‡‡ the daughter of the Apsaras Pramlochá (Márkańdeya).

* The "Savarga" of the former edition must have been a mere oversight. In two of my thirteen MSS., the name is Sarvatraga; that following being Sudharmátman. The *Váyu-puráńa* has Sarvavega, followed by Sudharman.

According to the *Bhágavata-puráńa*, VIII., XIII., 25, the eleventh Manu will engender Satyadharman and nine other sons.

† Sávarńa, in my copies.

‡ "Ritadháma", the name in the first edition, was simply a typographic error, I take it, as to its second syllable. One of my MSS. seems to have Kshatadháman. Similarly as in all my MSS but one, Ŕitadháman is the reading of the *Bhágavata-puráńa*, VIII., XIII., 29.

§ A single MS. has, like the *Váyu-puráńa*, Rohitas.

|| A fourth class of gods is here omitted. Ten of my MSS. call them Táras; one, Surúpas; one, Surápas; and one, Supáras. The *Váyu-puráńa* seems to have Suparvas.

¶ This name is implied, not expressed in full; the original being:

तपोधृतिर्द्युतिश्चान्यः सप्तमस्तु तपोधनः ।

** Of the Ŕishis under the twelfth Manu the *Bhágavata-puráńa*, VIII., XIII., 29, names only Tapomúrti, Tapaswin, and Ágnídhraka.

†† Devasávarńi: *Bhágavata-puráńa*, VIII., XIII., 31.

‡‡ Málini, in some MSS., as in the Calcutta edition, XCVIII., 6. It may be a Bengal corruption.

will be the Sutrámans,* Sukarmans, and Sudharmans;† their Indra will be Divaspati: the Ŕishis will be Nirmoha,‡ Tattwadarsin,§ Nishprakampa, Nirutsuka, Dhŕitimat, Avyaya, and Sutapas: and Chitrasena, Vichitra, and others, will be the kings.

In the fourteenth Manwantara, Bhautya ‖ will be the Manu;[1] Śuchi, the Indra: the five classes of gods will be the Chákshushas, the Pavitras, Kanishíhas, Bhrájiras,¶ and Váchávŕiddhas:** the seven Ŕishis †† will be Agnibáhu,‡‡ Śuchi, Śukra, Mágadha,§§ Gŕidhra,‖‖

[1] Son of Kavi, by the goddess Bhúti, according to the Váyu; but the Márkańdeya¶¶ makes Bhúti the son of Angiras, whose pupil, Śánti, having suffered the holy fire to go out in his master's absence, prayed to Agni, and so propitiated him, that he not only relighted the flame, but desired Śánti to demand a further

* For the "Sudhámans" of the former edition I find no warrant. Sutrámans is the name in the *Váyu-puráńa*. Two of my MSS. have Sudarmans.

† These are not recognised in the *Bhágavata-puráńa*, VIII., XIII., 33.

‡ One of my MSS. shows this name written over Nirmoka, the reading of the *Bhágavata-puráńa*, VIII., XIII., 34.

§ Tattwadarśa, the reading of the *Bhágavata-puráńa*, VIII., XIII., 33, occurs in a single copy.

‖ Indrasávarńi: *Bhágavata-puráńa*, VIII., XIII., 34.

¶ The *Váyu-puráńa* has Bhájiras or Bhájaras.

** This is the reading of the *Váyu-puráńa*, likewise. "Vávŕiddhas" is in the old edition: but it looks like an inadvertence only. Two of my MSS. have Váchávŕittas.

†† They are said to be Agnibáhu, Śuchi, Śuddha, Mágadha, and others, in the *Bhágavata-puráńa*, VIII., XIII., 35.

‡‡ Agniváyu is in one MS.

§§ In two of my MSS. is what looks like the meaningless name Mamádha.

‖‖ Such is the lection of two of my MSS.; while all the rest have Agnidhra,—as has the *Váyu-puráńa*,—or corruptions thereof.

¶¶ Chapter XCIX.

Yukta,* and Ajita:† and the sons of the Manu will be Uru,‡ Gabhira,§ Bradhna,‖ and others,¶ who will be kings, and will rule over the earth.[1]

At the end of every four ages** there is a disappearance†† of the Vedas; and it is the province of the seven Rishis to come down upon earth, from heaven, to give them currency again.‡‡ In every Kṛita age,

---

boon. Śánti accordingly solicited a son for his Guru; which son was Bhúti, the father of the Manu Bhautya.

[1] Although the Puráṅas which give an account of the Manwantaras agree in some of the principal details, yet, in the minor ones, they offer many varieties, some of which have been noticed. These chiefly regard the first six and the eighth. Except in a few individual peculiarities, the authorities seem to arrange themselves in two classes; one comprehending the Vishńu, Váyu, Kúrma, Bhágavata, and Márkańdeya; and the other, the Matsya, Padma, Brahma, and Hari Vaḿśa. The Márkańdeya, although it agrees precisely with the Vishńu in its nomenclature, differs from it, and from all, in devoting a considerable number of its pages to legends of the origin of the Manus, all of which are, evidently, of comparatively recent invention, and several of which have been, no doubt, suggested by the etymology of the names of the Manus.

---

* Two MSS. have Mukta.

† Arjita is the lection of two MSS.

‡ Úru, in a single copy.

§ Six MSS. give the synonymous Gambhira.

‖ One MS. has Budhna; one, Budhnya; one, Bandhra.

¶ These sons, agreeably to the *Bhágavata-puráńa*, VIII., XIII., 34, will be Urubuddhi, Gambhirabuddhi, and others. The *Váyu-puráńa* has, apparently, Ojaswin, Subala, and Bhautya.

** *Yuga.*

†† *Viplava.*

‡‡ Compare the *Mahábhárata*, *Śánti-parvan*, *ll.* 7660, quoted and translated in *Original Sanskrit Texts*, Part III., p. 90.

the Manu (of the period) is the legislator or author* of the body of law, the Smŕiti; the deities of the different classes receive the sacrifices during the Manwantaras to which they severally belong; and the sons of the Manu themselves, and their descendants, are the sovereigns of the earth for the whole of the same term. The Manu, the seven Ŕishis, the gods, the sons of the Manu, who are the kings, and Indra,† are the beings who preside over the world during each Manwantara.

An entire Kalpa,‡ O Brahman, is said to comprise a thousand ages,§ or fourteen Manwantaras;[1] and it is succeeded by a night of similar duration; during which he who wears the form of Brahmá, Janárdana, the substance of all things, the lord of all, and creator of all, involved in his own illusions, and having swallowed up the three spheres, sleeps upon the serpent Śesha, amidst the ocean.[2] Being, after that, awake, he, who

---

[1] A thousand ages of the gods and fourteen Manwantaras are not precisely the same thing, as has been already explained. (See Vol. I., p. 51, note 2.)

[2] The order of the text would imply, that, as Brahmá, he sleeps upon Śesha: but, if this be intended, it is at variance with the usual legend, that it is as Vishńu or Náráyańa that the deity sleeps in the intervals of dissolution. The commentator|| accordingly qualifies the phrase Brahmarúpadhara (ब्रह्मरूपधर) by

---

* "Legislator or author" is to translate *praśástri*, 'promulgator'.

† Śakra, in the original.

‡ For the names of twenty-eight Kalpas, as enumerated in the *Váyu-puráńa*, see Dr. Aufrecht's *Catalogus*, &c., pp. 51, 52.

§ To render *yuga*.

|| Rather, both the commentators.

is the universal soul, again creates all things, as they were before, in combination with the property of foulness (or activity): and, in a portion of his essence, associated with the property of goodness, he, as the Manus, the kings, the gods, and their Indras, as well as the seven Ṛishis, is the preserver of the world. In what manner Vishńu, who is characterized by the attribute of providence* during the four ages, effected their preservation, I will next, Maitreya, explain.

In the Kṛita age, Vishńu, in the form of Kapila and other (inspired teachers), assiduous for the benefit of all creatures, imparts to them true wisdom. In the Tretá age, he restrains the wicked, in the form of a universal monarch,[1] and protects the three worlds. In the Dwápara age, in the person of Veda-vyása, he divides the one Veda into four, and distributes it into innumerable† branches;‡ and, at the end of the Kali (or fourth age), he appears as Kalki, and reestablishes the iniquitous in the paths (of rectitude). In this man-

---

the term Divá (दिवा): 'Vishńu wears the form of Brahmá by day; by night, he sleeps on Śesha, in the person of Náráyańa:' रात्रौ श्रीनारायणरूपेण शेषाहौ शेते। This, however, may be suspected to be an innovation upon an older system; for, in speaking of the alternations of creation and dissolution, they are always considered as consentaneous with the day and night of Brahmá alone.

[1] As a Chakravartin.

---

* *Sthiti.*

† Literally, 'hundreds of', *śata.*

‡ For a more literal rendering of this paragraph, down to this point, see *Original Sanskrit Texts*, Part III., p. 20.

ner the universal spirit preserves, creates, and, at last, destroys, all the world.*

Thus, Brahman, I have described to you the true nature of that great being who is all things, and besides whom there is no other existent thing, nor has there been, nor will there be, either here or elsewhere. I have, also, enumerated to you the Manwantaras, and those who preside over them. What else do you wish to hear?

---

* एवमेतज्जगत्सर्वं परिपाति करोति च ।
हन्ति चान्तेऽप्यनन्तात्मा नास्त्यस्माद्व्यतिरिक्तं यत् ॥

CHAPTER III.

Division of the Veda into four portions, by a Vyása, in every Dwápara age. List of the twenty-eight Vyásas of the present Manwantara. Meaning of the word Brahma.

MAITREYA.—I have learned from you, in due order, how this world is Vishńu, (how it is) in Vishńu, (how it is) from Vishńu: nothing further is to be known. But I should desire to hear how the Vedas were divided, in different ages,* by that great being, in the form of Veda-vyása; who were the Vyásas of their respective eras; and what were the branches into which the Vedas were distributed.

PARÁŚARA.—The branches of the (great) tree of the Vedas are so numerous,† Maitreya, that it is impossible to describe them at length. I will give you a summary account of them.

In every Dwápara (or third) age, Vishńu, in the person of Vyása, in order to promote the good of mankind, divides the Veda, which is (properly, but) one, into many portions. Observing the limited perseverance, energy, and application of mortals, he makes the Veda fourfold, to adapt it to their capacities; and the bodily form which he assumes, in order to effect that classification, is known by the name of Veda-vyása.‡ Of the different Vyásas in the

* Yuga, rendered by "eras", just below.

† Literally, 'by thousands', *sahasraśah*.

‡ वीर्यं तेजो बलं चाल्पं मनुष्याणामवेक्ष्य वै ।
हिताय सर्वभूतानां वेदभेदान्करोति सः ।

present Manwantara,[1] and the branches which they have taught, you shall have an account.

Twenty-eight times have the Vedas been arranged, by the great Rishis, in the Vaivaswata Manwantara in the Dwápara age;[2] and, consequently, eight and twenty Vyásas have passed away; by whom, in their respective periods, the Veda has been divided into four. In the first Dwápara age, the distribution was made by Swayambhú (Brahmá) himself; in the second, the arranger of the Veda (Veda-vyása) was Prajápati (or Manu); in the third, Uśanas; in the fourth, Bŕihaspati; in the fifth, Savitŕi; in the sixth, Mŕityu (Death, or Yama); in the seventh, Indra; in the eighth, Vasishtha; in the ninth, Sáraswata; in the tenth, Tridháman; in the eleventh, Trivŕishan; † (in the twelfth), Bharadwája; : in the thirteenth, Antariksha; in the fourteenth, Vaprívan; § in the fifteenth, Trayyáruńa; [3] ‖

[1] The text has: 'Hear, from me, an account of the Vyásas of the different Manwantaras':

यस्मिन्मन्वन्तरे ये ये व्यासास्तांस्तान्निबोध मे ।

But this is inconsistent with what follows, in which the enumeration is confined to the Vaivaswata Manwantara.

[2] This name occurs as that of one of the kings of the solar

---

यथा स कुरुते तन्वा वेदमेकं पृथक्प्रभुः ।
वेदव्यासाभिधाना तु सा मूर्तिर्मधुविद्विषः ।

Vishńu is here called "the enemy of Madhu."

* A more exact translation of Paráśara's reply, breaking off here, will be found in *Original Sanskrit Texts*, Part III., pp. 20, 21.

† Three MSS. have Trivŕisha; and so has the *Kúrma-puráńa*.

: I ‌nd Bháradwája in six MSS.; and this lection seems best, as the nineteenth Vyása is called Bharadwája.

§ So read seven of my MSS.; while two give Vamrivan, and others, Vajrivan, Vyághrivan, Vapovan, &c. &c. Professor Wilson's "Vapra", now discarded, I have nowhere met with.

‖ Trayyárońi, in two MSS. Is the name Traiyáruńa, or Traijáruńi?

in the sixteenth, Dhananjaya; in the seventeenth, Kritanjaya; in the eighteenth, Ŕińajya;* (in the nineteenth), Bharadwája;† (in the twentieth), Gautama;‡ in the twenty-first, Uttama, also called Haryátman; (in the twenty-second), Vena,§ who is likewise named Rájaśravas;|| (in the twenty-third), Saumaśushmáyańa,¶ also Tŕińabindu;** (in the twenty-fourth), Ŕiksha,†† the descendant of Bhŕigu, who is known also by the name Válmíki; (in the twenty-fifth), my father, Śakti,‡‡

dynasty, and is included, by Mr. Colebrooke, amongst the per-

* The Translator has "Ŕińa", for which my MSS. furnish no warrant. Six of them exhibit Ŕińajya; two, this, with Ŕińadya written over; three, Kŕitin; others, Ŕińavya and Ŕińin.

† A single MS. has Bháradwája. See note ‡ in the last page.

‡ Substituted for Professor Wilson's "Gotama", which none of my MSS. countenances.

§ Exchanged for "Veńa", which is in but one of my MSS.

|| Almost as common a reading is Rájasravas: and one of my MSS. gives Vájasravas; another, Vájasrava. Again, three of them, including those accompanied by commentary B, have, instead of राजश्रवास्तु यः, वाजश्रवान्वयः, "of the line of Vájaśrava."

¶ Eight MSS. have Somaśushmáyańa; two, Somaśushmápańa; others, Somayushmáyana, Somoyushmápana, and Somaśushmáńaya. The Translator put "Somaśushmápańa". My conjectural Saumaśushmáyańa would be descendant of Somaśushma, mentioned in the *Śatapatha-bráhmańa*, XI., IV., 5, and elsewhere.

That the *Kúrma-puráńa* was compiled after our Puráńa had become corrupted, as to the name in question, might be inferred from my MSS., which read:

राजश्रवाश्चैव सोमशुष्मायणः परः ।

** According to the *Kúrma-puráńa*, Tŕińabindu was the twenty-third Vyása, Ushmápańa being the twenty-second. See note § in the next page.

†† In one MS., Ŕikshya; in another, Daksha.

‡‡ Three MSS. have Śaktri. In Vol. I., p. 8, the Translator, after speaking, in a note, of "Śakti, the son of Vasishtha," and father of Paráśara, calls him "Śakti or Śaktri;" touching the first of which, Śakti, I there hastily observe: "This is hardly the name of a male. The right

was the Vyása; I (was the Vyása of the twenty-sixth Dwápara), and was succeeded by Játúkarńa;* the Vyása (of the twenty-eighth), who followed him, was Kŕishńa Dwaipáyana. These are the twenty-eight elder Vyásas, by whom, in the preceding Dwápara ages, the Veda has been divided into four. In the next Dwápara, Drauńi (the son of Drońa) will be the Vyása, when my son, the Muni Kŕishńa Dwaipáyana, who is the actual Vyása, shall cease to be (in that character).[1]

---

sons of royal descent who are mentioned as authors of hymns in the Ŕig-veda.† Asiatic Researches, Vol. VIII., p. 383.‡

[1] A similar list of Vyásas is given in the Kúrma§ and Vá-

---

word seems to be Śaktri." On this observation Dr. Kern, in his meritorious edition of the *Bŕihat-sańhitá*, Preface, p. 31, comments in these words: "F. E. Hall remarks that Śakti is 'hardly the name of a male.' As if a male were intended! Śakti is the heavenly power of Indra-Agni." Assuredly, a male is intended; and Śaktiputra, as Parásara is called in the *Mahábhárata*, is not to be rendered, as by Dr. Kern, "the son of strength",—but "son of Śakti,"—unless we consent to regard the attribute of strength as offspring of Vasishtha. For Parásara, as son of Śakti, and grandson of Vasishtha, see the *Anukramańiká* to the *Ŕigveda*, on I., LXV., &c. &c. And the *Ŕigveda* itself—VII., XVIII., 21—makes mention of Parásara, no less than of Vasishtha, as if he were anything but a myth. Further, Śakti, as "the heavenly power of Indra-Agni," is, so far as I am at present informed, altogether a novelty.

* This is the reading of eleven of my MSS.; and the other two have Játúkarńya, which seems to be the lection of the *Váyu-puráńa*. Hence I have displaced Professor Wilson's "Jaratkáru."

† See the *Anukramańiká* to the *Ŕigveda*, on V., XXVII., and IX., CX. The Vaidik form of the name is Tryaruńa.

‡ Or *Miscellaneous Essays*, Vol. I., p. 23.

§ The list stands there as follows:

1. Swáyambhuva.	4. Bŕihaspati.
2. Prajápati.	5. Savitŕi.
3. Uśanas.	6. Mŕityu.

The syllable Om is defined to be the eternal monosyllabic Brahma.[1] The word Brahma is derived from

---

yu* Puráńas. Many of the individuals appear as authors of different hymns and prayers in the Vedas; and it is very possible that the greater portion, if not all of them, had a real existence; being the framers, or teachers, of the religion of the Hindus, before a complete ritual was compiled.

[1] We have already had occasion to explain the sanctity of this monosyllable (see Vol. I., p. 1, note 1), which ordinarily commences different portions of the Vedas, and which, as the text describes it, is identified with the supreme, undefinable deity, or Brahma. So, in the Bhagavad-gítá: †

ओमित्येकाक्षरं ब्रह्म व्याहरन्मामनुस्मरन् ।‡

'Repeating Om, the monosyllable, which is Brahma, and calling me to mind;' which is not exactly the same idea that is conveyed by Schlegel's version,§ 'Monosyllabum mysticum OM pronuntiando numen adorans, mei memor;' where 'numen ado-

---

7. Indra.
8. Vasishtha.
9. Sáraswata.
10. Tridháman.
11. Trivŕisha.
12. Śatatejas.
13. Dharma.
14. Tarakshu.
15. Trayyáruńi. (Traiyáruńi?)
16. Dhananjaya.
17. Kŕitanjaya.
18. Ŕitanjaya.
19. Bharadwája.
20. Gautama.
21. Rájaśravas.
22. Úshmápańa.
23. Tŕińabindu.
24. Válmíki.
25. Śakti.
26. Paráśara.
27. Jatúkarńa.
28. Kŕishńadwaipáyana.

None of these sages, it is observable, has more than one appellation. Noteworthy variants, in my MSS., are: Áruńi, for Trayyáruńi; Úshmánaya, for Úshmápańa. It is probable, that we should substitute, for Tarakshu, Surakshu, which appears to be the reading of the *Váyu-puráńa*.

* See Dr. Aufrecht's *Catalogus Cod. Manuscript.*, &c., pp. 59, 63.

† VIII., 13.

‡ This passage is referred to in the commentary.

§ P. 156 of the first edition; p. 60 of the second.

the root Bṛih (to increase); because it is infinite (spirit), and because it is the cause by which the Vedas (and all things) are developed.* Glory to Brahma, who is addressed by that mystic word, associated eternally with the triple universe,[1] and who is one with the four Vedas! Glory to Brahma, who, alike in the destruction and renovation of the world, is called the great and mysterious cause of the intellectual principle (Mahat); who is without limit in time or space, and exempt from diminution or decay; in whom (as connected with the property of darkness) originates

---

rana', although it may be defended as necessary to the sense, is not expressed by the words of the text, nor compatible with Hindu notions. In one of the MSS. employed, the transcriber has, evidently, been afraid of desecrating this sacred monosyllable, and has, therefore, altered the text, writing it

ध्रुवमेकाक्षरं ब्रह्म द्वापराद्रि व्यवस्थितम् ।

instead of

ध्रुवमेकाक्षरं ब्रह्म ओमित्येवं व्यवस्थितम् ।

[1] The daily prayers of the Brahman commence with the formula, Oṁ bhúr bhuvaḥ swar: 'Om, earth, sky, heaven.' These are the three mystical terms called Vyáhṛitis, and are scarcely of less sanctity than the Praṇava itself. Their efficacy, and the order of their repetition, preceding the Gáyatri, are fully detailed in Manu, II., 76—81. In the Mitákshará † they are directed to be twice repeated mentally, with Om prefixed to each; Oṁ bhúḥ, Oṁ bhuvaḥ, Oṁ swar; the breath being suppressed by closing the lips and nostrils: ओं भूः ओं भुवः ओं स्वरिति चौङ्कारादयुग्-नासिकास्यसंचाररहितं वायुं निरुध्य मनसा जपेत् ।

---

* बृहत्त्वाद्बृंहणत्वाच्च तद्ब्रह्मेत्यभिधीयते ।

Brahmá and Brahma are similarly etymologized in the *Váyu-puráṇa* and *Linga-puráṇa*, respectively. See Vol. I., p. 30, note *.

† Commenting on the *Yájnavalkya-smṛiti*, I., 23.

worldly illusion; and in whom resides the end of soul (fruition or liberation), through the properties of light and of activity (or goodness and foulness)! He is the refuge of those who are versed in the Sánkhya philosophy; of those who have acquired control over their thoughts and passions. He is the invisible, imperishable Brahma; varying in form, invariable in substance; the chief principle, self-engendered; who is said to illuminate the caverns of the heart; who is indivisible, radiant, undecaying, multiform. To that supreme Brahma be, for ever, adoration.

That form of Vásudeva, who is the same with supreme spirit, which is Brahma, and which, although diversified as threefold, is identical, is the lord who is conceived, by those that contemplate variety in creation, to be distinct in all creatures. He, composed of the Rig-, Sáma-, and Yajur-Vedas, is, at the same time, their essence, as he is the soul of all embodied spirits. He, distinguished as consisting of the Vedas, creates the Vedas, and divides them, by many subdivisions, into branches: he is the author* of those branches: he is those aggregated branches: for he, the eternal lord, is the essence of true knowledge.[1]†

---

[1] The form or sensible type of Vásudeva is here considered to be the monosyllable Om, and which is one with the three mystical words, Bhúh, Bhuvah, Swar, and with the Vedas. Consequently, the Vyáhritis and the Vedas are, also, forms of Vásudeva; diversified as to their typical character, but, essentially, one and the same.

* *Pradetri*, 'promulgator.'

† For another rendering of the Sanskrit of the latter half of this paragraph, see *Original Sanskrit Texts*, Part III., pp. 11, 12.

CHAPTER IV.

Division of the Veda, in the last Dwápara age, by the Vyása Krishńa Dwaipáyana. Paila made reader of the Ŕich; Vaiśampáyana, of the Yajus; Jaimini, of the Sáman; and Sumantu, of the Atharvan. Súta appointed to teach the historical poems. Origin of the four parts of the Veda. Sańhitás of the Ŕig-veda.

PARÁŚARA.—The original Veda, in four parts,* consisted of one hundred thousand (stanzas); and from it sacrifice of ten kinds,[1] the accomplisher of all desires (proceeded). In the twenty-eighth Dwápara†

[1] According to the Gŕihya portion of the Sáma-veda, there are five great sacrificial ceremonies: 1. Agnihotra, burnt-offerings, or libations of clarified butter on sacred fire; 2. Darśapaurńamása, sacrifices at new and full moon; 3. Chàturmásya, sacrifices every four months; 4. Paśuyajna or Aśwamedha, sacrifice of a horse or animal; and, 5. Soma-yajna, offerings and libations of the juice of the acid asclepias. These, again, are either Prákŕita, 'simple', or Vaikŕita, 'modified',‡ and, being thus doubled, constitute ten.§

* *Chatushpáda.* † In the original, *antara*, i. e., Manwantara.

‡ Rather, 'normal' and 'supplemental'.

§ The commentary says: यज्ञ: . . अग्निहोत्रदर्शपौर्णमासचातुर्मास्यपशुसोमा इति पञ्चविधः । स एव प्रकृतिविकृतिभेदेन दशविध इति । यद्वा गृह्योक्तैः पञ्चभिः सह दशविधत्वम् । Five sacrifices—but not said to belong to the *Sámaveda* ceremonial—are, thus, named, but not defined. The *paśu* of this nomenclature is, more usually, called *paśubandha* or *nirúd'hapaśubandha*. It is not to be confounded with the *aśwamedha*. To the five sacrifices in question, remarks the commentator, if we add the five mentioned in the *Gŕihya*, the ten of the text are completed. These five others—the *maháyajnas* of the *Sámaveda* ritual—are said, in Áśáditya's *Karmapradípabháshya*, to be the *bhútayajna*, *manushyayajna*, *pitŕiyajna*, *devayajna*, and *brahmayajna*. They are referred to in Chapter IX. of this Book. For the sacrifices generally, see Chapter XI., where I revert to this note.

age, my son Vyása separated the four portions of the Veda into four (Vedas). In the same manner as the Vedas were arranged by him, as Veda-vyása, so were they divided, (in former periods), by all the (preceding) Vyásas, and by myself; and the branches into which they were subdivided by him were the same into which they had been distributed in every aggregate of the four ages.* Know, Maitreya, the Vyása called Kŕishńa Dwaipáyana to be the deity† Náráyańa: for who else on this earth could have composed the Mahábhárata?[1] Into what portions the Vedas were arranged by my magnanimous son, in the Dwápara age, you shall hear.

When Vyása was enjoined, by Brahmá, to arrange the Vedas in different books, he took four persons, well read in those works, as his disciples. He appointed Paila reader of the Ŕig-;[2] Vaiśampáyana, of

---

[1] The composition of the Mahábhárata is always ascribed to the Vyása named Kŕishńa Dwaipáyana, the contemporary of the events there described. The allusion in the text establishes the priority of the poem to the Vishńu Puráńa.

[2] Or, rather, 'he took Paila as teacher.' The expression is: Ŕigvedaśrávakaṁ Pailaṁ jagráha sa mahámuniḥ:

ऋग्वेदश्रावकं पैलं जग्राह स महामुनिः ।

Śrávaka means, properly, 'he who causes to hear,' 'a lecturer,' 'a preacher;' although, as in the case of its applicability to the laity of the Buddhists and Jainas, it denotes a disciple. The commentator, however, observes, that the text is sometimes read ऋग्वेदपारगं,‡ 'one who had gone through the Ŕig-veda.'

---

* Yuga. † Prabhu.

‡ But the more ordinary reading is the one found in the Váyu-puráńa, from which work our text seems to be taken, largely, hereabouts.

the Yajur-; and Jaimini, of the Sáma-veda: and Sumantu, who was conversant with the Atharva-veda,[*] was also the disciple of the learned Vyása. He also took Súta, who was named Lomaharshańa,[†] as his pupil in historical and legendary traditions.[1][‡]

So, in the preceding verse, it is said: 'He took four persons, well read in the Vedas, as his disciples:'

स च शिष्यान्स जग्राह चतुरो वेदपारगान् ।

And again it is said: 'Sumantu, conversant with the Atharva-veda, was his disciple:'

• • • • • • तथैवाथर्ववेदवित् ।
सुमन्तुश्च शिष्योऽभूद्वेदव्यासस्य धीमतः ॥

It is clear, therefore, that the Vedas were known, as distinct works, before Krishńa Dwaipáyana; and it is difficult to understand how he earned his title of arranger, or Vyása. At any rate, in undertaking to give order to the prayers and hymns of which the Vedas consist, Paila and the others were rather his coadjutors than disciples; and it seems probable, that the tradition records the first establishment of a school, of which the Vyása was the head, and the other persons named were the teachers.

[1] The Itihása and Puráńas; understanding, by the former, legendary and traditional narratives. It is usually supposed, that, by the Itihása, the Mahábhárata is especially meant. But, although this poem is ascribed to Krishńa Dwaipáyana, the recitation of it is not attributed to his pupil, Romaharshańa or Lomaharshańa:

---

[*] The *Samhitás* thus disposed of are said, in the *Bhágavata-puráńa*, XII., VI., 52, 53, to be called, respectively, the Bahwrichá, the Nigada, the Chhandoga, and the Atharvángirasí.

This statement occurs in the passage referred to in Vol. I., Preface, p. XLIV.

[†] All my MSS. have Romaharshańa. Also see p. 64, 65, *infra*.

[‡] This chapter, thus far, will be found retranslated in *Original Sanskrit Texts*, Part III., pp. 21, 22.

There was but one Yajur-veda; but, dividing this into four parts, Vyása instituted the sacrificial rite that is administered by four kinds of priests: in which it was the duty of the Adhwaryu to recite the prayers (Yajusas,—or direct the ceremony); of the Hotri, to repeat the hymns (Richas); of the Udgátri, to chant other hymns (Sámans); and, of the Brahman, to pronounce the formulæ called Atharvans. Then the Muni, having collected together the hymns called Richas, compiled the Rig-veda; with the prayers and directions termed Yajusas he formed the Yajur-veda; with those called Sámans, the Sáma-veda; and with the Atharvans he composed the rules of all the ceremonies suited to kings, and the function of the Brahman agreeably to practice.[1*]

it was first narrated by Vaiśampáyana, and, after him, by Sauti, the son of Lomaharshaṅa.

[1] From this account, which is repeated in the Váyu Puráńa, it appears, that the original Veda was the Yajus, or, in other words, was a miscellaneous body of precepts, formulæ, prayers, and hymns, for sacrificial ceremonies; Yajus being derived, by the grammarians, from Yaj (यज्), 'to worship.' The derivation of the Váyu Puráńa, however, is from Yuj, 'to join,' 'to employ;' the formulæ being those especially applied to sacrificial rite, or set apart, for that purpose, from the general collection:

यच्छिद्रं च यजुर्वेदे तेन यज्ञमथायुजत् ।
युञ्जानः स यजुर्वेद इति शास्त्रविनिश्चयः ॥

Again:

यजुष्यति ह्यध्वरेष्वर्थेन वा युज्यते तु सः ।

The commentator on the text, however, citing the former of these

* Yathá-sthiti, 'according to a fixed rule.'

This vast original tree of the Vedas, having been divided, by him, into four principal stems, soon branched out into an extensive forest. In the first place, Paila divided the Ṛig-veda, and gave the two Saṁhitás (or collections of hymns) to Indrapramati* and to Báshkali.† Báshkali[1]‡ subdivided his Saṁhitá into four, which he gave to his disciples,§ Baudhya,

---

passages from the Váyu, reads it:

याजनादि यजुर्वेद इति शास्त्रस्य निश्चयः ।

confining the derivation to Yaj, 'to worship.' The concluding passage, relating to the Atharvan, refers, in regard to regal ceremonies, to those of expiation, Śanti, &c. The function of the Brahman (ब्रह्मत्वं • यथाविधि) is not explained; but, from the preceding specification of the four orders of priests who repeat, at sacrifices, portions of the several Vedas, it relates to the office of the one that is termed, specifically, the Brahman. So the Váyo has

ब्रह्मत्वमकारोद्यज्ञे वेदेनाथर्वणेन तु ।

'He constituted the function of the Brahman at sacrifices, with the Atharva-veda.

[1] Both in our text, and in that of the Váyu, this name occurs both Báshkala and Báshkali. Mr. Colebrooke writes it Báhkala and Báhkali.‖ Asiatic Researches, Vol. VIII., p. 374.¶

---

* Two of my MSS. have, here and below, Indrapramiti, a reading of no value.

† My MSS. all here give Báshkala. But see p. 49, note §, infra.

‡ Two MSS. here have Báshkala.

§ They are called, in the Váyu-puráńa, Bodhya, Agniśávara—in three MSS., by corruption, perhaps, of the Agnimáthara of two others,—Páráśara, and Yájnavalkya. The *Bhágavata-puráńa*, XII., VI., 55, has Bodhya, Yájnavalkya, Páráśara, and Agnimitra.

‖ Strictly, Báhkala and Báhkali, as transliterating the ungrammatical mislections बाःष्कल and बाःष्कलि.

¶ Or *Miscellaneous Essays*, Vol. I., p. 14.

Agnimáthara,* Yájnavalkya,† and Paráśara; and they taught these secondary shoots from the primitive branch. Indrapramati imparted his Saṁhitá to his son Máṅḍúkeya;‡ and it thence descended through successive generations, as well as disciples.[1]§ Vedamitra, (called also) Śákalya, studied the same Saṁhitá; but he divided it into five Saṁhitás, which he distributed amongst as many disciples, named, severally, Mudgala,

---

[1] The Váyu supplies the detail. Maṅḍukeya, or, as one copy writes, Márkaṅḍeya,¶ taught the Saṁhitá to his son Satyaśravas; he, to his son Satyahita; and he, to his son Satyaśri. The latter had three pupils: Śákalya, also called Devamitra** (sic in MS.); Rathántara;†† and another Báshkali, called also Bháradwája. The Váyu has a legend of Śákalya's death, in consequence of his being defeated, by Yájnavalkya, in a disputation at a sacrifice celebrated by Janaka.

---

* Agnimáchara, the lection of two MSS., and Agnimáthura, that of one, scarcely deserve noting.

† Professor Wilson had "Yajnawalka".

‡ The Translator put "Mánḍukeya", as the name is written in five of my thirteen MSS. See III., 8, of the *Prátiśákhya* of the *Ṛigveda*, edited by M. Regnier.

§ तस्य शिष्यप्रशिष्येभ्यः पुत्रशिष्यात्क्रमाद्ययौ ।

‖ According to the *Bhágavata-puráṅa*, XII., VI., 57, as explained by Śrídhara, Śákalya was son of Máṅḍúkeya.

¶ This is the reading of all the copies of the *Váyu-puráṅa* known to me.

** And so reads the *Bhágavata-puráṅa*, XII., VI., 56.

As the *Vishṅu-puráṅa* gives वेदमित्रस्तु शाकल्यः, so the *Váyu-puráṅa* gives देवमित्रस्तु शाकल्यः; and we here have, probably, only an epithet of Śákalya, or, at most, his secondary appellation.

†† See note †† in the next page.

Gokhalu,* Vátsya,† Śálíya, and Śiśira.[1] Śákapúrńi‡ made a different§ division of the original Sańhitá into three portions, and added a glossary (Nirukta), constituting a fourth.[2] The three Sańhitás

[1] These names, in the Váyu, are Mudgala, Golaka, Khálíya,|| Mátsya,¶ Śaiśireya.

[2] The commentator, who is here followed by Mr. Colebrooke, states, that he was a pupil of Indrapramati; but, from the Váyu, it appears, that Śákapúrńi was another name of Rathíntara, the pupil of Satyaśrí, the author of three Sańhitás and a Nirukta (or glossary); whence Mr. Colebrooke supposes him the same with Yáska. Asiatic Researches, Vol. VIII., p. 375.** It is highly probable, that the text of the Váyu may be made to correct that of the Vishńu, in this place, which is inaccurate, notwithstanding the copies agree. They read:

संहितात्रितयं चक्रे शाकपूर्णिरथेतरत् †† ।
निरुक्तमकरोत्तद्वच्चतुर्थं मुनिसत्तम ॥

* Probably it was from being misled by a smudged ख, that Professor Wilson deciphered "Goswalu", which I have corrected. Five of my MSS. have the word in the text; two corrupt it into Gohhalu; one, into Yokhalu; and four give Gomukha; one, Gálava. The *Bhágavata-puráńa*, XII., VI., 57, has Gokhalya. See, further, Professor Max Müller's *Ancient Sanskrit Literature*, p. 135, note 2, and p. 368, note 6.

† A single MS. has Śankha.

‡ Thus in four of my MSS., while the other nine have Śákapúńi.

Professor Max Müller — *Ancient Sanskrit Literature*, p. 153, note - asserts, that "there can be no doubt that Śákapúrńi is the same name as Śákapúńi." The former has much the air of being a corruption of the latter, due to popular etymology. The MSS. of the *Váyu-puráńa* almost everywhere have Śákapúńi; and so has Yáska.

§ See note †† in this page.

|| Two MSS. have Khálíya; others, Kháláya, Khaláya, and Swáloya.

¶ All my MSS. give Matsya.

** Or *Miscellaneous Essays*, Vol. I., p. 15.

Professor Roth - *Nirukta*, p. 222 - points out, that Śákapúńi is quoted by Yáska. The former cannot, therefore, be identical with the latter.

†† The bulk of MSS. at my disposal read शाकपूर्णिरथेतरः; and the

were given to his three pupils, Krauncha, Vaitálaki,*

Here, Śákapúrṇir atha-itaram is the necessary construction; but quere, if it should not be Śákapúrṇi Rathántaraḥ. The parallel passage in the Váyu is:

प्रोवाच संहितास्तिस्रः शाकपूर्णिरथान्तरः †।
निरुक्तं च पुनश्चक्रे चतुर्थं द्विजसत्तमाः ॥

Now, in describing the pupils of Satyaśrí, Rathántara was named clearly enough:

शाकल्यः प्रथमस्तेषां तस्मादन्यो रथान्तरः ‡।
बाष्कलिश्च भरद्वाज इति शाखाप्रवर्तकाः ॥§

In another passage it would seem to be implied, that this Báshkali was the author of the Saṁhitás; and Rathántara, of the Nirukta only:

बाष्कलिश्च भरद्वाजस्तिस्रः प्रोवाच संहिताः।
रथान्तरो निरुक्तं च पुनश्चक्रे चतुर्थकम् ॥||

resulting sense is: "Now, another, Śákapúṇi, made a triad of *Saṁhitás*, and made, likewise, a glossary, for a fourth *work*." The fact that the forementioned lection, with its awkwardly introduced 'now, another,' is the more ordinary one, lends considerable support to Professor Wilson's suggestion, that the text is here depraved.

* Bad readings are: Vaitálaki, Vaitáliki, Táluki, and Paitálaki; each in one manuscript.

† All my MSS. here give °रथीतरः. One of Professor Wilson's has शाकपूर्णरथान्तरः (*sic*).

‡ Such is, here, the prevailing lection: but रथीतरः occurs, also.

§ In the original, this passage precedes that quoted just above.

|| रथीतरः is the reading here, in all my five MSS., and so in every one of Professor Wilson's.

Rathántara is, without question, corrupted from Rathítara. As शाकपूर्णिरथीतरः, the reading of every one of my MSS., see note †, above—is an all but impossible compound name, and as the person intended is called, elsewhere in the *Váyu-puráṇa*, Rathítara simply, we must read शाकपूणी रथीतरः, 'Śákapúṇi, *that is to say*, Rathítara.' Śákapúṇi thus comes out a patronymic of Śákapúṇa,—a fact hitherto unnoticed, I believe. See Páṇini, IV., I., 95. In two of the three passages adduced, above,

and Baláka;* and a fourth, (thence named) Nirukta-

However this may be, his being the author of the Nirukta identifies him with Śákapúrńi, and makes it likely, that the two names should come in juxtaposition, in our text, as well as in the Váyu. It must be admitted, however, that there are some rather inexplicable repetitions in the part of the Váyu where this account occurs, although two copies agree in the reading. That a portion of the Vedas goes by the name of Rathantara† we have seen (Vol. I., p. 84); but, as far as is yet known, the name is confined to different prayers or hymns of the Úhya Gána of the Sáma-veda. The text of the Vishńu also admits of a different explanation regarding the work of Śákapúrńi; and, instead of a threefold division of the original, the passage may mean, that he composed a third Samhitá.‡ So Mr. Colebrooke says: "the *Vishńu puráńa* omits them [the Śákhás of Áśwaláyana

---

from the *Váyu-puráńa*, we find, similarly, mention of 'Báshkali, Bháradwája', *i. e.*, sprung from Bharadwája.

We are, then, to understand, that one and the same person is referred to in the *Bŕihaddevatá*, where it speaks of Śákapúńi and of Rathitara. See *Indische Studien*, Vol. I., p. 103.

Of the exceedingly rare work just named there is a MS. in the Bodleian Library, wittingly misrepresented, in Dr. Aufrecht's Catalogue, as the gift of Mr. William Walker.

* Instead of this, the *Bhágavata-puráńa*, XII., VI., 58, says, that Játúkarńya, disciple of Śákalya, digested a *Samhitá* and a *Nirukta*, and gave them to his disciples, Baláka, Paija, Vattála, and Viraja. The commentator explains that he divided his *Samhitá* into three.

One Játúkarńya succeeded, as a teacher, Yáska. *Bŕihad-árańyaka Upanishad*, II., VI., 3; IV., VI., 3.

† For the passage so called, see Vol. II., p. 343; supplementary note on p. 295, l. 9, *ibid*.

‡ संहितात्रितयम्, the reading of all my MSS., and also, apparently, of all seen by the Translator, can mean, in good Sanskrit, only 'three *Samhitás*',—not 'third *Samhitá*'. It would be interesting to know whether Colebrooke was acquainted with a different lection; as he very rarely trips in a matter of grammar. See Páńini, V., II., 43.

krit, had the glossary.[1]* In this way branch sprang from branch.† Another: Báshkali[2]§ composed three

---

and Śánkháyana], and intimates, that Śákapúrńi, a pupil of Indrapramati, gave the third varied edition from this teacher."|| The Váyu, however, is clear in ascribing three Samhitás, or Śákhás, to Śákapúrńi.

[1] In the Váyu, the four pupils of Śákapúrńi are called Kenava,¶ Dálaki,** Śatabaláka, and Naigama.

[2] This Báshkali may either be, according to the commentator,†† the pupil of Paila,—who, in addition to the four Samhi-

---

* क्रौञ्चो वैतालिकस्तद्वद्बलाकश्च महामतिः ।
निरुक्तकृच्चतुर्थोऽभूद्वेदवेदाङ्गपारगः ।

As the commentary observes, some MSS. begin the second line of this stanza with चतुर्थो निरुक्तकृत्तम ।

† इत्येताः प्रतिशाखाभ्योऽप्यनुशाखा द्विजोत्तम ।

‡ The original, unsupplemented by the commentary, does not discriminate this Báshkali from the one before mentioned:

बाष्कलिश्चापरास्तिस्रः संहिताः कृतवान्द्विज ।

See note †† in this page.

§ We read, in the *Bhágavata-puráńa*, XII., VI., 59:

बाष्कलिः प्रतिशाखाभ्यो वालखिल्याख्यसंहिताम् ।
चक्रे बालायनिर्भज्यः काशारश्चैव तां दधुः ॥

Báshkala had before been mentioned; and the Báshkali here spoken of is said, by Śrídhara, to have been his son: बाष्कलिः । पूर्वोक्तस्य बाष्कलस्य पुत्रः । It is stated, in this stanza, that Báshkali compiled a *Samhitá*, called Válakhilya, from all the aforesaid *Śákhás*; and that Báláyani (*sic*), Bhajya, and Kášára accepted it,—or read it, according to the commentator's gloss on दधुः, namely, तामादधुः । अधीतवन्तः ।

|| *Miscellaneous Essays*, Vol. I., p. 15.

¶ Two MSS. have Kaljava.

** One MS. has Dwáláki; and two, Vámana. Two, again, seem to intend Uddálaki. Uddálaka, son of Aruńa, is a well-known Vaidik personage.

†† The commentary remarks: बाष्कलिः पैलशिष्यः । चतस्रः संहितास्तस्य प्रसिद्धाः । स एवापरास्तिस्रः संहिताः कृतवान् । अपर एव

other Saṁhitás, which he taught to his disciples, Káláyani, Gárgya,* and Kathájava.[1]† These are they by whom the principal divisions of the Rich have been promulgated.[2]‡

tás previously noticed, compiled three others; or he may be another Báshkali, a fellow-pupil of Śákapúrṇi. The Váyu makes him a disciple of Satyaśrí, the fellow-pupil of Śákalya and Rathántara, and adds the name or title Bháradwája. §

[1] In the Váyu, they are called Nandáyaniya, Pannagári,|| and Árjava.

[2] Both the Vishṇu and Váyu Puráṇas omit two other principal divisions of the Rich, those of Áśwaláyana and Śánkháyana (or the Kaushítaki). Asiatic Researches, Vol. VIII., p. 375.¶ There is no specification of the aggregate number of Saṁhitás of the Rich, in our text, or in the Váyu; but they describe eighteen, including the Nirukta; or, as Mr. Colebrooke states,

बाष्कलसंहितास्तिस्रो बाष्कलिः । तच्छिष्याः कालायनिप्रमुखास्तथा । In other words, Báshkali, disciple of Paila, first redacted four *Saṁhitás*, and then three others. But there was a different Báshkali, Śákalya's fellow-student; and his disciples were Káláyani and the rest.

We are left to ascertain on what authority seven *Saṁhitás* are imposed on a single Báshkali.

* Son of Baláka, mentioned a little before. See the *Kaushítaki-bráhmaṇa Upanishad*, IV., 1.

† One of my MSS. exhibits Ájava, which looks like a mere miscript of the *Váyu-puráṇa's* Árjava.

‡ इत्येते बह्वृचाः प्रोक्ताः संहिता यैः प्रवर्तिताः ।

"These, by whom the *Saṁhitás* have been promulgated, were denominated Bahwṛichas."

Bahwṛicha is a general name for a teacher of the *Ṛigveda*.

§ See the second and third extracts from the *Váyu-puráṇa* at p. 46, note 2, *supra*.

|| In two MSS., Pannagárí.

¶ Or Colebrooke's *Miscellaneous Essays*, Vol. I., p. 15.

sixteen (Asiatic Researches, Vol. VIII., p. 374*); that is, omitting the two portions of the original as divided by Paila. The Kúrma Puráńa states the number at twenty-one;† but treatises on the study of the Vedas reduce the Śákhás of the Rich to five.‡

* Or Colebrooke's *Miscellaneous Essays*, Vol. I., p. 14.

† But it does not name them.

‡ The Śákalas, Báshkalas, Áśwaláyanas, Śáńkháyanas, and Máńdúkáyanas. So says the *Charańa-vyúha*.

CHAPTER V.

Divisions of the Yajur-veda. Story of Yájnavalkya: forced to give up what he has learned: picked up by others, forming the Taittiriya-yajus. Yájnavalkya worships the sun, who communicates to him the Vájasaneyi-yajus.

PARÁŚARA.—Of the tree of the Yajur-veda there are twenty-seven branches, which Vaiśampáyana, the pupil of Vyása, compiled, and taught to (as many) disciples.[1] Amongst these, Yájnavalkya, the

---

[1] The Váyu divides these into three classes, containing, each, nine, and discriminated as northern, middle and eastern:

उदीच्या मध्यदेश्याश्च प्राच्याश्चैव पृथग्विधाः ।

Of these the chiefs were, severally, Śyámáyani, Áruńi, and Ánalavi (or Álambi*). With some inconsistency, however, the same authority states, that Vaiśampáyana composed, and gave to his disciples, eighty-six Saṁhitás.†

---

* My MSS. have this reading.

† The *Váyu-puráńa* declares:

वैशम्पायनगोत्रोऽसौ यजुर्वेदं व्यकल्पयत् ।
षडशीतिस्तु येनोक्ता संहिता यजुषां शुभाः ॥
शिष्येभ्यः प्रददौ ताश्च जगृहुस्ते विधानतः ।
एकस्तत्र परित्यक्तो याज्ञवल्क्यो महातपाः ॥
षडशीतिश्च तस्यापि संहितानां विकल्पकाः ।
सर्वेषामेव तेषां वै त्रिधा भेदाः प्रकीर्तिताः ।
त्रिधा भेदास्तु ते प्रोक्ता भेदेऽस्मिन्नवमे शुभे ॥

Then follows the line quoted above, and the names of the disciples, Śyámáyani, &c.

These verses are thus edited, from Professor Wilson's MSS., in Dr. Aufrecht's *Catalogus*, &c., p. 55; and my five copies of the *Váyu-puráńa* are of no help towards mending them into something probable. The passage, as it stands, is, in part, ungrammatical and unintelligible; and it would be venturesome to guess at its full meaning, in its unamended state.

son of Brahmaráta,* was distinguished for piety and obedience to his preceptor.

It had been formerly agreed, by the Munis, that any one of them who, at a certain time, did not join an assembly held on mount Meru should incur the guilt of killing a Brahman within a period of seven nights.[1] Vaiśampáyana alone failed to keep the appointment, and, consequently, killed, by an accidental kick with his foot, the child of his sister. He then addressed his scholars, and desired them to perform the penance expiatory of Brahmanicide, on his behalf. Without any hesitation,† Yájnavalkya refused, and said: "How shall I engage in penance with these miserable and inefficient Brahmans?"‡ On which, his Guru, being incensed, commanded him to relinquish all that he had learned from him. "You speak contemptuously," he observed, "of these young Brahmans: but of what use is a disciple who disobeys my commands?" "I spoke," replied Yájnavalkya, "in perfect faith:§ but,

[1] The parallel passage in the Váyu rather implies, that the agreement was to meet within seven nights:

ततस्ते ऋषयः सर्वे वैशम्पायनवर्जिताः ।
प्रययुः सप्तरात्रेण यत्र संधिः कृतोऽभवत् ॥

* One MS. has Devaráta; and so reads the *Bhágavata-purána*, XII., VI., 64. Devaráta would be a violent synonym of Brahmaráta. Moreover, Daivaráti—patronymic of Devaráta—is a name of Janaka, Yájnavalkya's patron.

† These words should end the preceding sentence. The original runs:

चरध्वं मत्कृते सर्वे न विचार्यमिदं तथा ।

‡ He says: 'I will perform this sacred office': चरिष्येऽहमिदं व्रतम् ।

§ *Bhaktau*, "out of devotion *to thee*."

as to what I have read from you, I have had enough: it is no more than this—" (acting as if he would eject it from his stomach); when he brought up the texts of the Yajus, in substance stained with blood. He then departed. The other scholars of Vaiśampáyana, transforming themselves to partridges (Tittiri), picked up the texts which he had disgorged, and which, from that circumstance, were called Taittiríya;[1] and the disciples were called the Charaka professors* of the Ya-

[1] Also called the Black Yajus. No notice of this legend, as Mr. Colebrooke observes (Asiatic Researches, Vol. VIII., p. 376†), occurs in the Veda itself; and the term Taittiríya is more rationally accounted for in the Anukramańi, or Index, of the Black Yajus. It is there said, that Vaiśampáyana taught it to Yáska, who taught it to Tittiri, who, also, became a teacher; whence the term Taittiríya: for a grammatical rule explains it to mean, 'The Taittiríyas are those who read what was said or repeated by Tittiri:' तित्तिरिणा प्रोक्तमधीयते । तैत्तिरीयाः । Páńini, IV., III., 102. The legend, then, appears to be nothing more than a Pauráńik invention, suggested by the equivocal sense of Tittiri, a proper name, or a partridge.‡ Much of the mythos of the Hindus, and, obviously, of that of the Greeks and Romans, originates in this source. It was not confined, at least amongst the former, to the case that Creuzer specifies,—"Telle ou telle expression cessa d'être comprise, et l'on inventa des mythes pour éclaircir ces malentendus,"—but was wilfully perpetrated, even where the word was understood, when it afforded a favourable opportunity for a fable. It may be suspected, in the present instance, that the legend is posterior, not only to the Veda, but to the grammatical rule; or it would have furnished Páńini with a different etymology.

* *Charakádhwaryu.* † Or *Miscellaneous Essays*, Vol. I., p. 16.

‡ Compare Professor Max Müller's *History of Ancient Sanskrit Literature*, p. 174, note.

jus, from Charańa, ('going through' or 'performing' the expiatory rites enjoined by their master).[1]*

Yájnavalkya, who was perfect in ascetic practices,† addressed himself strenuously to the sun, being anxious to recover possession of the texts of the Yajus. "Glory to the Sun," he exclaimed, "the gate of liberation, the fountain of bright radiance, the triple source of splendour, as the Ŕig-, the Yajur-, and the Sáma-vedas! Glory to him, who, as fire and the moon, is one with the cause of the universe: to the sun, that is charged with radiant heat, and with the Sushumńa‡ ray, (by which the moon is fed with light): to him who is one with the notion of time, and all its divisions of hours, minutes, and seconds:§ to him who is to be

---

[1] This is another specimen of the sort of Paronomasia explained in the preceding note. The Charakas are the students of a Śákhá so denominated from its teacher Charaka. (Asiatic Researches, Vol. VIII., p. 377||). So, again, Páńini, IV., III., 107: 'The readers of that which is said by Charaka are Charakas:' चरकेण प्रोक्तं चरकाः। Charaka has no necessary connexion with Char, 'to go.' The Váyu states, they were also called Chaiakas, from Chai (चट्), 'to divide;' because they shared amongst them their master's guilt. 'Those pupils of Vaiśampáyana were called Chaiakas by whom the crime of Brahmanicide was shared; and Charakas, from its departure:'

---

* See the Translator's third note on Book IV., Chapter XXI.

† *Práńáyáma.* It is correctly rendered "suppression of breath", in Vol. II., p. 89.

‡ See Vol. II., p. 297, note *.

§ कलाकाष्ठानिमेषादिकालज्ञानात्मने नमः।

See Vol. I., p. 47.

|| Or Colebrooke's *Miscellaneous Essays*, Vol. I., p. 17.

meditated upon as the (visible) form of Vishńu, as the impersonation of the mystic Om:* to him who nourishes the troops of the gods, having filled the moon with his rays: who feeds the Pitŕis with nectar and ambrosia,† and who nourishes mankind with rain; who pours down, or absorbs, the waters, in the time of the rains, of cold, and of heat!‡ Glory be to Brahmá,§ the sun, in the form of the three seasons:|| him who alone is the dispeller of the darkness of this earth, of which he is the sovereign lord! To the god who is clad in the raiment of purity be adoration! Glory to the sun, until whose rising, man is incapable of devout acts, and water does not purify; and, touched by whose rays, the world is fitted for religious rites: to him who is the centre and source of purification!¶ Glory to Savitŕi, to Súrya, to Bháskara, to Vivaswat, to Áditya, to the first-born of gods or demons.** I adore the eye

---

वैशम्पायनशिष्यास्ते चरका: समुदाहृता: ।
ब्रह्महत्या तु यैश्चीर्णा चरणाच्चरका: स्मृता: ॥††

---

* In the original, *paramákshara*, "the supreme syllable."

† *Sudhámŕita*. See Vol. II., p. 300, note *.

‡ हिमाम्बुघर्मवृष्टीनां कर्ता हर्ता च य: प्रभु: ।

§ Vedhas, in the original.

|| *Kála*.

¶ सत्कर्मयोग्यो न जनो नैवाप: शौचकारकम् ।
यस्मिन्ननुदिते तस्मै नमो देवाय भास्वते ॥
स्पृष्टो यदंशुभिर्लोक: क्रियायोग्योऽभिजायते ।
पवित्रताकारणाय तस्मै शुद्धात्मने नम: ॥

** "Or demons" represents *ádi*, 'etc.'

†† The halves of this stanza are here transposed, if my MSS. are correct.

of the universe, borne in a golden car, whose banners scatter ambrosia."*

Thus eulogized by Yájnavalkya, the sun, in the form of a horse, (appeared to him, and) said: "Demand what you desire." To which the sage, having prostrated himself before the lord of day, replied: "Give me a knowledge of those texts of the Yajus with which (even) my preceptor is unacquainted." Accordingly, the sun imparted to him the texts of the Yajus called Ayátayáma (unstudied), which were unknown to Vaiśampáyana: and, because these were revealed by the sun, in the form of a horse, the Brahmans who study this portion of the Yajus are called Vájins (horses).† Fifteen branches of this school sprang from Kańwa and other pupils of Yájnavalkya.[1]

---

[1] The Váyu names the fifteen teachers of these schools, Kańwa, Vaidheya, Śálin, Madhyandina, Śápeyin,‡ Vidagdha, Uddálin,§ Támráyańi,|| Vátsya, Gálava,¶ Śaiśiri,** Átavya,†† Parńa, Virańa,‡‡ and Samparáyańa,§§ who were the founders of no fewer than 101 branches of the Vájasaneyi, or White Yajus. Mr. Colebrooke specifies several of these, as the Jábálas, Baudháyanas, Tápaniyas, &c. Asiatic Researches, Vol. VIII., p. 376."||||

---

* Yájnavalkya's hymn will be found in the *Bhágavata-puráńa*, XII., VI., 67–72.

† See, for a translation of nearly the whole of this chapter, Yájnavalkya's hymn excepted, *Original Sanskrit Texts*, Part III., pp. 32, 33.

‡ Two of my MSS. have Śápemin, a reading of no value.

§ This, as I judge from all my MSS., is an error for Uddala.

|| Similarly, this seems an oversight for Támráyańa.

¶ Golava is a variant.

** All my MSS. have Śaishiri.

†† Atavin is the most common reading; but Atavin and Átavin, also, are found.

‡‡ Viraúin is in all my MSS.

§§ The lection of four MSS. is चपरायणः, 'and Paráyańa.'

|||| Or *Miscellaneous Essays*, Vol. I., p. 17.

CHAPTER VI.

Divisions of the Sáma-veda: of the Atharva-veda. Four Pauráńik Saḿhitás. Names of the eighteen Puráńas. Branches of knowledge. Classes of Rishis.

YOU shall now hear, Maitreya, how Jaimini, the pupil of Vyása, divided the branches of the Sáma-veda. The son of Jaimini was Sumantu; and his son was Sukarman; who, both, studied the same Saḿhitá under Jaimini[1]. The latter* composed the Sáhasra Saḿhitá (or compilation of a thousand hymns, &c.), which he taught to two disciples, Hirańyanábha,—also named Kauśalya† (or, of Kośala),—and Paushyinji[2].‡ Fifteen disciples (of the latter) were the authors of as many Saḿhitás: they were called the northern chanters of

[1] The Váyu makes Sukarman the grandson of Sumantu; his son being called Sunwat.§

[2] Some copies read Paushpinji. The Váyu agrees with our text, but alludes to a legend of Sukarman having first taught a thousand disciples; but they were, all, killed by Indra, for reading on an unlawful day, or one when sacred study is prohibited.

* Sukarman, namely.

† One of my MSS. has Kaiśilya. The *Váyu-puráńa* reads Kauśilya, which looks less likely than Kauśalya to be correct.

‡ All my MSS. have Paushpinji. Paushyinji, a reading of no account, occurs in some copies of the *Váyu-puráńa*. The *Bhágavata-puráńa*—see p. 59, note *, *infra*,— has Paushpanji, a patronymic of Pushpanja. The meaning of Paushpinji is not evident; but it is, probably, the original name.

§ See p. 60, note ||, *infra*.

the Sáman.* As many more, also, the disciples of

---

* साहस्रं संहिताभेदं सुकर्मा तत्सुतस्ततः ।
चकार तं च तच्छिष्यौ जगृहाते महामती ॥
हिरण्यनाभः कौशल्यः पौष्पिञ्जिश्च द्विजोत्तम ।
उदीच्यसामगाः शिष्यास्तस्य पञ्चदश स्मृताः ॥
हिरण्यनाभात्तावत्यः संहिता यैर्द्विजोत्तमैः ।
गृहीतास्तेऽपि चोच्यन्ते पण्डितैः प्राच्यसामगाः ॥

The corresponding passage of the *Bhágavata-puráńa*,—XII., VI., 76–78,—runs thus:

सुकर्मा चापि तच्छिष्यः सामवेदतरोर्महान् ।
साहस्रं संहिताभेदं चक्रे साम्नां ततो द्विजः ॥
हिरण्यनाभः कौशल्यः पौष्यञ्जिश्च सुकर्मणः ।
शिष्यौ जगृहतुश्चान्य आवन्त्यो ब्रह्मवित्तमः ॥
उदीच्याः सामगाः शिष्या आसन्पञ्चशतानि वै ।
पौष्यञ्ज्यावन्त्ययोश्चापि तांश्च प्राच्यान्प्रचक्षते ॥

Śrídhara explains this to mean, that Hirańyanábha, Paushpanji, and Ávantya had, between them, five hundred disciples, first called northern, and, some of them, in time, eastern.

It seems possible that the name Ávantya grew out of a misreading of *távatyaḥ*,—which some of my MSS. corrupt into *trivantyaḥ*,—and the suggestion of Kauśalya; both which words stand only two lines apart, in the verses quoted from the *Vishńu-puráńa*. Ávantya does not appear in the *Váyu-puráńa*, an older work than either the *Vishńu* or the *Bhágavata*:

तस्य शिष्योऽभवद्धीमान्पौष्यिञ्जिर्द्विजसत्तमः ।
हिरण्यनाभः कौशिल्यो द्वितीयोऽभून्नराधिप ॥
अध्यापयत्तु पौष्यिञ्जिः सहस्रार्धं तु संहिताः ।
ते नाम्नोदीच्यसामानः शिष्याः पौष्यिञ्जिनः शुभाः ॥
शतानि पञ्च कौशिल्यः संहितानां च वीर्यवान् ।
शिष्या हिरण्यनाभस्य स्मृतास्ते प्राच्यसामगाः ॥

Here, distinctly, Paushpinji is said to have taught half a thousand *Samhitás*; and his disciples were called northerners: Hirańyanábha had five hundred *Samhitás*; and his disciples were known as easterlings.

Śrídhara tries to harmonise with the text he is editing that of the *Vishńu-puráńa*; quoting from it, in place of the fourth verse adduced above:

उदीच्याः सामगाः शिष्यास्तस्य पञ्च शतं स्मृताः ।

The reading शतं is seen, at once, to be incomparably better than

Hirańyanábha, were termed the eastern chanters of the Sáman, founding an equal number of schools. Lokákshi,* Kuthumi,† Kushídin,‡ and Lángali were the pupils of Paushyinji; and by them and their disciples many other branches were formed: whilst another scholar of Hirańyanábha, named Kriti,§ taught twenty-four Saḿhitás to (as many) pupils; and by them, again, was the Sáma-veda divided into numerous branches.[1] ‖

[1] The Váyu specifies many more names than the Vishńu; but the list is rather confused. Amongst the descendants of those named in the text, Ráyáńániya (or Ráńáyaniya), the son of Lokákshi, is the author of a Saḿhitá still extant; Saumitri, his son, was the author of three Saḿhitás: Parášara, the son of Kuthumi, compiled and taught six Saḿhitás: and Śáligotra, a son

---

[illegible]:; and 'five hundred', as the *Váyu-puráńa* shows, has to displace "fifteen". By the ordinary text, only thirty *Saḿhitás* are disposed of, out of the thousand. Both these better lections are in a single one of my thirteen copies of the *Vishńu-puráńa*; but the commentary adopts, uninquiringly, and without demur, what are now made out to be corruptions.

* Three MSS. have Langákshi; one has Laukákshi. The former of these readings seems to be the best of all.

† Scarcely worthy of mention are the variants Kuthami and Kuśumi.

‡ This is the prevailing lection; while three MSS. have Kusidin; two, Kuśidi; two, Kuchidi; one, Kuśádi. The *Váyu-puráńa* seems to give Kuśiti, in some MSS.; in others, Kuśin.

§ Two MSS. exhibit Kŕita; and this, according to the copies of it known to me, is the name, in the *Váyu-puráńa*.

‖ The history of the transmission of the *Sáma-veda* is briefly told as follows, in the *Bhágavata-puráńa*, XII., VI., 76—80. Jaimini had a son, Sumantu, whose son was Sunwat; and to each of them he gave a *Saḿhitá*. Sukarman, another disciple of Jaimini, divided the *Sáma-veda* into a thousand parts. His disciples were Hiraṅyanábha, Paushpanji, and Ávantya; and their disciples were, in all, five hundred.

I will now give you an account of the Saṁhitás of the Atharva-veda. The illustrious Muni Sumantu taught this Veda to his pupil Kabandha, who made it twofold, and communicated the two portions to Devadarśa* and to Pathya. The disciples of Devadarśa were Maudga,† Brahmabali, Śaulkáyani,‡ and Pippalá-

---

of Lángali, established, also, six schools.§ Kriti was of royal descent:

ततो हिरण्यनाभस्य कृतिः शिष्यो नृपात्मजः ।

He and Paushyinji were the two most eminent teachers of the Sáma-veda.

Paushpanji's disciples, to-wit, Laugákshi, Mángali, Kolya, Kuśida, and Kukshi, received, each, a hundred *Saṁhitás*; Hiraṇyanábha's disciple, Kṛita, twenty-four; and Ávantya's disciples, the rest.

We are not told who, or how many, these last were. They must have taken four hundred and seventy-six *Saṁhitás*, to make up the thousand into which the *Sámaveda* was partitioned by Sukarman.

* The *Váyu-puráṇa* has Vedasparśa. Śrídhara, commenting on the *Bhágavata-puráṇa*, XII., VII., 1, quotes a portion of our text, and reads Vedadarśa.

† One MS. has Maunda. The name, in the *Váyu-puráṇa*, is Moda.

‡ One MS. has Śaulkyáyani.

§ I do not find that Ráṇáyaniya is called son of Lokákshi: he seems to have been only his disciple. Nor is Saumitri represented as son of Ráṇáyaniya; and no writings are credited to him. Ráṇáyaniyi—son of Ráṇáyaniya—and he are merely stated to have been conversant with the *Sámaveda*. The Sanskrit runs:

राणायनीयिः सौमित्रिः सामवेदविशारदौ ॥

Again, instead of "Páráśara, the son of Kuthumi," I meet with Páráśarya Kauthuma and with Kauthuma Páráśarya, which perhaps intend Páráśarya, son of Kuthumi. Once more, the kinship of Lángali and Śálihotra,—a better reading than Śáligotra—is left unspecified: and each of them, we are told, published six *Saṁhitás*:

लाङ्गलिः शालिहोत्रश्च षट्प्रोवाच संहिताः ।

As to this line, at least, my MSS. of the *Váyu-puráṇa* must differ from those which were consulted by Professor Wilson.

da.* Pathya had three pupils, Jájali, Kumudádi,† and Śaunaka; and by all these were separate branches instituted. Śaunaka, having divided his Saṁhitá into two, gave one to Babhru, and the other to Saindhaváyana; and from them sprang two schools, the Saindhavas and the Munjakeśas.[1] ‡ The principal subjects of difference§ in the Saṁhitás of the Atharva-veda

---

[1] According to the commentator, Munjakeśa is another name for Babhru; but the Váyu seems to consider him as the pupil of Saindhava: but the text is corrupt:

शैन्धवो मुञ्जकेशाच भिन्नं चाथ द्विधा पुनः ।||

---

* Pishpaláda, though occurring in five of my MSS., and in some copies of the *Váyu-puráńa*, can be nothing but a clerical error.

† Kumudáhi is the reading of two MSS.; Kumudári, of one.

‡ The account of the *Atharvaveda* given in the *Bhágavata-puráńa*, XII., VII., 1—3, is, in substance, this. Sumantu had two disciples, Pathya and Vedadarśa. The disciples of the latter were Śaulkáyani, Brahmabali, Modosha, and Paippaláyani; and those of the former were Kumuda, Śunaka, and Jájali. Śunaka had two disciples, Babhru—son of Angiras,—and Saindhaváyana; and these were succeeded by the Sávarńyas and others.

I have availed myself of Śankara's supplementations, here and in note in p. 60, *supra*.

One MS. has, for Modosha, Modásha; another, Modiya. All my MSS., and likewise the printed editions, have the ungrammatical Pippaláyani, which I have corrected to Paippaláyani. The *Bhágavata-kathá-sangraha* gives, in my incorrect copies of it, Śaunakáyani, Brahmabali, Maudgaládi, and Pippaláyani, as the disciples of Vedadarśa.

§ "Subjects of difference" is the rendering of *vikalpaká*, 'divisions.'

|| Just before this line we read, almost in the words of the *Vishńu-puráńa*, as follows:

शौनकस्तु द्विधा कृत्वा ददावेकां तु बभ्रवे ।
द्वितीयां संहितां प्रादात्सैन्धवायनसंज्ञिते ॥

It is now patent why the Translator pronounced the text corrupt. Saindhaváyana and Saindhava cannot denominate the same teacher. The former must have been a descendant of the latter.

are the five Kalpas (or ceremonials): the Nakshatra Kalpa, (or rules for worshipping the planets); the Vaitána (Kalpa), (or rules for oblations, according to the Vedas generally); the Saṁhitá (Kalpa), (or rules for sacrifices, according to different schools); the Ángirasa (Kalpa), (incantations and prayers for the destruction of foes and the like); and the Śánti Kalpa, (or prayers for averting evil).[1]*

Accomplished in the purport of the Puráńas, Vyása compiled a Pauráńik Saṁhitá, consisting of historical and legendary traditions, prayers and hymns, and sacred chronology.[2]† He had a distinguished disciple,

[1] The Váyu has an enumeration of the verses contained in the different Vedas; but it is very indistinctly given, in many respects, especially as regards the Yajus. The Rich is said to comprise 8,600 Richas: the Yajus, as originally compiled by Vyása, 12,000; of which the Vájasaneyi contains 1,900 Richas and 7,000 Bráhmańas; the Charaka portion contains 6,026 stanzas; and, consequently, the whole exceeds 12,000 verses. The stanzas of the Sáman are said to be 8,014; and those of the Atharvan, 5,980. Mr. Colebrooke‡ states the verses of the whole Yajus to be 1,987; of the Śatapatha§ Bráhmańa of the same Veda, 7,624; and, of the Atharvan, 6,015.

[2] Or, of stories (Ákhyánas) and minor stories or tales (Upá-

* नक्षत्रकल्पो वेदानां संहितानां तथैव च।
चतुर्थः स्यादाङ्गिरसः शान्तिकल्पश्च पञ्चमः।
श्रेष्ठास्त्वथर्वणामेते संहितानां विकल्पकाः॥

The Translator consulted, for his intercalative explanations, those of the commentary; and this understands, by the second and third *kalpas*, the *Bráhmańas* of the *Atharvaveda*, and its *mantras*.

† आख्यानैश्चाप्युपाख्यानैर्गाथाभिः कल्पशुद्धिभिः।
पुराणसंहितां चक्रे पुराणार्थविशारदः॥

‡ *Miscellaneous Essays*, Vol. I., pp. 54, 60, 89.

§ "Satapatha" was, of course, an error of the press, in the first edition.

Súta, also termed Romaharshańa: and to him the great Muni communicated the Puráńas. Súta had six scholars, Sumati, Agnivarchas, Mitrayu* Śáḿśapáyana,† Akŕitabrańa,‡ (who is also called Kásyapa§), and Sávarńi. The three last composed three fundamental

khyánas); of portions dedicated to some particular divinity, as the

* One MS. has, here and below, Mitrayu, a reading which is seen in some copies of the *Váyu-puráńa*, as well.

† In one MS. is Śáḿśapáyani.

‡ One MS. has Kŕitabraña: but the reading is, perhaps, to be rejected. Akŕitabraña, however, renders the line which it begins hypermetrical:

अकृतव्रणोऽथ सावर्णिः षट्शिष्यास्तस्य चाभवन् ।

What is conclusive,—if the MSS. are not corrupt,—the *Váyu-puráńa* has the line

आत्रेयः सुमतिर्धीमान्काश्यपो ह्यकृतव्रणः ।

It is proved hereby, moreover, that Akŕitabraña sprang from Kaśyapa. Sumati is here called descendant of Atri, too.

For the reading Kŕitavrata, see note || in this page.

§ In the Sanskrit, Kaśyapa is not named here, but in the following sentence, which the translation abridges.

|| "Six persons received the Puráńas from Vyása, and were his pupils. Their names are Súta, Lomaharsha, Sumati, Maitreya, Siḿsapáyana, and Suvarńi." The Translator thus renders a passage from the *Agni-puráńa*, in the *Journal of the Asiatic Society of Bengal*, Vol. I., p. 84. Compare Professor Wilson's *Essays, Analytical, Critical, &c.*, Vol. I., p. 88.

Burnouf—in his edition of the *Bhágavata-puráńa*, Vol. I., Preface, pp. XXXIX., XL.—quotes the original of the passage thus rendered, and translates and annotates it, as follows:

प्राप्य व्यासात्पुराणादि सूतो वै लोमहर्षणः ।
सुमतिश्चाग्निवर्चाश्च मित्रयुः शांशपायनः ॥
कृतव्रतोऽथ सावर्णिः षट्शिष्यास्तस्य चाभवन् ।
शांशपायनादयश्चक्रुः पुराणानां तु संहिताः ॥
ब्राह्मादीनि पुराणानि हरिर्विद्या दशाष्ट च ।
महापुराणे चाग्नेये विद्यारूपो हरिः स्थितः ॥

"Lómaharchaṅa le Súta, après avoir reçu de Vyâsa les Puráṅas et le reste, eut six disciples, savoir: Sumati, Agnivartchas, Mitrayu,

Saṁhitás; and Romaharshaṅa himself compiled a

Śíva-gítá, Bhagavad-gítá, &c.; and accounts of the periods

Çâmçapâyana, Kritavrata et Sâvarńi. Çâmçapâyana et les autres firent des collections des Purâńas. Les Purâńas, dont le Brâhma est le premier, sont au nombre de dix-huit; c'est la science même qui n'est autre que Hari. En effet, dans le grand Purâńa nommé l'*Âgnéya*, Hari existe sous la forme de la science.'

"M. Wilson * * * * a cité ce texte qu'il regarde comme remarquable en ce qui touche à la question de l'origine des Purâńas. Mais soit qu'il ait eu sous les yeux un texte différent du nôtre, soit que quelque faute d'impression se soit glissée dans son travail, il fait deux personnages de Sûta et de Lômaharchańa, et il ne nomme pas Kritavrata. Au lieu de *Çâmçapâyana*, que donne également le Vâichńava, M. Wilson lit *Siṁsapâyana*, comme le Bhâgavata, et *Mâitrêya* au lieu du *Mitraya* ou *Mitrâyu* du Vâichńava. Ces différences viennent probablement de l'inattention des copistes qui ont compilé les index dont s'est servi M. Wilson pour ses analyses; quelle qu'en soit d'ailleurs la cause, je crois plus sûr de m'en tenir au texte que j'ai sous les yeux, que de faire deux personnages de Sûta et de Lômaharchańa. Mais je dois en même temps remarquer le peu d'accord qui se trouve entre les trois autorités originales dont je rapporte le témoignage, le Bhâgavata, le Vâichńava et l'Âgnêya. Les noms de *Trayyâruńi* et de *Hârita*, donnés par le Bhâgavata, ne reparaissent plus dans le Vâichńava ni dans l'Agnêya; d'autre part, le *Sumati*, l'*Agnivartchas* et le *Mitrâyu* de ces deux derniers ouvrages ne se trouvent pas dans le Bhâgavata. La liste de ce dernier Purâńa contient d'ailleurs un vice radical, qui consiste à faire deux personnages de Kaçyapa (qu'il faut lire, comme je vais le dire plus bas, *Kâçyapa*), et d'Akritavrańa. Quand on pourra comparer un plus grand nombre de textes indiens, et surtout de commentaires, peut-être résoudra-t-on ces difficultés, comme on peut le faire en ce qui touche Akritavrańa, qu'un commentateur nous apprend avoir été surnommé *Kâçyapa*, à cause sans doute de la famille à laquelle il appartenait; ainsi, le nom de *Trayyâruńi*, qui est patronymique, cache probablement le nom propre de *Sumati* ou d'*Agnivartchas*. *Trayyâruńi* rappelle le *Trayyaruńa* qui figure, selon Colebrooke, parmi les rois auteurs de quelques hymnes du Rigvêda (*Miscell. Essays*, t. I., p. 23); et *Hârita* est le nom d'un sage, auteur d'un Dharmaçâstra qui est quelquefois cité par Kullûka Bhaṭṭa, dans son Commentaire sur Manu", *etc.*

For Tryaruńa, the real Vaidik name, see p. 36, note †, *supra*; for Âtreya, the patronymic of Sumati, p. 64, note ‡, *supra*. According to

fourth, called Romaharshańiká;* the substance of which four Samhitás is collected into this (Vishńu Puráńa). †

The first of all the Puráńas is entitled the Bráhma. Those who are acquainted with the Puráńas enumerate eighteen, or, the Bráhma, Pádma, Vaishńava,‡ Śaiva,

called Kalpas, as the Bráhma Kalpa, Váráha Kalpa, &c.§

---

the Váyu-puráńa, Bháradwája is Agnivarchas's patronymic; Vásishṭha, Mitrayu's; and Sanmadatti, Sávarńi's.

The originators of the Puráńas are thus enumerated in the *Bhágavata-puráńa*, XII., VII., 5:

त्रय्यारुणिः कश्यपश्च सावर्णिरकृतब्रणः ।
वैशम्पायनहारीतौ षड्वै पौराणिका इमे ॥

So read, all but consentaneously, five MSS. which I have examined. One of them has Akritavrata, for Akritabrańa; and one has - like the *Bhágavata-kathá-sangraha* Śimśapáyana, for Vaiśampáyana. Śaimśapáyani is the name, in the *Váyu-puráńa*.

* काश्यपः संहिताकर्ता सावर्णिः शांशपायनः ।
रौमहर्षणिका चान्या तिसृणां मूलसंहिता ॥

"Káśyapa was compiler of a *Samhitá*: *and so was* Sávarńi, *and so* Śámśapáyana: and the *Romaharshańiká was* another *Samhitá*, the root of the three *just specified*."

The *Váyu-puráńa* says the same, in effect.

† The original of this paragraph, the scholia on it, and a translation of both, will be found in Burnouf's edition of the *Bhágavata-puráńa*, Vol. I., Preface, pp. XXXVII.—XXXIX.

‡ From the commentary: विष्णुपुराणं च क्वचिद् दशसाहस्रं क्वचिद्-ष्टसाहस्रमित्यादिविप्रतिपत्तौ षट्साहस्रमेव व्याख्यायते । We learn, from this, that the *Vishńu-puráńa* has been variously reputed as consisting of ten thousand stanzas, of eight thousand, and of six thousand. The scholiast accepts the most moderate estimate. It is a great reduction from twenty-three thousand. See Vol. I., Preface, p. XXXIV., note 2, extract from the *Matsya-puráńa*.

§ Most of this note is taken from the commentary, which remarks as follows: ब्राह्मणादिभिः सह पुराणसंहितां चक्रे । ब्राह्म इति शैवः । तत्र कृतोपलक्षणं मातृस्याख्यानवत् पुराणं । कुलकार्येषु वचनमुपाख्यानं प्रचक्षते । गाथा पितृपृथ्व्यादिगीताः । कल्पशुद्धिर्वाराहादिकल्पनिर्णयः ।

Bhágavata, Náradíya, Márkańdeya, Agneya, Bhavishyat, Brahma Vaivarta, Lainga, Váráha, Skánda, Vámana, Kaurma, Mátsya, Gárúda, Brahmáńda. The creation of the world, and its successive reproductions, the genealogies (of the patriarchs and kings), the periods of the Manus, and the transactions of the (royal) dynasties, are narrated in all these Puráńas.* This Puráńa which I have repeated to you, Maitreya, is called the Vaishńava, and is next, in the series, to the Pádma; and in every part of it, in its narratives of primary and subsidiary creation, of families, and of periods, the mighty Vishńu is declared, in this Puráńa[1].

The four Vedas, the (six) Angas (or subsidiary portions of the Vedas), (viz., Sikshá, rules of reciting the prayers, the accents and tones to be observed; Kalpa, ritual; Vyákarańa, grammar; Nirukta, glossarial comment; Chhandas, metre; and Jyotisha, astronomy), with Mímáḿsá (theology), Nyáya (logic), Dharma (the institutes of law), and the Puráńas, constitute the fourteen (principal) branches of knowledge: or (they are considered as) eighteen, (with the addition of these four), the Áyur-veda, (medical science, as taught by Dhanwantari), Dhanur-veda, (the science of archery or arms, taught by Bhrigu), Gándharva-(veda), (or the drama, and the arts of music, dancing, &c., of

[1] For remarks upon this enumeration, see Introduction.†

* See Vol. I., Preface, p. VII., note 1; and the supplementary annotation thereon, in p. 199, *ibid.* See, further, the note at the end of the present chapter.

† Vol. I., Preface, pp. XXIII. *et seq.*

which the Muni Bharata was the author), and the Artha Śástra, (or science of government, as laid down first by Bŕihaspati).*

There are three kinds of Ŕishis (or inspired sages): royal Ŕishis, (or princes who have adopted a life of devotion, as Viśwámitra), divine Ŕishis, (or sages who are demigods also, as Nárada), and Brahman Ŕishis, (or sages who are the sons of Brahmá, or Brahmans, as Vasishtha and others).[1]†

---

[1] A similar enumeration is given in the Váyu, with some additions. Ŕishi is derived from Ŕish, 'to go to', or 'approach.' The Brahmarshis, it is said, are descendants of the five patriarchs who were the founders of races or Gotras of Brahmans; or, Kaśyapa, Vasishtha, Bhŕigu, Angiras, and Atri. The Devarshis are Nara and Náráyańa, the sons of Dharma;‡ the Válikhilyas,§ who sprang from Kratu;‖ Kardama, the son of Pulaha; Kubera, the son of Pulastya¶; Achala, the son of Pratyúsha;** Parvata and Nárada, the sons of Kaśyapa. Rájarshis are Ikshwáku and other

---

* The definitions and other particulars enclosed within parentheses, in this and the following paragraph, are borrowed from the commentary.

† On these, and other descriptions of Ŕishis, see *Original Sanskrit Texts*, Part I., p. 109, note 11.

‡ See Vol. I., p. 111, note 1.

§ Such is the more ordinary spelling, in MSS. known to me. For the Válikhilyas, see the *Mahábhárata*, *Ádi-parvan*, Chapters XXX., XXXI. I am not aware that these pigmies had anything to do with the portion of Veda called Válakhilya. See p. 49, note §, *supra*.

‖ See Vol. I., p. 155.

¶ The original, as will be seen in the next page, has Paulastya; and this does not necessarily signify "son of Pulastya": but it does so, there. Kubera was Pulastya's grandson, and son of Viśravas, according to the *Bhágavata-puráńa*, IV., I., 36, 37. See Vol. I., p. 154, note 2.

** See Vol. II., p. 23.

I have, thus, described to you the branches of the Vedas, and their subdivisions; the persons by whom they were made; and the reason why they were made (or, the limited capacities of mankind). The same branches are instituted in the different Manwantaras.* The (primitive) Veda,† that of the progenitor of all things,‡ is eternal: these (branches) are but its modifications (or Vikalpas).§

---

princes. The Brahmarshis dwell in the sphere of Brahmá; the Devarshis, in the region of the gods; and the Rájarshis, in the heaven of Indra.‖

---

* सर्वमन्वन्तरेष्वेवं शाखाभेदाः समाः स्मृताः ।

† *Śruti*, in the Sanskrit.

‡ *Prájápatyá*, 'derived from Prajápati'.

§ See *Original Sanskrit Texts*, Part III., p. 11.

‖ The passage of the *Váyu-puráńa* is as follows:

त्रिधा ब्रह्मर्षयः पूर्वं तेभ्यो देवर्षयः पुनः ।
राजर्षयः पुनस्तेभ्य ऋषिप्रकृतयस्त्रयः ॥
तेभ्य ऋषिप्रकृतयो गुणिभिः संश्रितमतीः ।
कश्यपेषु वसिष्ठेषु तथा भृग्वङ्गिरोऽत्रिषु ॥
पञ्चस्वेतेषु जायन्ते गोत्रेषु ब्रह्मवादिनः ।
यस्मादृषन्ति ब्रह्माणं तेन ब्रह्मर्षयः स्मृताः ॥
धर्मस्याथ पुलस्त्यस्य क्रतोश्च पुलहस्य च ।
प्रत्यूषस्य प्रभासस्य कश्यपस्य तथा पुनः ॥
देवर्षयः सुतास्तेषां नामतस्तान्निबोधत ।
देवर्षी धर्मपुत्रौ तु नरनारायणावुभौ ॥
वालखिल्याः क्रतोः पुत्राः कर्दमः पुलहस्य तु ।
कुबेरश्चैव पौलस्त्यः प्रत्यूषस्याचलः स्मृतः ॥
पर्वतो नारदश्चैव कश्यपस्यात्मजावुभौ ।
ऋषन्ति देवान्यस्मात्ते तस्माद्देवर्षयः स्मृताः ॥
मानवे वैन्ये (??) वंशे ऐडे वंशे च ये नृपाः ।
ऐडा ऐक्ष्वाकनाभागा ज्ञेया राजर्षयस्तु ते ॥

I have, thus, related to you, Maitreya, the circumstances, relating to the Vedas, which you desired to hear. Of what else do you wish to be informed?[1]

---

[1] No notice is taken, here, of a curious legend which is given in the Mahábhárata, in the Gadá Parvan.* It is there said, that, during a great drought, the Brahmans, engrossed by the care of subsistence, neglected the study of the sacred books, and the Vedas were lost. The Rishi Sáraswata, alone, being fed with fish by his mother Saraswatí, the personified river so named, kept up his studies, and preserved the Hindu scriptures. At the end of the famine, the Brahmans repaired to him, to be taught; and sixty thousand disciples again acquired a knowledge of the Vedas from Sáraswata. This legend appears to indicate the revival, or, more probably, the introduction, of the Hindu ritual by the race of Brahmans, or the *people*, called Sáraswata: for, according to the Hindu geographers, it was the name of a nation, as it still is the appellation of a class of Brahmans who chiefly inhabit the Punjab. (Asiatic Researches, Vol. VII., p. 219;† Vol. VIII., pp. 338, 341.) The Sáraswata Brahmans are met with in many parts of India, and are, usually, fair-complexioned, tall, and handsome men. They are classed, in the Játi málás, or popular lists of castes, amongst the five Gauda Brahmans, and are divi-

---

ऋषय[illegible]त्मजा राजर्षयस्तथा ।
ब्रह्मलोकप्रतिष्ठास्तु स्मृता ब्रह्मर्षयोऽमलाः ॥
देवलोकप्रतिष्ठाश्च ज्ञेया देवर्षयः शुभाः ।
इन्द्रलोकप्रतिष्ठास्तु सर्वे राजर्षयो मताः ॥

The Translator omitted mention of the sons of Prabhása, here classed among the Devarshis, but not named. Prabhása was father of Viśwakarman. See Vol. II., p. 24.

Further, the Rájarshis are said to be Aidas, Aikshwákas, and Nábhágas,—kings sprung from Manu, Vena (??), and Idá.

* Or *Gadáyuddha-parvan*. It concludes the *Śalya-parvan*, beginning with its thirty-third chapter.

† Or Colebrooke's *Miscellaneous Essays*, Vol. II., p. 22.

ded into ten tribes. They are said, also, to be, especially, the Purohitas or family-priests of the Kshattriya or military castes;—(see the Játi málá, printed in Price's Hindee and Hindoostanee Selections, Vol. I., p. 280)—circumstances in harmony with the purport of the legend, and confirmatory of the Sáraswatas of the Punjab having been prominent agents in the establishment of the Hindu religion in India. The holy land of the Hindus, or the primary seat, perhaps, of Brahmanism, has, for one of its boundaries, the Saraswatí river. See Vol. II., p. 142, note 4.

Note referred to at p. 67, *supra*.

Burnouf, in his edition of the *Bhágavata-puráńa*, Vol. I., Preface, pp. XLIV.—LI., dwells at length on the definition of the term *Puráńa*. After citing, from the *Śabdakalpadruma*, a passage of the *Brahmavaivarta-puráńa*, where the topics of a Puráńa are said to be ten, he translates an extract from the *Bhágavata-puráńa*,—XII., VII., 8-19,—in which these topics are enumerated almost in the same manner. Subjoined is his translation, with the original prefixed.

पुराणलक्षणं ब्रह्मन्ब्रह्मर्षिभिर्निरूपितम् ।
शृणुष्व बुद्धिमाश्रित्य वेदशास्त्रानुसारतः ॥
सर्गोऽस्याथ विसर्गश्च वृत्ती रक्षान्तराणि च ।
वंशो वंशानुचरितं संस्था हेतुरपाश्रयः ॥
दशभिर्लक्षणैर्युक्तं पुराणं तद्विदो विदुः ।
केचित्पञ्चविधं ब्रह्मन्महदल्पव्यवस्थया ॥
अव्याकृतगुणक्षोभान्महतस्त्रिवृतोऽहमः ।
भूतसूक्ष्मेन्द्रियार्थानां संभवः सर्ग उच्यते ॥
पुरुषानुगृहीतानामेतेषां वासनामयः ।
विसर्गोऽयं समाहारो बीजाद्बीजं चराचरम् ॥
वृत्तिर्भूतानि भूतानां चराणामचराणि च ।
कृता स्वेन नृणां तत्र कामाच्चोदनयापि वा ॥
रक्षाच्युतावतारेहा विश्वस्यानुयुगे युगे ।
तिर्यङ्मर्त्यर्षिदेवेषु हन्यन्ते यैस्त्रयीद्विषः ॥
मन्वन्तरं मनुर्देवा मनुपुत्राः सुरेश्वराः ।
ऋषयोंऽशावताराश्च हरेः षड्विधमुच्यते ॥
राज्ञां ब्रह्मप्रसूतानां वंशस्त्रैकालिकोऽन्वयः ।
वंशानुचरितं तेषां वृत्तं वंशधराश्च ये ॥

नैमित्तिकः प्राकृतिको नित्य आत्यन्तिको लयः ।
संस्थेति कविभिः प्रोक्ता चतुर्धास्य स्वभावतः ॥
हेतुर्जीवोऽस्य सर्गादेरविद्याकर्मकारकः ।
यं चानुशयिनं प्राहुरव्याकृतमुतापरे ॥
व्यतिरेकान्वयो यस्य जाग्रत्स्वप्नसुषुप्तिषु ।
मायामयेषु तद्ब्रह्म जीववृत्तिष्वपाश्रयः ॥

"Écoute, ô Brâhmane (dit Sûta à Çâunaka), en y appliquant ton intelligence, la définition d'un Purâṅa, telle que l'ont donnée les Brahmarchis, d'accord avec les diverses écoles des Vêdas. La création de cet univers et la création distincte, l'existence, la conservation, les intervalles [de chaque Manu], la généalogie, l'histoire des familles postérieures, la destruction, la cause, la délivrance: voilà ce que les savants reconnaissent pour un Purâṅa, ouvrage qui a dix caractères particuliers. D'autres, distinguant les Purâṅas en grands et en petits, disent qu'un [petit] Purâṅa a cinq caractères. On entend par *Sarga*, création, l'origine du principe dit de l'Intelligence, qui vient du mouvement des qualités qui appartiennent à la Nature, celle du principe de la Personnalité qui est triple et qui sort de l'Intelligence, celle des molécules subtiles, celle des sens et des éléments grossiers. On entend par *Visarga*, création distincte, l'association de tous ces principes fécondés par Purucha association qui leur rappelle leur ancienne activité; il en résulte tout ce qui se meut comme ce qui ne se meut pas, de même qu'un germe sort d'un autre germe. Par *Vrĭtti*, existence, on entend que les êtres servent à l'existence les uns des autres, ceux qui ne se meuvent pas, à celle de ceux qui se meuvent; mais les moyens qu'a l'homme de soutenir son existence sont, par une suite de sa nature propre, volontaires ou nécessaires. La *Rakchâ* ou conservation de l'univers, c'est l'action d'Atchyuta (Vichṅu) qui descend, à chaque Yuga, dans des formes d'animaux, d'hommes, de Rĭchis, de Dêvas, pour anéantir les ennemis du triple Vêda. Par *Manvantara*, intervalle de chaque Manu, on entend une époque où se trouvent les six espèces d'êtres suivantes: un Manu, des Dêvas, des fils de Manu, des chefs de Suras, des Rĭchis, des incarnations partielles de Hari (Vichṅu). Par *Vaṁça*, généalogie, on entend la succession des rois, nés de Brahmâ, pendant les trois parties de la durée; et par *Vaṁçânutcharita*, histoire des familles postérieures, on entend la conduite de ceux qui ont perpétué les familles de ces rois. Les chantres inspirés nomment *Saṁsthâ*, destruction, la dissolution de cet univers qui est de quatre sortes, savoir: Nâimittika, Prâkrĭtika, Nitya et Atyantika, et qui résulte de sa nature propre. Par *Hêtu*, cause de la création et des autres états de l'univers, on entend l'âme individualisée qui accomplit des actes sous l'influence de l'Avidyâ (l'Ignorance). Cette cause, quelques-uns l'appellent le principe [intelligent] qui s'endort [au temps de la destruction de l'univers au sein de l'Être suprême]; d'autres, le principe [matériel] non développé. On entend par *Apâçraya*, délivrance, Brahma auquel il appartient d'être présent et absent tout à la fois, pendant que s'accomplissent les fonctions de la vie, de la veille, du sommeil et du sommeil profond, fonctions qui sont l'œuvre de Mâyâ."

This passage, and that from the *Brahmavaivarta-puráńa*, before adverted to, are of interest, as evincing the comparatively recent date of those compositions; only five constitutive and characteristic topics of a Puráńa being recognised by so late writers as the commentators on the *Amara-kośa*. See Vol. I., Preface, p. VII., where the commentators on Amarasiṃha are inadvertently identified, in respect of their views touching the subject-matters of a Puráńa, with the vocabularist himself.

CHAPTER VII.

By what means men are exempted from the authority of Yama, as narrated, by Bhíshma, to Nakula. Dialogue between Yama and one of his attendants. Worshippers of Vishńu not subject to Yama. How they are to be known.

MAITREYA.—You have, indeed, related to me, most excellent Brahman, all that I asked of you. But I am desirous to hear one thing which you have not touched on. This universe, composed of seven zones, with its seven subterrestrial regions, and seven spheres,—this whole egg of Brahmá,—is everywhere swarming with living creatures, large or small, with smaller and smallest, and larger and largest; so that there is not the eighth part of an inch in which they do not abound. Now, all these are captives in the chains of acts, and, at the end of their existence, become slaves to the power of Yama, by whom they are sentenced to painful punishments. Released from these inflictions, they are again born in the condition of gods, men, or the like; and, thus, living beings, as the Śástras apprise us, perpetually revolve. Now, the question I have to ask, and which you are so well able to answer, is, by what acts men may free themselves from subjection to Yama.

Parásara.—This question, excellent Muni, was once asked, by Nakula,[1] of his grandfather Bhíshma;

[1] Nakula is one of the Páńdava princes, and, consequently, grand-nephew, not grandson, of Bhíshma: he is great grandson of Parásara; and it is rather an anomaly for the latter to cite a conversation in which Nakula *formerly* bore a part.

and I will repeat to you the reply made by the latter.

Bhíshma said to the prince: "There formerly came, on a visit to me, a friend of mine, a Brahman, from the Kalinga country, who told me that he had once proposed this question to a holy Muni who retained the recollection of his former births, and by whom what was and what will be was accurately told. Being importuned by me, who placed implicit faith in his words, to repeat what that pious personage had imparted to him, he, at last, communicated it to me; and what he related I have never met with elsewhere.

"Having, then, on one occasion, put to him the same question which you have asked, the Kalinga Brahman recalled the story that had been told him by the Muni, —the great mystery that had been revealed to him by the pious sage who remembered his former existence, —a dialogue that occurred between Yama and one of his ministers.

"Yama, beholding one of his servants with his noose in his hand, whispered to him, and said: 'Keep clear of the worshippers of Madhusúdana. I am the lord of all men, the Vaishńavas excepted. I was appointed, by Brahmá,* who is reverenced by all the immortals, to restrain mankind, and regulate the consequences of good and evil in the universe. But he who obeys Hari, as his spiritual guide, is here independent of me; for Vishńu is of power to govern and control me. As gold is one sub-

* Dhátri, in the Sanskrit.

stance, still, however diversified as bracelets, tiaras,* or ear-rings, so Hari is one and the same, although modified in the forms of gods, animals, and man. As the drops of water, raised, by wind, from the earth, sink into the earth again, when the wind subsides, so the varieties of gods, men, and animals, which have been detached by the agitation † of the qualities, are reunited, when that disturbance ceases, with the eternal. He who, through holy knowledge, diligently adores the lotos-foot of that Hari, who is reverenced by the gods, is released from all the bonds of sin; and you must avoid him, as you would avoid fire fed with oil.'

"Having heard these injunctions of Yama, the messenger addressed the lord of righteousness, and said: 'Tell me, master, how am I to distinguish the worshipper of Hari, who is the protector of all beings?' Yama replied: 'You are to consider the worshipper of Vishńu him who never deviates from the duties prescribed to his caste; who looks with equal indifference upon friend or enemy; who takes nothing (that is not his own), nor injures any being. Know that person of unblemished mind to be a worshipper of Vishńu. Know him to be a devout worshipper of Hari, who has placed Janárdana in his pure mind, which has been freed from fascination, and whose soul is undefiled by the soil of the Kali age. Know that excellent man to be a worshipper of Vishńu, who, looking upon gold in secret, holds that which is another's wealth

* *Mukuta.*

† *Kalusha*, 'feculence'.

but as grass, and devotes all his thoughts to the lord. Pure is he as a mountain of clear crystal: for how can Vishńu abide in the hearts of men with malice, and envy, and other evil passions? The glowing heat of fire abides not in a cluster of the cooling rays of the moon. He who lives pure in thought, free from malice, contented, leading a holy life, feeling tenderness for all creatures, speaking wisely and kindly, humble and sincere, has Vásudeva ever present in his heart. As the young Śála-tree, by its beauty, declares the excellence of the juices which it has imbibed from the earth, so, when the eternal has taken up his abode in the bosom of any one, that man is lovely amidst the beings of this world. Depart, my servant, quickly from those men whose sins have been dispersed by moral and religious merit,[1] whose minds are daily dedicated to the imperceptible deity,* and who are exempt from pride, uncharitableness, and

---

[1] Or Yama and Niyama. The duties intended by these terms are variously enumerated. The commentator on the text specifies, under the first head, absence of violence or cruelty to other beings (Ahimsá), truth (Satya), honesty (Asteya), chastity (Brahmacharya), and disinterestedness, or non-acceptance of gifts (Aparigraha). Under Niyama are comprehended purity (Śaucha), contentment (Santosha), devotion† (Tapas), study of the Vedas (Swádhyáya), and adoration of the supreme (Íswara-prańidhána).

---

* "Imperceptible deity" here renders *achyuta*, on which term see Vol. I., p. 15, note 3.

† Rather, 'mortification'.

malice. In the heart in which the divine Hari, who is without beginning or end, abides, armed with a sword, a shell, and a mace, sin cannot remain; for it cannot coexist with that which destroys it: as darkness cannot continue in the world, when the sun is shining. The eternal makes not his abode in the heart of that man who covets another's wealth, who injures living creatures, who speaks harshness and untruth, who is proud of his iniquity, and whose mind is evil. Janárdana occupies not his thoughts who envies another's prosperity, who calumniates the virtuous, who never sacrifices, nor bestows gifts upon the pious, who is blinded by the property of darkness. That vile wretch is no worshipper of Vishńu, who, through avarice, is unkind to his nearest friends and relations, to his wife, children, parents, and dependants. The brute-like man whose thoughts are evil, who is addicted to unrighteous acts, who ever seeks the society of the wicked, and suffers no day to pass without the perpetration of crime, is no worshipper of Vásudeva. Do you proceed afar off from those in whose hearts Ananta is enshrined; from him whose sanctified understanding conceives the supreme male and ruler, Vásudeva, as one with his votary and with all this world. Avoid those holy persons who are constantly invoking the lotos-eyed Vásudeva, Vishńu, the supporter of the earth, the immortal wielder of the discus and the shell, the asylum of the world. Come not into the sight of him in whose heart the imperishable* soul resides; for he is defended from my power by the

* *Avyaya*. See Vol. I., p. 17., note *.

discus of his deity: he is designed for another world, (for the heaven of Vishńu).'

"'Such,' said the Kalinga Brahman, 'were the instructions communicated by the deity of justice, the son of the Sun, to his servants, as they were repeated, to me, by that holy personage, and as I have related them to you, chief of the house of Kuru' (Bhíshma). So, also, Nakula, I have faithfully communicated to you all I heard from my pious friend, when he came, from his country of Kalinga, to visit me. I have, thus, explained to you, as was fitting, that there is no protection, in the ocean of the world, except Vishńu; and that the servants and ministers of Yama, the king of the dead himself, and his tortures, are, all, unavailing against one who places his reliance on that divinity."*

I have, thus, resumed Parášara, related to you what you wished to hear, and what was said by the son of Vivaswat.[1] What else do you wish to hear?

---

[1] Or Vaivaswata. This section is called the Yama gítá.

* Kedava, in the original.

CHAPTER VIII.

How Vishńu is to be worshipped, as related, by Aurva, to Sagara. Duties of the four castes, severally and in common: also in time of distress.

MAITREYA.—Inform me, venerable teacher, how the supreme deity, the lord of the universe, Vishńu, is worshipped by those who are desirous of overcoming the world; and what advantages are reaped, by men assiduous in his adoration, from the propitiated Govinda.

PARÁŚARA.—The question you have asked was formerly put, by Sagara, to Aurva.[1] I will repeat to you his reply.

---

[1] Sagara, as we shall see,* was a king of the solar race. Aurva was a sage, the grandson of Bhŕigu.† When the sons

---

* Book IV., Chapter III.

† "In the *Mahábhárata*, *Ádi-parvan*, verse 2610, . . . we have the parentage of Aurva thus specified: 'Árushi, the daughter of Manu, was the wife of this sage [Chyavana, son of Bhŕigu]: the illustrious Aurva was born of her, having separated his mother's thigh.' In the *Harivaḿśa*, verse 1456, he seems to be identified with Ŕichika, father of Jamadagni; Ŕichika being *Aurva*, or the son of Úrva," &c. *Original Sanskrit Texts*, Part I., pp. 172, 173.

Subjoined are the originals of the passages here referred to:

आरुषी तु मनोः कन्या तस्य पत्नी मनीषिणः ।
और्वस्तस्यां समभवदूरुं भित्त्वा महायशाः ॥

Mahábhárata.

और्वस्यैवमृचीकस्य सत्यवत्यां महायशाः ।
जमदग्निस्तपोवीर्याज्जज्ञे ब्रह्मविदां वरः ॥

Harivaḿśa.

The name of the father of Jamadagni should, then, be read Úrva,—not Ûrva, nor Urva, nor Kuśa, as at p. 16, note †, &c., *supra*.

Sagara, having bowed down before Aurva, the

---

of king Kritavírya persecuted and slew the children of Bhrigu, to recover the wealth which their father had lavished upon them, they destroyed even the children in the womb. One of the women of the race of Bhrigu, in order to preserve her embryo, secreted it in her thigh (Úru), whence the child, on his birth, was named Aurva. From his wrath proceeded a flame, that threatened to destroy the world; but, at the persuasion of his ancestors, he cast it into the ocean, where it abode, with the face of a horse. Aurva was, afterwards, religious preceptor to Sagara, and bestowed upon him the Ágneyástra,* or fiery weapon, with

---

* The Translator—in Professor Johnson's *Selections from the Mahábhárata*, pp. 1, 7,—thus annotates on *sl.* 5107 of the *Ádi-parvan*: "Ágneyástra, 'the weapon of fire',—a kind of fire-arms. Fiery arms or rockets were, possibly, employed by the Hindus in remote antiquity, as well as in recent times; whence came the notion of certain mysterious weapons framed of the elements, and to be wielded only by deities and demigods. These make a great figure in the battle-scenes of the Mahábhárata and Rámáyaña, and, to readers who are not Hindus, spoil descriptions which would, else, be not without spirit. For a further account of these weapons, see Translation of the *Uttara Ráma Charitra*."

The further account here spoken of is found in Professor Wilson's *Specimens of the Hindu Theatre*, Vol. I., p. 297, second edition. "These weapons are of a very unintelligible character. Some of them are, occasionally, wielded as missiles; but, in general, they appear to be mystical powers exercised by the individual,—such as those of paralysing an enemy, or locking his senses fast in sleep, or bringing down storm and rain and fire from heaven. In the usual strain of the Hindu mythology, they are supposed to assume celestial shapes, endowed with human faculties, and, in this capacity, are alluded to in the text. The list of them, one hundred, is given in the first book of the *Rámáyaña*; and there, also, they are described as embodied, and address Ráma, saying: 'Command us, O Rághava, of mighty arm. Here we are, O chief of men: command us. What shall we do for thee?' The son of Raghu replied: 'Depart, all of you, and, in time of necessity, when called to mind, render me assistance.' They then circumambulated Ráma, and, having said *so be it*, received permission to depart, and went whence they came.' The Rámáyaña calls them, also, the sons of Kṛiśáśwa, and the

descendant of Bhṛigu, asked him what were the best

which he conquered the tribes of barbarians who had in-

sons of Jayá and Vijaya, the daughters of Prajápati. (*Rámáyaṇa*, Book I., Sections 20, 26, and 42.)"

For the armiform progeny of Kṛiśáśwa, see the present work, Vol. II., p. 29, text and note 2.

Mention is made of a similar mysterious weapon, in the *Bhágavata-puráṇa*, I., VII., 18—32. The text and Burnouf's translation here follow:

तमापतन्तं स विलक्ष्य दूरा-
त्कुमारहोद्विग्नमना रथेन ।
पराद्रवत्प्राणपरीप्सुरुर्व्यां
यावद्गमं रुद्रभयाद्यथार्कः ॥
यदाशरणमात्मानमैक्षत श्रान्तवाजिनम् ।
अस्त्रं ब्रह्मशिरो मेने आत्मत्राणं द्विजात्मजः ॥
अथोपस्पृश्य सलिलं संदधे तत्समाहितः ।
अजानन्नपि संहारं प्राणकृच्छ्र उपस्थिते ॥
ततः प्रादुष्कृतं तेजः प्रचण्डं सर्वतोदिशम् ।
प्राणापदमभिप्रेक्ष्य विष्णुं जिष्णुरुवाच ह ॥
कृष्ण कृष्ण महाबाहो भक्तानामभयंकर ।
त्वमेको दह्यमानानामपवर्गोऽसि संसृतेः ॥
त्वमाद्यः पुरुषः साक्षादीश्वरः प्रकृतेः परः ।
मायां व्युदस्य चिच्छक्त्या कैवल्ये स्थित आत्मनि ॥
स एव जीवलोकस्य मायामोहितचेतसः ।
विधत्से स्वेन वीर्येण श्रेयो धर्मादिलक्षणम् ॥
तथायं चावतारस्ते भुवो भारजिहीर्षया ।
स्वानां चानन्यभावानामनुध्यानाय चासकृत् ॥
किमिदं स्वित्कुतो वेति देवदेव न वेद्म्यहम् ।
सर्वतोमुखमायाति तेजः परमदारुणम् ॥
श्रीभगवानुवाच ।
वेत्थेदं द्रोणपुत्रस्य ब्राह्ममस्त्रं प्रदर्शितम् ।
नैवासौ वेद संहारं प्राणबाध उपस्थिते ॥
न ह्यस्यान्यतमं किंचिदस्त्रं प्रत्यवकर्शनम् ।
जह्यस्त्रतेज उन्नद्धमस्त्रज्ञोऽस्त्रतेजसा ॥
सूत उवाच ।
श्रुत्वा भगवता प्रोक्तं फाल्गुनः परवीरहा ।
स्पृष्ट्वापस्तं परिक्रम्य ब्राह्मं ब्राह्माय संदधे ॥

means of pleasing Vishńu, and what would be the

---

vaded his patrimonial possessions. Mahábhárata, Ádi Par-

संहत्यान्योन्यमुभयोस्तेजसी शरसंवृते ।
आवृत्य रोदसी खं च ववृधातेऽर्कवह्निवत् ॥
दृष्ट्वास्त्रतेजस्तु तयोस्त्रींल्लोकान्प्रदहन्महत् ।
दह्यमानाः प्रजाः सर्वाः सांवर्तकममंसत ॥
प्रजोपद्रवमालक्ष्य लोकव्यतिकरं च तम् ।
मतं च वासुदेवस्य संजहारार्जुनो द्वयम् ॥

"Mais l'assassin des enfants de Draupadî, qui avait mis pied à terre, troublé à la vue d'Ardjuna qui accourait de loin sur son char, s'enfuit pour sauver sa vie, de toute la rapidité de sa course, comme le soleil reculant de crainte devant Rudra (Çiva).

"Voyant que ses chevaux fatigués le laissaient sans ressource, le fils du Brâhmane songea, pour sauver sa vie, au javelot nommé Brahmaçiras (Tête de Brahmâ).

"Alors, dirigeant sa pensée sur cet objet, et s'étant plongé dans l'eau, il lança le javelot, quoiqu'il ignorât le moyen de le retenir, s'il venait à mettre en danger les êtres vivants.

"Il en sortit un feu indomptable qui enveloppait tout le ciel; alors prévoyant le danger qui menaçait les créatures, Ardjuna dit à Vichńu:

"Krichńa! Krichńa au bras puissant! toi qui donnes la sécurité à ceux qui te sont dévoués! tu es le seul qui puisses délivrer du monde les créatures qui y sont consumées.

"Oui, tu es le Seigneur suprême, Pourucha, ce premier être, supérieur à la Nature, qui se dégageant de Mâyâ par l'énergie de sa pensée, subsiste absolu en lui-même.

"C'est toi-même qui, par ta puissance, établis sous la forme de la loi et des autres avantages ce qui donne le salut au monde des créatures, dont l'intelligence est troublée par Mâyâ.

"De même, cette incarnation [sous laquelle tu te manifestes à mes yeux], tu l'as revêtue pour te charger du fardeau de la terre, et pour offrir un perpétuel sujet de méditations à ceux qui te connaissent et dont la pensée n'a pas d'autre objet que toi.

"Dieu des Dèvas! j'ignore quelle est cette merveille et quelle en est la cause; de tous côtés s'avance à ma rencontre un feu dont l'ardeur est intolérable.

"Bhagavat dit: Tu le connais; c'est le javelot de Brahmâ que le fils de Drońa vent t'opposer; mais lui-même ignore le moyen de le retenir, au moment où il va détruire les êtres.

"Certes, aucun autre javelot quel qu'il soit n'est capable de le domp-

6*

consequence of obtaining his favour. Aurva replied: "He who pleases Vishńu obtains all terrestrial enjoyments; heaven, and a place in heaven; and what is best of all, final liberation:* whatever he wishes, and to whatever extent, whether much or little, he receives it, when Achyuta is content with him. In what manner his favour is to be secured, that, also, I will, O king, impart to you, agreeably to your desire. The supreme Vishńu is propitiated by a man who observes

---

van,† Dána Dharma Parvan; Hari Vaḿśa.‡

[illegible]

ter; mais puisque tu en connais le secret, anéantis, avec un feu semblable, le feu de ce javelot déchaîné.

"Súta dit:

"À ces mots, Phálguna (Ardjouna), redoutable aux guerriers ennemis, portant de l'eau à ses lèvres et tournant autour de Krichńa, opposa le javelot de Brahmá au javelot de Brahmá.

"Les feux de ces deux javelots, avec les flèches dont ils étaient entourés, s'étant confondus l'un dans l'autre, comme le soleil et le feu [au temps de la destruction des mondes], augmentèrent de violence, enveloppant la terre, le ciel et l'atmosphère.

"En voyant l'immense éclat de ces javelots des deux guerriers, qui portaient l'incendie dans les trois mondes, toutes les créatures, consumées par le feu, crurent que le jour de l'embrasement de l'univers était arrivé.

"Ardjouna remarquant la détresse des créatures, le danger des trois mondes et l'intention du fils de Vasudéva, retint les deux javelots."

In stanzas 10—16 of the chapter following that just quoted from, the *brahmaśiras* is again introduced, with other fire-tipped darts.

It has been thought worth while to give the preceding passage at length, since it shows, quite as clearly as any other that I have met with, the sort of fiery weapon known to the Hindus of old times.

An interesting and learned disquisition on ancient and oriental firearms will be found in Sir Henry M. Elliot's *Bibliographical Index to the Historians of Muhammedan India*, Vol. I., Note H,—pp. 340-375.

* This expression here translates *nirváńa*.

† In *M.* 6340, the *brahmástra* is named.

‡ The *brahmaśiras* is spoken of in *M.* 1344.

the institutions of caste, order, and purificatory practices: no other path is the way to please him. He who offers sacrifices sacrifices to him; he who murmurs prayer prays to him; he who injures living creatures injures him: for Hari is all beings. Janárdana, therefore, is propitiated by him who is attentive to established observances, and follows the duties prescribed for his caste. The Brahman, the Kshattriya, the Vaiśya, and the Śúdra, who attends to the rules enjoined his caste,* best worships Vishńu. Keśava is most pleased with him who does good to others; who never utters abuse, calumny, or untruth;† who never covets another's wife or another's wealth, and who bears ill-will towards none; who neither beats nor slays any animate or inanimate thing; who is ever diligent in the service of the gods, of the Brahmans, and of his spiritual preceptor; who is always desirous of the welfare of all creatures, of his children, and of his own soul; in whose pure heart no pleasure is derived from the imperfections of love and hatred. The man, O monarch, who conforms to the duties enjoined, by scriptural authority, for every caste and condition of life is he who best worships Vishńu: there is no other mode."

Aurva having thus spoken, Sagara said to him: "Tell me, then, venerable Brahman, what are the duties of caste and condition:[1] I am desirous of know-

---

[1] Most of the Puráńas—especially the Kúrma, Padma, Vámana, Agni, and Garuda,—contain chapters, or sections, more or [illegible]

* *Dharma*, in the original.

† परापवादपैशुन्यमनृतं च न भाषते ।
अन्योद्वेगकरं चापि तोष्यते तेन केशवः ॥

ing them." To which Aurva answered and said: "Attentively listen to the duties which I shall describe, as those, severally, of the Brahman, the Kshattriya, the Vaisya,* and the Súdra. The Brahman should make gifts, should worship the gods with sacrifices, should be assiduous in studying the Vedas, should perform ablutions and libations with water, and should preserve the sacred flame. For the sake of subsistence, he may offer sacrifices on behalf of others, and may instruct them in the Śástras; and he may accept presents, of a liberal description, in a becoming manner (or, from respectable persons, and at an appropriate season). He must ever seek to promote the good of others, and do evil unto none; for the best riches of a Brahman are universal benevolence. He should look upon the jewels of another person as if they were pebbles, and should, at proper periods, procreate offspring by his wife. These are the duties of a Brahman.

"The man of the warrior-tribe should cheerfully

---

less in detail, upon the moral and ceremonial duties of the Hindus; and a considerable portion of the Mahábhárata, especially in the Moksha Dharma Parvan, is devoted to the same subject. No other Pauráńik work, however, contains a series of chapters exactly analogous to those which follow, and which contain a compendious and systematic description of the Ácháras, or personal and social obligations of the Hindus. The tenour of the whole is conformable to the Institutes of Manu; and many passages are the same.

---

* The Sanskrit has the shorter form, *Vid*.

give presents to Brahmans, perform various sacrifices, and study the scriptures. His especial sources of maintenance are arms and the protection of the earth. The guardianship of the earth is, indeed, his especial province. By the discharge of this duty a king attains his objects, and realizes a share of the merit of all sacrificial rites. By intimidating the bad, and cherishing the good, the monarch who maintains the discipline of the different castes secures whatever region he desires.

"Brahmá, the great parent of creation,* gave to the Vaiśya the occupations of commerce and agriculture, and the feeding of flocks and herds,† for his means of livelihood: and sacred study, sacrifice, and donation are, also, his duties, as is the observance of fixed and occasional rites.

"Attendance upon the three regenerate castes is the province of the Śúdra; and by that he is to subsist, or by the profits of trade, or the earnings of mechanical labour. He is, also, to make gifts; and he may offer the sacrifices in which food is presented, as well as obsequial offerings.[1]

[1] The Pákayajna,‡ or sacrifice in which food is offered, implies either the worship of the Viśwadevas, the rites of hospitality, or occasional oblations, on building a house, the birth of a child, or any occasion of rejoicing. It is to be understood, however, that this injunction intends his performing these ceremonies through the agency of a Brahman; as a Śúdra cannot repeat the

* *Loka-pitámaha.*

† *Páśupálya.*

‡ *Vide infra,* p. 110, note §; and p. 112, note §.

"Besides these, their respective obligations, there are duties equally incumbent upon all the four castes.* These are: the acquisition of property, for the support of their families; cohabitation with their wives, for the sake of progeny; tenderness towards all creatures, patience, humility, truth, purity, contentment, decency of deco-

---

Mantras, or prayers, that accompany them: and it might be a question how far he might be present; for he ought not even to hear such prayers repeated. The performance of funeral rites involves some personal share; and the Śúdra must present the cakes: but it must be done without Mantras; as the Mitákshará:† 'This rite (the presentation of cakes) must be performed by the Śúdras, without formulæ, on the twelfth day:' शूद्राणामप्येत-दमन्त्रकमवश्यं द्वादशेऽह्नि । The Váyu Puráńa directs the performance of the five great sacrifices by Śúdras, only omitting the Mantras:

शूद्रेणापि प्रकर्तव्याः पञ्चैते मन्त्रवर्जिताः ।

It may be suspected, that the Puráńas relaxed, in some degree, from the original rigour; for it may be inferred, that the great ceremonies were altogether withheld from Śúdras in the time of Manu, who declares, that none have any right or part (Adhikára) in his code, except those who perform rites with Mantras,—or the three regenerate castes (II., 16‡),—and denounces, as heinous sins, teaching the Vedas to Śúdras, performing sacrifices for them, or

---

* वायमानां च सर्वेषामेते सामान्यधर्मकाः ।

This comes, in the original, immediately after the stanza quoted in note *, p. 90.

† On the *Yájnavalkya-smŕiti*, I., 255.

‡ निषेकादिश्मशानान्तो मन्त्रैर्यस्योदितो विधिः ।
तस्य शास्त्रेऽधिकारोऽस्मिन् ज्ञेयो नान्यस्य कस्यचित् ॥

"For him whose rites, from fecundation to the cemetery, are enjoined *to be performed* with *mantras*, a title to *read* this *śástra* is to be recognized,—not for any one besides."

ration, gentleness of speech, friendliness; and freedom from envy and repining, from avarice, and from de-

---

taking gifts from them: X., 109, 110, 111.* Yájnavalkya,† however, allows them to perform five great rites with the Namaskára, or the simple salutation:

नमस्कारेण मन्त्रेण पञ्च यज्ञान् न हापयेत् ।

which Gotama confirms.‡ Some restrict the sense of Mantra, also, to the prayers of the Vedas, and allow the Śúdras to use those of the Puráńas; as Śúlapáńi: न वेदेष्वधिकारो शूद्रस्य विद्यते पुराणेष्वधिकारः । And the Tithi Tattwa is cited, in the Śúdra Kamalákara,§ as allowing them any Mantras except those of the Vedas: वैदिकेतरमन्त्रपाठे शूद्रस्याधिकारः ।

* प्रतिग्रहाद्याजनाद्वा तथैवाध्यापनादपि ।
प्रतिग्रहः प्रत्यवरः प्रेत्य विप्रस्य गर्हितः ॥
याजनाध्यापने नित्यं क्रियेते संस्कृतात्मनाम् ।
प्रतिग्रहस्तु क्रियते शूद्रादप्यन्त्यजन्मनः ॥
जपहोमैरपैत्येनो याजनाध्यापनैः कृतम् ।
प्रतिग्रहनिमित्तं तु त्यागेन तपसैव च ॥

"Among *these three acts, done against rule, namely*, accepting gifts, assisting to sacrifice, and teaching the Veda, the accepting of gifts is especially base *in this world, and*, in the world to come, is, to a Bráhman, matter of condemnation:

"*For that* the acts of assisting to sacrifice and teaching the Veda always have reference to the initiated; whereas the act of accepting gifts has reference even to the Śúdra, most low of birth.

"The sin committed in *wrongfully* assisting to sacrifice or in *wrongfully* teaching the Veda is expiated by oblations in the form of silent prayer; but *that* consequent on *illegally* accepting gifts, by relinquishment *of what is given* and by mortification."

Medhátithi, at variance with Kullúka, but more concinnously, reads the second stanza as above. On the beginning of the third he says: जपेन होमेन च पापमपैति विप्रकृति । In this interpretation of *japa-homa* I have not followed him.

† I., 121.

‡ अनुज्ञातोऽस्य नमस्कारो मन्त्रः । Gotama is thus cited by Śúlapáńi.

§ This is the popular title of the *Śúdra-dharma-tattwa*, by Kama-

traction. These, also, are the duties of every condition of life.*

"In times of distress, the peculiar functions of the castes may be modified, as you shall hear.† A Brahman may follow the occupations of a Kshattriya, or a Vaiśya; the Kshattriya‡ may adopt those of the Vaiśya; and the Vaiśya, those of the Kshattriya.§ But these two last should never descend to the functions of the Śúdra, if it be possible to avoid them[1]; and, if

[1] This last clause reconciles what would, else, appear to be an incompatibility with Manu, who permits the Vaiśya, in time

lakara Bhaṭṭa. The passages which the Translator refers to Śúlapáṇi and to the *Tithi-tattwa* occur there in these words, according to two manuscripts, with which agrees the Bombay edition of *Śaka* 1783, *fol.* 7 b: अथ कैश्चिदिमौ मन्त्रेण शूद्राणां एतच्च वैदिको मन्त्रो निषिद्धः। पौरा-णस्तु शूद्रैः पठनीयः।

न वेदेष्वधिकारो हि कश्चिच्छूद्रस्य विद्यते।
पुराणेष्वधिकारो मे दर्शितो ब्रह्मवैरिह॥

इति शूलपाणौ पाठोक्तिः। सोऽहमीदृशोऽन्वयम्। तिथितत्त्वे त्वार्तेषु वैदि-केतरमन्त्रपाठे शूद्रस्याधिकारः।

Śúlapáṇi's own words, in his *Dípakaliká*, a commentary on the *Yájnavalkya-smṛiti*, are: नमस्कारेण मन्त्रेण च वैदिकेन पौराणिकेन। Kamalákara considers them as based on the enunciation of the *Padma-puráṇa* which he adduces. It is a broken fragment of the Pauráṇik stanza which the Translator gives as the words of Śúlapáṇi.

* मैत्र्यस्पृहा तथा तद्वदकार्पण्यं नरेश्वर।
अनसूया च सामान्या वर्णानां कथिता गुणाः॥

† गुणास्तथापद्धर्मांश्च विप्रादीनामिमाञ्छृणु।

‡ *Rájanya*, in the original.

§ My MSS. contain nothing corresponding to the words "and the Vaiśya, those of the Kshattriya." Witness the original:

क्षात्रं कर्म द्विजस्योक्तं वैश्यकर्म तथापदि।
राजन्यस्य च वैश्योक्तं शूद्रकर्म न चैतयोः॥

that be not possible, they must, at least, shun the functions of the mixed castes. I will now, Rájá, relate to you the duties of the several Áśramas, or conditions of life."

---

of distress, to descend to the servile acts of a Śúdra. X., 98.*

---

* वैश्योऽजीवन्स्वधर्मेण शूद्रवृत्त्यापि वर्तयेत् ।
अनाचरन्नकार्याणि निवर्तेत च शक्तिमान् ॥

"A Vaiśya who does not derive subsistence from his proper duties may occupy himself with the functions even of a Śúdra; he not engaging in what ought not to be done: and, *when* possessed of a competency, let him desist."

CHAPTER IX.

Duties of the religious student, householder, hermit, and mendicant.

AURVA continued.—"When the youth has been invested with the thread (of his caste), let him diligently prosecute the study of the Vedas, in the house of his preceptor, with an attentive spirit, and leading a life of continence. He is to wait upon his Guru, assiduously observant of purificatory practices; and the Veda is to be acquired by him, whilst he is regular in the performance of religious rites. In the morning Sandhyá, he is first to salute the sun; in the evening, fire;* and, then, to address his preceptor with respect. He must stand, when his master is standing; move, when he is walking; and sit beneath him, when he is seated: he must never sit, nor walk, nor stand, when his teacher does the reverse. When desired by him, let him read the Veda attentively, placed before his preceptor; and let him eat the food he has collected as alms, when permitted by his teacher.[1] Let him bathe in water which has first been used for his preceptor's ablutions; and, every morning, bring fuel, and water, and whatsoever else may be required.

"When the scriptural studies appropriate to the

---

[1] These directions are the same as those prescribed by Manu, though not precisely in the same words: II., 175, et seq.

---

* उभे संध्ये रविं भूप तथैवाग्निं समाहितः ।

This seems to imply, that, alike morning and evening, he is to address the sun and fire. The commentary is here silent.

student have been completed, and he has received dismissal from his Guru, let the regenerate man enter into the order of the householder, and, taking unto himself, with lawful ceremonies, house, wife, and wealth, discharge, to the best of his ability, the duties of his station;[1] satisfying the manes with funeral cakes;[*] the gods, with oblations; guests, with hospitality; the sages, with holy study; the progenitors of mankind,[†] with progeny; the spirits, with the residue of oblations;[‡] and all the world, with words of truth.[2] A householder secures heaven by the faithful discharge of these obligations.[§] There are those who subsist upon alms, and lead an erratic life of self-denial, at the end of the term during which they have kept house. They wander over the world, to see the earth,

---

[1] So Manu, III., 4, &c.

[2] The great obligations, or, as Sir William Jones terms them, sacraments,—the Mahâyajnas, or great sacrifices,—are, according to Manu, but five: Brahmayajna, sacred study; Pitriyajna, libations to the manes; Devayajna, burnt-offerings to the gods; Baliyajna, offerings to all creatures; and Nriyajna, hospitality: III., 70, 71.|| The Prajápatiyajna, or propagation of offspring, and Satyayajna, observance of truth, are, apparently, later additions.

---

* *Nivápa.*

† My MSS. have Prajápati, namely, Brahmá.

‡ *Bali-karman*, 'an offering of food'.

§ प्राप्नोति लोकान्पुरुषो निजकर्मसमर्जितान् ।

|| अध्यापनं ब्रह्मयज्ञः पितृयज्ञस्तु तर्पणम् ।
होमो दैवो बलिर्भौतो नृयज्ञोऽतिथिपूजनम् ॥
पञ्चैतान्यो महायज्ञान्न हापयति शक्तितः ।
स गृहेऽपि वसन्नित्यं सूनादोषैर्न लिप्यते ॥

See p. 40, note §, *supra*; and p. 112, note §, *infra*.

and perform their ablutions, with rites enjoined by the Vedas, at sacred shrines,— houseless, and without food, and resting, for the night, at the dwelling at which they arrive in the evening. The householder is, to them, a constant refuge and parent:* it is his duty to give them a welcome, and to address them with kindness, and to provide them, whenever they come to his house, with a bed, a seat, and food. A guest disappointed by a householder, who turns away from his door, transfers to the latter all his own misdeeds, and bears away his religious merit.[1]† In the house of a good man, contumely, arrogance, hypocrisy, repining,‡ contradiction,§ and violence are annihilated: and the householder who fully performs this, his chief duty of hospitality, is released from every kind of bondage, and obtains the highest of stations, (after death).

"When the householder, after performing the acts incumbent on his condition, arrives at the decline of life, let him consign his wife to the care of his sons, and go, himself, to the forests.[2] Let him there subsist

[1] This is, also, the doctrine of Manu: III., 100.‖

[2] Manu, VI., 3, &c.

* To translate *yoni*.

† अतिथिर्यस्य भग्नाशो गृहात्प्रतिनिवर्तते ।
स तस्मै दुष्कृतं दत्त्वा पुण्यमादाय गच्छति ॥

This stanza is quoted in the *Hitopadeśa*: Book I., *ll.* 64. See Professor Johnson's second edition (1864), pp. 12, 13.

‡ *Paritápa.*

§ *Upaghdta.*

‖ शिलानप्युञ्छतो नित्यं पञ्चाग्नीनपि जुह्वतः ।
सर्वं सुकृतमादत्ते ब्राह्मणोऽनर्चितो वसन् ॥

upon leaves, roots, and fruit; and suffer his hair and beard to grow, and braid the former upon his brows; and sleep upon the ground. His dress* must be made of skin, or of Káśa or Kuśa grasses; and he must bathe thrice a day; and he must offer oblations to the gods and to fire, and treat all that come to him with hospitality. He must beg alms, and present food to all creatures; he must anoint himself with such unguents as the woods afford; and, in his devotional exercises,† he must be endurant of heat and cold. The sage who diligently follows these rules, and leads the life of the hermit (or Vánaprastha), consumes, like fire, all imperfections, and conquers, for himself, the mansions of eternity.

"The fourth order of men is called that of the mendicant; the circumstances‡ of which it is fit, O king, that you should hear from me. Let the unimpassioned§ man, relinquishing all affection for wife, children, and possessions, enter the fourth order.[1] Let him forego the three objects of human existence (pleasure, wealth, and virtue), whether secular or religious, and, indifferent to friends, be the friend of all living beings. Let him, occupied with devotion, abstain from wrong—in act, word, or thought,—to all creatures, human or brute; and equally avoid attachment

---

[1] Manu, VI., 33, &c.

---

* The original specifies his lower garment and his upper, *paridhána* and *uttaríyaka*.

† This expression is to render *tapas*.

‡ *Swarúpa*.

§ *Nirdhútamatsara*.

to any. Let him reside but for one night in a village, and not more than five nights, at a time, in a city; and let him so abide, that good-will, and not animosity, may be engendered.* Let him, for the support of existence, apply, for alms, at the houses of the three first† castes, at the time when the fires have been extinguished, and people have eaten. Let the wandering mendicant‡ call nothing his own, and suppress desire, anger, covetousness, pride, and folly. The sage who gives no cause for alarm to living beings need never apprehend any danger from them. Having deposited the sacrificial fire in his own person, the Brahman feeds the vital flame, with the butter that is collected as alms, through the altar of his mouth; and, by means of his spiritual fire, he proceeds to his own proper abode. But the twice-born man[1] who seeks

---

[1] The text uses the term Dwijáti, which designates a man of the three first castes. The commentator cites various authorities, to prove that its sense should be Brahman only, who, alone, is permitted to enter the fourth order.—

गतिश्चतुर्थाश्रमे नास्ति बाहुजवैश्ययोः क्वचित्।
तुर्याश्रमे गतिः प्रोक्ता मुख्यानां स्वयंभुवः॥

इति दत्तात्रेयोक्तेः। ब्राह्मणः प्रव्रजेद्गृहादिति यमसंवर्तबौधायनवचनाच्च। "'Entrance into the fourth order is never for the Kshattriya and Vaiśya. Entrance into the fourth order is for Brahmans, according to Swayambhú:' so says Dattátreya. 'Let the Brahman proceed from his dwelling' is, also, the expression of Yama, Samvarta, and Baudháyana.'" But this is not the general understand-

---

* तथा तिष्ठेद्यथा प्रीतिर्द्वेषो वास्य न जायते।

† Explanatory of the original, *prakata*.

‡ *Parivráj*.

for liberation, and is pure of heart, and whose mind is perfected by self-investigation, secures the sphere of Brahmá, which is tranquil, and is as a bright flame that emits not smoke."*

ing of the law; nor was it, originally, so restricted, apparently. Manu does not so limit it.

* मोक्षाश्रमं यश्चरते यथोक्तं
शुचिः सुसंकल्पितबुद्धियुक्तः ।
अनिन्धनं ज्योतिरिव प्रशान्तं
स ब्रह्मलोकं श्रयते द्विजातिः ॥

CHAPTER X.

Ceremonies to be observed at the birth and naming of a child. Of marrying, or leading a religious life. Choice of a wife. Different modes of marrying.

SAGARA then (addressed Aurva, and) said: "You have described to me, venerable Brahman, the duties of the four orders and of the four castes. I am now desirous to hear from you the religious institutes which men should individually observe, whether they be invariable, occasional, or voluntary. Describe these to me; for all things are known, chief of Bhṛigu's race, unto you." To this Aurva replied: "I will communicate to you, O king, that which you have asked,—the invariable and occasional rites which men should perform. Do you attend.

"When a son is born, let his father perform, for him, the ceremonies proper on the birth of a child, and all other initiatory rites, as well as a Śráddha, which is a source of prosperity.* Let him feed a couple of Brahmans, seated with their faces to the east; and, according to his means, offer sacrifices to the gods and progenitors. Let him present to the manes[1] balls

---

[1] To the Nándímukhas. The Pitṛis, or progenitors,† are so termed, here, from words occurring in the prayer used on the occasion of a festive Śráddha. Asiatic Researches, Vol. VII., p. 270.‡

* *Abhyudayátmaka.*

† The *Nándímukhas* are a special class of manes.

‡ Or Colebrooke's *Miscellaneous Essays*, Vol. I., p. 187.

of meat mixed with curds, barley, and jujubes, with the part of his hand sacred to the gods, or with that sacred to Prajápati.[1] Let a Brahman perform such a Śráddha, with all its offerings and circumambulations, on every occasion of good fortune.[2]

"Next, upon the tenth day (after birth), let the father give a name to his child,—the first term of which shall be the appellation of a god; the second, of a man; as Sarman or Varman: the former being the appropriate designation of a Brahman; the latter, of a warrior; whilst Gupta and Dása are best fitted for the

---

[1] With the Daiva tírtha, the tips of the fingers; or with the Prájápatya tírtha, the part of the hand at the root of the little finger. Manu, II., 58, 59.* The second is called, by Manu, the Káya tírtha, from Ka, a synonym of Prajápati.

[2] The Śráddha is, commonly, an obsequial or funeral sacrifice; but it implies offerings to the progenitors of an individual and of mankind, and always forms part of a religious ceremony, on an occasion of rejoicing, or an accession of prosperity; this being termed the Abhyudaya or Vriddhi Śráddha. Asiatic Researches, Vol. VII., p. 270.†

---

* ब्राह्मेण विप्रस्तीर्थेन नित्यकालमुपस्पृशेत् ।
कायत्रैदशिकाभ्यां वा न पित्र्येण कदाचन ॥
अङ्गुष्ठमूलस्य तले ब्राह्मं तीर्थं प्रचक्षते ।
कायमङ्गुलिमूलेऽग्रे दैवं पित्र्यं तयोरधः ॥

And we read, in the *Yájnavalkya-smŕiti*, I., 18, 19:

अन्तर्जानुः शुचौ देश उपविष्ट उदङ्मुखः ।
प्राग्वा ब्राह्मेण तीर्थेन द्विजो नित्यमुपस्पृशेत् ॥
कनिष्ठादेशिन्यङ्गुष्ठमूलान्यग्रं करस्य च ।
प्रजापतिपितृब्रह्मदेवतीर्थान्यनुक्रमात् ॥

† Or Colebrooke's *Miscellaneous Essays*, Vol. I., p. 187.

names of Vaiśyas and Śúdras.[1] A name should not be void of meaning; it should not be indecent, nor absurd, nor ill-omened, nor fearful; it should consist of an even number of syllables; it should not be too long, nor too short, nor too full of long vowels, but contain a due proportion of short vowels, and be easily articulated.* After this and the succeeding initiatory rites,[2] the purified youth is to acquire religious knowledge, in the mode that has been described, in the dwelling of his spiritual guide.

---

[1] So Manu, II., 30, 31, 32.† The examples given, in the comment, are Somaśarman, Indravarman, Chandragupta, and Śiva-dása,—respectively, appropriate appellations of men of the four castes.

[2] Or Saṁskáras; initiatory ceremonies, purificatory of the individual at various stages.

---

* नार्थहीनं न चाशस्तं नापशब्दयुतं तथा ।
नामङ्गल्यं जुगुप्स्यं वा नाम कुर्यात्समाक्षरम् ॥
नातिदीर्घं न ह्रस्वं वा नातिगुर्वक्षरान्वितम् ।
सुखोच्चार्यं तु तन्नाम कुर्याद्यत्प्रवणाक्षरम् ॥

† नामधेयं दशम्यां तु द्वादश्यां वास्य कारयेत् ।
पुण्ये तिथौ मुहूर्ते वा नक्षत्रे वा गुणान्विते ॥
मङ्गल्यं ब्राह्मणस्य स्यात्क्षत्रियस्य बलान्वितम् ।
वैश्यस्य धनसंयुक्तं शूद्रस्य तु जुगुप्सितम् ॥
शर्मवद्ब्राह्मणस्य स्याद्राज्ञो रक्षासमन्वितम् ।
वैश्यस्य पुष्टिसंयुक्तं शूद्रस्य प्रैष्यसंयुतम् ॥

Kullúka gives, as typical designations of persons of the four castes, Śubhaśarman, Balavarman, Vasubhúti, and Dínadása. The endings *śarman* and *deva* for names of Bráhmans, *varman* and *trátri* for those of Kshattriyas, *bhúti* and *datta* for those of Vaiśyas, and *dása* for those of Śúdras, are expressly sanctioned by the stanza which he cites from the lawgiver Yama:

शर्मा देवश्च विप्रस्य वर्मा त्राता च भूभुजः ।
भूतिर्दत्तश्च वैश्यस्य दासः शूद्रस्य कारयेत् ॥

"When he has finished his studies, and given the parting donation to his preceptor, the man who wishes to lead the life of a householder must take a wife. If he does not propose to enter into the married state, he may remain, as a student, with his teacher,—first making a vow to that effect,—and employ himself in the service of his preceptor and of that preceptor's descendants; or he may, at once, become a hermit,* or adopt the order of the religious mendicant, according to his original determination.[1]

"If he marry, he must select a maiden who is of a third of his age;[2] one who has not too much hair, but

[1] Or the vow or pledge he has taken, that he will follow, for life, the observances of the student, or ascetic; both of which are enumerated, in the Nirńaya Sindhu, as acts prohibited in the Kali age. A man is not to continue a student or Brahmachárin, i. e., a cœnobite, for life; nor is he to become a mendicant, without previously passing through the order of householder. In practice, however, the prohibition is, not unfrequently, disregarded.

[2] By this is to be understood, according to the commentator, merely a young girl, but, at the same time, one not immature; for, otherwise, he observes, a man of thirty—by which age he completes his sacred studies,—would espouse a girl of but ten years of age.† According to Manu,‡ however, the period of religious study does not terminate until thirty-six; and, in the East, a girl of twelve would be marriageable. The text of Yájnaval-

* *Vaikhánasa.* This term is synonymous with *vánaprastha.* *Vide* p. 95, *supra.*

† On the contrary, the commentator disallows, absolutely, even where the bridegroom is eight and forty, the marriage of a girl above ten years of age; on the ground that, after that period, she has her catamenia, &c. &c.

‡ III., 1.

is not without any; one who is not very black, or

---

kya* has merely the word Yaviyasi, 'a very young woman.' It

* I., 52:

अविप्लुतब्रह्मचर्यो लक्षण्यां स्त्रियमुद्वहेत् ।
अनन्यपूर्विकां कान्तामसपिण्डां यवीयसीम् ॥

Vijnáneśwara, Aparáditya, and Śúlapáńi, commentators on Yájnavalkya, leave his term *yavíyasí* unexplained.

The following dicta on the time when a female should marry are cited, by Jímútaváhana, in the *Dáyabhága*; pp. 272, 273, Calcutta edition of 1829. The first extract is from the *Vasishtha-smŕiti*, Chapter XVII.:

यावच्च कन्यामृतवः स्पृशन्ति
तुल्यैः सकामामपि याच्यमानाम् ।
तावन्ति भूतानि हतानि ताभ्यां
मातापितृभ्यामिति धर्मवादः ॥

"So many seasons of menstruation as overtake a maiden feeling the passion of love and sought in marriage by persons of suitable rank, even so many are the beings destroyed by both her father and her mother: this is a maxim of the law."

Paiṭhínasi is alleged as declaring: यावन्नोद्भिद्येते स्तनौ तावदेव देया । अथ ऋतुमती भवति दाता प्रतिग्रहीता च नरकमाप्नोति पितृपितामहप्रपितामहाश्च विष्ठायां जायन्ते । तस्मान्नग्निका दातव्या ।

"A damsel should be given in marriage, before her breasts swell. But, if she have menstruated [before marriage], both the giver and the taker fall to the abyss of hell; and her father, grandfather, and great-grandfather are born [insects] in ordure. Therefore she should be given in marriage while she is yet a girl.".

The preceding translations are taken from the *Two Treatises on the Hindu Law of Inheritance*, by Colebrooke, p. 186. His earlier renderings of the passages will be found in his *Digest of Hindu Law*, &c., London edition, Vol. II., p. 387.

In the *Panchatantra*,—III., *sl.* 213; p. 169, ed. Kosegarten,—we find the ensuing stanza:

वर्षमासाष्टका गौरी मासे रजसि रोहिणी ।
अव्यञ्जना भवेत्कन्या कुचहीना च नग्निका ॥

Nagniká is here vaguely said to signify a girl without breasts. This word, which Colebrooke renders by "yet a girl", is understood, by Vallabhagańi, to intend a maiden of eight years. If he be right, it is a synonym of *gauri*. No ordinary lexicographical authority seems to make the *nagniká* more than ten: see Colebrooke's *Amarakośa*, *sub voce*. But,

yellow-complexioned, and who is not, from birth, a

is worthy of remark, here, that neither that text, nor the text of Manu, nor the interpretation of our text, authorises the pre-

---

to judge from my next extract, the term appears to be, in some instances, as comprehensive as *kanyá*, 'virgin.'

In the *Nirńayasindhu* of Kamalákara,—Bombay edition of 1857, III. A, fol. 31 v and 32 r,—occurs the following extract, credited to the *Mahábhárata*:

त्रिंशद्वर्षः षोडशाब्दां भार्यां विन्देत नग्निकाम् ।
दशवर्षोऽष्टवर्षां वा धर्मे सीदति सत्वरः ।
अतो प्रवृत्ते रजसि कन्यां दद्यात्पिता सकृत् ॥

Whence came these lines? The first two look like a mixing up, from misrecollection, of the stanza cited in p. 104, note †, *infra*, with the *Anuśásana-parvan*, XLIV., 14, (Bombay edition), which runs thus:

त्रिंशद्वर्षो दशवर्षां भार्यां विन्देत नग्निकाम् ।
एकविंशतिवर्षो वा सप्तवर्षामवाप्नुयात् ॥

"Let a man of thirty years marry, for wife, a damsel of ten years; or let a man of twenty-one years secure a damsel of seven years."

The next quotation, also, is referred to the *Mahábhárata*:

सप्तसंवत्सरादूर्ध्वं विवाहः सार्ववर्णिकः ।
कन्यायाः शस्यते राजन्नन्यथा धर्मगर्हितः ॥

"The marriage, for all the castes, of a girl after *her* seventh year is commended, O king. *Her marriage* otherwise is reprobated by the law."

Of the first of the last three passages the first line is quoted,—immetrically, incorrectly, and, probably, from memory,—and without mention of its source, in Jagannátha Tarkapanchánana's *Vivádabhangárńava*. See Colebrooke's *Digest of Hindu Law*, &c., London edition, Vol. III., p. 398.

Mádhava says, in his commentary on the *Paráśara-smńiti*:

जन्मतो गर्भाधानाद्वा पञ्चमाब्दात्परं शुभम् ।
कुमारीवरणं दानं मेखलाबन्धनं तथा ॥

This approves the selection of a girl, for matrimony, at an interval of five years from the time she was born or conceived.

An extract from the *Jyotir-nibandha* may be added, for its superstitious oddity:

षडब्दमध्ये नोद्वाह्या कन्या वर्षद्वयं यतः ।
सोमो भुङ्क्ते ततस्तद्वद्गन्धर्वश्च तथानलः ॥

"A maiden should not be married within *her* sixth year: because Soma

cripple or deformed.* He must not marry a girl who is vicious, or unhealthy, of low origin, or labouring

sent practice of the nuptials of children.† The obligation imposed upon a man, of a life of perfect continence, until he is more than thirty, is singularly Malthusian.

[the Moon?] enjoys *her* for two years; then, in like manner, a *gandharva* and, similarly, Fire."

She has, thus, three unhuman husbands, before she is wived by a man. In the *Yájnavalkya-smṛiti*, I., 71, we read:

सोमः शौचं ददौ स्त्रीणां गन्धर्वश्च शुभां गिरम् ।
पावकः सर्वमेध्यत्वं मेध्या वै योषितो ह्यतः ॥

"On women Soma bestowed brilliancy; a *gandharva*, a pleasant voice; Fire, universal purity. Therefore are women truly pure."

The author of the *Mitákshará*, in commenting on this stanza, expresses himself much to the effect of the *Jyotir-nibandha*. His words are: परिणयनात्पूर्वं सोमगन्धर्ववह्नयः स्त्रियो भुक्त्वा यथाक्रमं तासां शौचमधुरवचनसर्वमेध्यत्वानि दत्तवन्तः ।

For similar ideas, see the *Panchatantra*, ed. Kosegarten, pp. 188, 189. An anonymous stanza is there given, authorising the nuptials of a damsel of eight years of age.

* The original has *adhikángí*, "possessing superfluous limbs."

† Professor Wilson must have overlooked "Manu", IX., 94:

त्रिंशद्वर्षो वहेत्कन्यां हृद्यां द्वादशवार्षिकीम् ।
त्र्यष्टवर्षोऽष्टवर्षां वा धर्मे सीदति सत्वरः ॥

"Let a man of thirty years wed a lovely maid of twelve; or a man of twenty-four, a maid of eight. *If his virtue is being impaired, let him be* expeditious."

The meaning seems to be, according to Kullúka, that, in case a young man is disposed to usurp on the rights of the married state, he should lose no time in taking a wife; provided, always, that his proficiency in scriptural knowledge is satisfactory.

In the *Nirńayasindhu's* citation of the preceding stanza, द्व्यष्टवर्षः, 'of sixteen years', is read for त्र्यष्टवर्षः, 'of twenty-four years.' But Medhátithi and Kullúka know nothing of this lection.

It has just been evinced, that, as to the marriage of an immature girl, venerable warrant is adducible for it, beyond the pages of the *Vishńu-puráńa*. The point, whether this work does not constructively furnish justification of such a practice, is discussed in a note near the end of Chapter XVI. of the present Book.

under disease;* one who has been ill brought up; one who talks improperly; one who inherits some malady from father or mother; one who has a beard, or who is of a masculine appearance; one who speaks thick, or thin, or croaks like a raven; one who keeps her eyes shut, or has the eyes very prominent; one who has hairy legs, or thick ancles; or one who has dimples in her cheeks, when she laughs.[1] Let not a wise and prudent man marry a girl of such a description: nor let a considerate man wed a girl of a harsh skin; or one with white nails; or one with red eyes, or with very fat hands and feet; or one who is a dwarf, or who is very tall; or one whose eyebrows meet, or whose teeth are far apart and resemble tusks. Let a householder marry a maiden† who is, in kin, at least five degrees remote from his mother, and seven from his father, with the ceremonies enjoined by law.[2]

"The forms of marriage are eight,—the Bráhma, Daiva, Ársha, Prájápatya, Ásura, Gándharva, Rákshasa, and Paiśácha; which last is the worst:[3] but

---

[1] For the credit of Hindu taste, it is to be noticed, that the commentator observes, the hemistich in which this last clause occurs is not found in all copies of the text.

[2] See Manu, III., 5, &c.

[3] These different modes of marriage are described by Manu, III., 27, &c.

---

* If only as doing away with something like tautology, the reading *atiroshiním*, 'very irascible,' is to be preferred to *atiroginím*. Just before we have *aroginím*, rendered "unhealthy".

† The term used hereabouts is *kanyá*.

the caste to which either form has been enjoined, as lawful, by inspired sages, should avoid any other mode of taking a wife. The householder who espouses a female connected with him by similarity of religious and civil obligations, and along with her discharges the duties of his condition, derives, from such a wife, great benefits."

CHAPTER XI.

Of the Sadácháras or perpetual obligations of a householder. Daily purifications, ablutions, libations, and oblations: hospitality: obsequial rites: ceremonies to be observed at meals, at morning and evening worship, and on going to rest.

SAGARA (again) said (to Aurva): "Relate to me, Muni, the fixed observances* of the householder, by attending to which he will never be rejected from this world or the next."

Aurva replied to him thus: "Listen, prince, to an account of those perpetual observances by adhering to which both worlds are subdued. Those who are called Sádhus (saints) are they who are free from (all) defects; and the term Sat means the same, or Sádhu. Those practices or observances (Ácháras†) which they follow are, therefore, called Sadácháras, 'the institutions or observances of the pious.'[1] The seven Rishis,

---

[1] Sir William Jones renders Áchára (आचार), 'the immemorial customs of good men'‡ (Manu, II., 6); following the explanation of Kullúka Bhatta, which is much the same as that of our text: आचारः कम्बलवल्कलाद्याचरणरूपः। साधूनां धार्मिकाणाम्। 'Áchára means the use of blankets, or bark, &c., (for dress), Sádhus are pious (or just) men.' Ácháras are, in fact, all ceremonial and

---

* *Sadáchára.*

† My MSS. have *ácharaṇa.*

‡ It is आचारः . . साधूनां that Sir William Jones thus renders. Colebrooke expresses *áchára* by "law", "conduct", "received usage", "established usage", "immemorial good customs", &c. &c. Medhátithi explains it by *vyavahára*, 'practice'.

the Manus, the patriarchs, are they who have enjoined and who have practised these observances. Let the wise man awake in the Muhúrta of Brahmá (or, in the third Muhúrta,—about two hours before sunrise*), and, with a composed mind, meditate on two of the objects of life (virtue and wealth), and on topics not incompatible with them. Let him, also, think upon desire, as not conflicting with the other two, and, thus, contemplate, with equal indifference, the three ends of life, for the purpose of counteracting the unseen consequences of good or evil acts. Let him avoid wealth and desire, if they give uneasiness to virtue; and abstain from virtuous or religious acts, if they involve misery, or are censured by the world.[1] † Having risen,

purificatory observances, or practices, not expiatory, which are enjoined either by the Vedas or the codes of law.

[1] That is, he may omit prescribed rites, if they are attended with difficulty or danger: he may forego ablutions, if they dis-

* Part of this is the commentator's explanation: ब्राह्मे मुहूर्ते । सूर्यो-दयात्पूर्वं तृतीये मुहूर्ते । Pitámaha is cited, in the *Śabdakalpadruma*, as ruling:

रात्रेश्च पश्चिमे यामे मुहूर्तो ब्राह्म उच्यते ।

† परित्यजेदर्थकामौ धर्मपीडाकरौ नृप ।
धर्ममप्यसुखोदर्कं लोकविक्रुष्टमेव च ॥

We read, to the same effect, and almost in the same words, in the *Laws of the Mánavas*, IV., 176:

परित्यजेदर्थकामौ यौ स्यातां धर्मवर्जितौ ।
धर्मं चाप्यसुखोदर्कं लोकविक्रुष्टमेव च ॥

This stanza Sir William Jones thus translates: "Wealth and pleasures, repugnant to law, let him shun, and even lawful acts which may cause future pain or be offensive to mankind."

Kullúka instances, as illustrative of the "lawful acts," etc., the giving away, in charity, of his entire possessions by a man on whom a large

he must offer adoration to the sun,* and then, in the south-west† quarter, at the distance of a bow-shot or more, or any where remote from the village,‡ void the impurities of nature. The water that remains after washing his feet he must not§ throw away into the court-yard of the house. A wise man will never void

---

agree with his health; and he may omit pilgrimage to holy shrines, if the way to them is infested by robbers.|| Again, it is enjoined, in certain ceremonies, to eat meat, or drink wine:¶ but these practices are generally reprehended by pious persons; and a man may, therefore, disregard the injunction.

---

family depends for subsistence, and the immolation of a cow on the *madhyamáshtaká* and other holydays. The *madhyamáshtaká* — sometimes called *mánsáshtaká* — falls, according to one authority, on the eighth day after the full moon in Mágha.

One occasion on which it seems that a cow was formerly slain, and that for purposes of hospitality, was a marriage. See Colebrooke's *Miscellaneous Essays*, Vol. I., pp. 203, 208.

* "Rising at break of day, let him go to stool", says the Sanskrit:

ततः कल्ये समुत्थाय कुर्यान्मैत्रं नरेश्वर ।

The Translator mistook, for *mitra*, 'the sun', *maitra*, n., 'alvine exoneration', which is said to come from *maitra*, m., 'the anus', of which the Sun is the guardian deity. Ratnagarbha etymologizes *maitra*. Also see the *Laws of the Mánavas*, IV., 152, and Kullúka's gloss thereon.

† I have corrected "south-east"; the original being *nairritya*m. This is a compromise between the directions to be observed by day and by night, or north and south, respectively. See the *Laws of the Mánavas*, IV., 50, and our text, just below.

‡ Thus, or by *gráma*, the commentator explains *bhú*, the word here used. The Sanskrit adds दूराद्वावसथात्, which means, according to the commentary, "*or, if that be impracticable, at least* away from the house."

§ I have inserted this word, translating *na*. Compare the *Laws of the Mánavas*, IV., 151.

|| Or by tigers. The commentary has: व्याघ्रचोराद्युपद्रवाकालतीर्थ-वसमयादि ।

¶ Drinking spirits at the *sautrámańí*, &c., says the commentator.

urine on his own shadow, nor on the shadow of a tree, nor on a cow, nor against the sun, nor on fire, nor against the wind,* nor on his Guru, nor on men of the three first castes;† nor will he pass either excrement in a ploughed field, or pasturage, or in the company of men, or on a high road, or in rivers and the like which are holy,‡ or on the bank of a stream, or in a place where bodies are burnt, or anywhere quickly.§ By day, let him void them with his face to the north, and, by night, with his face to the south, when he is not in trouble. Let him perform these actions in silence, and without delay; covering his head with a cloth, and the ground with grass. Let him not take, for the purposes of cleanliness, earth from an ant-hill, or a rat-hole,|| or from water, or from the residue of what has been so used, nor soil that has been employed to plaster a cottage, nor such as has been thrown up by insects,¶ or turned over by the plough. All such kinds of earth let him avoid as means of purification. One handful is sufficient, after voiding urine; three, after passing ordure: then, ten handfuls are to be rubbed over the left hand, and seven over both hands.** Let him, then, rinse his mouth with water

* See p. 140, *infra*, text and note —. † *Dwijáti.*

‡ "Places of pilgrimage", *tírtha*. Insert "or in water", *apsu*.

§ My MSS. give nothing corresponding to "or anywhere quickly." Probably the Translator read *ásu* for *apsu*. See the last note.

|| Literally, "dug up by a rat", *múshakotkháta*.

¶ अन्तःप्राण्यवपन्न. *Antaḥpráṇin* signifies *kíṭa*, "a worm", alleges the commentator. But he mentions a variant yielding *aṇupráṇin*, "a minute animal."

** एका लिङ्गे गुदे तिस्रो दश वामकरे तथा ।
हस्तद्वये च सप्तान्या मृदः शौचोपपादिकाः ॥

Compare, hereabouts, the *Vasishṭha-smṛiti*, Chapter VI.

that is pure, neither fetid, nor frothy, nor full of bubbles, and again use earth to cleanse his feet, washing them well with water. He is to drink water, then, three times, and twice wash his face with it; and, next, touch, with it, his head, the cavities of the eyes, ears, and nostrils,* the forehead,† the navel, and the‡ heart.¹§

¹ Many of these directions are given by Manu, IV.,

* Instead of "his head, the cavities of the eyes, ears and nostrils," read "the orifices of the head." The original,—see note §, below,—*śirshanyáni kháni*, is thus glossed by the commentator: शीर्षण्यानि । शिरःस्थानि । खानि । इन्द्रियच्छिद्राणि ।

† Read "head" *múrdhan*; and insert "arms", *báhú*.

‡ I should render *hṛidaya* by "breast".

§ त्रिः पिबेत्सलिलं तेन तथा द्विः परिमार्जयेत् ।
शीर्षण्यानि ततः खानि मूर्धानं च समालभेत् ।
बाहू नाभिं च तोयेन हृदयं चापि संस्पृशेत् ॥

Of all the ancient Hindu legislators, Daksha is most minutiose on the subject of daily ablution. His injunctions, as incorrectly cited by Ratnagarbha, I have rectified by reference to two manuscripts and the Calcutta edition of the *Daksha-smṛiti*; and I have compared them as quoted in various ceremonial treatises, more particularly in an ancient copy of Áśáditya's *Karmapradipabháshya*. The passage, as I would read it, is as follows:

प्रक्षाल्य हस्तौ पादौ च त्रिः पिबेदम्बु वीक्षितम् ।
संवृत्याङ्गुष्ठमूलेन द्विः प्रमृज्यात्ततो मुखम् ॥
संहताभिस्त्रिभिः पूर्वमास्यमेवमुपस्पृशेत् ।
ततः पादौ समभ्युक्ष्य अङ्गानि समुपस्पृशेत् ॥
अङ्गुष्ठेन प्रदेशिन्या घ्राणं पश्चादनन्तरम् ।
अङ्गुष्ठानामिकाभ्यां च चक्षुःश्रोत्रे पुनः पुनः ॥
कनिष्ठाङ्गुष्ठयोर्नाभिं हृदयं तु तलेन वै ।
सर्वाभिस्तु शिरः पश्चाद्बाहू चाग्रेण संस्पृशेत् ॥

"After bathing his hands and feet, let him thrice sip water in sight, *i. e.*, *any at hand*. Then let him compress his mouth, and rub it twice with the root of his thumb. Let him, likewise, touch his face with three *fingers* joined, and, next, wet his feet *again*, and touch his limbs im-

Having, finally, washed his mouth, a man is to clean and dress his hair, and to decorate his person, before a glass, with unguents, garlands, and perfumes.* He is, then, according to the custom† of his caste, to acquire wealth, for the sake of subsistence, and, with a lively faith, worship the gods.‡ Sacrifices with the acid juice, those with clarified butter, and those with offerings of food,§ are comprehended in wealth: wherefore, let men exert themselves to acquire wealth for these purposes.[1]

45, &c.||

[1] That is, wealth is essential to the performance of religious rites; and it is, also, the consequence of performing them. A

---

mediately afterwards, *let him touch* his nose with his thumb and fore-finger; and his eyes and ears, again and again, with his thumb and ring-finger; and his navel and breast, with the root of his little finger and thumb. Let him, afterwards, touch the crown of his head with all *his fingers*, and, finally, his arms."

The genuineness of the fourth line is open to suspicion. It is wanting in several places where these stanzas are adduced.

* आचान्तश्च ततः कुर्यात्पुमान्केशप्रसाधनम् ।
आदर्शाञ्जनमाङ्गल्यदूर्वाद्यालम्भनानि च ॥

Professor Wilson must have thought that he saw -माल्य-, instead of -माङ्गल्य-, in the original. For "garlands, and perfumes," read "sandal, *dúrvá*, &c." *Dúrvá* ordinarily means a certain sweet-scented grass. The oil expressed from it seems to be here denoted.

† *Dharma*, "duty".

‡ The original is simply *japet*, "let him pray inaudibly."

§ These sacrifices are called, in the original, *somasaṁsthá*, *haviḥsaṁsthá*, and *pákasaṁsthá*. On the meaning of *páka*, —'little', or 'good'— in *pákasaṁsthá*, see Professor Max Müller's *Ancient Sanskrit Literature*, p. 203; or Dr. Stenzler's edition of Áśvaláyana's *Gṛihyasútra*, Part II., p. 2, § 2, 3.

|| On the topic of ablution, see, particularly, *ibid.*, II., 60, 61; also, the *Yájnavalkya-smṛiti*, I., 20, *etc.*

"As preparatory to all established rites of devotion, the householder should bathe in the water of a river, a pond, a natural channel,* or a mountain torrent; or he may bathe upon dry ground, with water drawn from

householder should, therefore, diligently celebrate them, that he may acquire property, and, thus, be enabled to continue to sacrifice. According to Gautama,† there are seven kinds of each of the three sorts of sacrificial rites particularized in the text,—or those in which the Soma juice, oiled butter, or food, are presented. Of the latter, according to Manu, there are four varieties,—the offering of food to the Viśwadevas, to spirits, to deceased

* *Devakhátajala.*

† He is quoted, by the commentator, for his enumeration of sacrifices. These, as I find, on reference to the *Gautama-smṛiti*, are named as follows:

	Pákasaṃsthás.	*Haviḥsaṃsthás.*	*Somasaṃsthás.*
1.	*Ashṭaká.*	*Agnyádheya.*	*Agnishṭoma.*
2.	*Párvaṇa.*	*Agnihotra.*	*Atyagnishṭoma.*
3.	*Śráddha.*	*Darśapúrṇamásau.*	*Ukthya.*
4.	*Śrávaṇí.*	*Cháturmásyas.*	*Shoḍaśí.*
5.	*Ágraháyaṇí.*	*Ágrayaṇeshṭi.*	*Vájapeya.*
6.	*Chaitrí.*	*Nirúḍhapaśubandha.*	*Atirátra.*
7.	*Áśwayují.*	*Sautrámaṇí.*	*Aptoryáma.*

They have almost identical names, throughout, but are somewhat otherwise arranged, in Náráyaṇa's commentary on Śáṅkháyana's *Gṛihya-sútra*, as adduced by Dr. Stenzler, in the *Zeitschrift der Deutschen Morgenländischen Gesellschaft*, Vol. VII., p. 527, note 2. See, further, *ibid.*, Vol. IX., p. LXXIV. According to Ápastamba—see the *Taittiríya-saṃhitá and Commentary*, in the *Bibliotheca Indica*, Vol. I., p. 657,—several of the sacrifices of the first class bear appellations widely different from those given above. Baudháyana, quoted in the same place, gives them all still different names.

In note § to p. 40, *supra*, a passage is cited from Ratnagarbha, comparable to which, as concerns its groupment of sacrifices,—an understanding of which demands further inquiry,—I here quote another from Śankara's Commentary on the *Bṛihad-áraṇyaka Upanishad*, I., III., 1: न चाग्निहोत्रदर्शपूर्णमासचातुर्मास्यपशुबन्धसोमानां कर्मणां सतः काम्यनित्यत्वविवेकोऽस्ति।

a well, or taken from a river, or other source, where there is any objection to bathing on the spot.[1]* When bathed, and clad in clean clothes,† let him devoutly

---

ancestors, and to guests. II., 86.‡ The seven of Gautama§ are: offerings to progenitors on certain eighth days of the fortnight, at the full and change of the moon, at Śráddhas generally, and to the manes on the full moon of four different months, or Śrávańa, Agraháyańa, Chaitra, and Áświna.

[1] A person may perform his ablutions in his own house, if the weather, or occupation, prevents his going to the water. If he be sick, he may use warm water; and, if bathing be altogether injurious, he may perform the Mantra snána, or repeat the prayers used at ablution, without the actual bath.

---

* कूपेषूद्धृततोयेन स्नानं कुर्वीत वा भुवि ।
स्नायीतोद्धृततोयेन अथवा भुव्यसंभवे ॥

The commentator adds, — somewhat as in note 1 in this page, — that he is permitted to take water to his house, for bathing, if he must; that he may substitute warm water, when necessary, for cold; and that, in exigency, it is lawful for him to make shift with a *mantra-snána*, — in other words, to commute ablution for a prayer. Compare Colebrooke's *Miscellaneous Essays*, Vol. I., pp. 124, 136.

† The commentator observes, that the bathing and worship here described belong to noon-day.

‡ Four *pákayajnas* are there spoken of; but their names are not specified in the text. Kullúka says they are the *vaiśwadevahoma*, *balikarman*, *nityaśráddha*, and *atithibhojana*. These are four out of five *pákayajnas* which belong to a classification different from, and later than, that which Gautama recognizes. See p. 40, note §; and p. 93, notes 2 and ‡, *supra*: also, Kullúka on the *Laws of the Mánavas*, III., 67; Dr. Stenzler's edition of Áśwaláyana's *Grihyasútra*, Part II., p. 6, § 1; and Professor Max Müller's *Ancient Sanskrit Literature*, p. 93.

§ The third and fourth *pákayajnas* or *pákasaṁsthás*, in Ápastamba, correspond with the first and second of Gautama. The remaining five are called *aupásanahoma*, *vaiśwadeva*, *másí śráddham*, *sarpabali*, and *íśánabali*.

offer libations to the gods, sages,* and progenitors, with the parts of the hand severally sacred to each. He must scatter water thrice, to gratify the gods; as many times, to please the Ṛishis; and once, to propitiate Prajápati: he must, also, make three libations, to satisfy the progenitors. He must then present, with the part of the hand sacred to the manes, water to his paternal grandfather and great-grandfather, to his maternal grandfather, great-grandfather, and his father; and, at pleasure, to his own mother, and his mother's mother† and grandmother, to the wife of his preceptor, to his preceptor, his maternal uncle, and other relations,[1] to a dear friend, and to the king. Let him, also, after libations have been made to the gods and the rest, present others, at pleasure, for the benefit of all beings, reciting inaudibly this prayer: 'May the

---

[1] The whole series is thus given by Mr. Colebrooke: Asiatic Researches, Vol. V., p. 367.‡ Triple libations of tila (sesamum seeds) and water are to be given to the father, paternal grandfather, and great-grandfather; to the mother, maternal grandfather, great-grandfather, and great great-grandfather: and single libations are to be offered to the paternal and maternal grandmother and great-grandmother, to the paternal uncle, brother, son, grandson, daughter's son, son-in-law, maternal uncle, sister's son, father's sister's son, mother's sister, and other relatives. With exception of those, however, offered to his own immediate ancestors, which are obligatory, these libations are optional, and are rarely made.

---

* *Ṛishis.*

† *Pramátṛi.* This word has escaped the lexicographers.

‡ Or *Miscellaneous Essays*, Vol. I., p. 145.

gods, demons,* Yakshas, serpents, Gandharvas, Rákshasas, Piśáchas, Guhyakas,† Siddhas, Kúshmáńdas,‡ trees, birds, fish,§ all that people the waters, or the earth, or the air, be propitiated by the water I have presented to them! This water is given, by me, for the alleviation of the pains of all those who are suffering in the realms of hell. May all those who are my kindred, and not my kindred, and who were my relations in a former life, all who desire libations from me, receive satisfaction from this water! May this water and sesamum, presented by me, relieve the hunger and thirst of all who are suffering from those inflictions, wheresoever they may be!"[1]‖ Presentations of water, given in the manner, O king, which I have described, yield gratification to all the world; and the sinless man who, in the sincerity of faith, pours out these voluntary libations obtains the merit that results from affording nutriment to all creatures.

"Having, then, rinsed his mouth, he is to offer water to the sun, touching his forehead with his hands joined, and with this prayer: 'Salutation to Vivaswat, the radiant, the glory of Vishńu; to the pure illu-

---

[1] The first part of this prayer is from the Sáma-veda, and is given by Mr. Colebrooke. Asiatic Researches, Vol. V., p. 367.¶

---

* *Asura.*

† Servants of Kubera. Colebrooke calls them "unmelodious guardians of the celestial treasure." *Miscellaneous Essays*, Vol. I., p. 146.

‡ See Vol. I., p. 166.

§ There is no word for this, in the original.

‖ Several of my MSS. omit the stanza which this sentence translates.

¶ Or *Miscellaneous Essays*, Vol. I., p. 146.

minator of the world; to Savitri, the granter of the fruit of acts!"* He is, then, to perform the worship of the house, presenting to his tutelary deity† water, flowers, and incense. He is, next, to offer oblations with fire, not preceded by any other rite, to Brahmá.[1]‡ Having invoked Prajápati, let him pour oblations,§ reverently, to his household gods,‖ to Kásyapa, and to Anumati,[2] in succession. The residue of the obla-

---

[1] The rite is not addressed to Brahmá, specially; but he is to be invoked to preside over the oblations offered to the gods and sages, subsequently particularized.

[2] Kásyapa, the son of Kasyapa, is Áditya,¶ or the Sun. Anumati** is the personified moon, wanting a digit of full. The objects and order of the ceremony here succinctly described differ from those of which Mr. Colebrooke gives an account (Asiatic Researches, Vol. VII., p. 236††), and from the form of oblations given by Ward (Account of the Hindus, Vol. II., p. 477); but, as

---

* नमो विवस्वते ब्रह्मभास्वते विष्णुतेजसे ।
जगत्सवित्रे शुचये सवित्रे कर्मदायिने ॥

The commentator prefers the reading ब्रह्मन्भास्वते, but notes ब्रह्म-भास्वते.

† *Abhishta-sura.*

‡ अपूर्वमग्निहोत्रं च कुर्यात्प्राग्ब्रह्मणे ततः ।

Apúrva the commentator elucidates by *ananyaprakritika*: *vide supra*, p. 40, notes 1 and ‡. A variant, he says, is *appúrva*, 'previously sprinkled.' For the *agnihotra*, here spoken of, see p. 40, note 1; and p. 113, note †, *supra*.

§ *Áhuti.*

‖ *Grihya.*

¶ For the twelve Ádityas, see Vol. II., p. 27, and pp. 284 *et seq.*

** See Vol. I., p. 153; and Vol. II., p. 261: also, Goldstücker's *Sanskrit Dictionary*, *sub voce*.

†† Or *Miscellaneous Essays*, Vol. I., p. 152.

tion let him offer to the earth, to water, and to rain,* in a pitcher at hand; and to Dhátri and Vidhátri, at the doors of his house; and, in the middle of it, to Brahmá. Let the wise man also offer the Bali, consisting of the residue of the oblations, to Indra, Yama,† Varuńa, and Soma,‡ at the four cardinal points of his dwelling,§ the east and the rest; and, in the north-east quarter, he will present it to Dhanwantari.[1] After having thus worshipped the domestic deities, he will, next, offer part of the residue to all the gods (the Viswadevas); then, in the north-west quarter, to Váyu

observed by Mr. Colebrooke, oblations are made "with such ceremonies, and in such form as are adapted to the religious rite which is intended to be subsequently performed." Asiatic Researches, Vol. VII., p. 237.||

[1] See, also, Manu, III., 84, &c., and the Asiatic Researches, Vol. VII., p. 275.¶

---

* The ordinary reading is:

तथैव मणिकेऽद्भ्योऽथ पर्जन्याय विनिक्षिपेत् ।

But the commentator notes a variant, पृथ्वीपर्जन्याद्भ्यः, which Professor Wilson seems to have preferred. And he explains मणिके — above rendered "in a pitcher at hand",—by जलाधारसन्निधौ, 'near a pond.'

Personifications are, of course, intended here. The commentator calls these offerings the *bhútayajna*. This is the same as the *baliyajna*. See p. 93, notes 2 and , *supra*.

† *Dharmarája*, in the original. ‡ Substituted for Indu.

§ The Sanskrit of this sentence begins:

शृणुष्व पुरुषव्याघ्र दिग्देवानपि मे गृह्य ।

"Hear from me, man-tiger, the house's gods of the quarters, also."

The Translator rarely renders the vocatival epithets with which this work abounds; and these constitute one of its quaintest features.

|| Or *Miscellaneous Essays*, Vol. I., p. 153.

¶ Or Colebrooke's *Miscellaneous Essays*, Vol. I., p. 191.

(wind); then, in all directions, to the points of the horizon,* to Brahmá, to the atmosphere,† and to the sun; to all the gods,‡ to all beings, to the lords of beings, to the Pitṛis, to twilight.§ Then, taking other rice,[1] let the householder, at pleasure, cast it upon a clean spot of ground, as an offering to all beings; repeating, with collected mind, this prayer: 'May gods, men, animals, birds, saints,¶ Yakshas, serpents, demons, ghosts, goblins,** trees, all that desire food given by me; may ants,†† worms, moths,‡‡ and other insects, hungered, and bound in the bonds of acts; may all obtain satisfaction from the food left them by me, and enjoy happiness! May they who have neither mother, nor father, nor relations, nor food, nor the means of preparing it, be satisfied and pleased with the food presented for their contentment!'[2] Inasmuch

---

[1] Or this ceremony may be practised instead of the preceding.

[2] This prayer is said, by Mr. Colebrooke, to be taken from the Puráńas (Asiatic Researches, Vol. VII., p. 275).§§ He translates

---

* निर्वपेद्विश्वेदेवे च कर्म कुर्यादतः परम् ।
वायवे वायवे दिक्षु समस्तासु ततो दिशाम् ॥

† *Antariksha.*

‡ *Viśve deváh.*

§ My MSS. concur in reading:

यक्ष्माय च समुद्दिश्य बलिं दद्यान्नरेश्वर ।

There is nothing, here, of "twilight". *Yakshman*, in this passage, may be Consumption, personified as a divinity. The commentary is silent.

‖ *Anna*, 'food', as just below; not, necessarily, 'rice'.

¶ *Siddha.*

** *Daitya, preta*, and *piśácha.*

†† *Pipiliká*, 'termites'.

‡‡ *Patanga.*

§§ Or *Miscellaneous Essays*, Vol. I., p. 192.

as all beings, and this food, and I, and Vishńu, are not different, I, therefore, give, for their sustenance, the food that is one with the body of all creatures. May all beings that are comprehended in the fourteen orders of existent things[1] be satisfied with the food bestowed, by me, for their gratification, and be delighted!' Having uttered this prayer, let the devout believer cast the food upon the ground, for the nourishment* of all kinds of beings: for the householder is, thence, the supporter of them all. Let him scatter food upon the ground, for dogs, outcasts,† birds, and all fallen and degraded‡ persons.

"The householder is then to remain, at eventide, in his court-yard, as long as it takes to milk a cow,[2]—or

---

the last clause: "May they, who have neither * * * * * * food, nor means of obtaining it." In our text, the phrase is

येषां * * * * * * * * *
नैवान्नसिद्धिर्न तथान्नमस्ति ।

which the commentator explains by येषामन्नं नास्ति येषां च सान्न-पात्रे नान्न सिद्धिः पाकसाधनं नास्तीत्यर्थः; understanding Anna siddhi to mean 'means of dressing food,' Páka sádhana. The following passages of the prayer are, evidently, peculiar to the Vishńu Puráńa.

[1] Either fourteen classes of Bhútas (or spirits); or the same number of living beings,—or eight species of divine, one of human, and five of animal, creatures.

[2] This, according to the commentator, is equal to the fourth part of a Ghaṭiká, which, considering the latter synonymous with

---

* Upakára. † Chańḍála.

‡ Apátra. Some MSS. have apútra, 'souless'. The former term imports 'undeserving of exequial offerings',—śrāddhāyogya,—says commentary B.

longer, if he pleases,—to await the arrival of a guest. Should such a one arrive, he is to be received with a hospitable welcome; a seat is to be offered to him, and his feet are to be washed, and food is to be given him with liberality,* and he is to be civilly and kindly spoken to; and, when he departs, to be sent away, by his host, with friendly wishes.† A householder should ever pay attention to a guest who is not an inhabitant of the same village, but who comes from another place, and whose name and lineage are unknown. He who feeds himself, and neglects the poor and friendless stranger in want of hospitality, goes to hell. Let a householder who has a knowledge of Brahmá‡ reverence a guest, without inquiring his studies, his school, his practices, or his race.'[1] §

Muhúrta, or one thirtieth of the day and night, would be twelve minutes.‖

[1] These precepts, and those which follow, are of the same tenour as those given by Manu, on the subject of hospitality (III., 99, &c.), but more detailed.

---

* *Śraddhá.* Elsewhere the Translator renders this word by "faith".

† अध्वनश्चानुयानेन प्रीतिमुत्पादयेद्गृही ।

It is, thus, directed, that, when the guest departs, his host should bear him company,—for a short distance, only, of course. The less common reading *anuyánena* must yield the same sense. The unique lection *anupánena* might move an imaginative speculator to attribute the idea of the stirrup-cup to the ancient Hindus.

‡ The Sanskrit directs the householder to reverence his guest 'by regarding *him as if he were* Hiraṇyagarbha,'—*hiraṇyagarbha-buddhyá*.

§ "School," "practices," and "race" here render *gotra*, *charaṇa*, and *kula*, 'stock,' 'school', and 'family'. The commentator gives *charaṇa* two meanings,—*vedántaraśákhá* and *áchára*.

‖ See Vol. I., p. 47, note 2.

"A householder should, also, at the perpetual Śráddha,* entertain another Brahman who is of his own country, whose family and observances are known, and who performs the five sacramental rites.† He is, likewise, to present, to a Brahman learned in the Vedas, four handfuls of food, set apart with the exclamation Hanta;‡ and he is to give, to a mendi-

---

* *Pitrartham*, 'for the sake of the manes'. It is explained by *nitya-śráddhártham*, in the commentary.

† *Vide supra*, p. 93, note 2.

‡ अन्नाग्रं च समुद्धृत्य हन्तकारोपकल्पितम् ।
निर्वापभूतं भूपाल श्रोत्रियायोपपादयेत् ॥

"Let him, O king, also set apart the choicest of food, and present *it*, by way of appropriation, hallowed by the utterance *hanta*, to a Bráhman versed in holy writ."

The commentator says: अन्नाग्रं भोजनात्पूर्वमुद्धृतम् । तच्चोक्तम् ।

ग्रासमात्रा भवेद्भिक्षा अग्रं ग्रासचतुष्टयम् ।
अग्राण्येव तु चत्वारि हन्तकारं प्रचक्षते ॥

मनुष्येभ्यो हन्तेति मन्त्रेणोपकल्पितमन्नं हन्तकारोपकल्पितम् । निर्वापभूतं पृथक्कृत्य स्थापितम् ।

A stanza, the same in meaning as the one here quoted, is adduced, from Hemachandra's scholiast, in Messrs. Boehtlingk and Rieu's edition of the *Abhidhánachintámaṇi*, p. 366:

ग्रासप्रमाणा भिक्षा स्यादग्रं ग्रासचतुष्टयम् ।
अग्रं चतुर्गुणं प्राहुर्हन्तकारं द्विजोत्तमाः ॥

Annágra and *hantakára*, rendered by 'the choicest of food' and 'the utterance *hanta*', have, thus, denoted specific quantities,—four mouthfuls and sixteen. But neither of these acceptations—which are, probably, of late date,—seems to be intended in the passage under annotation. One or other of them is there impossible.

The following is taken from the *Bṛihad-áraṇyaka Upanishad*,—V., VIII.: वाचं धेनुमुपासीत । तस्याश्चत्वारः स्तनाः स्वाहाकारो वषट्कारो हन्तकारः स्वधाकारः । तस्यै द्वौ स्तनौ देवा उपजीवन्ति स्वाहाकारं च वषट्कारं च हन्तकारं मनुष्याः स्वधाकारं पितरः । तस्याः प्राण ऋषभो मनो वत्सः । "One should reverence speech as a cow. Here *are*

cant[*] religious student, three handfuls† of rice, or according to his pleasure, when he has ample means.‡ These, with the addition of the mendicant before described, are to be considered as guests; and he who treats these four descriptions of persons with hospitality acquits himself of the debt due to his fellow-men.§ The guest who departs, disappointed, from any house, and proceeds elsewhere, transfers his sins to the owner of that mansion, and takes away with him such a householder's merits.|| Brahmá,¶ Prajápati, Indra,** fire, the Vasus, the Sun, are present in the person of

---

four dugs: the utterance *swáhá*, the utterance *vashat*, the utterance *hanta*, the utterance *swadhá*. By two of her dugs, the utterance *swáhá* and the utterance *vashat*, the gods are sustained; by the utterance *hanta*, man; by the utterance *swadhá*, the manes. Life is her bull; the organ of imagination, *her* calf."

Of *swáhá* and *vashat* Śrídhara says: स्वाहां हविर्दीयते देवेभ्यः; of *hanta*, हन्त इति मनुष्येभ्योऽन्नं प्रयच्छन्ति; of *swadhá*, स्वधाकारेण हि पितृभ्यः स्वधां प्रयच्छन्ति ।

For Swáhá and Swadhá, see Vol. I., p. 109; for Vashat, Vol. II., p. 23, notes 3 and §.

* *Parivráj*.

† *Grása*, 'mouthfuls'.

‡ इच्छया च नरो दद्याद्विभवे सत्यवारितम् ।

§ इत्येतेऽतिथयः प्रोक्ताः प्रागुक्ता भिक्षवश्च ये ।
चतुरः पूजयित्वैतान्नृयज्ञर्णात्प्रमुच्यते ॥

"These *are* called guests: and one showing honour to the four above-mentioned eleemosynaries acquits," &c.

The commentator says that these persons are: the unknown Bráhman, the known Bráhman, the Bráhman versed in holy writ, and the mendicant religious student.

|| This is almost a verbal repetition of what we have had before. *Vide supra*, p. 94, text and note †. The Sanskrit here runs thus:

अतिथिर्यस्य भग्नाशो गृहात्तस्मात्पराङ्मुखः ।
स दत्त्वा दुष्कृतं तस्मै पुण्यमादाय गच्छति ॥

¶ Dhátri, in the original.

** Substituted for Śakra.

a guest, and partake of the food (that is given to him). Let a man, therefore, be assiduous in discharging the duties of hospitality: for he who eats his food, without (bestowing any upon) a guest, feeds only upon iniquity.

"In the next place, the householder must provide food for a married damsel remaining in her father's dwelling;* for any one who is ill; for a pregnant woman; for the aged, and the infants (of his house); and then he may eat, himself. He who eats, whilst these are yet unfed, is guilty of sin (in this life), and, when he dies, is condemned, in hell, to feed upon phlegm. So, he who eats without performing ablutions is fed, (in hell), with filth; and he who repeats not his prayers,† with matter and blood; he who eats unconsecrated food, with urine; and (he who eats) before the children and the rest (are fed, is stuffed, in Tartarus), with ordure. Hear, therefore, O king of kings, how a householder should feed, so that, in eating, no sin may be incurred, that invariable health and increased vigour may be secured, and all evils and hostile machinations may be averted.‡ Let the householder, having bathed, and offered libations to the gods§ and manes, and decorated his hand with jewels, proceed to take his meal, after having repeated the

* *Suvásiní.*

† The *gáyatrí* and so forth, the commentator says.

‡ अवाग्वारिस्थाभिव वैरिपक्षाभिचारिका ।

The gloss on this line is as follows: वारिस्थमुखाकृष्ट सक्त धारिता: । वैरिपक्षाभ्युत्पन्नरोगाणामभिचारिका विनाशयित्री ।

§ Insert 'Rishis'.

(introductory) prayers, and offered oblations with fire, and having given food to guests, to Brahmans, to his elders, and to his family. He must not eat with a single garment on, nor with wet hands and feet, but dressed in clean clothes, perfumed, and wearing garlands of flowers: he must not eat with his face to any intermediate point of the horizon, but fronting the east or the north:* and thus, with a smiling countenance, happy and attentive, let him partake of food, of good quality, wholesome, boiled with clean water,† procured from no vile person, nor by improper means, nor improperly cooked.‡ Having given a portion to his hungry companions, let him take his food, without reproach,§ out of a clean handsome vessel, which must not be placed upon a low stool|| (or bed). He must not eat in an unfit place, or out of season,¶ or in an incommodious attitude;** nor must he first cast any of his meal into the fire. Let his food be made holy with suitable texts; let it be good of its kind: and

* The directions he must face when bathing. See the *Laws of the Mánavas*, II., 61: and compare VIII., 87. Also *vide infra*, p. 127.

† "Boiled with clean water" translates प्रोक्षितं प्रोक्षणोदकैः, "sprinkled with water for sprinkling,"—with a view to ceremonial purification.

‡ नैव जुगुप्सावदसंस्कृतं, "not disgusting, nor unhallowed." This is to be substituted for "nor by improper means, nor improperly cooked." I find but one reading.

§ *Akupita*, 'undisturbed by wrath.'

|| *Ásandí*, 'wooden, three-legged, &c.' says the commentary: दारुमयं त्रिपदादि ।

¶ *Nákále*: as at noon, or either of the twilights, it is said. The commentator adds a variant, *nákáśe*, 'not in the open air.'

** *Atisankírṇe*, "in a place much littered over", I should think. The commentator says nothing.

it must not be stale, except in the case of fruit or meat;[1] nor must it be of dry vegetable substances, other than jujubes[2] or preparations of molasses; but never must a man eat of that of which the juices have

---

[1] By stale,* as applied to meat, is intended, in this place, probably, meat which has been previously dressed, as part of an offering to the gods or manes; meat which is dressed in the first instance for an individual being prohibited; as by Yájnavalkya:† वृथामांसं वर्जयेत् । 'Let him avoid flesh killed in vain;' or, 'that which is not the residue of an offering to the gods, &c.': देवाद्यर्चनावशिष्टं यन्न भवति ।‡ So, also, Manu, V., 7.§

[2] By dried vegetables, &c., (शुष्कशाकादिकं), is to be understood unboiled vegetables, or pot-herbs dressed without being sprinkled with water: जलोपसेकं विना पक्वम् ।‖ Instead of बदरिकेभ्यः,¶ 'Jujubes,' the reading is, sometimes, हरितकेभ्यः,** myro-

---

* *Paryushita* means 'kept over night'. See the *Mitákshará* on the *Yájnavalkya-smŕiti*, I., 167; and Śridhara on the *Bhagavad-gítá*, XVII., 10.

† I., 167, 168.

‡ This is the *Mitákshará's* elucidation of the words of Yájnavalkya.

§ Add IV., 213. But V., 34, is most explicit on the enormity of the offence here denounced:

न तादृशं भवत्येनो मृगहन्तुर्धनार्थिनः ।
यादृशं भवति प्रेत्य वृथामांसानि खादतः ॥

"The sin of him who kills deer for gain is not so heinous, with respect to *the punishment in* another life, as that of him who eats flesh-meat in vain, *or, not previously offered as a sacrifice.*" Sir William Jones's Translation.

‖ The commentary farther says, that the bare mention of 'pot-herbs, &c.' implies, that they are unaccompanied by fried grain and the like: धानादिकं सक्त्वादिकं निषेधति शेषः ।

¶ I nowhere find this reading, but बादरिकेभ्यः, 'preparations of jujubes,' according to the gloss, बदरविकारेभ्यः.

** The reading preferred by the commentator, and explained by चष्यलेह्यादिभ्यः, "things to be licked, and the like, uncooked."

been extracted.[1] Nor must a man eat so as to leave no residue (of his meal), except in the case of flour-cakes,* honey, water, curds, and butter.† Let him, with an attentive mind, first taste that which has a sweet flavour: he may take salt and sour things, in the middle course, and finish with those which are pungent and bitter. The man who commences his meal with fluids, then partakes of solid food, and finishes with fluids again, will ever be strong and healthy. In this manner, let him feed without fault, silent, and contented with his food; taking, without uttering a word, to the extent of five handfuls, for the nutriment of the vital principle.‡ Having eaten sufficiently, the householder is, then, to rinse his mouth, with his face turned towards the east or the north;§ and, having again sipped water, he is to wash his hands, from the wrist downwards.‖ With a pleased and tranquil spirit, he is, then, to take a seat,¶ and call to memory his tutelary deity;** and then he is thus to pray: 'May fire, excited by air, convert this food into the earthly ele-

balans.' The other term, गुडपक्वैः, is explained 'sweetmeats.'†† The construction here, however, is somewhat obscure.

[1] As oil-cake, or the sediment of anything after expression.

* The first edition exhibits "flour, cakes"; a typographical oversight. The Sanskrit word is *saktu*.

† *Sarpis*, 'clarified butter.'

‡ *Prasiddhi*.

§ *Vide supra*, p. 125, note *.

‖ "From the wrist downwards" is to render *mûlataḥ*, which the commentary explains by *kaphoṇi-paryantam*, 'as far as the elbow.'

¶ *Kritâsana-parigrahaḥ*, 'his wife being seated.'

** *Abhishṭa-devatâ*, in the plural.

†† मधुकादिभ्यः । गुडमयेभ्य इति पाठे च एवार्थः । Commentary.

ments of this frame, and, in the space afforded by the ethereal atmosphere, cause it to digest, and yield me satisfaction!* May this food, in its assimilation, contribute to the vigour of the earth, water, fire, and air of my body, and afford unmixed† gratification!‡ May Agasti, Agni, and submarine fire effect the digestion of the food of which I have eaten! May they grant me the happiness which its conversion into nutriment engenders; and may health (ever) animate my form! May Vishńu, who is the chief principle of all invested with bodily structure and the organs of sense, be propitiated by my faith in him, and influence the assimilation of the invigorating food which I have eaten! For, verily, Vishńu is the eater, and the food, and the nutriment:§ and, through this belief, may that which

---

* अग्निराप्याययत्वन्नं पार्थिवं पवनेरितः ।
दत्तावकाशं नभसा जरयत्वस्तु मे सुखम् ॥

The comment on this runs thus: पवनेरितो वह्निर्नभसा दत्तावकाशं मया भुक्तमन्नं जरयतु । ततश्चान्नरसेन पार्थिवं देहधातुमाप्याययत्विति । According to this, the stanza signifies: "May fire, excited by air, effect the digestion of *any* food under heaven, *eaten by me*; *and then* may it, *viz.*, *fire*, *by the juices of food*, prosper the earthy *elements of* my body: may there be happiness to me!" Independently of the scholiast, however, one would feel inclined to translate as follows: "May fire, excited by air, prosper *all* earthy food under heaven, *and* cause *it* to be digested: may there be happiness to me!"

† *Avyáhata*, 'uninterrupted.'

‡ Nearly all my MSS. here interpolate, if they do not substitute for what just precedes, as follows:

प्राणापानसमानानामुदानव्यानयोस्तथा ।
अन्नं पुष्टिकरं चास्तु ममास्त्वव्याहतं सुखम् ॥

The copies containing the commentary give this unimportant stanza, but in such a way, in some, that it is doubtful as to its genuineness. It is left unexplained. For अव्याहत, &c., see Goldstücker's *Sanskrit Dictionary*, *sub voce*.

§ Read "digestion", *parińáma*.

I have eaten be digested!"*

"Having repeated this prayer, the householder should rub his stomach with his hand, and, without indolence, perform such rites as confer repose; passing the day in such amusements as are authorized by holy writings and are not incompatible with the practices of the righteous, until the Sandhyá, when he must engage in pious meditation.† At the Sandhyá at the close of the day, he must perform the usual rites before the sun has quite set; and, in the morning, he must perform them before the stars have disappeared.[1]‡ The morning and evening rites must never

---

[1] So Manu, II., 101,§ and IV., 93.||

---

* विष्णुः समस्तेन्द्रियदेहदेही-
प्रधानभूतो भगवान्यथैकः ।
सत्येन तेनाग्रमशेषमेत-
दारोग्यदं मे परिणाममेतु ॥
विष्णुरत्ता तथैवान्नं परिणामश्च वै यथा ।
सत्येन तेन मे भुक्तं जीर्यत्वन्नमिदं तथा ॥

The first stanza should, rather, be rendered: "Just as the holy Vishńu, the ultimate source of all the organs of sense, bodies, and embodied *souls*, *is* one, *so*, by this truth, may all this food, health-giving, be digestible to me." For *pradhána*, see Vol I., p. 20, note *.

† ततः संध्यामुपतिष्ठेत्समाहितः ।

‡ दिनान्तसंध्यां सूर्येण पूर्वामृक्षैर्युतां बुधः ।
उपतिष्ठेद्यथान्यायं सम्यगाचम्य पार्थिव ॥

As bearing on this, the commentator adduces a couplet from some *Smriti*:

प्रातः संध्यां सनक्षत्रामुपासीत यथाविधि ।
सादित्यां पश्चिमां संध्यामर्धास्तमितभास्कराम् ॥

§ पूर्वां संध्यां जपंस्तिष्ठेत्सावित्रीमार्कदर्शनात् ।
पश्चिमां तु समासीनः सम्यगृक्षविभावनात् ॥

|| उत्थायावश्यकं कृत्वा कृतशौचः समाहितः ।
पूर्वां संध्यां जपंस्तिष्ठेत्स्वकाले चापरां चिरम् ॥

be neglected, except at seasons of impurity,* anxiety, sickness, or alarm. He who is preceded by the sun, in rising, or sleeps when the sun is setting,—unless it proceed from illness and the like,—incurs guilt which requires atonement;† and, therefore, let a man rise before the sun, in the morning, and sleep not until after he has set.‡ They who sinfully omit both the morning§ and the evening service go, after death, to the hell of darkness.|| In the evening, then, having again dressed food, let the wife (of the householder), in order to (obtain the fruit of) the Vaiśwadeva rite, give food, without prayers,¶ to outcasts and unclean spirits.** Let the householder himself, according to his means, again show hospitality to any guest who may arrive; welcoming him with the salutation of evening,†† water for his feet, a seat, a supper, and a bed. The sin of want of hospitality to a guest who comes after sunset is eight times greater than that of turning away one

---

* *Sútakásaucha*. *Sútaka* is ceremonial uncleanness resulting from the birth of a child; *asaucha*, that resulting from death. Commentary.

† Compare the *Laws of the Mánavas*, II., 221:

सूर्येण ह्यभिनिर्मुक्तः शयानोऽभ्युदितश्च यः ।
प्रायश्चित्तमकुर्वाणो युक्तः स्यान्महतैनसा ॥

‡ तस्मादनुदिते सूर्ये समुत्थाय महीपते ।
उपतिष्ठेन्नरः संध्यामस्वपंश्च दिवाकरम् ॥

§ See, on the sinfulness of this omission, Vol. II., p. 252.

|| *Támisra*. See Vol. II., p. 215, notes || and ¶.

¶ Instead of पत्न्यमन्त्रवत्, "wife", "without prayers", some MSS. read पत्न्या सार्धं, 'with his wife.' The commentator notices this variant.

** In the original, श्वपचादिभ्यः. *Ádi*, 'etc.', is here rendered by "unclean spirits."

†† *Prahwa-swágatokti* means 'a salutation and a welcome'; *prahwa* being explained by *prahwatwa*, *i. e.*, *pranáma*. But, in several MSS., the reading is *prahwah*, 'complaisant.'

who arrives by day. A man should, therefore, most especially show respect to one who comes to him in the evening, for shelter; as the attentions that gratify him will give pleasure to all the gods. Let the householder, then, according to his ability, afford a guest food, pot-herbs, water, a bed, a mat, or, if he can do no more, ground on which to lie.*

"After eating his evening meal, and having washed his feet, the householder is to go to rest. His bed is

---

* शयनस्रस्तरमहीप्रदानैरथवापि तम् ।

So read most of my MSS. The commentary says: शयनं कम्बलादि । स्रस्तरः कटतृणादिः । मही स्थानमात्रमपि । Several MSS. of the text, and one of the commentary, have *prastara*, for *srastara*; one MS. has *srastara* altered into *saṁstara*, 'a couch'; and one has *swastara*. "Bed" denotes, then, 'a blanket, &c.'; and the *srastara*, which the Translator calls "mat", consists of 'a mat, straw, etc.' In the *Laws of the Mánavas*, II., 204, the reading, according to Kullúka, is *srastara*; but he does not explain it. Sir William Jones gives "a pavement of stones." Medhátithi has the lection *prastara*, which he defines to be: कुशादितृणास्तीर्णं आस्तरः, 'a rug strewed with *darbha* or other grass.' In Gulzár Paṇḍit's Hindi version of the *Mánavadharmaśástra*, *srastara* is rendered *chaṭái*, 'mat'. In the unfinished Calcutta translation of the same Code,—made, I am told, by Táráchandra Chakravartin,—this term is interpreted "a seat made of sprouts and leaves", with the following comment: "*Srastara* is a word which is not much in use. It is not found in the Sanskrita dictionaries commonly consulted, nor even in the voluminous compilation of Dr. Wilson; and yet, unaccountable as the thing must appear, the word is left unexplained by the commentator [Kullúka]. We have found it, however, with the meaning given above, in a dictionary which was compiled and published some years ago, and is entitled *Prádakshiṇa-śabdámbudhi*. These circumstances considered, it will not appear improbable, that Sir William Jones took it to be a mistake, in the manuscript, for *prastara*, 'stone': or that he found the word to be *prastara*, in his manuscript, and gave the rendering accordingly." The *Śabdámbudhi*, ed of 1856, defines *srastara* 'seat', 'support for sitting.' Finally, *srastara*, on the faith of the *Śabdakalpadruma*, is found in the *Śuddhitattwa*, and is equivalent to *ásana*, 'seat.'

The word *prastara* recurs in p. 150, *infra*.

to be entire, and made of wood;* it is not to be scanty, nor cracked, nor uneven, nor dirty, nor infested by insects, nor without a bedding: and he is to sleep with his head either to the east or to the south: any other position is unhealthy. In due season, a man should approach his wife, when a fortunate asterism† prevails, in an auspicious moment, and on even nights,‡ if she is not unbathed,§ sick, unwell,‖ averse, angry,¶ pregnant,** hungry, or over-fed. He should be, also, free from similar imperfections, should be neatly attired and adorned, and animated by tenderness and affection.†† There are certain days on which unguents, flesh, and women are unlawful; as the eighth and fourteenth lunar days, new moon and full moon,[1] and the

[1] So Manu, IV., 128.‡‡

---

* This will do, in default of one of ivory, observes the commentator. A variant is *ekadárumaya*, 'made of a single pine', apparently. Oriental cots are light and easily portable.

† *Punnámayrikshe*. The asterisms referred to are, according to the commentator, ten in number: Aświni, Kríttiká, Rohiṇí, Punarvasu, Pushya, Hasta, Anurádhá, Śravaṇá, Púrvabhádrapadá, Uttarabhádrapadá.

‡ ओजयुग्मासु रात्रिषु. Commentary: ऋतुकालमारभ्य षष्ठ्यादि-षु रात्रिषु । तथापि ओजासु युग्मासु यथाक्रमं शुभाशिवार्थः 1.

§ After her courses. Commentary. ‖ *Rajaswalám*, 'menstruous.'

¶ There is an omission, here, of "not an object of evil report," *aprasastám*; *aprasasta* meaning, the scholiast says, परिवादादिदूषित.

** The original adds other epithets, besides the two that follow in the translation:

नाहृष्टां नान्यकामां नाकामां नान्ययोषितम् ।
क्षुत्क्षामामतिभुक्तां वा स्वयं चैभिर्गुणैर्युतः ॥

†† स्नातः स्रग्गन्धधृक्प्रीतो नाध्मातः क्षुधितोऽपि वा ।
सकामः सानुरागश्च व्यवायं पुरुषो व्रजेत् ॥

‡‡ अमावास्याष्टमी च पौर्णमासी चतुर्दशी ।
ब्रह्मचारी भवेन्नित्यमप्यृतौ स्नातको द्विजः ॥

entrance of the sun into a new sign. On these occasions, the wise will restrain their appetites, and occupy themselves in the worship of the gods, as enjoined by holy writ, in meditation, and in prayer: and he who behaves differently will fall into a hell where ordure will be his food.* Let not a man stimulate his desires by medicines, nor gratify them with unnatural objects,† or in public or holy places. Let him not think incontinently of another's wife, much less address her to that end; for such a man will be born, in future life, as a creeping insect.‡ He who commits adultery is punished both here and hereafter: for his days, in this world, are cut short; and, when dead, he falls into hell. Thus considering, let a man approach his own wife in the proper season, or even at other times."§

---

* This clause about punishment is not found in my MSS.

† Two terms used in the original—for which see note § in the present page,—are thus expounded by the commentator: अन्ययोनौ । अजादियोनौ । अयोनौ । मुखादौ । See, further, Goldstücker's *Sanskrit Dictionary*, article अयोनि.

‡ This explanation of the text is taken from the commentary.

§ The conclusion of this chapter is much abridged, as here translated. The original is as follows:

चतुर्दश्यष्टमी चैव अमावास्याथ पूर्णिमा ।
पर्वाण्येतानि राजेन्द्र रविसंक्रान्तिरेव च ॥
तैलस्त्रीमांससंभोगी पर्वस्वेतेषु वै पुमान् ।
विण्मूत्रभोजनं नाम प्रयाति नरकं मृतः ॥
अशेषपर्वस्वेतेषु तस्मात्संयमिभिर्बुधैः ।
भाव्यं सच्छास्त्रदेवेज्याध्यानजप्यपरैर्नरैः ॥
नान्ययोनावयोनौ वा नोपयुक्तौषधस्तथा ।
द्विजदेवगुरूणां च व्यवायी नाश्रमे भवेत् ॥
चैत्यचत्वरतीर्थेषु गोष्ठे नैव चतुष्पथे ।
नैव श्मशानोपवनसलिलेषु महीपते ॥

सोपपर्वस्वथैतेषु नैव भूपाल संयतः ।
गच्छेद्व्यवायं मतिमान्न भूपोद्धारयोषितः ॥
पर्वस्वभिगमोऽधन्यो दिवा पापप्रदो नृप ।
भुवि रोगावहो नृणामप्रशस्तो जलाशये ॥
परदारान्न गच्छेच्च मनसापि कदाचन ।
किमु वाचास्थिबन्धोऽपि नास्ति तेषु व्यवायिनाम् ॥
मृतो नरकमभ्येति हीयतेऽत्रापि चायुषः ।
परदाररतिः पुंसामुभयत्रापि भीतिदा ॥
इति मत्वा स्वदारेषु ऋतुमत्सु बुधो व्रजेत् ।
यथोक्तदोषहीनेषु सकामेष्वनृतावपि ॥

CHAPTER XII.

Miscellaneous obligations, purificatory, ceremonial, and moral.

AURVA continued.—"Let a respectable householder ever venerate the gods, kine, Brahmanas, saints,* aged persons, and holy teachers. Let him observe the two daily Sandhyás, and offer oblations to fire. Let him dress in untorn garments, use delicate herbs and flowers, wear emeralds and other precious stones, keep his hair smooth and neat, scent his person with agreeable perfumes, and always go handsomely attired, decorated with garlands of white flowers.† Let him never appropriate another's property, nor address him with the least unkindness. Let him always speak amiably, and with truth, and never make public another's faults. Let him not desire another's prosperity, nor seek his enmity. Let him not mount upon a crazy vehicle, nor take shelter under the bank of a river, (which may fall upon him). A wise man will not form a friendship, nor walk in the same path, with one who is disesteemed, who is a sinner, or a drunkard,‡ who has many enemies, or who is lousy,§ with a harlot, or her gallant, with a pauper,|| or a liar, with a prodi-

---

* *Siddha.*

† सदानुपहते वस्त्रे प्रशस्ताश्च तथौषधीः ।
गारुडानि च रत्नानि बिभृयात्प्रयतो नरः ॥
प्रसिग्धामलकेशश्च सुगन्धश्चारुवेषधृक् ।
सिताः सुमनसो हृद्या बिभृयाच्च नरः सदा ॥

‡ *Patita* and *unmatta.*

§ *Atikiśaka*, 'very verminous.'

|| *Kshudra.* It is glossed स्वल्पलाभोत्सिक्त, 'elated by petty gain.'

gal, a slanderer, or a knave. Let not a man bathe against the strength of a rapid stream, nor enter a house on fire, nor climb* to the top of a tree, nor (in company) clean his teeth or blow† his nose, nor gape without covering his mouth, nor clear his throat,‡ nor

---

* As will be seen below, to climb a tree to any height, apparently, is considered to be objectionable. The heterogeneous collection of maxims dictated by prudence, propriety, and superstition, of which this chapter is, in good part, made up, may be fitly accompanied by the subjoined extract from Varadarája's *Girváńapadamanjarí*, or, as the work is called, in one copy, Dhuńḍhirája's *Girváńavágmanjarí* or *Girváńaśabdapadamanjarí*: सर्वत्र दुराचाराः सन्त्येव । तथा हि । द्रविडदेशे स्त्री मातुलकन्यापरिणयनं दुराचारः । • • • • मध्यदेशे हलाचरणं दुराचारः । कर्णाटकदेशे स्नानं विना भोजनं दुराचारः । ताम्रपात्रे मद्यादिनिक्षेपणं दुराचारः । महाराष्ट्रे वर्णिकृतभक्षणं दुराचारः । श्रीशैलपरितश्च कन्यिकाया विवाहकरणं दुराचारः । • • • • द्रविडकेरलयोः सर्वासां कुचमर्दनं दुराचारः । पथि पर्युषितान्नभक्षणं दुराचारः । केरलदेशे उपरिसुरतं दुराचारः । कोङ्कणदेशे गृहारोहणं दुराचारः । गुर्जरदेशे चर्मोदकपानं तृतीयदिने रजस्वलास्नानं दुराचारः । उत्तरदेशे स्त्री मांसभक्षणं दुराचारः । पर्वतदेशे कश्चित्स्त्री देवरेण सुतोत्पत्तिर्दुराचारः । क्वचित्कूर्ममांसभक्षणं दुराचारः । • • • • सिंधगंगादेशे सदा तैलक्षेपणं दुराचारः । गौडदेशे वेदत्यागो दुराचारः । कान्यकुब्जदेशे पलाण्डुतपभक्षणं दुराचारः । विवाहादौ भोजनसमये परस्परस्पर्शनं दुराचारः । उत्कलदेशे मुखसुरतं दुराचारः । गौडद्राविडकेरलोत्कलमैथिलेषु मत्स्यमांसमधुमोदनभक्षणं दुराचारः । सर्वेषां पथि ताम्बूलभक्षणं दुराचारः । मगधे वर्णसंकरत्वं दुराचारः । सर्वेषामप्यद्यापाणीग्रहणं दुराचारः । काश्मीरदेशीया स्त्री केवलं यवनभाषा । अनुचितं दुराचाराणां सर्वत्रैव नास्ति । Thus read, in combination, my two MSS., so far as they are legible. The book from which this passage is taken emanated, at least in one of its two forms, from Mahárásḥṭra; and it imparts instructive hints as to the opinions, on the dark side, entertained, by certain Hindus, of certain others.

† The verb here used is *kush*, 'to scratch.' The commentary says न कुष्णीयात् । नोत्किरेत् ।

‡ Read 'not sigh'. The substantive here used is *śwása*.

cough, nor laugh loudly, nor emit wind with noise, nor bite * his nails, nor cut grass, nor scratch the ground,[1] nor put his beard into his mouth, nor crumble a clod of clay; nor look upon the chief planetary bodies,† when he is unclean.‡ Let him not express disgust at a corpse; for the odour of a dead body is the produce of the moon. Let (a decent man) ever avoid, by night, the place where four roads meet, the village-tree,§ the grove adjacent to the place where bodies are burnt, and a loose woman. Let him not pass across the shadow of a venerable person, of an image of a deity, of a flag,|| of a heavenly lumi-

---

[1] Manu, IV., 71. ¶ "He who breaks clay, or cuts grass, or bites his nails, will speedily fall to ruin."

---

* *Khâdayet*. But a common reading is *uddayet*. He is, then, not to snap his nails, apparently.

† ज्योतींष्यमेध्यः शस्तानि । But the commentator notes a variant, ज्योतींष्यमेध्याशस्तानि, which he takes to mean ज्योतींषि चक्षुःप्रतिकूलानि अमेध्यानि पुरीषादीनि अशस्तानि अमङ्गलानि; that is to say, "*things* injurious to the eyes, filthy, and inauspicious."

But compare the *Mânavadharmaśâstra*, IV., 142:

न चापि पश्येदशुचिः सुस्थो ज्योतिर्गणान्दिवि ।

‡ Here follows the line:

नग्नां परस्त्रियं चैव सूर्यं चास्तमनोदये ।

Other objects forbidden to be looked at are, thus, 'another's naked wife, and the sun at its setting or rising.'

According to the *Laws of the Mânavas*, IV., 53, a man may not see even his own wife in a state of nudity.

§ *Chaitya-taru*. I find a variant, *chaitya-tama*, 'the interior of a temple', perhaps.

|| The original words, occurring in the midst of a compound, are *devadhwaja*, which may mean 'the banner of a god'.

In the former edition there was an unintentional comma after "image".

¶ लोष्टमर्दी तृणच्छेदी नखखादी च यो नरः ।
स विनाशं व्रजत्याशु सूचकोऽशुचिरेव च ॥

nary.[1] Let him not travel alone through a forest, nor sleep* by himself in an empty house.[2] Let him keep remote from hair, bones, thorns, filth, remnants of offerings, ashes,† chaff, and earth[3] wet with water in which another has bathed. Let him not receive the protection of the unworthy, nor attach himself to the dishonest. Let him not approach a beast of prey;‡ and let him not tarry long, when he has risen from sleep. Let him not lie in bed, when he is awake; nor encounter fatigue, when it is time to rest.§ A prudent

---

[1] Manu, IV., 130.||

[2] Ib., id., 57.¶

[3] Ib., id., 78.**

---

* I find *vaset*, 'dwell.'

† *Balibhasma.*

‡ Preferably, 'a vicious beast'; *vyála* being interpreted *dushía-mriga.*

§ अतीव जागरस्वप्ने तद्वत्स्थानासने बुधः ।
न सेवेत तथा शय्यां व्यायामं च नरेश्वर ॥

"Let the wise man shun excess as to watching and sleeping: likewise, as to standing and sitting; *and* so, as to *his* bed and as to labour, O King."

One MS. has *jágaraswapnau*, which we should rather expect. Perhaps the writer preferred jingle to good grammar. Further, several MSS. read *snána*, 'bathing', for *sthána*, 'standing'; and one gives *chiram*, 'for a long time', instead of *tathá*, 'so.' The scholiast says: अतीव जागरादीनि न सेवेत नाभ्यसेत् । स्थानं गतिनिवृत्तिम् । आसनमुपवेशनम् । शय्यामिति शयनव्यवाययोरुपलक्षणम् । व्यायामं श्रमम् ।

|| देवतानां गुरो राज्ञः स्नातकाचार्ययोस्तथा ।
नाक्रामेत्कामतश्छायां बभ्रुणो दीक्षितस्य च ॥

According to Kullúka and Medhátithi, idols are intended by the first word of this stanza.

¶ नैकः सुप्याच्छून्यगेहे शयानं न प्रबोधयेत् ।

** अधितिष्ठेन्न केशांस्तु न भस्मास्थिकपालिकाः ।
न कार्पासास्थि न तुषान्दीर्घमायुर्जिजीविषुः ॥

man will avoid, even at a distance, animals with tusks and horns; and he will shun exposure to frost, to wind,* and to sunshine. A man must neither bathe, nor sleep, nor rinse his mouth,† whilst he is naked;[1] he must not wash his mouth, nor perform any sacred rite, with his waistband unfastened; and he must not offer oblations to fire, nor sacrifice to the gods, nor wash his mouth, nor salute a Brahman, nor utter a prayer,‡ with only one garment on.§ Let him never associate with|| immoral persons: half an instant is the limit for the intercourse¶ of the righteous with them. A wise man will never engage in a dispute with either his superiors or inferiors: controversy and marriage are to be permitted only between equals. Let not a prudent man enter into contention: let him avoid unprofitable enmity. A small loss may be endured; but he should shun the wealth that is acquired by hostility.

"When a man has bathed, he must not wipe his limbs with a towel or with** his hands; nor shake his hair, nor rinse his mouth before he has risen.†† Let

---

[1] Manu, IV., 45.‡‡

---

* Read 'the east wind', *puro-váta*.

† *Upaspriśet* is so explained by the commentator.

‡ As the original of "nor salute a Brahman, nor utter a prayer", I find, with क॰ प्रवर्तेत in the context, द्विजवाचनके जपे, "nor engage in prayer which he has procured to be said by the twice-born." The commentator explains द्विजवाचनके by पुण्याहवाचने. The prayer referred to is, thus, understood to be that at a ceremony for which the Bráhmans have pronounced a certain day to be lucky.

§ Compare p. 136, *supra*. || *Sahásita*. ¶ *Sannikarsha*. ** *Snánaśáṭí*.

†† The Sanskrit has only *utthitah*, implying 'after he has stood up'.

‡‡ नाश्नीयादेकवासा न नग्नः स्नानमाचरेत्।

him not (when sitting,) put one foot over another, nor stretch forth* his foot, in the presence of a superior, but sit, with modesty, in the posture called Vírásana (or, on his knees). He must never pass round a temple upon his left hand,† nor perform the ceremony of circumambulating any venerable object in the reverse direction. A decent man will not spit, nor eject any impurity, in front of the moon, fire, the sun, water, wind, or any respectable person;[1] nor will he void urine standing, nor upon the highway. He will never step over phlegm, ordure, urine, or blood: nor is the expectoration of the mucus of the throat‡ allowable at the time of eating, offering sacrifices or oblations, or repeating prayers,§ or in the presence of a respectable person.

"Let not a man treat women with disrespect; nor let him put entire‖ faith in them. Let him not deal impatiently with them,¶ nor set them over matters of

[1] Manu, IV., 52."

* This—*prasárayet*—is the commentator's explanation of *nayet*.

† अपसव्यं न गच्छेच्च देवागारचतुष्पथान् ।

‡ Add 'or nose'. The original is श्लेष्मशिंघाणकोत्सर्गः. Commentary A adds: सिंघाणकं पुतम् । सिंघाणो नासिकोद्भवः । सिंघाणकं कठिनः श्लेष्मा । पुतमिति केचित् ।

§ बलिमङ्गलजप्यादौ न होमे ।

‖ This all-important qualification is not in the original.

¶ न चेर्ष्युर्भवेत् । The commentary gives *írshu* = *asahishńu*.

" प्रत्यग्निं प्रति सूर्यं च प्रति सोमोदकद्विजान् ।
प्रति गां प्रति वातं च प्रज्ञा नश्यति मेहतः ॥

Compare p. 110, *supra*.

importance.* A man who is attentive to the duties of his station will not go forth from his house without

---

* The Hindus, in their literature, here and there manifest a due esteem for womankind. In the subjoined extract from the *Mahábhárata* it is to be hoped that their misogyny found its utmost limit. These verses—selected from a slanderous effusion of a member of the celestial *demi-monde*, the *apsaras* Panchachúdá,—are to be met with in the *Anuśásana-parvan*, *ll.* 2212—2230 (Chapter XXXVIII., *ll.* 11—29, in the Bombay edition of *Śaka* 1784—5.).

कुलीना रूपवत्यश्च नाथवत्यश्च योषितः ।
मर्यादासु न तिष्ठन्ति स दोषः स्त्रीषु नारद ॥
अनर्थित्वान्मनुष्याणां भयात्परिजनस्य च ।
मर्यादायाममर्यादाः स्त्रियस्तिष्ठन्ति भर्तृषु ॥
न भयान्नाप्यनुक्रोशान्नार्थहेतोः कथंचन ।
न ज्ञातिकुलसंबन्धात्स्त्रियस्तिष्ठन्ति भर्तृषु ॥
यौवने वर्तमानानां मृष्टाभरणवाससाम् ।
नारीणां स्वैरवृत्तीनां स्पृहयन्ति कुलस्त्रियः ॥
पङ्गुष्वथ च देवर्षे ये चान्ये कुत्सिता नराः ।
स्त्रीणामगम्यो लोकेऽस्मिन्नास्ति कश्चिन्महामुने ॥
यदि पुंसां गतिर्ब्रह्मन्कथंचिन्नोपपद्यते ।
अप्यन्योन्यं प्रवर्तन्ते न हि तिष्ठन्ति भर्तृषु ॥
अलाभात्पुरुषाणां हि भयात्परिजनस्य च ।
वधबन्धभयाच्चापि स्वयंगुप्ता भवन्ति ताः ॥
नाग्निस्तृप्यति काष्ठानां नापगानां महोदधिः ।
नान्तकः सर्वभूतानां न पुंसां वामलोचनाः ॥
इदमन्यच्च देवर्षे रहस्यं सर्वयोषिताम् ।
दृष्ट्वैव पुरुषं हृद्यं योनिः प्रक्लिद्यते स्त्रियाः ॥
कामानामपि दातारं कर्तारं मनसां प्रियम् ।
रक्षितारं न मृष्यन्ति स्वभर्तारमलं स्त्रियः ॥
न कामभोगान्बहुलान्नालंकारार्थसंचयान् ।
तथैव बहु मन्यन्ते यथा रत्यामनुग्रहम् ॥
अन्तकः पवनो मृत्युः पातालं वडवामुखम् ।
क्षुरधारा विषं सर्पो वह्निरित्येकतः स्त्रियः ॥

"Women, though born in noble families, *themselves* beauteous, and married *to worthy husbands*, remain not within the bounds of duty: this, Nárada, is the fault of women.

"From the want of a motive *for deviation*, or through fear of the

saluting the chaplets,* flowers, gems, clarified butter, and venerable persons in it. At proper seasons, he will salute, respectfully, the places where four roads meet, when engaged† in offering oblations with fire. Let him liberally relieve the virtuous who are poor, and reverence those who are learned in the Vedas.‡

people or of their kindred, unbridled women may remain within the bounds of duty, *faithful* to their husbands.

"But neither through fear *of moral law*, nor through severe reprehension, nor from any motive of *regard for* wealth, nor on account of their connexion with kindred and family, are women constant to their husbands.

"Matrons envy women who live by prostitution the *bloom of* youth they possess, and the food and apparel they receive.

"Though men be lame, divine Sage! or otherwise contemptible, there is not any man, in this world, great Sage! insufferable to women.

"If they have no possible access to men, *O thou inspired by* Brahmá! they seduce each other: truly, they are not constant to their husbands.

"From not finding men, or through fear of their kindred, or apprehension of stripes or confinement, they guard themselves.

"But fire is not satiated with wood, nor the ocean with rivers, nor death with all beings, nor woman with man.

"This, divine Sage! is another hidden quality of all women: at the very sight of a handsome man, the heart of a woman melts with desire.

"Women bear not much *affection to* their husbands, though giving them what they desire, doing what they wish, and protecting them *from danger*.

"They do not so much value the gratification of their wishes, abundance of ornaments, or hoards *of wealth*, as they do sensual pleasures.

"Final destiny, wind, death, the infernal regions, the fire of the ocean, the edge of a razor, poison, venomous serpents, and *devouring* fire, all united, are *no worse than* women."

This translation is by Colebrooke, and may be found in his version of Jagannátha Tarkapanchánana's *Digest of Hindu Law*, Vol. II., pp. 393, 394, London edition.

* *Mangalya.*

† Read "and will engage"; the Sanskrit being होमपरो भवेत्.

‡ दीनानभ्युद्धरेत्साधूनुपासीत बहुश्रुतान् ।

"Let him aid the needy; and let him reverence the virtuous, *if* very learned."

This is in accord with the commentary, which says: साधूनेव बहुश्रुतानुपासीत नेतरान् ।

He who is a worshipper of the gods and sages, who gives cakes and water to the manes, and who exercises hospitality, obtains the highest regions, (after death). He who* speaks wisely, moderately, and kindly, goes to those worlds which are the inexhaustible sources of happiness. He who is intelligent, modest, devout,† and who reverences wisdom, his superiors,‡ and the aged, goes to§ heaven.

"On the days called Parvans, on periods of impurity, upon unseasonable thunder, and the occurrence of eclipses or atmospheric portents,|| a wise man must desist from the study of the Vedas.[1] The pious man who suppresses anger and envy, who is benevolent to all, and allays the fears of others, secures, as the least of his rewards, enjoyment in Swarga.¶ A man should carry an umbrella, as a defence against sun and rain; he should bear a staff, when he goes by night, or through a wood; and he should walk in shoes, if he desires to keep his body from harm. As he goes along, he should not look up, or about him,"** or

[1] Manu, IV., 101, &c. The legislator is much more copious, on this subject, than the author of the Puráńa.

* In the Sanskrit, काले यतात्मा यः, "the person of subdued affections who, at the *proper time*."

† *Kshamáyukta*, 'forbearing.' Here follow two untranslated epithets, *ástika* and *vinayávanita*, 'pious' and 'meek'.

‡ *Abhijana*; his 'family', perhaps.

§ Insert 'the highest', *uttama*.

|| "Or atmospheric portents" is to render *ádika*, 'etc.'

¶ धर्मं चरति यः कुर्वन्सर्वमन्युरमत्सरी ।
भीताश्वासनकृत्साधुः स्वर्गस्तस्याल्पकं फलम् ॥

** *Tiryach*.

afar off, but keep his eyes upon the ground, to the extent of a couple of yards.*

"The householder who expels all sources of imperfection is, in a great degree, acquitted of the three ordinary objects of existence,—desire, wealth, and virtue;† sinless amongst the sinful; speaking amicably to all men; his whole soul melting with benevolence; final felicity is in his grasp.‡ The earth is upheld by the veracity of those who have subdued their passions, and, following righteous practices, are never contaminated by desire, coveteousness, and wrath.§ Let, therefore, a wise man (ever) speak the truth, when it is agreeable; and, when the truth would inflict pain, let him hold his peace. Let him not utter that which, though acceptable, would be detrimental; for it were better to speak that which would be salutary, although it should give exceeding offence.[1]|| A considerate

---

[1] So Manu, IV., 138.¶ "Let him say what is true; but let him say what is pleasing. Let him speak no disagreeable truth; nor let him speak agreeable falsehood. This is a primeval rule."**

---

* *Yuga-mátra*, defined by *hasta-chatushtaya*.

† दोषहेतूनशेषांश्च वश्यात्मा यो निरस्यति ।
तस्य धर्मार्थकामानां हानिर्नाल्पापि जायते ॥

‡ पापेऽप्यपापः परुषेऽप्यभिधत्ते प्रियाणि यः ।
मैत्रीद्रवान्तःकरणस्तस्य मुक्तिः करे स्थिता ॥

§ ये कामक्रोधलोभानां वीतरागा न गोचरे ।
सदाचारस्थितास्तेषामनुभावधृता मही ॥

|| प्रियं युक्तं हितं नैतदिति मत्वा न तद्वदेत् ।
श्रेयस्तत्र हितं वाच्यं यद्यप्यत्यन्तमप्रियम् ॥

¶ सत्यं ब्रूयात्प्रियं ब्रूयान्न ब्रूयात्सत्यमप्रियम् ।
प्रियं च नानृतं ब्रूयादेष धर्मः सनातनः ॥

** This is Sir William Jones's rendering.

man will always cultivate, in act, thought, and speech, that which is good for living beings, both in this world and in the next."[1]

[1] Thus the preceding chapter agrees, in many respects, very closely with the contents of the fourth book of the Institutes of Manu, on economics and private morals, will be evident from the instances cited of some of the parallel passages. Several others might have been adduced.

CHAPTER XIII.

Of Śráddhas or rites in honour of ancestors, to be performed on occasions of rejoicing. Obsequial ceremonies. Of the Ekoddishṫa or monthly Śráddha, and the Sapiṅḋana or annual one. By whom to be performed.

AURVA continued.—"The bathing of a father, without disrobing, is enjoined, when a son is born; and he is to celebrate the ceremony proper for the event,* which is the Śráddha offered upon joyous occasions.[1]

---

[1] The offerings of the Hindus to the Pitṛis partake of the character of those of the Romans to the lares and manes, but bear a more conspicuous part in their ritual. They are said, indeed, by Manu (III., 203†), in words repeated in the Váyu and Matsya Puráńas, and Hari Vaṁśa, to be of more moment than the worship of the gods:

दैवकार्यादपि सदा पितृकार्यं विशिष्यते ।‡

These ceremonies are not to be regarded as merely obsequial; for, independently of the rites addressed to a recently deceased relative,—and, in connexion with him, to remote ancestors, and to the progenitors of all beings, —which are of a strictly obsequial or funeral description, offerings to deceased ancestors, and the Pitṛis in general, form an essential ceremony, on a great variety of festive and domestic occasions. The Nirńaya Sindhu, in a passage referred to by Mr. Colebrooke (Asiatic Researches, Vol. VII.§), specifies the following Śráddhas: 1. The Nitya, or perpetual; daily offerings to ancestors in general: 2. The Naimittika, or occasional; as the Ekoddishṫa, or obsequial offerings

---

* Expressed, in the original, by *játa-karman*, for which see Colebrooke's *Digest, &c.*, Vol. III., p. 104, note †.

† दैवकार्याद्द्विजातीनां पितृकार्यं विशिष्यते ।

‡ *Harivaṁśa, śl.* 1006. § Or *Miscellaneous Essays*, Vol. I., p. 160, note.

With composed mind, and thinking on nothing else, the Brahman should offer worship to both the gods and progenitors, and should respectfully circumambulate, keeping Brahmans on his left hand, and give them food.* Standing with his face to the east,† he should present, with the parts of the hand sacred to the gods

---

on account of a kinsman recently deceased: 3. The Kámya, voluntary; performed for the accomplishment of a special design (अभिमतसिद्धये): 4. The Vriddhi; performed on occasions of rejoicing or prosperity: 5. The Sapiṅḋana; offerings to all individual and to general ancestors: 6. The Párvaṅa Śráddha; offerings to the manes, on certain lunar days called Parvans, or day of full moon and new moon, and the eighth and fourteenth days of the lunar fortnight: 7. The Goshṭhi; for the advantage of a number of learned persons, or of an assembly of Brahmans, invited for the purpose: 8. The Śuddhi; one performed to purify a person from some defilement,—an expiatory Śráddha: 9. The Karmánga; one forming part of the initiatory ceremonies, or Saṁskáras, observed at conception, birth, tonsure, &c.: 10. The Daivika; to which the gods are invited: 11. The Yátrá Śráddha; held by a person going a journey: and, 12. The Pushṭi Śráddha; one performed to promote health and wealth. Of these, the four which are considered the most solemn are the rite performed for a parent, or near relative, lately deceased; that which is performed for kindred, collectively; that observed on certain lunar days; and that celebrated on occasions of rejoicing: अत्र पार्वणैकोद्दिष्टवृद्धिसपिण्डीकरणाख्यं चतुर्विधमेव मुख्यम् । Nirṅaya Sindhu, p. 271.

---

* युग्मान्दैवान् पित्र्यांश्च सव्यप्रसव्यक्रमाद्विजान् ।
पूजयेद्भोजयेच्चैव तन्मना नान्यमानसः ॥

"With mind *intent* thereon, *i.e.*, *on the son born, and* on nothing else, let him duly circumambulate—keeping *them* on *his* left—Bráhmans, in couples, those *set apart for the service* of the gods and those *set apart for the service* of the manes; and let him worship and feed *those same Bráhmans*."

† Add "or to the north"; for the original has प्राङ्मुखोदङ्मुखोऽपि वा ।

and* to Prajápati, balls of food,[1] with curds, unbruised grain, and jujubes; and should perform, on every accession of good fortune, the rite by which the class of progenitors termed Nándímukha is propitiated.[2] A

[1] Manu directs the balls to be made from the remainder of the clarified butter constituting the previous oblation to the gods. III., 215.† Kullúka Bhaíía explains, however, the oblation to consist partly of Anna (अन्न),—food, or boiled rice. The latter is the article of which the balls chiefly consist. Yájnavalkya‡ directs them to be made of rice and sesamum-seeds. The Váyu Puráńa adds, to these, two ingredients, honey and butter: but various kinds of fruit, of pulse, and of grain, and water, frankincense, sugar, and milk, are, also, mixed up in the Pińdas. Their size, also, differs; and, according to Angiras, as quoted by Hemádri, in the Śráddha Mayúkha,§ they may be of the dimension of the fruit of the jujube, or of the hog-plum, of the fruit of the Bel, or of the wood-apple, or of a fowl's egg. Some authorities direct Pińdas of a different size for different Śráddhas; prescribing them no larger than the wood-apple, at the first or pure funereal ceremony, and as big as a cocoa-nut, at the monthly and annual Śráddha. In practice, the Pińda is, usually, of such a magnitude, that it may be conveniently held by the hand.

[2] We have, here, the authority of the text for classing the Nándímukhas amongst the Pitris (see p. 98, *supra*). The verse is:

नान्दीमुखः पितृगणस्तेन श्राद्धेन पार्थिव ।
प्रीयते तत्तु कर्तव्यं पुरुषैः सर्ववृद्धिषु ॥

* The original has *vá*, 'or'; the injunction allowing an option. The expressions here connected are *daivatírtha* and *kúya*, on which *vide supra*, p. 99, notes 1 and *. The *daivatírtha* is sometimes called the *tírtha* of the Rishis,—*ársha*.

† पीतु तस्माद्धविःशेषात्पिण्डान्कृत्वा समाहितः ।
औदकेनैव विधिना निर्वपेद्दक्षिणामुखः ॥

‡ ?

§ This work has Nílakańtha for its author. Hemádri wrote the *Śráddhakalpa*.

householder should diligently worship the Pitṙis so named, at the marriage of a son or daughter, on entering a new dwelling, on giving a name to a child, on performing his tonsure and other purificatory ceremonies,* at the binding of the mother's hair during gestation, or on (first) seeing the face of a son, or the like. The Śráddha on such occasions, however, has been briefly alluded to. Hear now, O king, the rules for the performance of obsequial rites.

"Having washed the corpse with holy water, decorated it with garlands, and burnt it without the village, the kinsmen, having bathed with their clothes on, are to stand with their faces to the south, and offer libations (to the deceased), addressing him by name, and adding, 'wherever thou mayest be.'[1] They then re-

---

And the same Gańa or class is presently again named:

नान्दीमुखः पितृगणः पूजयेत्प्रयतो गृही ।

The Mantra of the Vriddhi or festival Śráddha is, also, said, in the Nirńaya Sindhu, to be नान्दीमुखेभ्यः पितृभ्यः स्वाहा । According to the authorities, however, which are cited in that work, there seems to be some uncertainty about the character of the Nándimukhas; and they are addressed both as Pitṙis and gods; being, in the former case, either the ancestors prior to the great-grandfather,—ancestors collectively, or a certain class of them; and, in the latter, being identified with the Viśwadevas, or a class of them called also Úrdhwavaktra. The term Nándimukha is, also, applied to the rite itself, or to the Vriddhi Śráddha, and to one addressed to maternal ancestors. Nirńaya Sindhu, pp. 268, &c.

[1] "An oblation of water must be next presented from the joined palms of the hand, naming the deceased and the family

---

* *Chúdákarmádika*

turn, along with the cattle (coming from pasture), to the village, and, upon the appearance of the stars, retire to rest, sleeping on mats spread upon the earth.* Every day (whilst the mourning lasts), a cake (or ball) of food[1] is to be placed on the ground, (as an offering) to the deceased; and rice,† without flesh, is to be daily‡ eaten. Brahmans are to be fed for as many days as the mourner pleases; for the soul of the defunct derives satisfaction accordingly as his relatives are content with their entertainment.§ On the first day, or the third, or seventh, or ninth (after the death

---

from which he sprung, and saying, 'May this oblation reach thee.'" Asiatic Researches, Vol. VII., p. 244.‖ The text has:

यत्र तत्र स्थितायैतदमुकायेति वादिनः ।

[1] The proper period of mourning is ten days, on each of which, offerings of cakes and libations of water are to be made to the deceased, augmenting the number of cakes each day, so that, on the last day, ten cakes are presented. When the period is shorter, the same number of ten cakes must be distributed amongst the several days; or they may be, all, presented on one day. Nirńaya Sindhu, p. 429.

---

* कटधर्मासनाः कुर्युर्भूमौ स्रस्तरशायिनः ।

Here—compare p. 131, note, *supra*,—we encounter the unusual vocable *srastara*, with the variants *prastara*, *saṁstara*, and *swastara*. Commentary A has *srastara*; commentary B, *prastara*: but, as both give the same definition, तृणशय्या, it is presumable that one or other of them is sophisticated as to the term defined.

On the expression कटधर्माणम् the commentator remarks मितशयनादि.

† So the commentator explains *bhakta*.

‡ *Divá*, 'by day.'

§ प्रेततृप्तिं तथा याति बन्धुवर्गेण भुञ्जता ।

‖ Or Colebrooke's *Miscellaneous Essays*, Vol. I., pp. 159, 160.

of a person), his kinsmen should change their raiment,* and bathe out of doors, and offer a libation of water, with (tila) sesamum-seeds. On the fourth day,[1] the ashes and bones should be collected; after which the body of one connected with the deceased by offerings of funeral cakes may be touched (by an indifferent person, without thereby incurring impurity); and those who are related only by presentation of water† are qualified for any occupation.[2] The former class of

---

[1] It should be, more correctly, on that day on which the mourning ceases, or, as previously mentioned, the first, third, seventh, or ninth: but the authorities vary; and, besides these, the second and fourth days, and certain days of the fortnight or month, are specified. Nirńaya Sindhu, p. 432.

[2] They are no longer unclean. The Sapińdas, or those connected by offerings of cakes to common ancestors, extend to seven degrees, ascending or descending; the Samánodakas, or those similarly connected by presentations of water, to fourteen degrees.‡

---

* The words वस्त्रत्यागं • कृत्वा imply that the clothes should be laid aside for the second funeral ablution. As we have seen just above, they are to be retained during the first. According to some MSS., however, which have

ततोऽनु बन्धुवर्गेषु भुवि दद्युस्तिलोदकम् ।

instead of

वस्त्रत्यागं बहिः स्नानं कृत्वा दद्युस्तिलोदकम् ।

there is no bathing prescribed for this latter occasion.

† *Samánasalila* It means the same as *samánodaka*.

‡ In the *Mitákshará*, where it expatiates on the *Yájnavalkya-smriti*, II., 136, the following lines are quoted from Brihan-Manu:

सपिण्डता तु पुरुषे सप्तमे विनिवर्तते ।
समानोदकभावस्तु निवर्तेताचतुर्दशात् ।
जन्मनाम्नोः स्मृतेरेके तत्परं गोत्रमुच्यते ॥

"The relation of the *sapińdas* (or, kindred connected by the funeral ablation,) ceases with the seventh person: and that of *samánodakas* (or,

relatives may use beds;* but they must still refrain from unguents and flowers, and must observe continence, after the ashes and bones have been collected, (until the mourning is over). When the deceased is a child,† or one who is abroad,‡ or who has been degraded, or a spiritual preceptor,§ the period of uncleanness is but brief,‖ and the ceremonies with fire and water are discretional.¶ The food of a family in which a kinsman is deceased is not to be partaken of for ten days;[1] and, during that period, gifts, acceptance, sacrifice, and sacred study are suspended. The

---

[1] That is, a mere guest, or stranger, is not to partake of it. The food directed to be given to Brahmans is given, in general, only to the relatives of the deceased who are already unclean. In this respect, our text and the modern practice seem to differ

---

those connected by a common libation of water,) extends to the fourteenth degree; or, as some affirm, it reaches as far as the memory of birth and name extends. This is signified by *gotra* (or, the relation of family-name)." Colebrooke's *Two Treatises on the Hindu Law of Inheritance*, pp. 351, 352.

Compare the *Laws of the Mánavas*, V., 60.

* Add 'and seats', *ásana*.

† That has not yet cut its teeth, says the commentator.

‡ And has been so for upwards of a year, the commentary adds.

As explanatory of what is meant by "abroad", the following stanza is cited:

महानद्यन्तरं यत्र गिरिर्वा-व्यवधायकः ।
वाचो यत्र विभिद्यन्ते तद्देशान्तरमिष्यते ॥

§ *Guru*. A common variant, and preferred by commentary A, is *muni*.

‖ *Sadyas*. It is stated, by the scholiast, that it lasts only three nights, for one who dies abroad.

¶ बाले देशान्तरस्थे च पतिते च गुरौ मृते ।
सद्यः शौचं तथेच्छातो जलाग्न्युद्बन्धनादिषु ॥

After "brief" read: "likewise, optionally, as regards persons who *die from* water, fire, or hanging."

term of impurity for a Brahman is ten days;* for a Kshattriya,† twelve; for a Vaiśya, half a month; and a whole month, for a Śúdra.[1] On the first day (after uncleanness ceases), the nearest relation of the deceased should feed Brahmans at his pleasure, but in uneven numbers, and offer to the deceased a ball of rice upon holy grass: placed near the residue of the food that has been eaten. After the guests have been fed, the mourner, according to his caste, is to touch water, a weapon, a goad, or a staff; as he is purified by such contact. He may then resume the duties prescribed for his caste, and follow the avocation ordinarily pursued by its members.

"The Śráddha enjoined for an individual§ is to be repeated on the day of his death, (in each month, for a year),[2] but without the prayers and rites performed

---

from the primitive system, as described by Manu, III., 187.|| The eleventh or twelfth day is the term on which the Śráddha which crowns the whole of the funeral rites is to be performed, and when Brahmans are to be invited. Nirńaya Sindhu, p. 437.

[1] The number of Pińdas, however, is, for each case, the same, or ten. Nirńaya Sindhu, p. 429.

[2] So Manu, III., 251.¶ It may be doubted if the monthly

---

* The ceremonial uncleanness of the Brahman lasts as long as that of the Kshattriya, according to my MSS., which here read:

[illegible]राशौचं राजन्यस्याथ वैश्यकम् ।

But the Translator has the support of the *Mánavadharmaśástra*, V., 83.

† *Rájanya*, in the original. ‡ *Darbha*.

§ This phrase is to render *ekoddishta*.

|| पूर्वेद्युरपरेद्युर्वा श्राद्धकर्मण्युपस्थिते ।
निमन्त्रयीत त्र्यवरान्सम्यग्विप्रान्यथोदितान् ॥

¶ ?

on the first occasion, and without offerings to the Viśwadevas.* A single ball of food is to be offered to the deceased, as the purification of one person; and Brahmans are to be fed.† The Brahmans are to be asked, by the sacrificer, if they are satisfied; and, upon their assent, the prayer 'May this ever satisfy such a one' (the deceased,) is to be recited.‡

"This is the Śráddha called Ekoddishťa, which is to be performed (monthly,) to the end of a twelvemonth (from the death of a person); at the expiration of which, the ceremony called Sapińdana§ is to be observed. The practices of this rite are the same as those of the monthly obsequies; but a lustration is to be made with four vessels of water, perfumes, and sesamum. One of these vessels is considered as dedicated to the deceased; the other three, to the progenitors in general; and the contents of the former are

---

Śráddha was part of the ancient system, although Kullúka Bhaťťa supposes it to be referred to (v. 248), and supplies the fancied omission of the text.

---

* मृताहनि च कर्तव्यमेकोद्दिष्टमतः परम्।
आह्वानादिक्रियादैवनियोगरहितं हि तत्॥

The commentator says that the Viśwa devas are here intended; and the Translator has substituted his explanation.

† एकोऽर्घस्तत्र दातव्यस्तथैवैकं पवित्रकम्।
प्रेताय पिण्डो दातव्यो भुक्तवत्सु द्विजातिषु॥

‡ प्रश्नश्च तत्राभिरतिर्यजमानैर्द्विजन्मनाम्।
अक्षय्यममुकस्येति वक्तव्यं विरतौ तथा॥

§ The term here used, in the original, is *sapińdíkarańa*, as a little below.

to be transferred to the other three,* by which the deceased becomes included in the class of ancestors, to whom worship is to be addressed, with all the ceremonies of the Śráddha. The persons who are competent to perform the obsequies (of relations connected by the offering of the cake) are the son, grandson, great-grandson, a kinsman of the deceased,† the descendants of a brother, or the posterity of one allied by funeral offerings. In absence of all these, (the ceremony may be instituted) by those related by presentations of water only, or those connected, by offerings of cakes or water, to maternal ancestors. Should both families (in the male line) be extinct, the last obsequies may be performed by women, or by the associates of the deceased in religious or social institutions,‡ or by any one who becomes possessed of the property of a deceased kinsman.§

"Obsequial rites are of three descriptions,—initiative, intermediate, and subsequent.[1] The first are those which are observed after the burning (of the corpse),

---

[1] Púrva, 'first'; Madhyama, 'middle'; and Uttara, 'last'.

---

* पार्वं प्रेतस्य तस्यैव पार्वणप्रयुतं तथा ।
त्रिष्वेतेष्वपि पार्वेषु प्रेतपार्वं नृप स्थितु ॥

† *Bandhu*. "*Bandhu*, cognate or distant kin, corresponding nearly to the Cognati of the Roman law." Colebrooke's *Two Treatises on the Hindu Law of Inheritance*, p. 359, note.

‡ The phrase "associates of the deceased," &c. is to represent *sanghátántargata*, on which the commentator observes: संघातः सार्वो धार्मिकसमुदायः । तत्र मृतस्य तद्गतैः । प्रेतक्रियार्थैस्तर्वः । समानप्रवरसमानग्रामस्थादिरूपः संघात इति केचित् ।

§ *Uttama-bandhu*.

until the touching of water, weapons, &c., (or, until the cessation of uncleanness); the intermediate ceremonies are the Śráddhas called Ekoddishťa, which are offered every month; and the subsequent rites are those which follow the Sapińdíkarańa, when the deceased is admitted amongst the ancestors of his race: and the ceremonies are, thenceforth, (general or) ancestral. The first set of rites (as essential) are to be performed by the kindred of the father or mother,—whether connected by the offering of the cake or of water,—by the associates of the deceased,* or by the prince who inherits his property. The first and the last rites are, both, to be performed by sons and other relations, and by daughter's sons, and their sons; and so are the sacrifices on the day of the person's death. The last class, or ancestral rites, are to be performed annually, with the same ceremonies as are enjoined for the monthly obsequies; and they may be, also, performed by females. As the ancestral rights are, therefore, most universal, I will describe to you, O king, at what seasons, and in what manner, they should be celebrated."†

* *Sanghátántargata.*

† तस्मादुत्तरसंज्ञा या क्रिया तां शृणु पार्थिव ।
यदा यदा च कर्तव्या विधिना येन चानघ ॥

CHAPTER XIV.

Of occasional Śráddhas or obsequial ceremonies: when most efficacious, and at what places.

AURVA proceeded.—"Let the devout performer of an ancestral oblation[1] propitiate Brahmá, Indra, Rudra,

---

[1] We may here take the opportunity of inquiring who are meant by the Pitris: and, generally speaking, they may be called a race of divine beings, inhabiting celestial regions of their own, and receiving into their society the spirits of those mortals for whom the rite of fellowship in obsequial cakes with them, the Sapińdikarańa, has been duly performed. The Pitris collectively, therefore, include a man's ancestors; but the principal members of this order of beings are of a different origin. The Váyu, Matsya, and Padma Puráńas, and Hari Vaḿśa, profess to give an account of the original Pitris. The account is much the same, and, for the most part, in the same words, in all. They agree* in distinguishing the Pitris into seven classes; three of which are without form (अमूर्तयः), or composed of intellectual, not elementary, substance, and assuming what forms they please; and four are corporeal (समूर्तयः). When they come to the enumeration of the particular classes, they somewhat differ; and the accounts, in all the works, are singularly imperfect. According to a legend given by the Váyu and the Hari Vaḿśa, the first Pitris were the sons of the gods. The gods, having offended Brahmá, by neglecting to worship him, were cursed, by him, to become fools; but, upon their repentance, he directed them to apply to their sons, for instruction. Being taught, accordingly, the rites of ex-

---

* From the *Harivaḿśa*, *ll.* 939:

इत्येते वसतां श्रेष्ठ स्वर्गे पितृगणाः स्मृताः ।
चत्वारो मूर्तिमन्तो वै त्रय एषाममूर्तयः ॥

the Aświns,* the sun, fire, the Vasus, the winds,† the Viśwadevas, the sages, birds, men, animals,‡ reptiles,§

---

piation and penance, by their sons, they addressed them as fathers; whence the sons of the gods were the first Pitris.

ते पुत्रास्तनुमन्त्रीता लब्धसंज्ञा दिवौकसः ।
यूयं वै पितरोऽस्माकं यैर्वयं प्रतिबोधिताः ॥||

So the Matsya has:

मन्वन्तरेषु जायन्ते पितरो देवसूनवः ।

'The Pitris are born, in the Manwantaras, as the sons of the gods.' The Hari Vaḿśa¶ makes the sons assume the character of fathers; addressing them, 'Depart, children:'

गम्यतां पुत्रका एवं पुत्रकास्ते गता ।

Again, the Váyu Puráńa declares the seven orders of Pitris to have been, originally, the first gods, the Vairájas, whom Brahmá, with the eye of Yoga, beheld in the eternal spheres, and who are the gods of the gods:

लोकाः सान्तानिका नाम यत्र तिष्ठन्ति भास्वराः ।
ते वैराजा इति ख्याता देवानां दिवि देवताः ॥

* * * * * * * * * * * * * *

आदिदेवा इति ख्याता महात्मानो महौजसः । **

* * * * * * * * * * * * * *

तेषां सप्त समाख्याता गणास्ते लोकपूजिताः ।
अमूर्तयस्त्रयस्तेषां चत्वारश्च समूर्तयः ॥

Again, in the same work, we have the incorporeal Pitris called Vairájas,†† from being the sons of the Prajápati Virája:‡‡

---

* Násatyas, their synonym, in the original.

† *Máruta* is the Sanskrit expression. For the Maruts, or Márutas, deities so called, see Vol. II., p. 79.

‡ *Paśu*.

§ *Sarisŕipa*.

|| This is from the *Váyu-puráńa*. Compare the *Harivaḿśa*, *śl*. 917, 918.

¶ *Śl*. 912.

** Here I have filled out a line which Professor Wilson, it should seem, was not enabled, from the illegibleness of his MSS., to decipher in its entirety.

†† See Vol. II., p. 227, text and note 1.

‡‡ For "the patriarch Vairája", see Vol. I., p. 177; and Vol. II., p. 66, and p. 262, note †. From Vol. I., p. 104, note 2, and p. 106, note 1, it

progenitors, and all existent things, by offering adoration to them monthly, on the fifteenth day of the

---

अमूर्तय: पितृगणा: पुत्रास्ते वै प्रजापते: ।
विराजस्य द्विजा: श्रेष्ठा वैराजा इति विश्रुता: ॥

The Matsya agrees with this latter statement, and adds, that the gods worship them:

अमूर्तय: पितृगणा विराजस्य प्रजापते: ।
यजन्ति यान्देवगणा वैराजा इति विश्रुता: ॥

The Hari Vaṁśa* has the same statement, but more precisely distinguishes the Vairájas as one class only of the incorporeal Pitṛis. The commentator† states the same, calling the three incorporeal Pitṛis, Vairájas, Agnishwáttas, and Barhishads;‡ and the four corporeal orders, Sukálas, Ángirasas, Suswadhas,§ and Somapas. The Vairájas are described as the fathers of Mená,|| the mother of Umá. Their abode is variously termed the Sántánika, Sanátana, and Soma loka.¶ As the posterity of Virája, they are the Somasads of Manu.** The other classes of Pitṛis

---

seems that Vairája is one with Manu. Who, then, is the *prajápati* Vairája? And was Vairája corrupted into Virája? Nílakaṅṭha says that Virája's sons were *mánasáh*, which term he explains by *manomátrataríra*. Arjuna Miśra, another scholiast on the *Harivaṁśa*, identifies Virája with Brahmá.

* *Śl.* 935, 936:

लोका: सनातना नाम यत्र तिष्ठन्ति भास्वरा: ।
अमूर्तय: पितृगणास्ते वै पुत्रा: प्रजापते: ॥
विराजस्य द्विजश्रेष्ठ वैराजा इति विश्रुता: ।
यजन्ति तान्देवगणा विधिदृष्टेन कर्मणा ॥

† Nílakaṅṭha.

‡ See Vol. I., p. 158, note 2.

§ *Vide infra*, p. 164, note **.

|| A different paternity is assigned to Mená in Vol. I., pp. 156, 157. Also *vide infra*, p. 162, note ||.

¶ For their residence in the Tapoloka, &c., see Vol. II., p. 227, text and note 1.

** In III., 195, we read that the Somasads were sons of Viráj:

विराट्सुता: सोमसद: साध्यानां पितर: स्मृता: ।
अग्निष्वात्ताश्च देवानां मारीचा लोकविश्रुता: ॥

See note ‡‡ in the preceding page.

moon's wane (or dark fortnight),* or on the eighth day of the same period in certain months,† or at particular‡ seasons, as I will explain.

the three Puráńas agree with Manu in representing as the sons of the patriarchs, and, in general, assign to them the same offices and posterity.§ They are the following:—

Agnishwáttas—sons of Maríchi, and Pitřis of the gods (Manu,‖ Matsya, Padma): living in Soma-loka, and parents of Achchhodá (Matsya, Padma, Hari Vaḿśa¶). The Váyu** makes them residents of Viraja-loka, sons of Pulastya,†† Pitřis of the demigods and demons, and parents of Pívarí; omitting‡‡ the next order of

* This, the commentator observes, is the *darśa-śráddha*.

† For these months,—three, or four, according to different authorities,—*vide infra*, p. 168, text and note ‡.

‡ *Kámya*.

§ In the *Márkańdeya-puráńa*, XCVI., 40—42, the Agnishwáttas, Barhishads, Ájyapas, and Somapas are attached to the east, south, west, and north, respectively.

‖ See the quotation in note ‖ in the preceding page.

¶ *Śl*. 953, 954:

लोकाः सोमपदा नाम मरीचेर्यत्र वै सुताः ।
पितरो दिवि वर्तन्ते देवास्तानाभजन्त्युत ॥
अग्निष्वात्ता इति ख्याताः सर्व एवामितौजसः ।
एतेषां मानसी कन्या अच्छोदा नाम निम्नगा ॥

** विरजा नाम ते लोका दिवि रोचन्ति ते नवाः ।
अग्निष्वात्ताः सुताश्च पितरो भास्करप्रभाः ॥
तान् वै दानवयक्षा रक्षोगन्धर्वकिंनराः ।
भूतसर्पपिशाचाश्च भावयन्ति फलार्थिनः ॥
एते पुत्राः समाख्याताः पुलहस्य प्रजापतेः ।
पञ्च एते गणा लोका धर्ममूर्तिधराः शुभाः ॥
एतेषां मानसी कन्या पीवरी नाम विश्रुता ।
योगिनी योगपत्नी च योगमाता तथैव च ॥

†† My MSS. have Pulaha. See the last note.

‡‡ Without doubt, there is a hiatus in my MSS. of the *Váyu-puráńa*. These contain, nearly word for word, the three lines—all but their

"When a householder finds that any circumstance has occurred, or a distinguished guest has arrived, on

---

Pitṛis, to whom these circumstances more accurately refer. The commentator on the Hari Vaṁśa* derives the name from Agnishu (अग्निषु), 'in or by oblations to fire,' and Átta (आत्ताः), 'obtained,' 'invoked.'

Barhishads—sons of Atri, and Pitṛis of the demons (Manu†): sons of Pulastya, Pitṛis of the demons, residents in Vaibhrája,‡ fathers of Pívari (Matsya, Padma, Hari Vaṁśa§).

---

opening, विरजा दिवि – ending the extract in note § in p. 165, *infra*; and there was, probably, mention, in what preceded, of the Barhishads. These personages were, then, it seems, regarded as sons of Vasishṭha, as dwellers in Jyotirbhásin, and as parents of a mind-born daughter by name Go. It should be added, that my MSS. of the *Váyu-puráṇa* elsewhere mention the Barhishads again and again; as in the line:

अग्निष्वात्ता बर्हिषदः पितरो द्विविधाः स्मृताः ।

Also see Vol. II., p. 303, notes 1 and च.

* अग्निषु अग्निसाध्येषु कर्मसु आत्ताः गृहीताः पित्र्यादिष्विति । Nílakaṇṭha.

† III., 196:

दैत्यदानवयक्षाणां गन्धर्वोरगरक्षसाम् ।
सुपर्णकिंनराणां च स्मृता बर्हिषदोऽत्रिजाः ॥

‡ Nílakaṇṭha, commentator on the *Harivaṁśa*, glosses this word thus: वैभ्राजा इति । विभ्राजः सूर्यस्तेन वैभ्राजाः ।

§ *Sl.* 974—977:

वैभ्राजा नाम लोकास्ते दिवि भान्ति सुदर्शनाः ।
यत्र बर्हिषदो नाम पितरो दिवि विश्रुताः ॥
तान्दानवगणाः सर्वे यक्षगन्धर्वराक्षसाः ।
नागाः सर्पाः सुपर्णाश्च भावयन्त्यमितौजसः ॥
इति पुत्रा महात्मानः पुलस्त्यस्य प्रजापतेः ।
महात्मानो महाभागास्तेजोयुक्तास्तपस्विनः ॥
एतेषां मानसी कन्या पीवरी नाम विश्रुता ।
योगा च योगिपत्नी च योगिमाता तथैव च ॥

Also see note ‡ in the preceding page.

which account ancestral ceremonies are appropriate, he should celebrate them.* He should offer a volun-

---

These three are the formless or incorporeal Pitris.

Somapas,—descendants of Bhrigu, or sons of Kavi by Swadhá, the daughter of Agni;† and Pitris of the Brahmans (Manu‡ and Váyu Puráńa§). The Padma calls them Ushmapas. The Hari Vaḿśa|| calls the Somapas—to whom it ascribes the same de-

---

* यत्रार्हमावर्त्तं पूर्वं पितृइमथवा पितृम् ।
श्राद्धं कुर्वीत विद्वांश्च * * * * * ॥

† Swadhá appears, in Vol. I., p. 109, as daughter of Daksha and Prasúti. For her husbands, *vide ibid.*, pp. 156, 157. Also *vide supra*, p. 159, note ‡, *ad finem*.

Nílakańtha, commentator on the *Harivaḿśa*, says that Hirańyagarbha, mentioned in the passage in note ||, below, intends Agni: कवेर्दुहितरि स्वधायाम् । हिरण्यगर्भस्याग्नेः सुताः ।

‡ III., 197, 198:

सोमपा नाम विप्राणां क्षत्रियाणां हविर्भुजः ।
वैश्यानामाज्यपा नाम शूद्राणां तु सुकालिनः ।
सोमपास्तु कवेः पुत्रा हविष्मन्तोऽङ्गिरःसुताः ।
पुलस्त्यस्याज्यपाः पुत्रा वसिष्ठस्य सुकालिनः ॥

§ My five MSS. of the *Váyu-puráńa* do not here tally with those on which Professor Wilson depended.

|| *Śl.* 997—999:

तत्पश्चा ये स्वधायां ते सोमपा वै कवेः सुताः ।
हिरण्यगर्भस्य सुताः शूद्रास्तान्भावयन्त्युत ॥
मानसा नाम ते लोका यत्र तिष्ठन्ति ते दिवि ।
तेषां वै मानसी कन्या नर्मदा सरितां वरा ॥
यां भावयन्ति भूतानि दक्षिणापथवासिनीम् ।
अभिधी यवदूताः सा पुरुकुत्सपरिग्रहः ॥

The Somapas are here—as in the *Matsya-puráńa*,—said to dwell in Mánasa, and to have the river Narmadá for mind-born daughter. In *Śl.* 941, Moná, too, is their mind-born daughter. But *vide supra*, p. 159, note ||. Compare, also, note ‡ in p. 165, *infra*.

tary sacrifice, upon any atmospheric portent,* at the equinoctial and solstitial periods, at eclipses of the sun

---

scent as the Váyu,—the Pitris of the Śúdras; and the Sukálas, the Pitris of the Brahmans.†

Havishmats‡—in the solar sphere, sons of Angiras, and Pitris of the Kshattriyas (Manu,§ Váyu,|| Matsya, Padma, Hari Vamśa¶).

---

* *Vyatipáta.* On the malignant aspect so called, an astrological *yoga*, see Professor Whitney's comment at p. 236 of the American translation of the *Súrya-siddhánta*: or Colebrooke's *Miscellaneous Essays*, Vol. I., p. 167; Vol. II., p. 363.

† In the *Nirńayasindhu*, III., B, fol. 11 r, Bombay edition, the *Nandi-puráńa*—not called an Upapuráńa—is quoted as follows:

अग्निष्वात्ता ब्राह्मणानां पितरः परिकीर्तिताः ।
राज्ञां बर्हिषदो नाम विशां काव्याः प्रकीर्तिताः ।
सुकालिनस्तु शूद्राणां व्यामा म्लेच्छान्त्यजातिषु ॥

Here the Agnishwáttas are declared to be the *pitris* of the first caste; the Barhishads, of the second; the Kávyas, of the third; the Sukálins, of the fourth; and the Vyámas,—'Fumes', mere smoke,—of *mlechchhas* and the lowest castemen.

Of the Vyámas I know of no mention except in passages from the *Nandi-puráńa*, for which see Dr. Aufrecht's *Catalogus*, &c., p. 81; also, note || in the next page, and p. 166, *infra*, note ‡.

‡ Here I have corrected "Havishmantas". § See the next note.

|| As is seen in note ‡ in the preceding page, a Havishmat is synonymously denominated a Havirbhuj. A third designation is Upahúta, which occurs in the following passage and elsewhere:

मरीचिगर्भांल्लोकान्समाश्रित्य दिवि स्थिताः ।
एते ह्यङ्गिरसः पुत्राः साध्यैः सह विवर्धिताः ॥
उपहूताः स्मृतास्ते तु पितरो भास्वरा दिवि ।
तान्क्षत्रियगणाः श्राद्धे भावयन्ति फलार्थिनः ॥
एतेषां मानसी कन्या यशोदा नाम विश्रुता ।
पत्नी सा विश्वमहतः स्नुषा वै विश्वशर्मणः ॥

These beings are here said to inhabit Marichigarbha, and to have a mind-born daughter Yaśodá.

Nilakańtha thus comments on the first term in this passage: मरीचिगर्भान् । सूर्यरश्मिमध्यस्थान् ।

¶ In *ll.* 986—990, we have almost the very words of the extract in the

and moon, on the sun's entrance into a zodiacal sign, upon unpropitious aspects* of the planets and as-

---

Ájyapas—sons of Kardama, Pitris of the Vaiśyas, in the Kámaduha-loka† (Manu,‡ &c.); but the lawgiver calls them the sons of Pulastya.§ The Pitris of the Vaiśyas are called Kávyas, in the Nandi Upapuráńa;|| and, in the Hari Vaḿśa¶ and its comment, they are termed Suswadhas,** sons of Kardama, descended from Pulaha.

---

preceding note; except that the line is omitted which names the *pitris* under description, and that Yaśodá is said to be daughter-in-law of Vŕiddhaśarman.

* "Unpropitious aspects" is to represent *pidá*, which signifies 'occultation.'

† This seems to be a mistake. The *Matsya-puráńa* has Kámadugha; with which compare the *Mahábhárata*, *Vana-parvan*, *śl.* 15460. In the *Harivaḿśa*, the name is Kámaga. See note ¶ in this page.

‡ *Vide supra*, p. 162, note ‡.

§ We read, in the *Váyu-puráńa*:

आज्यपा नाम पितरः कर्दमस्य प्रजापतेः ।
समुत्पन्नस्य पुलहादुत्पन्नास्तस्य वै सुताः ॥
लोकेष्वेतेषु वर्तन्ते कामगेषु विहङ्गमाः ।
एतान्वैश्यगणाः श्राद्धे भावयन्ति फलार्थिनः ॥
एतेषां मानसी कन्या विरजा नाम विश्रुता ।
ययातेर्जननी साध्वी पत्नी सा नहुषस्य तु ॥

It is stated here,—compare note ¶, below,—that the Ájyapas live in Kámaga, and that they have a mind-born daughter Virajá.

|| See note † in the last page, and p. 166, note ‡, *infra*; also, Vol. I., Preface, p. LXXXVII.

¶ *Śl.* 993—996.

सुस्वधा नाम पितरः कर्दमस्य प्रजापतेः ।
समुत्पन्नास्तु पुलहाद्ब्रह्मणो द्विजसत्तमाः ॥
लोकेषु दिवि वर्तन्ते कामगेषु विहङ्गमाः ।
तांश्च वैश्यगणास्तात भावयन्ति फलार्थिनः ॥
तेषां वै मानसी कन्या विरजा नाम विश्रुता ।
ययातेर्जननी ब्रह्मवादिनी नहुषस्य च ॥

** My best MSS. yield Sumedhas, which reading seems to be preferred by Arjuna Miśra. The *Matsya-puráńa* appears to exhibit Swaswadhas.

terisms, on dreaming unlucky dreams, and on eating the grain of the year's harvest.* The Pitris derive sa-

---

Sukálins—sons of Vasishtha, and Pitris of the Śúdras (Manu† and Váyu Puráńa‡). They are not mentioned in the Padma. The Matsya inserts the name and descent, but specifies them as amongst the incorporeal Pitris:

अमूर्तिमन्तः पितरो वसिष्ठस्य सुकालिनः ।
नाम्ना तु मानसाः सर्वे सर्वे ते धर्ममूर्तयः ॥

It may be suspected that the passage is corrupt. The Hari Vaṁśa§ makes the Sukálas sons of Vasishtha, the Pitris of the Brahmans; and gives the title of Somapas to the Pitris of the Śúdras. In general, this work follows the Váyu, but with omissions and transpositions, as if it had carelessly mutilated its original.

---

* *Navasasyágama.*

† See note ‡ in page 162, *supra.*

‡ They are there called Sukálas:

सुकाला नाम पितरो वसिष्ठस्य प्रजापतेः ।
हिरण्यगर्भस्य सुताः शूद्रास्तान्भावयन्त्युत ॥
मानसा नाम ते लोका वर्तन्ते यत्र ते दिवि ।
एतेषां मानसी कन्या नर्मदा सरितां वरा ।
सा भावयति भूतानि दक्षिणापथगामिनी ॥
जननी त्रसदस्योर्हि पुरुकुत्सपरिग्रहः ।

The personages here spoken of are said to have their home in Mánasa; and a mind-born daughter is affiliated on them, in the form of the river Narmadá. Compare note ‖ in p. 162, *supra.*

For discrepancies between this extract and that in the next note, additional to those pointed out by the Translator, *vide supra*, p. 160, note ‡.

The *Matsya-puráńa*, by evident corruption, gives the Sukálins—as it calls them—the synonym Mánasas.

§ *Śl.* 965, 966:

सुकाला नाम पितरो वसिष्ठस्य प्रजापतेः ।
निरता दिवि लोकेषु ज्योतिर्भासिषु भार्गव ॥
सर्वकामसमृद्धेषु द्विजास्तान्भावयन्त्युत ।
तेषां वै मानसी कन्या गौर्नाम्ना दिवि विश्रुता ॥

tisfaction, for eight years, from ancestral offerings upon the day of new moon when the star of the conjunc-

Besides these Pitris or progenitors, other heavenly beings* are, sometimes, made to adopt a similar character. Thus, Manu † says: "The wise call our fathers Vasus; our paternal grandfathers, Rudras; our paternal great-grandfathers, Ádityas; agreeably to a text of the Vedas:" that is, these divine beings are to be meditated upon, along with, and as not distinct from, progenitors. Hemádri quotes the Nandi Upapuráńa‡ for a different practice, and directs Vishńu to be identified with the father; Brahmá, with the grandfather; and Śiva, with the great-grandfather. This, however, is Śaiva innovation. The Vaishńavas direct Aniruddha to be regarded as one's-self; and Pradyumna, Sankarshaña, and Vásudeva, as the three ancestors. Again, they are identified with Varuńa, Prájápatya, and Agni; or, again, with months, seasons, and years. Nirńaya Sindhu, p. 284. It may be doubted how far any of these correctly represent the original notions inculcated by the texts of the Vedas, from which,§ in the most essential particulars, they are derived.

* Also *vide supra*, p. 98, note †; p. 163, note †. The Saumyas and Kávyas are mentioned in Vol. II., p. 303, text and note 1; also, with the Agnidagdhas and Anagnidagdhas, in the *Mánavadharmaśástra*, III., 199:

अग्निदग्धानग्निदग्धान्काव्यान्बर्हिषदस्तथा ।
अग्निष्वात्तांश्च सौम्यांश्च विप्राणामेव निर्दिशेत् ॥

In Goldstücker's *Sanskrit Dictionary*, the Agnidagdhas are said to be certain *pitris* "who, when alive, kept up the household flame, and presented oblations with fire"; the Anagnidagdhas, *pitris*, "apparently, who, when alive, did not observe religious rites."

† III., 284:

वसून्वदन्ति वै पितॄन्रुद्रांश्चैव पितामहान् ।
प्रपितामहांस्तथादित्याञ्छ्रुतिरेषा सनातनी ॥

‡ Some extracts from the *Nandi-puráńa*,—as Hemádri, like the *Nirńayasindhu*, calls the work here named,—and further particulars touching the *pitris*, will be found in a note at the end of the volume.

For the *Nandi-puráńa*, *vide supra*, p. 163, note †.

§ Where?

tion[1] is Anurádhá,* Viśákhá, or Swáti; and, for twelve years, when it is Pushya, Árdrá,† or Punarvasu. It is not easy‡ for a man to effect his object, who is desirous of worshipping the Pitris, or the gods, on a day of new moon when the stars are those of Dhanishthá, Púrvabhádrapadá, or Śatabhishaj.§ Hear, also, an account of another class of Śráddhas, which afford especial contentment to progenitors,‖ as ex-

---

[1] When the Yogatárá, or principal star seen, is the chief star or stars of these asterisms or lunar mansions, respectively. See the table given by Mr. Colebrooke: Asiatic Researches, Vol. IX., p. 346.¶ The first three named in the text are stars in Scorpio, Libra, and Arcturus; the second three are stars in Cancer, Orion, and Gemini; and the third are stars in the Dolphin, Pegasus, and Aquarius.

---

* The Sanskrit has its synonym, Maitra.

† Raudra, its synonym, is the word used in the original.

‡ वासवाजैकपादर्क्षे पितॄणां तृप्तिमिच्छताम् ।
वारुणं वाप्यमावास्या देवानामपि दुर्लभा ॥

"For those who wish to propitiate the progenitors, or the gods, a day of new moon under the asterism Vásava, or Ajaikapád, or Varuńa, is hard to find."

Compare what is said of Dhanishthá in p. 169, *infra*.

§ Substituted for "Śatábhishá". The three names in the Sanskrit are as in the last note. The commentator wrongly interprets Vásava by Jyeshthá.

‖ नवस्वृक्षेष्वमावास्या यदैतेष्ववनीपते ।
तदा तृप्तिमदं श्राद्धं पितॄणां शृणु चापरम् ॥

"When, O king, the day of new moon *falls* under *any of* these nine asterisms, then exequial rites *are* propitiatory of the progenitors. And listen further."

This stanza comes immediately after that in note ‡, above. The Translator passed by the first line of it, and connected the second with what follows; namely:

गीतं सनत्कुमारेण यथैलाय महात्मने ।
पृच्छते पितृभक्ताय प्रश्रयावनताय च ॥

¶ Or *Miscellaneous Essays*, Vol. II., table opposite p. 372.

plained, by Sanatkumára, (the son of Brahmá), to the magnanimous Purúravas,* when, full of faith and devotion to the Pitris, he inquired (how he might please them). The third lunar day of the month Vaiśákha (April, May), and the ninth of Kárttika (October, November), in the light fortnight; the thirteenth of Nabha (July, August), and the fifteenth of Mágha (January, February), in the dark fortnight; are called, by ancient teachers, the anniversaries of the first day of a Yuga or age (Yugádya), and are esteemed most sacred. On these days, water mixed with sesamum-seeds should be regularly presented to the progenitors of mankind; as well as on every solar and lunar eclipse; on the eighth lunations of the dark fortnights of Agraháyańa, Pausha, and Mágha† (November—February);‡ on the two days commencing the solstices, when the nights

* Called, in the Sanskrit, by his metronym, Aila, i. e., son of Ilá.

† For an account of the *mahávishuva* festival, see Professor Wilson's *Essays and Lectures*, &c., Vol. II., pp. 181, 182. Also *vide supra*, p. 106, note †.

‡ The text has only "on the three eighth days after the full moon", त्रिष्वष्टकासु; the months not being specified: but their names are stated in recent copies of commentary A,—though not in old ones, nor in commentary B,—in the following couplet, professedly taken from the *Kúrma-puráńa*:

मार्गशीर्षे तथा पुष्ये माघमासे तथैव च ।
तिस्रोऽष्टकाः समाख्याताः कृष्णपक्षे च सूरिभिः ॥

The months here named are Márgaśirsha, Pushya,—a rare substitute for Pausha,—and Mágha. I have, accordingly, corrected the Translator's "Agraháyańa, Mágha, and Phálguna (December—February)."

According to Áśwaláyana's *Gŕihya-sútra*, II., IV., 1, the great *ashtakás* are four in number, coming in the frosty and the dewy seasons, that is to say, in Márgaśirsha, Pausha, Mágha, and Phálguna. Śánkháyana, in his *Gŕihya-sútra*, recognizes but three. See Dr. Stenzler's *Áśwaláyana*, Part II., p. 71; also, Kullúka and Medhátithi on the *Mánavadharmaśástra*, IV., 150.

and days alternately begin to diminish; on those days which are the anniversaries of the beginning of the Manwantaras; when the sun is in the path of the goat; and on all occurrences of meteoric phenomena.* A Śráddha at these seasons contents the Pitŕis for a thousand years: such is the secret which they have imparted. The fifteenth day of the dark half of the month Mágha, when united with the conjunction of the asterism over which Varuńa presides (Śatabhishaj †), is a season of no little sanctity, when offerings are especially grateful to the progenitors. Food and water presented by men who are of respectable families, when the asterism Dhanishthá is combined with the day of new moon, content the Pitŕis for ten thousand years; whilst they repose for a whole ‡ age, when satisfied by offerings made on the day of new moon when Árdrá is the lunar mansion. §

---

* चन्द्रसूर्ययो ग्रहणानि यत्र
द्विषुवद्द्वयायनद्वयं च ।
मन्वन्तरादिषु युगादिषु च
छाया गजस्य व्यतिपातकाल: ॥

These verses occur in only a few of my MSS. Commentary B recognizes them, but in silence; while commentary A omits them. Professor Wilson's translation supposes readings materially different from those here given.

On *Chháyá gajasya*, "the shadow of the elephant", see Vol. II., p. 264, note *; and pp. 276, 277; also, the *Laws of the Mánavas*, III., 274. For *vyatipáta*,—the same as *vyatipáta*,—see p. 163, note *, *supra*.

Compare, respecting the seasons most appropriate for exequial offerings, the *Laws of the Mánavas*, III., 122, 276; IV., 150; also, the *Yájnavalkya-smŕiti*, I., 217, 218.

† Altered from "Śatabhishá."

‡ *Samagra*. There is a variant, *sahasra*, 'a thousand.'

§ नवैव पैत्रादपदाशु पूर्वा:
श्राद्धे तदा चाक्षयतां पितृभ्य: ।

"He who, after having offered food and libations to the Pitŕis, bathes in the Ganges, Satlaj,* Vipáśá (Beas), Saraswatí,† or the Gomatí at Naimisha,‡ expiates all his sins. The Pitŕis also say: 'After having received satisfaction for a twelvemonth, we shall further derive gratification by libations offered, by our descendants, at some place of pilgrimage, at the end of the dark fortnight of Mágha.'§ The songs of the Pitŕis confer purity of heart, integrity of wealth, prosperous seasons, perfect rites, and devout faith,—all that men can desire. Hear the verses that constitute those songs, by listening to which all those advantages will be secured, O prince, by you:|| 'That enlightened

---

श्राद्धं परां तृप्तिमुपैति तेन
युगं समग्रं पितरः स्वपन्ति ॥

This is the only reading that I find; and the asterism mentioned is Púrvabhádrapadá,—not "Árdrá", which, on a rapid glance, might be surmised in the first line.

* Śatadrú, in the original.

† See, for the Śatadrú, Vipáśá, and Saraswatí rivers, Vol. II., pp. 130, 131, and 142—144.

‡ In the Sanskrit, *Naimisha-gomatí*, the Gomatí of the country—apparently—in which lies the Naimisha forest, as distinguished from the better-known Gomatí in Oude; for which see Vol. II., p. 146, text and note 3. A third Gomatí, a feeder of the Sindhu, is spoken of in the *Ŕigveda*, X., LXXV, 6. For the locality of Naimisha, see Professor Wilson's *Essays, Analytical*, &c., Vol. I., p. 137.

§ मघास्वथ पैतृपितरः सदैव
वर्षासु तृप्तिं समवाप्य भूयः ।
माघासितान्ते शुभतीर्थतोयै-
र्यास्याम तृप्तिं तनयादिदत्तैः ॥

No other reading appears in my MSS.; and I would substitute, in lieu of "satisfaction for a twelvemonth", "satisfaction under *the asterism* Maghá during the rainy season."

Compare the *Laws of the Mánavas*, III., 273.

|| What follows is known as the *Pitŕi-gítá*.

individual who begrudges not his wealth, but presents us with cakes, shall be born in a distinguished family. Prosperous and affluent shall that man ever be, who, in honour of us, gives to the Brahmans, if he is wealthy, jewels, clothes, land, conveyances, wealth, or any valuable presents; or who, with faith and humility, entertains them with food, according to his means, at proper seasons. If he cannot afford to give them dressed food, he must, in proportion to his ability, present them with unboiled grain,* or such gifts, however trifling, as he can bestow. Should he be utterly unable even to do this, he must give to some eminent Brahman, bowing at the same time before him, sesamum-seeds adhering to the tips of his fingers, and sprinkle water to us, from the palms of his hands, upon the ground;† or he must gather, as he may,‡ fodder for a day, and give it to a cow; by which he will, if firm in faith, yield us satisfaction. If nothing of this kind is practicable, he must go to a forest, and lift up his arms to the sun and other regents of the spheres,§

---

* *Dhánya-mána*, *i. e.*, as much as a man can eat, says the commentator.

† तिलैः सप्ताष्टभिर्वापि समवेताञ्जलाञ्जलीन् ।
अभिनम्रः समुद्दिश्य भुव्यस्माकं प्रदास्यति ॥

Instead of "and sprinkle", &c., read: "or, bowing in devotion, he will offer to us, by name, on the ground, handfuls of water, with seven or eight grains of sesamum."

‡ "Whencesoever *he can*", *yataḱ kutaśchit*.

§ *Lokapála*. This word, it should seem, more properly designates the four superintendents named in Vol. II., pp. 66 and 261–263. But it is also used, as here, for *dikpála*. The *dikpálas* – see Vol. II., pp. 117, 118; also, p. 118, *supra*, – are, at least in the later Hindu writings, eight in number. I owe to Dr. Muir the indication of a passage in the *Taittiríya-bráhmańa*, – III., XI., 5, – where seven *devatás* or deities are

and say, aloud: I have no money, nor property, nor grain,* nor anything whatever fit for an ancestral offering. Bowing, therefore, to my ancestors, I hope the progenitors will be satisfied with these arms tossed up in the air in devotion.' These are the words of the Pitŕis themselves; and he who endeavours, with such means as he may possess, to fulfil their wishes, performs the ancestral rite called a Śráddha."

---

assigned as follows: Agni, to the east; Indra, to the south; Soma, to the west; Mitra and Varuńa, to the north; Bŕihaspati, to the region above; and Aditi, to the region here below.

For a long list of *lokapálas*, see Professor Wilson's *Select Specimens of the Theatre of the Hindus*, Vol. I., p. 219, note ‡.

* My MSS., and likewise the commentator, have *dhana* only; reading:

न मेऽस्ति वित्तं न धनं न चान्यत् ।

It may be conjectured that the Translator, supposing the lection to be न धान्यं, wrote "nor grain", and forgot to strike it out, when he came to prefer "nor property."

CHAPTER XV.

What Brahmans are to be entertained at Śráddhas. Different prayers to be recited. Offerings of food to be presented to deceased ancestors.

AURVA proceeded:—"Hear, next, O prince, what description of Brahman should be fed at ancestral ceremonies.* He should be one studied in various triplets of the Rig- and Yajur Vedas;[1] one who is

[1] The Brahmans here particularized are termed Triṅáchiketa, Trimadhu, and Trisuparńa, and are so denominated, according to the commentator, from particular parts of the Vedas. The first is so called from studying or reciting three Anuvákas of the Káthaka branch of the Yajur-veda, commencing with the term Triṅáchiketa; the second, from three Anuvákas of the same Veda, beginning Madhuváta, &c.; and the third, from a similar portion, commencing Brahmavan namámi. † The first and third terms

* The *párvaṇa-śráddha* is here described, says the scholiast.

† The commentator's words are: द्वितीयकाठककाण्डस्थत्रिणाचिकेताः। तदध्यायी तद्व्रतवांश्च त्रिणाचिकेतः। मधु वाता इति तृचाध्यायी तद्व्रतश्च त्रिमधुः। ब्रह्मेतन्मामित्यनुवाकत्रयाध्यायी तद्व्रतश्च त्रिसुपर्णः। The *triṅáchiketa* is, thus, said to be so called from three *anuvákas* of the second *Káṭhaka*, denominated *triṅáchiketas*; the *trimadhu*, from three *ṛiches*, beginning with the words *madhu vátáḥ*; and the *trisuparńa*, from three *anuvákas*, beginning with the words *brahmaitan mámi*.

Of the passage referred to the *Káṭhaka* I am unable to say anything at present. The three versicles opening with the words *madhu vátáḥ* appear first in the *Ṛigveda*, as I., XC., 6–8; and they reappear in the White *Yajurveda*, as XIII., 27–29. The position of the Vaidik passage alleged to be connected with the *trisuparńa* has not been traced out.

Aparárka, commenting on the *Yájnavalkya-smṛiti*, I., 200, gives this definition of *trimadhu*, denoting a person: त्रिमधुत्रयाध्यायी व्रतं कृत्वा-पञ्चाग्निमेव वेदमात्रमधीते च त्रिमधुः।

acquainted with the six supplementary sciences of the Vedas;[1]* one who understands the Vedas; one who practises the duties they enjoin;[2] one who exercises

---

occur in Manu, III., 185; and Kullúka Bhaṭṭa explains Trińáchiketa to mean a portion of the Yajur-veda, and the Brahman who studies it; and Trisuparńa, a part of the Ŕich, and the Brahman who is acquainted with it. The Nirńaya Sindhu explains the terms in a like manner, but calls the Trisuparńa, as well as the Trińáchiketa, prayers, portions of the Yajus. The Trimadhu it assigns to the Ŕich. Other explanations are also given to the terms Trińáchiketa and Trisuparńa; the first being explained a Brahman who thrice performs the ceremony called Chayana;† and the last, one who, after the seven ascending generations, worships the Pitŕis termed Somapas.‡ These explanations are, however, considered less correct than the preceding, and which are thus given in the authority cited: त्रिणाचिकेतस्त्रिसुपर्णौ यजुर्वेदैकदेशौ तद्व्रतेन तदध्यायिनौ । . . . . त्रिमधु ऋग्वेदैकदेशस्तदध्यायी ।

[1] For the six Angas, see p. 67, *supra*.

[2] So the commentator§ distinguishes the Vedavit,—the Brah-

---

* *Shaḍangavit.*

† त्रैविद्याचिकेतं चयनं चितः क्रमव्याख्यातार्थमाह: । And herewith agrees Śankara, where commenting on the *Kaṭha Upanishad*, I., 17, त्रिणाचिकेतः । त्रिःकृत्वो नाचिकेतोऽग्निश्चितो येन स त्रिणाचिकेतस्तद्विज्ञानस्तदध्ययनस्तदनुष्ठानवान्वा ।

‡ यस्य सप्त पूर्वे सोमपाः स त्रिसुपर्ण इति बोपदेवः । "He of whom seven forefathers have drunk the juice of the moon-plant is a *trisuparńa*: so *says* Bopadeva." These words occupy the blank, indicated by asterisks, in the passage quoted at the end of the note here supplemented; and the definitions preceding them are referred to the same author.

§ His words are: वेदवित् । वेदार्थविचारकः । श्रोत्रियः । तदर्थानुष्ठाता । In the *Mitákshará*, I., 219, we read: श्रोत्रियः । श्रुताध्ययनसंपन्नः । Kullúka, on the *Mánavadharmaśástra*, III., 128, says: छन्दोमात्राध्यायी श्रोत्रियः । Medhátithi has: श्रोत्रियः । छान्दसः छान्दसमस्याङ्गसहितां शाखामधीते यः ।

penance;* a chanter of the principal Sáma-veda,¹ an officiating priest,† a sister's son, a daughter's son, a son-in-law, a father-in-law, a maternal uncle, an ascetic,‡ a Brahman who maintains the five fires,§ a pupil, a kinsman;‖ one who reverences his parents.¶ A man should first employ the Brahmans first specified in the (principal) obsequial rite; and the others, (commencing with the ministering priest), in the subsidiary ceremonies** instituted to gratify his ancestors.

---

man who understands the meaning of the text of the Vedas,—from the Śrotriya, who practises the rites he studies.

¹ Portions of the Sáman contained in the Áraṅyaka are called the Jyeshṫha, 'elder' or 'principal', Sáman.††

---

* *Yogin.*

† *Ritwig.*

‡ *Tapo-nishṫha.*

§ According to Ánanda, the five fires, spoken of in the *Kaṫha Upanishad*, III., 1, are called *gárhapatya*, *dakshiṅágni*, *áhavaníya*, *sabhya*, and *ávasathya*. Also see the *Mitákshará*, I., 221. The more technical name of the *dakshiṅágni* or *dakshiṅa* is *anváhiryapachana*; as we learn from the *Chhándogya Upanishad*, IV., XII., 1. The three first-named fires, out of the five, are the principal. See, regarding them, the Translator's last note on Chapter VI. of Book IV.

‖ *Sambandhin*, 'a relation by marriage.'

¶ Compare the *Laws of the Mánavas*, III., 148.

** *Anukalpa.*

†† The commentator says that the *jyeshṫha-sáman* opens with the *rich* beginning with the words *múrdhánam divaḣ*: मूर्धानं दिव इत्यादृचि-ष्वगीतं ज्येष्ठसाम । तद्गाता ज्येष्ठसामगः । Professor Wilson should seem to have preferred the authority of Kullúka, who thus explains the term *jyeshṫha-sámaga*, occurring in the *Mánavadharmaśástra*, III., 185: ज्येष्ठसामानि चारण्यके गीयन्ते । तेषां गाता । The stanza in question is found in the *Rigveda*, VI., VII., 1; and it is met with twice in the *Sámaveda*,—as I., 67, and as II., 490.

"A false friend, a man with ugly nails* or black teeth,† a ravisher, a Brahman who neglects the service of fire and sacred study, a vender of the Soma-plant, a man accused of any crime, a thief, a calumniator, a Brahman who conducts religious ceremonies for the vulgar; one who instructs his servant in holy writ, or is instructed in it by his servant; the husband of a woman who has been formerly betrothed to another; a man who is undutiful to his parents;‡ the protector of the husband of a woman of the servile caste,§ or the husband of a woman of the servile caste;|| and a Brahman who ministers to idols¶—are not proper persons to be invited to an ancestral offering.[1] On the first day, let a judicious man invite eminent teachers of the Vedas,** and other Brahmans, and, according to their directions, determine what is

---

[1] Manu, III., 150, &c.

---

* *Kunakhin*. The commentator explains this term to mean 'with nails naturally bad.' Neither Kullúka nor Medhátithi justifies Sir William Jones's rendering, "a man with whitlows on his nails." See his Translation of "Menu", III., 153.

† 'A eunuch', *kliba*, is omitted.

‡ Rather, an 'abandoner' of them, *ujjhaka*.

§ *Vrishali-súti-poshtri*, "the supporter of the offspring of a *vrishali*", who seems to be a woman sprung from a man that has lost caste.

Professor Wilson read, for *súti*, *pati*, which I find in some MSS. But the gloss, शूद्रापत्यपोषक, shows that *pati* is a clerical error.

|| *Vrishali*.

¶ *Devalaka*. He must have been so for three years, says the commentator, to incur disqualification. And yet an idol was reputed so holy that it was sacrilege to pass over its shadow. *Vide supra*, p. 137, text, and p. 138, note ||.

** *Śrotriya*. *Vide supra*, p. 174, note §.

to be dedicated to the gods, and what to the Pitṛis.* Associated with the Brahmans, let the institutor of an obsequial rite abstain from anger and incontinence.† He who, having eaten, himself, in a Śráddha, and fed Brahmans, and appointed them to their sacred offices, is guilty of incontinence, thereby sentences his progenitors to shameful suffering.‡ In the first place, the Brahmans before described are to be invited: but those holy men§ who come to the house without an invitation are, also, to be entertained. The guests are to be reverently received with water for their feet, and the like; and the entertainer, holding holy grass in his hand,|| is to place them, after they have rinsed their mouths, upon seats. An uneven number of Brahmans is to be invited in sacrifices to the manes; an even, or uneven, number, in those presented to the gods; or one only, on each occasion.[1]¶

"Then let the householder, inspired by religious faith, offer oblations** to the maternal grandfather,

---

[1] As two, or five, at a ceremony dedicated to the gods; three, at the worship of the Pitṛis. Nirṇaya Sindhu, p. 311.

---

* कथयेच्च तदैवैषां नियोगान्पितृदैविकान् ।

† Add 'fatigue', *áyása*; also, "this is a great offence on that occasion", दोषश्च महानयम् ।

‡ श्राद्धे नियुक्तो भुक्त्वा तु भोजयित्वा नियुज्य च ।
व्यवायी रेतसो गर्ते मज्जयत्यात्मनः पितॄन् ॥

§ *Yatis*; these being Brahmans, as the original conditions.

|| *Pavitra-páṇi*; literally, 'pure-handed'.

¶ It is directed, in the *Yájnavalkya-smṛiti*, I., 227:
युग्मान्दैवे यथाशक्ति पित्र्येऽयुग्मांस्तथैव च ।

** *Śráddha*.

along with the worship of the Viśwadevas,[1] or the ceremony called Vaiśwadeva,* (which comprehends offerings to both paternal and maternal ancestors, and to ancestors in general).† Let him feed the Brahmans who are appropriated to the gods and to maternal ancestors, with their faces to the east; and those set apart for the paternal ancestors and ancestors in general, with their faces to the north.‡ Some say, that

---

[1] The worship of the Viśwadevas§ (see p. 158, *supra*) forms a part of the general Śráddhas, and of the daily sacrifices of the householder. According to the Váyu, this was a privilege conferred upon them, by Brahmá and the Pitṛis, as a reward for religious austerities practised, by them, upon Himálaya. Their introduction as a specific class seems to have originated in the custom of sacrificing to the gods collectively, or to all the gods,|| as the name Viśwadevas implies. They appear, however, as a

---

* तथा मातामहश्राद्धं वैश्वदेवसमन्वितम् ।
कुर्वीत भक्तिसंपन्नस्तन्त्रं वा वैश्वदेविकम् ॥

† "It consists in oblations to the gods, to the manes, and to the spirits." Colebrooke's *Miscellaneous Essays*, Vol. I., p. 188.

‡ The original passage, in correct MSS., runs thus:

प्राङ्मुखान्भोजयेद्विप्रान्देवानामुभयार्थकान् ।
पितृमातामहानां च भोजयेच्चाप्युदङ्मुखान् ॥

"For both *sets of his ancestors* let him feed, with *their* faces to the east, Bráhmans *retained* for the gods *called Viśwadevas*; and let him also feed, with *their* faces to the north, *Bráhmans retained* for *his* paternal and maternal manes."

The Translator, corrected above, transposed "east" and "north".

Comment: उभयार्थकान् । पितृमातामहीयवैश्वदेवार्थकान् । पितृमा-तामहयोरर्थकांश्चोदङ्मुखान्भोजयेदित्यन्वयः ।

Compare the *Yájnavalkya-smṛiti*, I., 228:

द्वौ दैवे प्राक्त्रयः पित्र्य उदगेकैकमेव वा ।

§ See note at the end of this chapter.

|| So the term signifies, literally: but I have never found it expressed by the compound "Viśwadevas", as it is by Professor Wilson.

the viands of the Śráddha should be kept distinct for these two sets of ancestors; but others maintain, that they are to be fed with the same food, at the same tinne.* Having spread Kuśa grass for seats,† and offered libations‡ according to rule, let the sensible

---

distinct class, in the Vedas;§ and their assumption of this character is, therefore, of ancient date. The daily offering to them is noticed by Manu, III., 90,|| 121;¶ and offerings to 'the gods' are, also, enjoined at the beginning and end of a Śráddha. Kullúka Bhaṭṭa understands, here, the Viśwadevas; and it probably is so: but, in another verse, different divinities are specified: "First, as it is ordained, having satisfied Agni, Soma, and Yama, with clarified butter, let him proceed to satisfy the manes of his progenitors."** Verse 211.†† Manu also directs them to be worshipped first and last in order. See Asiatic Researches, Vol. VII., pp. 265, 271, &c.‡‡

---

* पृथक्तयोः केचिदाहुः श्राद्धस्य करणं नृप ।
एकत्रैकेन पाकेन वदन्त्यन्ये महर्षयः ॥

† *Vishṭara.* ‡ *Arghya.*

§ Professor Wilson has elsewbere observed, that "The Viśwadevas are, sometimes, vaguely applied to divinities in general; but they also form a class, whose station and character are imperfectly noticed, but who are entitled, at most religious rites, to share in the solemnity." Translation of the *Rigveda*, Vol. I., p. 9, note b.

Bhaga, Mitra, Aditi, Daksha, Asridh, Aryaman, Varuṇa, Soma, and the Aświns, named together in the *Rigveda*, LXXXIX., 3, are said to be considered as Viśwa devas.

Of all these Daksha alone is included in any of the various lists of post-vaidik Viśwa devas collected in the last note in p 183, *infra.*

|| विश्वेभ्यश्चैव देवेभ्यो बलिमाकाश उत्क्षिपेत् ।
दिवाचरेभ्यो भूतेभ्यो नक्तंचारिभ्य एव च ॥

¶ See Vol. II., p. 23, note §. ** Sir William Jones's translation.

†† अग्नेः सोमयमाभ्यां च कृत्वाप्यायनमादितः ।
हविर्दानेन विधिवत्पश्चात्संतर्पयेत्पितॄन् ॥

‡‡ Or Colebrooke's *Miscellaneous Essays*, Vol. I., pp. 181, 186, &c.

man invoke the deities, with the concurrence of the Brahmans who are present.[1] Let the man who is acquainted with the ritual offer a libation to the gods, with water and barley; having presented to them flowers,* perfumes, and incense.† Let him offer the same to the Pitŕis, placed upon his left; and, with the consent (of the Brahmans), having first provided seats of Kuśa‡ grass doubled, let him invoke, with (the usual) prayers, the manes (to the ceremony), offering a libation, on his left hand, of water and sesamum. He will then, with the permission of the Brahmans, give food to any guest who arrives at the time, or who is desirous of victuals, or who is passing along the road:§ for holy saints and ascetics,‖ benefactors

---

[1] The text is तदनुज्ञया, 'with *their* assent;' but no noun occurs, in the sentence, with which the relative is connected. It must mean the Brahmans, however; as in this passage of Vŕiddha Paráśara: "Let the sacrificer place his left hand on the Brahman's right knee, and say, 'Shall I invoke the Viśwadevas?' And, being desired to invoke them, let him address them with the two Mantras, 'Viśwadevas, he is come!' 'Viśwadevas, hear him!'"

ततः सव्यं करं न्यस्य विप्रदक्षिणजानुनि ।
देवानावाहयिष्येऽहमिति वाचमुदीरयेत् ॥
आवाहयेदनुज्ञातो विश्वे देवास आगत ।
विश्वे देवाः शृणुतेममिति मन्त्रद्वयं पठेत् ॥¶

---

* *Srag*, 'garlands.'

† Add 'lights', *dípa*.

‡ *Darbha*, in the original.

§ काले तथातिथिं प्राप्तमन्नकामं नृपाध्वगम् ।

‖ The original has only one word, *yogin*, for "holy saints and ascetics."

¶ Bŕihat-Paráśara's *Dharmaśástra*, V., 184, 185.

of mankind, are traversing this earth, disguised in various shapes.'[1] On this account, let a prudent man welcome a person who arrives at such a season: for inattention to a guest frustrates the consequences of an ancestral offering.

"The sacrificer is then to offer food, without salt or seasoning,[*] to fire,[2] three several times, with the consent of the assistant Brahmans; exclaiming, first: 'To fire, the vehicle of the oblations;[†] to the manes! Swáhá!' Next, addressing the oblation:[‡] to Soma, the lord of the progenitors,[§] and giving the third to Vaivaswata.[||] He is then to place a very little of the residue of the oblation[¶] in the dishes of the Brahmans; and, next, presenting them with choice viands, well-dressed and seasoned, and abundant, he is to request them, civilly, to partake of it at their pleasure."[**] The

---

[1] This notion occurs, more than once, in the Váyu, in nearly the same words:

सिद्धा हि विप्ररूपेण चरन्ति पृथिवीमिमाम् ।
तस्मादतिथिमायान्तमभिगच्छेत्कृताञ्जलिः ॥

[2] This places the initiatory oblations noticed by Manu (see p. 176, note 1, *supra*) subsequent to the offerings to the Viswadevas.

---

[*] *Vyanjana*; explained, by the scholiast, to denote pot-herbs and the like.

[†] *Kavya*.

[‡] *Áhuti*.

[§] *Pitrimat*, 'attended by the manes.'

[||] The commentator observes: वैवस्वताय यमायेति पृथगाहुतिः [illegible] ।

[¶] *Huta*.

[**] ततोऽन्नमिष्टमत्यर्थमभीष्टमपि सत्कृतम् ।
दत्त्वा जुषध्वमिच्छातो वाच्यमेतदनिष्ठुरम् ॥

Brahmans are to eat of such food attentively, in silence, with cheerful countenances, and at their ease. The sacrificer is to give it to them, not churlishly, nor hurriedly,* but with devout faith.

"Having, next, recited the prayer for the discomfiture of malignant spirits,[1] and scattered sesamum-seeds upon the ground, the Brahmans (who have been fed) are to be addressed,† in common with the ancestors (of the sacrificer), in this manner: 'May my father, grandfather, and great-grandfather, in the persons of these Brahmans, receive satisfaction! May my father, grandfather, and great-grandfather derive nutriment from these oblations to fire!‡ May my father, grandfather, and great-grandfather derive satisfaction from the balls of food placed, by me, upon the ground! May my father, grandfather, and great-grandfather be pleased with what I have, this day, offered§ them in faith! May my maternal grandfather, his father, and his father, also enjoy contentment from my offerings! May all the gods|| experience gratifi-

[1] The Rakshoghna Mantra,—the extinguishing of a lamp lighted to keep off evil spirits, which is accompanied by a Mantra, or prayer. Asiatic Researches, Vol. VII., p. 274.¶

* अक्रुद्धता चात्वरता ।

† *Dhyeya*, 'to be meditated on.'

‡ पिता पितामहश्चैव तथैव प्रपितामहः ।
मम तृप्तिं प्रयान्त्वग्निहोमाप्यायितमूर्तयः ॥

§ For *ihāhṛita*, 'here offered,' there is a variant, *udāhṛita*, 'spoken.'

|| *Viśve devāḥ.*

¶ Or Colebrooke's *Miscellaneous Essays*, Vol. I., p. 191.

cation, and all evil beings* perish! May the lord of sacrifice,† the imperishable‡ deity Hari, be the accepter of all oblations made to the manes or the gods! § And may all malignant spirits,|| and enemies of the deities,¶ depart from the rite!'

"When the Brahmans have eaten sufficiently, the worshipper must scatter some of the food upon the ground, and present them, individually, with water, to rinse their mouths. Then, with their assent, he may place upon the ground balls made up of boiled rice and condiments, along with sesamum-seeds. With the part of his hand sacred to the manes he must offer sesamum-seeds, and water from his joined palms; and, with the same part of his hand, he must present cakes to his maternal ancestors.** He should, in lonely places, naturally beautiful, and by the side of sacred streams, diligently make presents (to the manes and

---

* *Yátudhána.* See Vol. II., p. 293, note, near the foot of the page.

† *Yajneśwara.* See Vol. II., p. 124, note ‡.

‡ *Avyayátman*, 'immutable.' See Vol. I., p. 17, note *.

§ This is to translate हव्यसमस्तकव्यभोक्ता ।

|| *Rakshas.*

¶ "Enemies of the gods" renders *asura.*

** तृप्तेषु तेषु विकिरेदन्नं विप्रेषु भूतले ।
दद्याच्चाचमनार्थाय तेभ्यो वारि सकृत्सकृत् ॥
सुतृप्तैस्तैरनुज्ञातः सर्वेणान्नेन भूतले ।
सतिलेन ततः पिण्डान्सम्यग्दद्यात्समाहितः ॥
पितृतीर्थेन सलिलं दद्याच्च जलाञ्जलीन् ।
मातामहेभ्यस्तेनैव पिण्डांस्तीर्थेन निर्वपेत् ॥

"Instead of "Then, with their assent," &c., read: "Authorised by them, *they being* fully satisfied, let him, collectedly, then duly offer, on the ground, funeral cakes *made* of all *sorts of* food and of sesamum."

the Brahmans).[1]* Upon Kuśa† grass, the tips of which are pointed to the south, and lying near the fragments (of the meat), let the householder present the first ball of food, consecrated‡ with flowers and incense, to his father; the second, to his grandfather; and the third, to his great-grandfather: and let him satisfy those who are contented with the wipings of his hand, by wiping it with the roots of Kuśa grass.[2]§ After presenting balls of food to his maternal ancestors, in the same manner, accompanied by perfumes and incense, he is to give to the principal Brahmans water, to rinse their mouths; and then, with attention and piety, he is to give the Brahmans|| gifts, according to his power, soliciting their benedictions, accompanied

---

[1] Part of this passage is in the words of Manu, III., 207:

अवकाशेषु चोक्षेषु नदीतीरेषु चैव हि ।

It is omitted in the MSS. in the Bengali character.

[2] Manu, III., 216.¶

---

* दक्षिणाप्रवणं चैव प्रयत्नेनोपपादयेत् ।
अवकाशेषु चोक्षेषु जलतीरेषु चैव हि ॥

"And he should carefully select a southerly slope, in a pure place, and also by the side of water."

Compare the *Yájnavalkya-smriti*, I., 227:

परिश्रुते शुचौ देशे दक्षिणाप्रवणे तथा ।

† *Darbha*, its synonym, in the original; and so just below, and frequently.

‡ *Pújita*.

§ दर्भमूले लेपभुजः प्रीणयेल्लेपघर्षणैः ।

|| *Pitribhyah*, 'to the manes,' whom the Bráhmans represent. *Vide supra*, p. 182.

¶ न्युप्य पिण्डांस्ततस्तांस्तु प्रयतो विधिपूर्वकम् ।
तेषु दर्भेषु तं हस्तं निमृज्याल्लेपभागिनाम् ॥

with the exclamation 'Swadhá!'[1]* Having made presents to the Brahmans,† he is to address himself to the gods,‡ saying: 'May they who are the Viśwadevas be pleased with this (oblation)!' Having thus said, and the blessings to be solicited having been granted by the Brahmans, he is to dismiss first the paternal ancestors, and then the gods. The order is the same with the maternal ancestors and the gods, in respect to food, donation, and dismissal. Commencing with the washing of the feet, until the dismissing of the gods and Brahmans, the ceremonies are to be performed first for paternal ancestors, and then for ancestors on the mother's side.§ Let him dismiss the

---

[1] "Then let the *Bráhmans* address him, saying *swadhá*; for,

---

* सुस्वधेत्याशिषा युक्तां दद्याच्छक्त्या च दक्षिणाम् ।

We are to read, then: "and let him give, according to his ability, a present, accompanied with the benediction *suswadhá*."

† 'To them', agreeably to the Sanskrit. See note ‖ in the preceding page.

‡ *Vaiśwadevika.*

§ तथेति चोक्ते तैर्विप्रैः प्रार्थनीयास्तथाशिषः ।
पश्चाद्विसर्जयेद्देवान्पूर्वं पैत्र्यान्महामते ॥
मातामहानामप्येवं सह देवैः क्रमः स्मृतः ।
भोजने च स्वशक्त्या च दाने तद्वद्विसर्जने ॥
आपादशौचनात्पूर्वं कुर्याद्देवद्विजन्मसु ।
विसर्जनं तु प्रथमं पैत्रमातामहेषु वै ॥

"And, 'so be it' having been uttered by those Bráhmans, blessings are, likewise, to be solicited: *and then* let him dismiss, first, the *Bráhmans entertained in the service* of the manes, *and*, afterwards, those *entertained in the service* of the gods, O great-souled. For the maternal ancestors, too, along with the gods,—*all these being represented by Bráhmans*,—the order is laid down the same, as to food, donation according

Brahmans with kindly speeches and profound respect, and attend upon them at the end of the Śráddha, until permitted, by them, to return. The wise man will then perform the invariable worship* of the Viśwadevas, and take his own meal, along with his friends,† his kinsmen, and his dependants.

"In this manner, an enlightened householder will celebrate the obsequial worship of his paternal and maternal ancestors, who, satisfied by his offerings, will grant him all his desires. Three things are held pure at obsequies,—a daughter's son,‡ a Nepal blanket,

---

in all ceremonies relating to deceased ancestors, the word *swadhá* is the highest benison."§ Manu, III., 252.||

---

to ability, and, in like manner, as to dismissal. *In the Vaiśwadeva ceremony*, let him first do *everything*, beginning with the purification of the feet, for the Bráhmans *entertained in the service* of the gods; but *let him first grant* dismissal to the *personated* paternal ancestors and maternal ancestors."

On this passage the commentator remarks as follows: विश्वे यथार्हं सर्वेष्विति । अनेन विसर्जनमपि पितृपूर्वकमिति । ततोऽन्यत्सर्वं दैवपूर्वमेवेत्यर्थादुक्तम् । एतमेवार्थं वैश्वदेवतन्त्रमपेक्ष्याह । पादादीति । पादप्रक्षालनात्प्रभृति देवार्थानां ब्राह्मणानां सर्वं प्रथमं कुर्यात्ततः पितृवर्गीयाणां ततो मातामहवर्गीयाणामिति । विसर्जनं त्विति । दक्षिणाया उपलक्षणं पूर्वमेवोक्तत्वात् ।

* *Nitya-kriyá.*

† *Pújya* = *mánya*. Commentary.

‡ The MSS. have both *dauhitraḥ* and *dauhitram*. And see note † in the next page.

§ This is Sir William Jones's rendering.

|| स्वधास्त्वित्येव तं ब्रूयुर्ब्राह्मणास्तदनन्तरम् ।
स्वधाकारः परा ह्याशीः सर्वेषु पितृकर्मसु ॥

and sesamum-seeds;[1] and the gift, or naming, or sight,

---

[1] We have, here, the words of Manu:

त्रीणि श्राद्धे पवित्राणि दौहित्रः कुतपस्तिलाः।

III., 235. 'Three things are held pure, at such obsequies,—the daughter's son, the Nepal blanket, and sesamum-seed.' Sir William Jones's translation of these terms rests upon the explanation of Kullúka Bhaṭṭa of this and the verse preceding:

व्रतस्थमपि दौहित्रं श्राद्धे यत्नेन भोजयेत्।
कुतपं चासने दद्यात्तिलैश्च विकिरेन्महीम्॥*

'Let him give his daughter's son, though a religious student, food at a Śráddha, and the blanket for a seat,' &c. The commentator on our text says,† that some understand, by Dauhitra, clarified butter made from the milk of a cow fed with grass gathered on the day of new moon; and some explain it a plate, or dish, of buffalo-horn.‡ Kutapa he interprets by Ashṭama Muhúrta, the eighth hour of the day, or a little after noon; although he admits, that some render it a blanket made of goat's wool.§

---

* III., 234.

† His words are: दौहित्रो दुहितुः सुतः। कुतपोऽष्टमो मुहूर्तः। दौहित्रमिति पाठे दौहित्रं घृतमित्येके।

अमावास्यागते सोमे या च खादति गोतृणम्।
दौहित्री सा मता तस्या घृतं दौहित्रमुच्यते॥

इति। दौहित्रं खड्गपात्रमिति केचित्। केचित्तु कुतपमपि छागलोमज कम्बलमाहुः। My oldest and best MSS. have अष्टमा घटिका, instead of अष्टमो मुहूर्तः. See Vol. I., p. 47, note 2; also, p. 190, note 2, *supra*.

The *Nirṇayasindhu* quotes, as follows, from the *Brahmaṇḍa-puráṇa*:

अमावास्यागते सोमे या खादयति गोतृणम्।
तस्या गोर्यद्भवेत्क्षीरं तद्दौहित्रमुदाहृतम्॥

‡ Read 'rhinoceros-horn.' So explains the *Kalpataru*, says the *Nirṇayasindhu*: दौहित्रं खड्गपात्रमिति कल्पतरुः।

§ Thus Vijnáneśwara understands it, in his comment on the *Yájnavalkya-smṛiti*, I., 186: कुतपः। पार्वतीयच्छागरोमनिर्मितः कम्बलः। And similarly Aparárka. Also see the *Śabdakalpadruma*, *sub voce*.

of silver (is, also, propitious).[1] The person offering a Śraddha should avoid anger, walking about, and hurry: these three things are very objectionable.* The Viśwadevas, and paternal and maternal ancestors, and (the living members of) a man's family, are, all, nourished by the offerer of ancestral oblations.

"The class of Pitŕis derives support from the moon; and the moon is sustained by acts of austere devotion.† Hence, the appointment of one who practises austerities ‡ is most desirable. A Yogin set before a

---

These explanations are also noticed in the Nirńaya Sindhu, p. 302; and, upon the authority of the Matsya Puráńa, Kutapa is said to mean eight things which equally consume (Tap) all sin (Ku), or, — noon, a vessel of rhinoceros-horn, a Nepal blanket, silver, holy grass, sesamum, kine, and a daughter's son:

मध्याह्नः खड्गपात्रं च तथा नेपालकम्बलः ।
रौप्यं दर्भास्तिला गावो दौहित्रश्चाष्टमः स्मृतः ॥ §
पापं कुत्सितमित्याहुस्तस्य संतापकारिणः ।
अष्टावेते यतस्तस्मात्कुतपा इति विश्रुताः ॥ ||

[1] So the Matsya Puráńa has 'the gift, sight, and name, of silver are desired:'

रजतस्य तथा दानं दर्शनं नाम चेष्यते । ¶

The notion originates with Manu, III., 202.**

---

* क्रोधोऽध्वगमनं राजेन्द्र त्रयमेतन्न शस्यते ।

† सोमाधारः पितृगणो योगाधारश्च चन्द्रमाः ।

See Vol. II., pp. 298—303; and compare Vol. I., p. 90.

‡ *Yogin.*

§ I find दौहित्रं चाष्टमं स्मृतम्, also.

|| Quoted in the *Nirńayasindhu.*

¶ This line is cited by the commentator.

** राजतैर्भाजनैरेषामथो वा रजतान्वितैः ।
वार्यपि श्रद्धया दत्तमक्षयायोपकल्पते ॥

thousand Brahmans enables the institutor of obsequial rites to enjoy all his desires."[1]*

[1] The same doctrine is inculcated by the Váyu Puráńa:† but it appears to be a Pauráńik innovation; for Manu places the Brahman intent on scriptural knowledge and on austere devotion on a level, and makes no mention of the Yogin. III., 134.‡

* सहस्रस्यापि विप्राणां योगी चेत्पुरतः स्थितः ।
सर्वान्भोक्तॄंस्तारयति यजमानं तथा नृप ॥

Instead of "enables," &c., read "saves all the eaters, *and*, likewise, the sacrificer."

† Cited thus, in the commentary:

यस्मै प्रीताः पुनः सोमं पितरो योगमास्थिताः ।
आप्याययन्ति योगेन त्रैलोक्यं तेन जीवति ॥

Just before, the scholiast quotes the ensuing stanza,—*Ll.* 939—from the *Harivaṁśa*:

एतेऽस्मिंस्तरस्मात योगिनां योगवर्धनाः ।
आप्याययन्ति ये पूर्वं सोमं योगबलेन वै ॥

In these passages, the manes are represented as nourishing the moon by their devotion of *yoga*.

‡ ज्ञाननिष्ठा द्विजाः केचित्तपोनिष्ठास्तथापरे ।
तपःस्वाध्यायनिष्ठाश्च कर्मनिष्ठास्तथापरे ॥

Note referred to at pp. 178, 179, *supra*.

The names and functions of the post-vaidik Viśwa devas are set forth, in the *Likhita-smŕiti*, as follows:

क्रतुर्दक्षो वसुः सत्यः कालः कामो धुरिरोचनौ ।
पुरूरवा माद्रवाश्च विश्वे देवाः प्रकीर्तिताः ॥
* * * * * * * * * * * * * * *
इष्टिश्राद्धे क्रतुर्दक्षो वसुः सत्यश्च दैविके ।
कालः कामोऽग्निकार्येषु काम्येषु धुरिरोचनौ ।
पुरूरवा माद्रवाश्च पार्वणेषु नियोजयेत् ॥

Here the Viśwa devas are said to be Kratu, Daksha, Vasu, Satya, Kála, Káma, Dhuri, Rochana, Purúravas, and Mádravas; ten, in all.

In Hemádri's *Śráddhakalpa*, the *Bŕihaspati-smŕiti* is named as the source of these lines:

क्रतुर्दक्षो वसुः सत्यः कामः कालस्तथैव च ।
धुनिश्च रोचनश्चैव तथा चैव पुरूरवाः ।
आर्द्रवश्च इतीमे तु विश्वे देवाः प्रकीर्तिताः ॥

As well as of these:

इष्टिश्राद्धे क्रतुर्दक्षः सत्यो नान्दीमुखे वसुः ।
नैमित्तिके कालकामौ काम्ये च धुनिरोचनौ ।
पुरूरवा आर्द्रवश्चैव पार्वणे समुदाहृतौ ॥

This last extract, slightly varied, is, in the *Śráddhatattva*, likewise credited to Bríhaspati.

And the following verses are professedly taken, by Hemádri, from the *Śankha-smṛiti*:

इष्टिश्राद्धे क्रतुर्दक्षः संकीर्त्यौ वैश्वदेविके ।
नान्दीमुखे सत्यवसू काम्ये च धुरिरोचनौ ॥

But I can find nothing of the sort in Bríhaspati and Śankha.

In the *Agni-puráńa*, we read, according to Colebrooke's best MS., copied in the time of Akbar:

क्रतुर्दक्षो वसुः सत्यः कालः कामस्तथा धुनिः ।
रोचकश्चार्द्रवाश्चैव तथा चान्यः पुरूरवाः ।
विश्वे देवा भवन्त्येते दश सर्वत्र पूजिताः ॥
विश्वेदेवौ क्रतुदक्षौ सर्वास्विष्टिषु विश्रुतौ ।
नित्यं नान्दीमुखश्राद्धे वसुसत्यौ च पैतृके ॥
नवान्नालम्भने देवौ कामकालौ सदैव हि ।
अपि कन्यागते सूर्ये श्राद्धे वा धुनिरोचनौ ।
पुरूरवार्द्रवाश्चैव विश्वेदेवौ च पर्वणि ॥

The last half of this extract, slightly varied, is quoted in the *Nirńayasindhu*, in Rámakríshńa's *Śráddhagańapati*, and in other works, as from the *Áditya-puráńa*.

The ensuing enumeration is referred, in the *Rájyábhishekapaddhati*, to the *Agni-puráńa*; but I have not been able to find it there:

क्रतुर्दक्षो वसुः सत्यः कामः कालो धुरिर्जयः ।
पुरूरवा माद्रवाश्च विश्वे देवाश्च रोचनः ॥

Here the Viśwe devas number eleven; the additional one being Jaya.

In the *Nirńayasindhu* and *Vratakamalákara*, we meet with the subjoined verses, taken, perhaps, from the *Vasishtha-saṁhitá*:

क्रतुर्दक्षो वसुः सत्यः कालः कामो मुनिस्तथा ।
धूलिमाश्चार्द्रवश्चैव रोचमानस्तथैव च ।
एते स्वामभिवदन्तु विश्वे देवास्तथा दश ॥

The name Muni, in the first line, looks exceedingly like a mere clerical error.

We read, farther, in the *Sárasangraha*:

पुरूरवा माद्रवाश्च कुरुवौ पर्वपवाः ।
मात्रिके वसुसत्यौ च काम्ये तु धुरिरोचनौ ॥
कालकामौ तु निवेधौ वृद्धिकार्ये त्रिलोचन ।
पित्रे ईष्टाः सत्याख्याताः श्राद्धकर्मसु सर्वदा ॥

We have, thus, to choose between Dhuri, Dhwani, and Muni; between Rochana, Rochaka, Rochamána, and the Lochana of some MSS.; between Purúravas and Dhritimat; and between Mádravas, Ádravas, Ándrava, and Manuja. I incline to think that the मा-, in the reading पुरूरवा मा-द्रवाश्च, may have been corrupted out of धा-, and this out of च. The *Nirńayasindhu*, like other treatises, in quoting the second passage which Hemádri refers to Bŕihaspati, and the extract from the *Agni-puráńa*, gives, instead of the immetrical पुरूरवा चार्द्रवश्चैव, and पुरूरवामा-द्रवाश्च, पुरूरवार्द्रवौ चैव. Possibly, this originated from पुरूरवो-द्रवौ चैव, which yields, at all events, in lieu of two unintelligible names, two intelligible,—Purúravas and Adrava. The termination of the nonmeaning Mádravas and Ádravas was, perhaps, suggested by that of Purúravas.

The *Váyu-puráńa*, in my MSS., declares:

क्रतुर्दक्षः श्रवः सत्यः कालः कामो धुनिस्तथा ।
कुरुवानमवांश्चैव रोचमानश्च ते दश ।
धर्मपुत्राः सुता ह्येते विश्वायां जज्ञिरे शुभाः ॥

Here the Viśwe devas, called sons of Dharma and Viśwá,—see Vol. II., pp. 21, 22,—are said to be ten in number, namely: Kratu, Daksha, Śrava, Satya, Kála, Káma, Dhuni, Kuruvat, Amavat, and Rochamána.

Śrava, possibly, here grew out of Vasu, with its consonants transposed. Dhuni, again, could easily be corrupted from Dhuri; or *vice versa*. See Vol. II., p. 23, note §. For Kuruvat it is obvious to propose Puruvat,—the original, perhaps, of the readings Purúravas and Dhŕitimat; as Amavat may have been of Ádravas, &c.

It is a suggestive fact, that none of the dozen or more law-books which I have examined for the Viśwe devas refers to these verses,—the oldest, not impossibly, of all that are cited in this note. Is this omission to be accounted for by the desuetude of the *Váyu-puráńa*? And can that work be more ancient than the *Likhita-smŕiti*, in the form of it which has been derived to us?

Perhaps it was even some older work than the *Váyu-puráńa* that led Sankara—in his commentary on the *Bŕihad-árańyaka Upanishad*, I., IV., 12,—to count Viśwá's sons, the Viśwe devas, at thirteen.

In the *Harivanśa*, *ll.* 11541—4, I make out, as the result of collating several MSS.:

विश्वे देवाश्च विश्वाख्या धर्मोद्भूता इति श्रुतिः ।
दक्षश्चैव महाबाहुर्वसुश्च सुत एव च ॥
सुधर्मा च महाबाहुः शङ्खपाच्च महायशाः ।
पृथुश्चैव महाबाहुर्वपुष्मांश्च तथैव च ॥
चाक्षुषस्य मनोरेते तथानन्तमहारणौ ।
विश्वावसुसुपर्वाणौ निष्कुम्भश्च महायशाः ॥
रुरुश्च धर्मपुत्रो वै भास्करप्रतिमद्युतिः ।
विश्वेदेवास्त्विमाख्याता विश्वेशा धर्मसुतान् ॥

Here, subject to correction, I read the names of thirteen Viśwe devas, to-wit: Daksha, Vasu, Suta, Sudharman, Śankhapád, Prithu, Vapushmat, Ananta, Mahárańa, Viśwávasu, Suparvan, Nishkumbha, and Ruru. The first seven are said to be connected with the Manu Chákshusha. *Vide supra*, p. 11.

It is alleged, by the Translator,—Vol. II., p. 22, note 1,—that there are twelve Viśwe devas, according to the *Matsya-puráńa*. The passage, in that work, which names these supernals,—but without numbering them,—is much too corrupt, in my MSS., to invite conjectural mending. For the most part, if not throughout, it has, without question, a close genetic relationship to the last extract transcribed.

CHAPTER XVI.

Things proper to be offered, as food, to deceased ancestors: prohibited things. Circumstances vitiating a Śráddha: how to be avoided. Song of the Pitṛis or progenitors, heard by Ikshwáku.

AURVA continued.—"Ancestors are satisfied, for a month, with offerings of rice or other grain,* with clarified butter,[1] with fish, or the flesh of the hare, of birds, of the hog, the goat, the antelope,† the deer,‡ the Gayal,§ or the sheep, or with the milk of the cow, and its products.[2] They are for ever satisfied with

---

[1] See Manu, III., 266, &c. The articles are much the same; the periods of satisfaction somewhat vary.

[2] The expression Gavya (गव्य) implies all that is derived from a cow: but, in the text, it is associated with 'flesh'; and, as the commentator observes, some consider the flesh of the cow to be here intended: मांससम्बन्धपाठाद्गव्यमित्येके ।|| But this, he adds, relates to other ages.¶ In the Kali or present age, it implies milk and preparations of milk.** The sacrifice of a cow or calf formed part of the ancient Śráddha. It then became typical; or, a bull was turned loose, instead of being slaughtered: and

---

* There is nothing, in the original, corresponding to "offerings of rice or other grain." The scholiast, however, suggests such an addition.

† *Aiṇa*, adjective of *eṇa*.

‡ *Ruru*; explained, in the commentary, by *prishata*. In Vol. I., p. 73, it is translated "antelope".

§ *Gavaya*.

|| The commentator here refers, in terms, to a variant of the text.

¶ तत्तु युगान्तरविषयमेव ।

** The five pure products of the cow are milk, curds, butter, her urine, and her dung.

flesh (in general), and with that of the long-eared white goat,* in particular. The flesh of the rhinoceros, the Kálaśáka (pot-herb), and honey are, also, especial sources of satisfaction to those worshipped at ancestral ceremonies. The birth of that man is the occasion of satisfaction to his progenitors, who performs, at the due time, their obsequial rites at Gayá. Grains that spring up spontaneously,† rice growing wild,‡ panic§ of both species (white or black||), vegetables that grow in forests,¶ are fit for ancestral oblations; as are barley, wheat, rice, sesamum, various kinds of pulse,** and mustard.†† On the other hand, a

---

this is still practised, on some occasions.‡‡ In Manu, the term Gavya is coupled with others, which limit its application:

---

* *Vṛiddhrinasa.* Some, according to the commentator, understand this word to denote a bird with a dark throat, a red head, and white wings.

† *Prasátiká.* The scholiast says: प्रशातिका हैयधान्यादि । चार-चर्णीतिचकृष्णा: । श्वेतशूका इति केचित् । Commentary A.

‡ नीवारा रक्तशूका: । Commentary A. In the comment on the text of Vol. I., p. 95, *nívára* is defined चारस्था नीवारा:.

§ *Śyámáka.*

|| So adds the commentator.

¶ *Vanaushadhi.*

** The original specifies *priyangu*, *mudga*, *nishpáva*, and *kovidára*. *Nishpáva* is said, in one commentary, to be the same as *valla*; in the other, the same as *śimbya*: and a gloss gives *yugapatra* as the synonym of *kovidára*. For these and other vegetable products named in this chapter, see the list in Vol. I., p. 95.

†† Unlike the list referred to in the preceding note, this does not profess to be exhaustive. In the former, we find the names of fourteen articles; in the latter, the names of twelve. This mentions five species of grains,—*prasátiká*, *mudga*, *nishpáva*, *kovidára*, and *sarshapa*,—omitted in the other; while the remaining seven species are common between both.

‡‡ See Colebrooke's *Miscellaneous Essays*, Vol. I., p. 177.

householder must not offer any kind of grain that is not consecrated, by religious ceremonies, on its first coming into season;* nor (the pulse called) Rája-másha,† nor millet,‡ nor lentils, nor gourds,§ nor garlic, nor onions,|| nor nightshade,¶ nor camels' thorn,** nor salt, nor the efflorescence of salt deserts,†† nor red vegetable extracts,‡‡ nor anything that looks like salt,§§ nor anything that is not commendable: nor is water fit to be offered at a Śráddha, that has been brought by night, or has been abandoned, or is so little as not to satisfy a cow, or smells badly, or is covered with froth. The milk of animals with undi-

---

संवत्सरं तु गव्येन पयसा पायसेन च ।

"A whole year with the milk of cows, and food made of that milk."|||| III., 271.

---

* अकृताग्रयणं यच्च धान्यजातं नरेश्वर ।
* * * * * * * * निवर्जयेत् ॥

† *I. e.*, *másha* not black, according to the commentator.

‡ *Ásu.* Commentary A gives *china* as its synonym; B defines it by *sukshma-śáli*. In the comments on the text of Vol. I., pp. 94, 95, it is said, equivalently, to be *kshudra-śáli*, 'small rice'; while *chinaka* is explained to be *ásu-tulya*.

§ *Alábu*.

|| Insert 'carrots' (?), *piṇḍamúlaka*. The commentary explains the word by पिण्डाकारमूलकं, 'a bulbous root.'

¶ *Gándháraka.* शाकभेदः काशिकं वा । Commentary.

** *Karambha.* करम्भाणि दधिशर्करा लाजाः । शाकभेद इत्येके । Commentary.

†† *Aushara.*

‡‡ आरक्तांश्चैव निर्यासान्.

§§ प्रत्यक्षलवणानि, which the commentator defines to be चक्षुर्ग्राह्यल-वणानि.

|||| Sir William Jones.

vided hoofs, of a camel, a ewe, a deer,[*] or a buffalo, is unfit for ancestral oblations. If an obsequial rite is looked at by a eunuch, a man ejected from society,[†] an outcast, a heretic, a drunken man, or one diseased, by a cock,[‡] a naked ascetic,[1] a monkey, a village-hog,[§] by a woman in her courses or pregnant,[||] by an unclean person, or by a carrier of corpses,[¶] neither gods nor progenitors will partake of the food. The ceremony should, therefore, be performed in a spot carefully enclosed.[**] Let the performer cast sesamum on the ground, and drive away malignant spirits.[††] Let him not give food that is fetid, or vitiated by hairs or insects, or mixed with acid gruel,[‡‡] or stale.[§§] Whatever suitable food is presented with pure faith, and with the enunciation of name and race,[|| ||] to ancestors,

---

[1] Nagna is, literally, 'naked', but, as explained in the following chapter, means a Jaina mendicant. No such person is included, by Manu (III., 239, &c.), amongst those who defile a Śráddha by looking upon it. The Váyu contains the same prohibition: नग्नादयो न पश्येयुः ।

---

[*] The original word is márga. But there is a variant, chhága, 'of a goat.'

[†] Apaviddha; defined स्वजनपरित्यक्तः. [‡] Khikandku.

[§] I have corrected the printer's blunder "a village-bag"; the original being grámya-súkara.

[||] Sútiká. This, according to the commentator, is a woman ceremonially unclean by reason of recent childbirth.

[¶] Mritahára; explained by शवनिर्हरणवृत्तिः, in the commentary.

[**] तस्मात्परिश्रिते कुर्याच्छ्राद्धं श्रद्धासमन्वितः ।

[††] Yátudhána. See Vol. II., p. 292, near the foot.

[‡‡] Abhishava; synonymized by kánjika, in the commentary.

[§§] Paryushita. The scholiast says it means पक्वं रात्र्यन्तरितम् । Also vide supra, p. 176, note *. [|| ||] Gotra.

at an obsequial oblation, becomes food to them (or, gives them nourishment).* In former times, O king of the earth, this song† of the Pitris was heard by Ikshwáku,‡ the son of Manu, in the groves of Kalápa, (on the skirts of the Himálaya mountains§): 'Those of our descendants shall follow a righteous path, who shall reverently present us with cakes at Gayá. May he be born in our race, who shall give us, on the thirteenth of Bhádrapada and Mágha,‖ milk, honey, and clarified butter; or when he marries a maiden,¶ or

---

* श्राद्धसमन्वितैर्दत्तं पितृभ्यो नामगोत्रतः ।
यदाहारास्तु ते जातास्तदाहारत्वमेति तत् ॥

† *Gáthá.*

‡ See, for him, Book IV., Chapter I.

§ It is a village there, says the scholiast, from whom this parenthesis is borrowed. His words are: कलापो हिमवत्पार्श्ववर्ती ग्रामविशेषः । The village of Kalápa is mentioned in Book IV., Chapter IV., *ad finem.*

‖ The words "of Bhádrapada and Mágha" correspond to वर्षासु च मघासु च, which means, "during the rainy season, and under *the asterism* Maghá." Only one period, however, is intended; and that is during the month of Bhádrapada, according to the scholiast: वर्षासु । भाद्रपदे मघागमये त्रयोदश्यां श्राद्ध । Compare note § to p. 170, *supra.*

¶ *Gauri.* In definition of this term, the commentator adduces, from some unnamed *Smriti*, the ensuing stanza:

अष्टवर्षा भवेद्गौरी नववर्षा तु रोहिणी ।
दशवर्षा भवेत्कन्या अत ऊर्ध्वं रजस्वला ॥

It appears, herefrom, that *gauri* signifies a girl of eight years; *rohiṇi*, one of nine; and *kanyá*, one of ten; after which age, a female is to be considered as a woman.

With this the stanza which I have quoted from the *Panchatantra*, in p. 109, note *, *supra*, is unaccordant, as regards the *rohiṇi*.

For what seems to be intended for the above, cited in a corrupt and curtailed form by Vallabhagaṇi, see Goldstücker's *Sanskrit Dictionary*, *sub voce* वरवस्.

By its acceptance of the strains of the *pitris*, our text sanctions the marriage of a *gauri*. We have seen that this technicality is held to denote a maiden of eight; I nowhere find that it means a damsel more

liberates a black bull,[1] or performs any domestic ceremony agreeable to rule, accompanied by donations to the Brahmans!'"[2]*

---

[1] Níla vrisha. But this animal is not altogether, or always, black. In the Brahma Puráńa, as quoted in the Nirńaya Sindhu,† it is said to be of a red colour, with light face and tail, and white hoofs and horns; or, a white bull, with black face, &c.; or, a black bull, with white face, tail, and feet.‡

[2] Very full descriptions of the Śráddha occur in almost all

---

advanced; and it may be doubted whether the compiler of the *Vishńu-puráńa* took a different notion of its import.

Kanyá—*vide supra*, pp. 102–105,—is often used in the vaguer sense of 'virgin'. Such may, then, be a *gaurí*.

The commentator quotes, as follows, from the lawgiver Samvarta:

गौरीं ददन्नाकपृष्ठं वैकुण्ठं याति रोहिणीम् ।
कन्यां ददद्ब्रह्मलोकं रौरवं तु रजस्वलाम् ॥

"He who gives away a *gaurí* goes to Nákapṛishṭha; *he who gives away a rohiṇí*, to Vaikuṇṭha; he who gives away *a kanyá*, to Brahmaloka; but *he who gives away* a damsel whose courses have commenced, to Raurava."

Nákapṛishṭha is the highest heaven of the three specified. Raurava is a hell: see Vol. II., p. 216.

Ratnagarbha would have proved himself inconsistent indeed, if, while citing the two preceding stanzas with tacit approval, he had expressed himself as represented in note 2 to p. 101, *supra*.

* I find only this reading:

यजेत वाश्वमेधेन विधिवद्दक्षिणावता ।

This is to be rendered: "or offers a hippocaust accompanied by remuneration agreeably to rule."

† The *Brahma-puráńa* is there quoted much to this effect. The *Brahmáńḍa-puráńa*—with many other authorities,—is adduced, by Hemádri, as follows:

लोहितो यस्तु वर्णेन मुखे पुच्छे च पाण्डुरः ।
श्वेतः खुरविषाणाभ्यां स नीलो वृष उच्यते ॥
चरणाश्च मुखं पुच्छं यस्य श्वेतानि गोपतेः ।
लाक्षारससवर्णश्च तं नीलमिति निर्दिशेत् ॥

‡ In the *Áchárachandriká*, bulls of different colours are appropriated to different castes.

the Puráńas,—especially in the Váyu, Kúrma, Márkańdeya, Vámana, and Garuda. The Matsya and Padma (Srishti Khańda) contain descriptions which are much the same as that of the Váyu. The accounts of the Brahma, Agni, and Varáha are less full and regular than in some of the others; and in none of them is the subject so fully and perspicuously treated as in our text. For satisfactory information, however, the Śráddha Mayúkha and the Nirńaya Sindhu should be consulted.*

* The prime authority on the subject of obsequies is, beyond all question, the voluminous *Śráddhakalpa* of Hemádri,—a work which the *Śráddhamayúkha* and *Nirńayasindhu* perpetually lay under contribution.

CHAPTER XVII.

Of heretics, or those who reject the authority of the Vedas: their origin, as described by Vasishṭha to Bhíshma: the gods, defeated by the Daityas, praise Vishṇu: an illusory being, or Buddha, produced from his body.

PARÁŚARA.—Thus, in former days, spake the holy Aurva to the illustrious monarch Sagara, when he inquired concerning the usages proper to be practised (by mankind): and thus I have explained to you the whole of those observances against which no one ought to transgress.*

MAITREYA.—You have told me, venerable sir, that an ancestral rite is not to be looked upon by certain persons, amongst whom you mentioned such as were apostates. I am desirous to learn whom you intended by that appellation;† what practices bestow such a title upon a man; and what is the character of the individual to whom you alluded.

PARÁŚARA.—The Rig-, Yajur-, and Sáma-Vedas constitute the triple covering of the several castes; and the sinner who throws this off is said to be naked (or apostate).‡ The three Vedas are the raiment of all the orders§ (of men); and, when that is discarded,

---

* मयाप्येतदशेषेण कथितं भवतो द्विज ।
समुल्लङ्घ्य सदाचारं कश्चिन्नाप्नोति शोभनम् ॥

† षण्ढापविद्धप्रमुखा विदिता भगवन्मया ।
उदक्याद्याश्च मे सर्वे नग्नमिच्छामि वेदितुम् ॥

‡ ऋग्यजुःसामसंज्ञेयं त्रयी वर्णावृतिर्द्विज ।
एतामुज्झति यो मोहात्स नग्नः पातकी स्मृतः ॥

§ *Varṇa.*

they are left bare.[1] On this subject hear what I heard my grandfather, the pious Vasishtha, relate to the magnanimous Bhíshma:

There was, formerly, a battle between the gods and demons,* for the period of a divine year, in which the gods were defeated by the demons† under the command of Hráda.[2] The discomfited deities fled to the northern shore of the milky ocean,‡ where, engaging in religious penance, they thus prayed to Vishńu: "May

[1] This idea is expressed in nearly the same terms, in the Váyu Puráńa:

सर्वेषामेव भूतानां त्रयी संवरणं स्मृता ।
परित्यजन्ति ये मोहात्ते वै नग्नादयो जनाः ॥

"The three Vedas are the covering of all beings; and they who throw it off, through delusion, are called Nagnas, naked." The notion is, probably, original with neither of the Puráńas; and the metaphorical sense of the term is not that in which it was first employed: ascetics, whether of the Bauddha or of the Digambara order of Jainas, being, literally, Nagnas,—or, going naked. The qualified application of it, however, was rendered necessary by the same practice being familiar to ascetics of the orthodox faith. To go naked was not necessarily a sign of a heretic; and, therefore, his nudity was understood to be, rejecting the raiment of holy writ. Thus, the Váyu Puráńa extends the word to all ascetics—including naked Brahmans,—who practise austerities fruitlessly, that is, heretically or hypocritically:

वृथादण्डी वृथामुण्डी वृथानग्नश्च यो द्विजः ।
वृथाव्रती वृथाजापी ते वै नग्नादयो जनाः ॥

"The Brahman who unprofitably bears a staff, shaves his head, goes naked, makes a vow, or mutters prayers,—all such persons are called Nagnas and the like."

[2] A son of Hirańyakaśipu (Vol. II., p. 30).

* *Asura.* † *Daitya.* ‡ See Vol. II., p. 200.

the first of beings, the divine Vishńu, be pleased with the words that we are about to address to him, in order to propitiate the lord of (all) worlds; from which mighty cause all (created things) have originated, and into whom they shall again dissolve! Who is able to declare his praise? We, who have been put to shame by the triumph of our foes, will glorify thee, although thy true power and might be not within the reach of words.* Thou art earth, water, fire, air, ether, mind,† crude matter,‡ and (primeval) soul.§ All this elementary creation, with or without visible form, is thy body; all, from Brahmá to a stock,|| diversified by place and time. Glory to thee, who art Brahmá, thy first form, evolved from the lotos springing from thy navel, for the purpose of creation! Glory to thee,¶ who art Indra,** the sun, Rudra, the Vasus,†† fire,‡‡ the winds,§§ and even, also, ourselves! Glory to thee, Go-

---

* [illegible]

"*Albeit* thy real selfhood *is* not within the scope of words, yet we, whose might has been destroyed by discomfiture at the hands of our enemies, *being* solicitous of *renewed* welfare, will, *according to our understanding*, laud thee."

The commentator explains this stanza in detail.

† *Antahkarańa*. ‡ *Pradhána*. See Vol. I., p. 20, note *.

§ *Puṁs*. It is qualified by *tatpara*, 'superior thereto', *viz.*, to *pradhána*.

|| आब्रह्मस्तम्बपर्यन्तम् । We have, here, the very words with which the *Sánkhya-pravachana*, III., 47, begins.

¶ Supply 'identical with the gods', *devátman*.

** Śakra, in the original.

†† See, for the Vasus, Vol. II., pp. 22, 23.

‡‡ I find 'the Aświns'; for whom *vide supra*, p. 21.

§§ 'The Maruts.' See Vol. II., p. 79.

vinda, who art all demons, whose essence is arrogance and want of discrimination, unchecked by patience or self-control!* Glory to thee, who art the Yakshas, whose nature is charmed with sounds, and whose frivolous hearts perfect knowledge cannot pervade!† Glory to thee, who art all fiends that walk by night, sprung from the quality of darkness, fierce, fraudulent, and cruel!‡ Glory to thee, Janárdana, who art that piety which is the instrument of recompensing the virtues of those who abide in heaven!§ Glory to thee, who art one with the saints, whose perfect nature is ever blessed, and traverses, unobstructed, all permeable elements!|| Glory to thee, who art one with the serpent-race, double-tongued, impetuous, cruel, insatiate of enjoyment, and abounding with wealth! Glory to thee, who art one with the Rishis, whose nature is free from sin or defect, and is identified with wisdom and tranquillity! Glory to thee, O lotos-eyed, who art one with time, the form that devours, without remorse, all created things, at the ter-

---

* दम्भप्रायमसंबोधि तितिक्षादमवर्जितम्।
यद्रूपं तव गोविन्द तस्मै दैत्यात्मने नमः॥

† नातिज्ञानवहा यस्मिन्नाड्यः स्तिमिततेजसि।
शब्दादिलोभि यत्तस्मै तुभ्यं यक्षात्मने नमः॥

‡ क्रौर्यमायामयं घोरं यच्च रूपं तवासितम्।
निशाचरात्मने तस्मै नमस्ते पुरुषोत्तम॥

§ स्वर्गस्थधर्मिसद्धर्मफलोपकरणं तव।
धर्माख्यं च तथा रूपं नमस्तस्मै जनार्दन॥

|| हर्षप्रायमसंसर्गि गतिमद्गमनादिषु।
सिद्धाख्यंच यद्रूपं तस्मै सिद्धात्मने नमः॥

mination of the Kalpa!* Glory to thee, who art Rudra, the being that dances (with delight), after he has swallowed up all things,—the gods and the rest,—without distinction! Glory to thee, Janárdana, who art man, the agent in developing the results of that activity which proceeds from the quality of foulness! Glory to thee, who art brute animals, the universal spirit that tends to perversity, which proceeds from the quality of darkness, and is encumbered with the twenty-eight kinds of obstructions![1]† Glory to thee, who art that chief spirit which is diversified in the vegetable world, and which, as the essence‡ of sacrifice, is the instrument of accomplishing the perfection of the universe! Glory to thee, who art everything, and whose primeval form is the objects of perception, and heaven, and animals, and men, and gods!§ Glory to thee, who art the cause of causes, the supreme spirit; who art distinct from us and all beings composed of intelligence and matter and the like, and with whose

---

[1] See Vol. I., p. 71, note 2.

---

* भक्षयत्यथ कल्पान्ते भूतानि यद्वारितम् ।
त्वद्रूपं पुण्डरीकाक्ष तस्मै कालात्मने नमः ॥

For Puṇḍaríkáksha, see Vol. I., p. 2, note 1.

† अष्टाविंशद्वधोपेतं यद्रूपं तामसं तव ।
उन्मार्गगामि सर्वात्मंस्तस्मै पश्वात्मने नमः ॥

Some MSS. have the reading अष्टाविंशद्विधोपेतं, to which the commentator, followed by the Translator, gives the preference.

‡ *Anga*.

§ तिर्यङ्मनुष्यदेवादि व्योमशब्दादिकं च यत् ।
रूपं तवादेः सर्वस्य तस्मै सर्वात्मने नमः ॥

primeval nature there is nothing that can be compared! We bow to thee, O lord, who hast neither colour, nor extension, nor bulk,* nor any predicable qualities; and whose essence,† purest of the pure, is appreciable only by holy sages.‡ We bow to thee, in the nature of Brahma, uncreated, undecaying;§ who art in our bodies, and in all other bodies, and in all living creatures; and besides whom there is nothing else. We glorify that Vásudeva, the (sovereign) lord (of all), who is without soil, the seed of all things, exempt from dissolution, unborn, eternal; being, in essence, the supreme condition of spirit,‖ and, in substance,¶ the whole of this (universe)."

Upon the conclusion of their prayers,** the gods beheld the sovereign deity Hari, armed with the shell, the discus, and the mace, riding on Garuda. Prostrating themselves before him, they addressed him, and said: "Have compassion upon us, O lord, and protect us, who have come to thee for succour from the Daityas! They have seized upon the three worlds, and appropriated the offerings which are our portion, taking care not to transgress the precepts of the Veda. Although we, as well as they, are parts of thee, of whom all beings consist, yet we behold the world impressed by the ignorance of unity, with the belief of

---

* *Ghana.*

† *Rúpa.*

‡ *Paramarshi.*

§ *Avyaya.* See Vol. I., p. 17, note *.

‖ *Paramapadátmavat.*

¶ *Rúpa* is here rendered by both "essence" and "substance".

** *Stotra.*

its separate existence. Engaged in the duties of their respective orders,* and following the paths prescribed by holy writ, practising, also, religious penance, it is impossible for us to destroy them. Do thou, whose wisdom is immeasurable,† instruct us in some device by which we may be able to exterminate the enemies of the gods‡!"

When the mighty Vishńu heard their request, he emitted from his body an illusory form,§ which he gave to the gods, and thus spake: "This deceptive vision|| shall wholly beguile the Daityas; so that, being led astray from the path of the Vedas, they may be put to death: for all gods, demons, or others, who shall be opposed to the authority of the Veda, shall perish by my might, whilst exercised for the preservation of the world. Go, then, and fear not. Let this delusive vision precede you: it shall, this day, be of great service unto you, O gods!"¶

* *Varńa.* † *Ameyátman.* ‡ *Asura.*

§ *Máyámoha*, "the deluder by illusion." || *Máyámoha.*

¶ Most of my MSS., including all those accompanied by the commentary, here add:

पराशर उवाच ।
इत्युक्ताः प्रणिपत्यैनं ययुर्देवा यथागतम् ।
मायामोहोऽपि तैः सार्धं ययौ यत्र महासुराः ॥

CHAPTER XVIII.

Buddha goes to the earth, and teaches the Daityas to contemn the Vedas: his sceptical doctrines: his prohibition of animal sacrifices. Meaning of the term Bauddha. Jainas and Bauddhas: their tenets. The Daityas lose their power, and are overcome by the gods. Meaning of the term Nagna. Consequences of neglect of duty. Story of Śatadhanu and his wife Śaibyá. Communion with heretics to be shunned.

PARÁŚARA.—After this, the great delusion,* having proceeded (to earth), beheld the Daityas, engaged in ascetic penances, upon the banks of the Narmadá river;[1] and, approaching them, in the semblance of a naked mendicant,† with his head shaven, and carrying a bunch of peacock's feathers,[2] he thus addressed them, in gentle accents: "Ho, lords of the Daitya race, wherefore is it that you practise these acts of penance?

---

[1] The situation chosen for the first appearance of the heresy agrees well enough with the great prevalence of the Jaina faith in the west of India, in the eleventh and twelfth centuries (Asiatic Researches, Vol. XVI., p. 818), or, perhaps, a century earlier, and is a circumstance of some weight, in investigating the date of the Vishńu Puráńa.

[2] A bunch of peacock's feathers is still an ordinary accompaniment of a Jaina mendicant. According to the Hindí poem, the Příthu Rai Charitra, it was borne by the Buddhist Amara Simha. But that work is not, perhaps, very good authority for Bauddha observances,—at least, of an ancient date.

---

* *Máyámoha.* † *Digambara.*

Is it with a view to recompense in this world? or in another?" "Sage," replied the Daityas, "we pursue these devotions, to obtain a reward hereafter. Why should you make such an inquiry?"* "If you are desirous of final emancipation," answered the seeming ascetic,† "attend to my words; for you are worthy of a revelation‡ which is the door to ultimate felicity. The duties that I will teach you are the secret path to liberation: there are none beyond, or superior to, them.§ By following them you shall obtain either heaven or exemption from future existence. You, mighty beings, are deserving of such (lofty) doctrine." By such persuasions, and by many specious arguments,|| did this delusive being mislead the Daityas from the tenets of the Vedas; teaching, that the same thing might be for the sake of virtue and of vice; might be, and might not be; might, or might not, contribute to liberation; might be the supreme object,¶ and not the supreme object; might be effect, and not be effect; might be manifest, or not be manifest; might be the duty of those who go naked, or who go clothed in much raiment. And so the Daityas were seduced from their proper duties by the repeated lessons of their illusory preceptor, maintaining the equal truth

* पारत्र्यफललाभाय तपश्चर्या महामते।
अस्माभिरियमारब्धा किंवा तेऽत्र विवक्षितम्॥

† *Máyámoha.* ‡ *Dharma.*

§ धर्मो विमुक्तेरर्होऽयं नैतस्मादपरः परः।

|| एवंप्रकारैर्बहुभिर्युक्तिदर्शनचर्चितैः।

¶ *Paramártha.*

of contradictory tenets;[1]* and they were called Arhatas,[2] from the phrase he had employed, of "Ye are worthy (Arhatha) of this great doctrine,"—that is, of the false doctrines which he persuaded them to embrace.†

The foes of the gods‡ being, thus, induced to apostatize from the religion of the Vedas, by the delusive person (sent by Vishńu), became, in their turn, teachers of the same heresies, and perverted others; and these, again, communicating their principles to others, by whom they were still further disseminated, the Ve-

---

[1] In this and the preceding contradictions it is probable that the writer refers, although not with much precision, to the sceptical tenets of the Jainas, whence they are called, commonly, Syádvádins, assertors of probabilities, or of what may be. These usually form seven categories, or: 1. a thing is; 2. it is not; 3. it is, and it is not; 4. it is not definable; 5. it is, but is not definable; 6. it is not, neither is it definable; 7. it is, and it is not, and is not definable. Hence the Jainas are also termed Saptavádins and Saptabhangins, assertors and oppugners of seven propositions. Asiatic Researches, Vol. XVII., p. 271;§ and Transactions of the Royal Asiatic Society, Vol. I., p. 555.‖

[2] Here is further confirmation of the Jainas being intended by our text; as the term Arhat is, more particularly, applied to them, although it is also used by the Buddhists.

---

* एवमनेकान्तवादं च मायामोहेन नैकधा ।
तेन दर्शयता दैत्याः स्वधर्मास्त्याजिता द्विज ॥

† अर्हथैनं महाधर्मं मायामोहेन ते यतः ।
प्रोक्तास्तमाश्रिता धर्ममार्हतास्तेन तेऽभवन् ॥

‡ *Asura.*

§ Or Professor Wilson's collected essays, Vol. I., pp. 315, 316.

‖ Or Colebrooke's *Miscellaneous Essays*, Vol. I., pp. 386, 387.

das were, in a short time, deserted by most of the Daitya race. Then the same deluder, putting on garments of a red colour, assuming a benevolent aspect, and speaking in soft and agreeable tones, addressed others of the same family, and said to them: "If, (mighty) demons, you cherish a desire either for heaven or for final repose,* desist from the iniquitous massacre of animals (for sacrifice), and hear (from me what you should do). Know that all (that exists) is composed of discriminative knowledge.† Understand my words; for they have been uttered by the wise. This world subsists without support,‡ and, engaged in the pursuit of error, which it mistakes for knowledge, as well as vitiated by passion and the rest, revolves in the straits of existence." In this manner, exclaiming to them, "Know!" (Budhyadhwam), and they replying, "It is known" (Budhyate), these Daityas were induced, by the arch-deceiver, to deviate from their religious duties§ (and become Bauddhas), by his repeated argu-

---

* *Nirváńa.*

† *Vijnána.* The commentator explains this term by *buddhi.* He says that the doctrine of the Yogácháras—a sect of Bauddhas,—is here set forth. According to Colebrooke,—*Miscellaneous Essays*, Vol. I., p. 391,—the Yogácháras "except internal sensation or intelligence (*vijnána*), and acknowledge all else to be void. They maintain the eternal existence of conscious sense alone."

‡ This is the faith of the Mádhyamikas, agreeably to the scholiast. These "maintain that all is void (*sarva śúnya*); following, as it seems, a literal interpretation of Buddha's *sútras.*" Colebrooke's *Miscellaneous Essays*, Vol. I., p. 391. See, further, on the Yogácháras and Mádhyamikas, Burnouf's *Introduction à l'Histoire du Buddhisme Indien*, Vol. I., pp. 449 *et seq.*

§ I find no reading but this:

एवं बुध्यत बुध्यध्वं बुध्यतैवमितीरयन् ।
मायामोहः स दैतेयान्धर्ममत्याजयन्निजम् ॥

ments and variously urged persuasions.[1] When they had abandoned their own faith, they persuaded others to do the same: and the heresy spread; and many deserted the practices enjoined by the Vedas and the laws.

The delusions of the false teacher paused not with the conversion of the Daityas to the Jaina and Bauddha* heresies; but, with various erroneous tenets,† he prevailed upon others to apostatize, until the whole were led astray, and deserted the doctrines and observances inculcated by the three Vedas. Some then spake evil of the sacred books; some blasphemed the gods; some treated sacrifices and other devotional ceremonies with scorn; and others calumniated the Brahmans. "The precepts," they cried, that lead to the injury of

---

[1] We have, therefore, the Bauddhas noticed as a distinct sect. If the author wrote from a personal knowledge of Buddhists in India, he could not have written much later than the tenth or eleventh century.

"Saying 'thus understand, understand, understand thus,' he, the deluder by illusion, caused the Daiteyas—*i. e., sons of Diti*—to forsake their own religion."

The commentary recognises *budhyata*, not *budhyate*; as it says: बुध्यं बुध्यतेत्येव बुध्यस्वेति बौद्धपदनिर्वचनमर्थः ।

Burnouf, evidently without looking at the original of the passage here rerendered, departs still further from its literal sense than Professor Wilson, for whose "arch-deceiver" (*mahámoha*) he boldly substitutes Bouddha: "Connaissez (*budhyadhwam*), s'écriait le Buddha aux Démons qu'il voulait séduire. Cela est connu (*budhyate*), répondirent ses auditeurs." *Introduction à l'Histoire du Buddhisme Indien*, Vol. I., note 1 in pp. 70, 71.

* The translation adds the words "Jaina" and "Bauddha" to the original.

† The commentator explains: लोकायतिकमतभेदैः, "with varieties of the secularist belief."

animal life (as in sacrifices,) are highly reprehensible. To say, that casting butter into flame is productive of reward, is mere childishness. If Indra, after having obtained godhead by multiplied rites, is fed upon the wood used as fuel in holy fire, he is lower than a brute, which feeds, at least, upon leaves. If an animal slaughtered in religious worship is, thereby, raised to heaven, would it not be expedient for a man who institutes a sacrifice to kill his own father for a victim? If that which is eaten by one, at a Śráddha, gives satisfaction to another, it must be unnecessary for one who resides at a distance to bring food for presentation in person."[1]* "First, then, let it be determined what may be (rationally) believed by mankind; and then," said their preceptor, "you will find, that felicity may be expected from my instructions. The words of authority do not, mighty Asuras, fall from heaven: the text that has reason is, alone, to be acknowledged by me, and by such as you are."[2] By such and similar lessons the

---

[1] That is, according to the commentator, a Śráddha may be performed, for a man who is abroad, by any of his kinsmen who are tarrying at home: it will be of equal benefit to him as if he offered it himself; he will equally eat of the consecrated food.†

[2] We have, in these passages, no doubt, allusion to the Bár-

---

* तृप्तये जायते पुंसो भुक्तमन्येन चेत्ततः ।
दद्याच्छ्राद्धं श्रद्धयान्नं न वहेयुः प्रवासिनः ॥

† अन्येन श्राद्धेऽन्नं भुक्तमथच तृप्तये चेज्जायते तर्हि प्रवासिनोऽन्नं न वहेयुः । किंतु स्वधार्मिकाः पुत्रादिबन्धुभिः श्राद्धं दद्यात् । Commentary.

For the real meaning of the verse thus explicated, which the Translator misunderstood, see note * in p. 214, infra.

Daityas were perverted, so that not one of them admitted the authority of the Vedas.

---

haspatyas, or followers of Bṛihaspati, who seem to have been numerous and bold at some period anterior to the fourteenth century. Asiatic Researches, Vol. XVI., p. 5.*

---

* Or Professor Wilson's collected essays, Vol. I. pp. 6—7.

I subjoin Dr. Muir's translation of a metrical passage, quoted in the *Sarvadarśanasangraha*, purporting to represent the views of Bṛihaspati:

"There is no heaven, no final liberation, no soul [which continues to exist] in another world, nor any ceremonies of castes or orders which are productive of future reward.

"The Agnihotra sacrifice, the three Vedas, the mendicant's triple staff (*tridaṇḍa*), and the practice of smearing with ashes, are the means of livelihood ordained, by the Creator, for men who have neither understanding nor energy.

"If [it be true, that] an animal slaughtered at the Jyotishṭoma sacrifice is [in consequence,] exalted to heaven, why does not the worshipper immolate his own father?

"If a *śrāddha* (offering of food to the manes) satiates even defunct creatures, it is quite superfluous to furnish people who are setting out upon a journey with any provisions; [as their friends who remain behind can offer food to them].

"Since [as you say,] persons in heaven are filled by oblations presented upon earth, why is not food similarly offered [by those below,] to people on the roof of the house?

"While a man does live, let him live merrily, let him borrow money, and swallow clarified butter. How can a body return to Earth, after it has once been reduced to ashes?

"If a man goes to another world, when he quits his body, why does not affection for his kindred impel him to come back?

"Hence, ceremonies for the dead are a mere means of livelihood devised by the Brahmans, and nothing else.

"The three composers of the Veda were buffoons, rogues, and goblins. Every one has heard of *jarbhari*, *turphari*, and such other [nonsensical] exclamations of the Pandits.

"It is well known, that, in an *aśwamedha* (horse-sacrifice), the embraces of the horse must be received by the queen; and it is, in like manner, well known what other sorts of things, also, are to be grasped by these

When the Daityas had thus declined from the path of the holy writings, the deities took courage, and gathered together for battle. Hostilities, accordingly, were renewed: but the demons were now defeated and slain by the gods, who had adhered to the righteous path. The armour of religion, which had formerly protected the Daityas, had been discarded by them; and upon its abandonment followed their destruction.[1]*

[1] We may have, in this conflict of the orthodox divinities and heretical Daityas, some covert allusion to political troubles,

buffoons. In the same way, the eating of flesh is prescribed by these goblins." *Journal of the Royal Asiatic Society*, Vol. XIX., pp. 299—301.

Dr. Muir's learned and instructive notes must, for want of space, be omitted.

* The original of these two paragraphs has been more accurately rendered, by Dr. Muir, as follows: "The great Deceiver, practising illusion, next beguiled other Daityas by means of many other sorts of heresy. In a very short time, these Asuras (= Daityas), deluded by the Deceiver, abandoned the entire system founded on the ordinances of the triple Veda. Some reviled the Vedas; others, the gods; others, the ceremonial of sacrifice; and others, the Brahmans. This (they exclaimed,) is a doctrine which will not bear discussion: the slaughter [of animals, in sacrifice,] is not conducive to religious merit. [To say, that] oblations of butter consumed in the fire produce any future reward, is the assertion of a child. If Indra, after having attained to godhead by numerous sacrifices, feeds upon *śamí* and other woods, then an animal which eats leaves is superior to him. If it be a fact, that a beast slain in sacrifice is exalted to heaven, why does not the worshipper slaughter his own father? If a man is really satiated by food which another person eats, then *śráddhas* should be offered to people who are travelling abroad; and they, trusting to this, should have no need to carry any food along with them. After it has been settled, that this doctrine is entitled to credence, let the opinions which I express be pondered, and received as conducive to happiness. Infallible utterances do not, great Asuras, fall from the skies: it is only assertions founded on reasoning that are ac-

Thus, Maitreya, (you are to understand, that) those who have seceded from their original belief are said to be naked, because they have thrown off the garment of the Vedas. According to the law, there are four conditions (or orders of men of the three first castes),—the religious student, the householder, the hermit, and the mendicant.* There is no fifth state; and the unrighteous man who relinquishes the order of the householder, and does not become either an anchoret or a mendicant, is (also,) a naked (seceder). The man who neglects his permanent observances for one day and night, being able to perform them, incurs, thereby, sin for one day; and, should he omit them, not being in trouble, for a fortnight, he can be purified only by arduous expiation. The virtuous must (stop to) gaze upon the sun, after looking upon a person who has allowed a year to elapse without the observance of the

---

growing out of religious differences, and the final predominance of Brahmanism. Such occurrences seem to have preceded the invasion of India by the Mohammedans, and prepared the way for their victories.

---

cepted by me, and by other [intelligent] persons like yourselves. Thus, by numerous methods, the Daityas were unsettled by the great Deceiver; so that none of them any longer regarded the triple Veda with favour. When the Daityas had entered on this path of error, the deities mustered all their energies, and approached to battle. Then followed a combat between the gods and the Asuras; and the latter, who had abandoned the right road, were smitten by the former. In previous times, they had been defended by the armour of righteousness which they bore; but, when that had been destroyed, they, also, perished." *Journal of the Royal Asiatic Society*, Vol. XIX., p. 302.

For the remainder of this note, see the end of the volume.

* *Pariorájí.*

perpetual ceremonies; and they must bathe, with their clothes on, should they have touched him: but, for the individual himself, no expiation has been declared. There is no sinner, upon earth, more culpable than one in whose dwelling the gods,* progenitors, and spirits† are left to sigh, unworshipped. Let not a man associate, in residence, sitting, or society,‡ with him whose person, or whose house, has been blasted by the sighs of the gods, progenitors, and spirits. Conversation, interchange of civilities,§ or association|| with a man who, for a twelvemonth, has not discharged his religious duties, is productive of equality of guilt; and the person who eats in the house of such a man, or sits down with him, or sleeps on the same couch with him, becomes like him, instantaneously. Again; he who takes his food without showing reverence to the gods, progenitors, spirits, and guests, commits sin. How great is his sin! The Brahmans, and men of the other castes, who turn their faces away from their proper duties, become heretics, and are classed with those who relinquish pious works. Remaining in a place where there is too great an intermixture of the four castes is detrimental to the character of the righteous.

---

* Insert 'Ṛishis'.

† *Bhūta.*

‡ *Parichchhada.*

§ *Anupraśna.*

|| Here insert, by transfer, the words "for a twelvemonth." The original runs:

संभाषणानुप्रश्नादि सहास्यां चैव कुर्वतः ।
जायते तुल्यता पुंसस्तेनैव द्विज वत्सरम् ॥

The commentator says: संवत्सरं कुर्वतः । तेन । नग्नेन ।

Men fall into hell, who converse with one who takes his food without offering a portion to the gods, the sages,* the manes, spirits, and guests. Let, therefore, a prudent person carefully avoid the conversation, or the contact, and the like, of those heretics who are rendered impure by their desertion of the three Vedas. The ancestral rite, although performed with zeal and faith, pleases neither gods nor progenitors, if it be looked upon by apostates.†

It is related, that there was, formerly, a king named Śatadhanu, whose wife, Śaibyá, was (a woman) of great virtue. She was devoted to her husband, benevolent, sincere, pure, adorned with every female excellence, with humility, and discretion.‡ The Raja and his wife daily worshipped the god of gods, Janárdana, with pious meditations, oblations to fire, prayers, gifts, fasting, and every other mark of entire faith, and exclusive devotion. On one occasion, when they had fasted on the full moon of Kárttika, and had bathed in the Bhágírathí, they beheld, as they came up from the water, a heretic approach them, who was the friend of the Raja's military preceptor.§ The Raja, out of respect to the latter, entered into conversation with the heretic; but not so did the princess. Reflecting that she was observing a fast, she turned from him, and cast

---

* *Rishi.*

† श्रद्धावद्भिः कृतं यत्नाद्देवान्पितृपितामहान्
न प्रीणयति तच्छ्राद्धं यद्येभिरवलोकितम् ॥

‡ पतिव्रता महाभागा सत्यशौचदयान्विता ।
सर्वलक्षणसंपन्ना विनयेन नयेन च ॥

§ *Chápáchárya*; literally, 'archery-master.'

her eyes up to the sun. On their arrival at home, the husband and wife, as usual, performed the worship of Vishńu, agreeably to the ritual. After a time, the Raja, triumphant over his enemies, died; and the princess ascended the funeral-pile of her husband.

In consequence of the fault committed by Śatadhanu, by speaking to an infidel, when he was engaged in a solemn fast, he was born again, as a dog. His wife was born as the daughter of the Raja of Káśí, with a knowledge of the events of her preexistence, accomplished in every science,* and endowed with every virtue. Her father was anxious to give her, in marriage, to some suitable husband: but she constantly opposed his design; and the king was prevented, by her, from accomplishing her nuptials.† With the eye of divine intelligence, she knew that her own husband had been regenerate as a dog; and, going, once, to the city of Vaidiśá, she saw the dog, and recognized her former lord in him. Knowing that the animal was her husband, she placed upon his neck the bridal garland, accompanying it with the marriage-rites and prayers:‡ but he, eating the delicate food presented to him, expressed his delight, after the fashion of his species. At which she was much ashamed, and, bowing reverently

---

* *Vijnána.*

† तां पिता दातुकामोऽभूद्वराय विनिवारितः ।
तयैव तन्व्या विरतो विवाहारम्भतो नृपः ॥

‡ The original has:

ददौ तस्मै वराहारं सत्कारप्रवणं शुभम् ।

"She bestowed on him excellent cates and kind treatment."

This is instead of "she placed - - prayers." The cates are referred to just below.

to him, thus spake to her degraded* spouse: "Recall to memory, illustrious prince, the ill-timed politeness on account of which you have been born as a dog, and are now fawning upon me. In consequence of speaking to a heretic, after bathing in a sacred river, you have been condemned to this abject birth. Do you not remember it?" Thus reminded, the Raja recollected his former condition, and was lost in thought, and felt deep humiliation. With a broken spirit, he went forth from the city, and, falling dead in the desert, was born anew, as a jackal. In the course of the following year, the princess knew what had happened, and went to the mountain Koláhala, to seek for her husband. Finding him there, the lovely daughter of the king of the earth said to her lord, thus disguised as a jackal: "Dost thou not remember, O king, the circumstance of conversing with a heretic, which I called to thy recollection, when thou wast a dog?" The Raja, thus addressed, knew that what the princess had spoken was true, and, thereupon, desisted from food, and died. He then became a wolf; but his blameless wife knew it, and came to him in the lonely forest, and awakened his remembrance of his original state. "No wolf art thou," she said, "but the illustrious sovereign Śatadhanu. Thou wast then a dog, then a jackal, and art now a wolf." Upon this, recollecting himself, the prince abandoned his life, and became a vulture; in which form his lovely queen still found him, and aroused him to a knowledge of the past. "Prince," she exclaimed, "recollect yourself: away with this uncouth form, to which the sin of

* *Kuyonija.*

conversing with a heretic has condemned you!" The Raja was next born as a crow; when the princess, who, through her mystical powers, was aware of it, said to him: "Thou art now, thyself, the eater of tributary grain, to whom, in a prior existence, all the kings of the earth paid tribute."[1] Having abandoned his body, in consequence of the recollections excited by these words, the king next became a peacock, which the princess took to herself, and petted, and fed, constantly, with such food as is agreeable to birds of its class. The king of Káśí[*] instituted, at that time, the solemn sacrifice of a horse. In the ablutions with which it terminated,[†] the princess caused her peacock to be bathed; bathing, also, herself: and she then reminded Satadhanu how he had been successively born as various animals. On recollecting this, he resigned his life. He was, then, born as the son of a person of distinction;[‡] and, the princess now assenting to the wishes of her father to see her wedded, the king of Káśí caused it to be made known, that she would elect a bridegroom from those who should present themselves as suitors

---

[1] There is a play upon the word Bali, which means 'tribute', or 'fragments of a meal, scattered abroad to the birds', &c.

[*] The original has जनको राजा, 'King Janaka'; thus revealing the monarch's name. This Janaka is nowhere else mentioned in the Vishṇu-purāṇa.

[†] Avabhṛitha. See the Laws of the Mánavas, XI., 83.

[‡] We read, in the Sanskrit:

कवे च जनकस्यैव पुरोऽसौ कुमद्राजन: ।

"And he was born as son of the very magnanimous Janaka."

Here, then, emerges still another Janaka; unless we suppose the princess to have married her own brother or half-brother.

for her hand.* When the election took place, the princess made choice of her former lord, who appeared amongst the candidates, and again invested him with the character of her husband. They lived happily together;† and, upon her father's decease, Śatadhanu ruled over the country of Videha.‡ He offered many sacrifices, and gave away (many) gifts, and begot sons, and subdued his enemies in war; and, having duly exercised the sovereign power, and cherished (benignantly,) the earth, he died, as became his warrior-birth,§ in battle. His queen again followed him in death, and, conformably to sacred precepts, once more mounted, cheerfully, his funeral pile. The king, then, along with his princess, ascended beyond the sphere of Indra, to the regions where all desires are for ever gratified,‖ ob-

---

* ततः सा पितरं तन्वी विवाहार्थमचोदयत् ।
स चापि कारयामास पिता तस्याः स्वयंवरम् ॥

† बुभुजे च तया सार्धं सभोगाख्यं नृपः ।

"And the prince, with her, governed Sabhoga."

Of this country I know of no other notice. There are obvious objections to reading स भोगाख्यम्; and I find no lection संभोगाख्यम्.

‡ The text seems to point to some close connexion between Káśi, Vaidiśá, and Videha. For Káśi, see Vol. II., p. 163, notes 12 and *; and, for Videha, *ibid.*, p. 165, notes 9 and ¶.

Vidiśá—perhaps intended by Vaidiśá,—is mentioned in Vol. II., p. 150, note 6. The word Vaidiśá may be due to the confounding, by ignorant or heedless copyists, of the *i* with the *ai* of old MSS. transcribed by them. Every one who has used such MSS., or has had to do with mediæval inscriptions, must have encountered, repeatedly, the particle वि so written as to be all but, if not quite, undistinguishable from वै, and *vice versa*. Perhaps the unjustifiable Triyáruṇa may now be accounted for: *vide supra*, foot of p. 37. Also see p. 158, note ‡‡; and Burnouf's *Introduction*, &c., Vol. I., p. 86, note 2, on Viśálá and Vaiśáli.

§ This phrase is an expansion of *dharmatas*.

‖ This translates *lokán kámaduhah*. For the region called by the equivalent name Kámaduha, *vide supra*, p. 164, Translator's note.

taining ever-during and unequalled happiness in heaven, the perfect felicity that is the rarely realized reward of conjugal fidelity.[1] *

Such, Maitreya, is the sin of conversing with a heretic, and such are the expiatory effects of bathing after the solemn sacrifice of a horse,† as I have narrated them to you. Let, therefore, a man carefully avoid the discourse or contact of an unbeliever, especially at seasons of devotion, and when engaged in the performance of religious rites preparatory to a sacrifice.‡ If it be necessary that a wise man should look at the sun, after beholding one who has neglected his domestic ceremonies for a month, how much greater need must there be of expiation, after encountering one who has wholly abandoned the Vedas, one who is supported by infidels, or who disputes the doctrines of holy writ? Let not a person treat with even the civility of speech, heretics, those who do forbidden acts, § pretended saints,‖ scoundrels, sceptics,[2] ¶ and hypocrites. Intercourse with such

---

[1] The legend is peculiar to the Vishńu Puráńa, although the doctrine it inculcates is to be found elsewhere.

[2] Haitukas, 'causalists;' either the followers of the Nyáya or

---

* स्वर्गाद्यव्ययमतुलं दाम्पत्यमतिदुर्लभम् ।
प्राप्तं पुण्यफलं प्राप्य संशुद्धिं तां द्विजोत्तम ॥

† तथाश्वमेधावभृथस्नानमाहात्म्यमेव च ।

‡ विशेषतः क्रियाकाले यज्ञादौ चापि दीक्षितः ।

§ *Vikarmastha.*

‖ *Baidálavratika.* The original of "hypocrites" is *bakavritti.*

¶ The patrons of the Veda, like their analogues of all times and climes, have a just dread of the exercise of right reason; and *haituka*, or 'rationalist', is, of course, a designation of evil omen to orthodox Hindus. The annexed extract from the *Virodhapadamanjarí* of Varadarája, or

iniquitous wretches, even at a distance,—all association

'logical' philosophy, or Bauddhas; those who take nothing upon authority, and admit nothing that cannot be proved: or it is ex-

---

Varada Bhaṭṭa,—*vide supra*, p. 136, note *,—may remind the reader of Sir William Hamilton's demolition, quotationwise, of the mathematics. One hapless logician, we here read, was cursed to become a jackal; while another was transformed into a ghoul. A person who addicts himself to the Nyáya is to be reckoned a dog: and Śankara Áchárya is said to stigmatize such a one as a bull sans tail and horns. The extract here follows:

किंच तर्कवैशेषिकादीन्यपि कानिचिद्दर्शनानि निषिद्धानि दृश्यन्ते । तथा हि । आदिपर्वणि [*ll.* 4192–6] भीष्मोत्पत्तिकथनानन्तरं पाण्डुः कुन्तीं प्राह ।

स वै दीर्घतमा नाम शापादृषिरजायत ।
स पुत्राञ्जनयामास गौतमादीन्महायशाः ।
लोभमोहाभिभूतास्तु पुत्रास्ते गौतमादयः ॥ इति ।

अत एव हयशीर्षपञ्चरात्रे ।

कपिलश्चाक्षपादश्च नास्तिको नग्न एव च ।
अपथस्तामसा एते शास्त्रमेषां विमोहनम् ॥ इति ।

मोक्षधर्मे [Read *Anuśásana-parvan*, *ll.* 9195—6] ।

आन्वीक्षिकीं तर्कविद्यामनुरक्तो निरर्थिकाम् ।
हेतुवादान्ब्रुवन्सत्सु विजेता ब्राह्मणादिषु ॥
तस्येयं फलनिष्पत्तिः सृगालत्वं मम द्विज ।
न तर्कशास्त्रदग्धाय न वाच्यं पिशुनाय च ॥ इति ।

दानधर्मे ।

आन्वीक्षिक्यां सदासक्तं नरं श्वानं च तं विदुः ।

आदित्यपुराणे ।

बौद्धा वैशेषिका जैना भविष्यन्ति कलौ युगे ।

पद्मपुराणे ।

कणादं गौतमं शक्तिमुपमन्युं च जैमिनिम् ।
अपथस्तामसा एते शास्त्रमेषां विमोहनम् ।
मत्कथ्याचार्यविभ्रतिरीतिरभेदो मम गोपितः ॥ इति ।

रामायणेऽयोध्याकाण्डे ।

धर्मशास्त्रेषु मुख्येषु विद्यमानेषु दुर्बुधाः ।
बुद्धिमान्वीक्षिकीं प्राप्य निरर्थं प्रवदन्ति ते ॥

with schismatics,—defiles. Let a man, therefore, care-

---

plained, those who, by argument, cast a doubt upon the efficacy

अवेत्यपण्डितमानी यो ब्राह्मणो वेदनिन्दकः ।
आन्वीक्षिकीं तर्कविद्यामनुरक्तो निरर्थिकाम् ॥
हेतुवादान्प्रवक्ता तु विजेता हेतुवादिकः ।
आक्रोष्टा चातिवक्ता च ब्राह्मणानां सदैव हि ॥
सर्वाभिशङ्की मूढश्च बालश्च कटुवागपि ।
बोद्धव्यस्तादृशस्तात नरश्वानं च तं विदुः ॥
यथा श्वाभिमतं दुष्टं हन्तुं चैवाभिसृज्यते ।
एवं संभाषणार्थाय स हि शास्त्रवधाय च ॥ इति ।

मिताक्षरायाम् ।

हैतुकान्बकवृत्तींश्च वाङ्मात्रेणापि नार्चयेत् ।

तर्काप्रतिष्ठानादिति व्याससूत्रम् (II., I., 11) । नैषा तर्केण मतिरापनेया इति श्रुतिः [*Katha Upanishad*, II., 9] । पाद्मे पार्वतीं प्रतीश्वर आह ।

मच्छक्त्यावेशितैर्विप्रैः संप्रोक्तानि ततः परम् ।
कणादेन तु संप्रोक्तं शास्त्रं वैशेषिकं महत् ॥
गौतमेन तथा न्यायं सांख्यं तु कपिलेन वै ।
द्विजन्मना जैमिनिना पूर्वं वेदमयार्थतः ॥
निरीश्वरेण वादेन कृतं शास्त्रं महत्तमम् ॥ इति ।

पराशरोपपुराणे ।

अक्षपादप्रणीते च काणादे सांख्ययोगयोः ।
त्याज्यः श्रुतिविरुद्धोंऽशः श्रुत्येकशरणैर्नृभिः ।
जैमिनीये च वैयासे विरुद्धांशो न कश्चन ॥ इति ।

काशीमाहात्म्ये । तर्कशास्त्रं पठित्वा तत्परिभाव्य महातार्किको जातः । तदनन्तरमसंख्याममन्तरादिकं कृत्वा मातुलानां भक्षणं कृत्वा स्थितवान् । चहर्यन्देशे कांसगृध्रोपरि महापिशाचो भूत्वा ब्रह्मकल्पपर्यन्तं स्थितः । द्विजवेतालो नाम कश्चन ब्राह्मण इत्यादि सर्वत्र श्रूयते । अत एव बृहदारण्यकभाष्ये आचार्यचरणैरुक्तम् । पुच्छविषाणरहितास्तार्किकबलीवर्दाः प्रत्यवतिष्ठन्त इति । तस्माद्वैशेषिके तर्के चातुर्यं न पठनीयमित्येव प्रतीयते ।

Varadarája's citations and references are careless in the extreme. To the source of the extract which he professes to take from the *Rámáyańa* a clue is indicated by the verses wrongly attributed to the *Moksha-dharma*; and the line which he assigns to the *Mitáksharú* is the very passage of the *Vishńu-puráńa* to which this note is appended.

fully avoid them.*

These, Maitreya, are the persons called naked, the meaning of which term you desired to have explained. Their very looks vitiate the performance of an ancestral oblation: speaking to them destroys religious merit for a whole day. These are the unrighteous heretics to whom a man must not give shelter,† and speaking to whom effaces whatever merit he may, that day, have obtained. Men, indeed, fall into hell, as the consequence of only conversing with those who unprofitably‡ assume the twisted hair and shaven crown; with those who feed without offering food to gods, spirits, and guests;§ and those who are excluded from the presentation of cakes and libations of water to the manes.||

---

of acts of devotion."

---

* दूरादपास्यः संपर्कः सहास्यापि च पापिभिः ।
पाषण्डिभिर्दुराचारैस्तस्मात्तान्परिवर्जयेत् ॥

† एते पाषण्डिनः पापा न ह्येतानालपेद्बुधः ।

This is the only reading that I find. Professor Wilson may have read *áśrayet*, for *álapet*; mistaking its meaning.

‡ *Vṛithá.*

§ मोघाशिनामविज्ञापितृनिराकृतानाम् ।

|| This last explanation is the only one given by the commentator,— in a line in the midst of an anonymous metrical quotation:

बहिष्कृतैः पितृभिश्च सत्कर्मसु च वैगुणः ।

But see the *Mánavadharmaśástra*, XII., 111, and Kullúka's gloss thereon.

In his *Essays, Analytical*, &c., Vol. I., pp. 5—7, Professor Wilson has given an account of the measures which he took, in India, towards preparing the materials that served as the basis of his Analyses of the Puráńas, a series of papers ultimately abandoned unfinished. Under his oversight, we read, "indices were drawn up in Sanskrit. To convert them into English, I employed several native young men, educated in the Hindu College, and well conversant with our language; and to them the Pandits explained the summary which they had compiled. The original and translation were examined by myself, and corrected wherever necessary. When any particular article appeared to promise interest or information, I had that translated in detail, or translated it myself; in the former case, revising the translation with the original."

From among all the works thus dealt with, none was the object of greater care than the *Vishńu-puráńa*. Of this a very large part was thought worthy of unabridged reproduction in English. Out of the scattered portions left untranslated, the longest occurs in the Book here completed, embracing Chapters VIII.—XVIII.

This being an appropriate place for a general note, and it being of interest to know the relation of the present version to that made in India, I shall here add a few specimens of the latter,—now the property of the India Office Library,—indicating the locality of the corresponding passages in the former.

Vol. I., p. 67, l. 6 *ab infra*.

"As the characteristics of seasons are seen (to be the same and identical in all their returnings), so in that manner they are the same in every beginning of the Yugs, &c. Thus, he creates, again and again, on the commencement of the Kalpas. This (Brahmá) is desirous of creating, has the power of so doing, and is joined with the power of making creations."

Vol. II., p. 273, l. 6.

"He who thinks on Vásudeva during his prayers, sacrifices, and worship, despises even the state of Mahendra."

Vol. II., p. 241, l. 5.

"In the same manner, O Maitreya, as the sun shines here in the midday, so does he shine in the other Dwipas in the midnight. He is always seen opposite, in the time of his setting and rising, (whether seen) from the cardinal points or the corners. Whoever observes the sun from any place, he is rising there; and wherever he disappears, he is setting there. The sun is constantly present, and is neither setting nor rising (in any place, in reality). The ideas of his setting and rising are obtained merely from his being either visible or invisible (in any particular place)."

Vol. II., p. 244, l. 6.

"The rays of the sun and fire, identical with light and heat, pervade, during both day and night, being mingled with each other."

Vol. II., p. 281, note *.

"Both these waters are productive of virtue and destructive of sin. These waters, O Maitreya, are of the Mandákiní; and it is the bathing in them that is called *Divyasnána*."

Vol. II., p. 309, l. 4 *ab infra.*

"When the world, being freed from works, is rendered void of defects, pure in its real form, and identical with knowledge, then the tree of desire produces no fruits, and all distinctions of matter are lost."

Vol. II., p. 330, l. 8.

"The earth, feet, legs, buttocks, thighs, belly, &c., are, thus, depending upon one another. In the same manner, therefore, as this palanquin is upon my shoulder, so you do bear a load, also."

Vol. III., p. 17, l. 7.

"In the Raivata Manwantara, he, the Vishńu, who is the superior of all the Devatás, was born in the womb of Sambhúti, with the Rájasagańa, under the title of Mánasa."

Vol. III., p. 65, l. 1.

"A fourth Samhitá was written by Romaharshańa, called Romaharshańiká. The essence of these four Samhitás, O Muni, or Maitreya, I have given in this Vishńu Puráńa, which I shall communicate to you."

Further, we have, in Vol. III., "Bhagadheya" *for* "Nábhanidishťa", p. 13, last line; "twenty-one", p. 23, l. 5; "Medhátithi", p. 25, l. 3; "Savarga", p. 27, l. 2; an omission of "Táras", p. 27, l. 6 and note ||; &c. &c. &c.

———

VISHŃU PURÁŃA.

BOOK IV.

CHAPTER I.

Dynasties of kings. Origin of the solar dynasty from Brahmá. Sons of the Manu Vaivaswata. Transformations of Ilá or Sudyumna. Descendants of the sons of Vivaswat: those of Nedishíha. Greatness of Marutta. Kings of Vaiśáli. Descendants of Śaryáti. Legend of Raivata: his daughter Revati married to Balaráma.

MAITREYA.—Venerable preceptor, you have explained to me the perpetual and occasional ceremonies which are to be performed by those righteous individuals who are diligent in their devotions; and you have, also, described to me the duties which devolve upon the several castes, and on the different orders of the human race. I have now to request you will relate to me the dynasties (of the kings who have ruled over the earth).[1]

---

[1] The complete series of the different dynasties is found elsewhere only in the Váyu, the Brahmáńda (which is the same), the Matsya, and the Bhágavata Puráńas. The Brahma Puráńa and the Hari Vaḿśa, the Agni, Linga, Kúrma, and Garuda Puráńas have lists of various extent, but none beyond the families of Páńdu and Kŕishńa. The Márkańdeya contains an account

Parášara.—I will repeat to you, Maitreya, an account of the family of Manu, commencing with Brahmá, and graced by a number of religious, magnanimous,* and heroic princes. Of which it is said: "The lineage of him shall never be extinct, who daily calls to mind the race of Manu, originating with Brahmá."[1] Listen, therefore, Maitreya, to the (entire) series† of the princes of this family, by which all sin shall be effaced.

Before (the evolution of) the mundane egg, existed Brahmá, who was Hirańyagarbha, the form of (that supreme) Brahma which consists of Vishńu as identical with the Rig-, Yajur-, and Sáma-‡ (Vedas); the primeval, uncreated cause§ of all worlds. From the right thumb of Brahmá was born the patriarch Daksha:[2] his daughter was Aditi, who was the mother‖ of

---

of a few of the kings of the solar dynasty alone; and the Padma, of a part of the solar and lunar princes only, besides accounts of individuals. In the Rámáyańa, Mahábhárata, and in the other Puráńas, occasional short genealogies and notices of individual princes occur. In general, there is a tolerable conformity: but this is not invariably the case; as we shall have occasion to observe.

[1] In the historical passages of all the Puráńas in which such occur, and, especially, in the Vishńu and Váyu, verses, apparently the fragments of a more ancient narrative, are frequently cited. It may, also, be noticed, as a peculiarity of this part of the Puráńa, that the narration is in prose.

[2] Daksha is elsewhere said to have been one of the mind-born sons of Brahmá, or to have been the son of the Prachetasas. See Vol. II., p. 9, note 1.

---

* *Víra*, which the commentator defines by *utsáhavat*, 'energetic'.

† *Ánupúrví*, 'succession.' ‡ The original adds 'etc.' § *Ádibhúta*.

‖ The father being Kaśyapa, according to the *Bhágavata-puráńa*, IX., I., 10.

the Sun.* The Manu (Vaivaswata) was the son of the celestial luminary; and his sons[1] were Ikshwáku,

---

[1] According to the nomenclature sometimes followed, and, as we shall have reason to conclude, intended in this place, there are ten sons of Manu. The commentator regards them, however, as but nine; considering Nábhága-nedishtha but one name, or, Nedishtha the father of Nábhága.† The number is generally stated to be nine; although there is some variety in the names, particularly in this name, which occurs Nabhágadishta, Nábhágarishta;‡ and also separated, as Nábhága, Nabhaga, or Nabhága; Nedishtha, Dishta, and Arishta: the latter, as in the Kúrma, distinctly stated, नाभागो ह्यरिष्टः । Again, नेदिष्टः सुमनाः श्रुतः । Brahma Puráńa. The commentator on the Hari Vaḿśa quotes the Vedas for Nábhágadishta: नाभानेदिष्ठं वै मानवमिति श्रुतेः ।§ But the name occurs as Nábhánedishtha in the Aitareya Bráhmańa of the Ṙigveda, where a story is told of his being excluded from all share of his inheritance, on the plea of his being wholly devoted to a religious life: नाभानेदिष्ठं वै मानवं ब्रह्मचर्यं वसन्तं भ्रातरो निरभजन् । See, also, Asiatic Researches, Vol. VIII., p. 384.¶ The name, as ordinarily written, Na-bhága, 'no-share,' has, nevertheless, an obvious connexion with the legend. The name of Nṙiga is found only in our text, the Padma, and the

---

* *Vivaswat*; and so in the next sentence.

For Vivaswat's wives, *vide supra*, p. 20, text and note 1.

† नाभागस्य पिता नेदिष्ठ इत्यर्थः । क्वचिन्नेदिष्ठस्थाने दिष्ट इत्यपि संज्ञा । Dishta is here recognized as a substitute, "somewhere", for Nedishtha. *Vide infra*, p. 240, notes 2, †, ††, and ‡‡.

‡ Corrected from "Nábhágarishtha".

§ This quotation is from Nílakańtha on the *Harivaḿśa*, *śl.* 614. Only I find, invariably, the reading नाभानेदिष्ठं, yielding Nábhánedishtha.

‖ V., 14. On the Nabánazdista of the ancient Pársís, see Professor R. Roth, *Zeitschrift der Deutschen morgenländischen Gesellschaft*, Vol. VI., pp. 243—247.

¶ Or Colebrooke's *Miscellaneous Essays*, Vol. I., p. 25.

Nŕiga,* Dhŕishńa, Śaryáti,† Narishyanta, Práḿśu, Nábhága, Nedishtha,‡ Karúsha,§ and Pŕishadhra.

Bhágavata: the Váyu has Najava. Práḿśu is, also, the reading of the Váyu and Agni, but not of the rest,¶ which have Vena, Vanya, Dańda, Kuśanábha, or Kavi, in its place. The Mahábhárata, Ádi Parvan,** p. 113, has: Vena,†† Dhŕishńu, Narishyanta, Nábhága, Ikshwáku, Karúsha, Śaryáti, Ilá, Pŕishadhra, and Nábhágárishta. The Padma Puráńa, in the Pátála Khańda, says there were 'ten,'‡‡ and names them Ikshwáku, Nŕiga, Dishta, Dhŕishta, Karúsha, Śaryáti, Narishyanta, Pŕishadhra, Nábhága, and Kavi.

* *Vide supra*, p. 13, note ††; *et infra*, p. 256, notes * and §.

† Several MSS. have Saryáti.

‡ Substituted, here and in numerous instances below, for the unmeaning "Nedishta". § In three MSS. I find Kárúsha.

|| This seems to have been mistaken for Nahava, into which one of Professor Wilson's MSS. corrupts Nahusha, itself an error for Nabhaga.

¶ But see note ‡‡, below.

** *Śl.* 3140—3142. The last person of this group is called, in the text, the tenth; and Nilakańtha, the commentator, says, of him: चतुर्दशा-नाभागारिष्टौ ऽयं नामानामितरि द्वन्द्वः। We are to understand, then, by नाभागारिष्टो, not one name, but an irregular combination of two.

†† The commentator Arjuna Miśra here reads Veńu.

‡‡ And so says the *Bhágavata-puráńa*,—IX., I., 11, 12,—which gives the same names, save Nabhaga for Nábhága. At VIII., XIII., 2, 3, it has, among ten names, both Nabhaga and Nábhága, omitting Nŕiga; and it puts Vasumat for Kavi. *Vide supra*, p. 14, note *.

Like our text at pp. 13, 14, *supra*, the *Márkańdeya-puráńa*, LXXIX., 11, 12, says that the Manu had nine sons: Ikshwáku, Nabhaga, Dhŕishta, Śaryáti, Narishyanta, Nábhága, Dishta, Karúsha, and Pŕishadhra. The Calcutta edition of the *Márkańdeya-puráńa* has, here, such bad readings as Śarmáti, Kurúsha, and Prushadhra. See, likewise, the same Puráńa, CXI., 4, 5.

In the *Harivaḿśa*, 613, 614, the names, in the best MSS., are, substantially, as in the *Márkańdeya-puráńa*; except that, instead of Nábhága and Dishta, we find Práḿśu and Nábhágárishta, with the variant Dańda and Nedishtha. Further, Dhŕishńu is a common substitute for its synonym Dhŕishta.

Before their birth, the Manu, being desirous of sons, offered a sacrifice* (for that purpose,) to Mitra and Varuńa; but, the rite being deranged, through an irregularity of the ministering priest, a daughter, Ilá,† was produced.[1] Through the favour of the two divinities,

---

[1] तत्रापहुते होतुरपचारादिला नाम कन्या बभूव । "That sacrifice being wrongly offered, through the improper invocations of the Hotri," &c.‡ It is also read अपहुते, 'frustrated.' This is rather a brief and obscure allusion to what appears to be an ancient legend, and one that has undergone various modifications.§

The Váyu-puráńa has two several lists of the sons of the Manu. The first names Ikshwáku, Nabhaga, Dhrishńu, Śaryáti, Narishyanta, Nábhága Arishía, Karúsha, Prishadhra, and Práńśu: the second, Ikshwáku, Nabhaga, Dhrishńa, Śaryáti, Narishyanta, Práńśu, Nábhága Arishía, Karúsha, and Prishadhra.

As each of these lists distinctly states that it reckons up only ten persons, we are to find but one in नाभागो ऽरिष्टः, which stands, here, in lieu of the more ordinary नाभागारिष्टः.

See the preceding page, note **; also, p. 240, note ‖, and p. 250, note *, infra.

* Ishti.

† See the references in note * to p. 236, infra; also, Professor Wilson's Translation of the Rigveda, Vol. I., p. 82, note a.

‡ It is to this effect that the passage is to be understood, if we read अपहुते, which lection the commentator prefers: तत्रिकमर्त्यापि मनुपत्न्या कन्यार्थं प्रार्थितस्य होतुरपचारात्कन्यासंकल्पकृपात् । अपहुते विफले जाते सति कन्याभूत् । He adds: अपहुतेरिति पाठे ऽपचाराद्धोमाद्वेतोरित्यर्थः । I nowhere find Professor Wilson's reading अपहुते.

§ Premising the names of the Manu's ten sons, the Bhágavata-puráńa, IX., I., 13—16, says, as translated by Burnouf:

"Avant leur naissance, quand le Manu n'avait pas encore d'enfants, le bienheureux Vasishtha, ce puissant sage, avait célébré le sacrifice de Mitra et de Varuńa, pour lui donner des fils.

"Alors Çraddhá, la femme du Manu, qui s'était soumise au vœu du lait, s'étant rendue auprès de l'officiant, se jeta à ses pieds, et le supplia de lui donner une fille.

"Mais à l'instant où le Bráhmane faisant les fonctions d'officiant,

however, (her sex was changed, and) she became a man, named Sudyumna. At a subsequent period, in con-

---

According to the Matsya, no change of sex took place, in the first instance. The eldest son of Manu was Ida or Ila (इड or इल), whom his father appointed sovereign of the seven Dwípas. In his progress round his dominions, Ila came to the forest of Śambhu or Śiva; entering into which, he was changed to a female, Ilá, agreeably to a promise made, formerly, by Śiva to Párvatí,—who had been, once, unseasonably broken in upon by some sages,*—that such a transformation should be inflicted on every male who trespassed upon the sacred grove. After a season, the brothers of Ila sought for him, and, finding him thus metamorphosed, applied to Vasishtha, their father's priest, to know the cause. He explained it to them, and directed them to worship Śiva and his bride. They did so, accordingly; and it was announced, by the deities, that, upon the performance of an Aśwamedha by Ikshwáku, Ila should become a Kimpurusha, named Sudyumna, and that he should be a male one month, and a female another month, alternately. The Váyu, which is followed by most of the other authorities, states, that, upon Manu's offering their share of the sacrifice to Mitra and Varuńa, instead of a boy, a girl was born; according to the Vedas: इला जज्ञे इति श्रुतिः । Manu desired her to follow him:

तामिलेत्येव होवाच मनुर्दण्डधरः प्रभुः ।
अनुगच्छामि भद्रं ते तमिला प्रत्युवाच ह ॥

Whence her name Ilá (from ila or ida, 'come'). There, however, Manu propitiates Mitra and Varuńa; and the girl Ilá is

---

venait de recevoir ses instructions de celui qui récite le Yadjus, et tenait entre ses mains l'offrande, l'attention qu'il donnait à la prière de Çraddhá, lui fit commettre une erreur dans la manière dont il prononça le mot Vachat.

"La méprise de l'officiant donna lieu à la naissance d'une fille qui fut nommée Ilâ."

* In Ilávrita, the scholiast says.

sequence of (becoming subject to the effects of) a malediction once pronounced by Śiva,* Sudyumna was

changed into the boy Ila, or Sudyumna, by their favour: as the Márkańdeya:†

तथेति ताभ्यामुक्ते तु देवाभ्यां सैव कन्यका ।
इला इल: समभवत्सुद्युम्न इति विश्रुत: ॥

Sudyumna's subsequent change to a female again is told much as in the Matsya; but his being alternately male and female is not mentioned in the Váyu, any more than it is in our text. The Bhágavata agrees, in that respect, with the Matsya; but it has, evidently, embellished the earlier part of the legend, by the introduction of another character, Śraddhá, the wife of the Manu. It is said, that it was by her instigation,—as she was desirous of having a girl,—that the ministering Brahmans altered the purpose of the rite; in consequence of which a girl, instead of a boy, was born. The similarity of the name has induced the learned author of the Origin of Pagan Idolatry to conceive that he has found the Ila of the Hindus in the Il or Ilus of the Phœnicians. "The Phenician *Il* is the masculine *Ila* of the Hindoos and Indo-Scythæ; and *Ila* was a title of Menu or Buddha, who was preserved in the ark, at the time of the deluge." Vol. I., p. 156. And he thence concludes, that Ila must be Noah; whilst other circumstances in his Phœnician history identify him with Abraham. Vol. I., p. 159. Again: "*Ilus* or *Il* * * is a regular Cuthic name of Buddha, which the Phenicians, I have no doubt, brought with them from their settlements on the Erythrêan sea: for Buddha or Menu, in the character of Ila, is said to have married his own daughter, Ila, who is described as the offspring of an ancient personage that was preserved in an ark, at the time of the general deluge." Vol. I., p. 223. Now, whatever connexion there may be between the names of Ila, Il, Ilus, Ilium, Ilá 'the earth,' and Ilos 'slime,' there is no very obvious

* *Íśwara*, in the original.

† CXI., 11, 12.

again transformed to a woman, in the vicinity of the hermitage of Budha, the son of (the deity of) the Moon. Budha saw and espoused her, and had, by her, a son named Purúravas.* After his birth, the illustrious† Rishis, desirous of restoring Sudyumna to his sex, prayed to the mighty Vishńu,‡ who is the essence of the four Vedas,§ of mind,|| of everything, and of nothing;¶ and who is in the form of the sacrificial

---

resemblance between the Pauráńik legends of Ilá and the Mosaic record; nor do the former authorise the particulars of Ila stated by Mr. Faber, on the authority, probably, of Colonel Wilford. The Manu Satyavrata, who was preserved in the ark, is never called Ila; nor is he the father of Ilá. Buddha was not so preserved; nor is Ila ever a title of Buddha. Budha (not Buddha), the husband of Ilá, never appears as her father; nor is he a Manu; nor is she the daughter of any ancient personage preserved in an ark. There is not, therefore, as far as I am aware, any circumstance in the history of Ila or Ilá which can identify him either with Abraham or Noah.

---

* [illegible] तस्यां बुधः पुरूरवसमात्मजमुत्पादयामास।

Thus it is indicated, observes the commentator, that the Solarian race sprang from the Lunarian.

For Ilá and Purúravas, see Chapter VI. of this Book. Ilá is dwelt on, in great detail, by Burnouf, in his *Bhágavata-puráńa*, Vol. III., Preface, pp. LXX.—XCII.

See, for another version of the original, Dr. Muir's *Original Sanskrit Texts*, Part I., p. [illegible].

† *Amitatejas.*

‡ In all my MSS., Vishńu is qualified, first of all, as 'identical with sacrifice,' *ishťimaya.*

§ The epithet 'one with the law', *dharmamaya*, here follows, in nearly all my MSS.

|| Here all my best MSS. insert 'identical with intelligence', *jnánamaya.*

¶ This is not in all MSS.

male;* and, through his favour, Ilá once more became Sudyumna; (in which character) he had three sons, Utkala, Gaya, and Vinata.[1]

In consequence of his having been, formerly, a female, Sudyumna was excluded from any share in his paternal dominions: but his father, at the suggestion of Vasishtha, bestowed upon him the city Pratishthána;[2] and he gave it to Purúravas.†

---

[1] The Matsya calls the name of the third, Haritáśwa; the Váyu, &c., Vinatáśwa; the Márkańdeya,‡ Vinaya; and the Bhágavata,§ Vimala. All but the last agree in stating that Utkala (Orissa) and Gayá (in Behar) are named after the two first. The Matsya calls the third the sovereign of the east, along with the Kauravas; the Váyu makes him king of the west.‖ The Bhágavata calls them, all three, rulers of the south.¶

[2] The authorities agree in this location of Sudyumna. Pratishthána** was situated on the eastern side of the confluence of the Ganges and Jumna, the country between which rivers was the territory of the direct male descendants of Vaivaswata. In the

---

* *Yajnapurusha.* See Vol. I., p. 61, note 1; p. 163, note *; and pp. 180, 181: also, Vol. II., p. 136.

† One MS. has Purushavara.

‡ CXI., 15.

§ IX., I. 41.

‖ The *Váyu-puráńa* says:

उत्कलस्योत्कलं राष्ट्रं विनताश्वस्य पश्चिमम् ।
दिक्पूर्वा तस्य राजर्षेर्गयस्य तु गया पुरी ॥

We are, thus, told, that the kingdom of Vinatáśwa lay to the west of Utkala.

With this compare the *Harivaṁśa*, *ll.* 632; and the *Linga-puráńa*, Prior Section, LXV., 37.

¶ दक्षिणापथराजानो बभूवुर्धर्मवत्सलाः ।

Vide infra, p. 240, note .

** See Burnouf's *Bhágavata-puráńa*, Vol. III., Preface, pp. XCVII., XCVIII.

Of the other sons of the Manu, Přishadhra, in consequence of (the crime of) killing a cow,* was degraded

---

Hari Vaḿśa,† it is said that he reigned in Pratishťhána, having killed Dhřishťaka, Ambarísha, and Dańda:

सुद्युम्नः कारयामास प्रतिष्ठाने नृपक्रियाम् ।
धृष्टकाम्बरीषञ्च दण्डकेति हतत्रयः ॥

M. Langlois had,‡ no doubt, सुतत्रयः in his copy; as he renders it:§ 'Il donna * * * naissance à trois enfants;' though, as he observes, Hamilton‖ had called these the sons of Ikshwáku. The Brahma Puráńa has not this passage; nor does the commentator on the Hari Vaḿśa give any explanation: neither does anything of the kind occur elsewhere. We have, however, subsequently, in the text,¶ Dańda named as a son of Ikshwáku; and, in the Padma Puráńa, Sřishťi Khańda, and in the Uttara Káńda of the Rámáyańa, we have a detailed narrative of Dańda, the son of Ikshwáku, whose country was laid waste by an imprecation of Bhárgava, whose daughter** that prince had violated. His kingdom became, in consequence, the Dańdaka forest. The Mahábhárata, Dána Dharma,†† alludes to the same story. If, therefore, the preferable reading of the Hari Vaḿśa be Suta, 'son,' it is at variance with all other authorities. At the same time, it

---

* The Sanskrit has 'his teacher's cow'.

† Śl. 637.

‡ Since he puts "Dandaca", a word of three syllables, it is more than probable that he followed some such reading as दण्डकेति हि त्रयः, which I find to be the most ordinary. In some MSS., दण्डकेति सुताख्ययः occurs. The lection हतत्रयः is of no account. It seems like a corruption of the last syllables of दण्डकेतीह हि त्रयः, which is read in one of Professor Wilson's MSS.

§ Vol. I., p. 54.

‖ The fact as to Mr. Hamilton's statement is more correctly expressed in these words: "Fr. Hamilton dit que ce roi, et par conséquent ses frères, étaient fils d'Ikchwâcou." See *Genealogies of the Hindus*, &c., p. 64.

¶ *Vide infra*, p. 259.

** Abjá, by name.

†† A part of the *Śánti-parvan*.

to the condition of a Śúdra.[1] From Karúsha descended the mighty warriors* termed Kárúshas, (the

must be admitted, that the same work is singular in asserting any collision between Daṅḋa and his brothers and Sudyumna; and the passage seems to have grown out of that careless and ignorant compilation which the Hari Vaṁśa so perpetually presents. It is, not improbably, a gratuitous perversion of this passage in the Matsya:

नाभागस्याम्बरीषस्तु धृष्टस्य च सुतत्रयम् ।

'Ambarísha was the son of Nábhága;† and Dhṙishṫa had three sons.'‡

[1] This story has been modified, apparently, at different periods, according to a progressive horror of the crime. Our text simply states the fact. The Váyu says he was hungry, and not only killed, but ate, the cow of his spiritual preceptor, Chyavana. In the Márkaṅdeya,§ he is described as being out a hunting, and killing the cow of the father of Bábhravya, mistaking it for a Gavaya or Gayal. The Bhágavata,|| as usual, improves upon the story, and says that Pṙishadhra was appointed, by his Guru, Vasishṫha, to protect his cattle. In the night, a tiger made his way into the fold; and the prince, in his haste, and in the dark, killed the cow upon which he had fastened, instead of the tiger. In all the authorities, the effect is the same; and the imprecation of the offended sage degraded Pṙishadhra to the caste of a Śúdra. According to the Bhágavata, the prince led a life of devotion, and, perishing in the flame of a forest, obtained final liberation. The obvious purport of this legend, and of some that follow, is, to account for the origin of the different castes from one common ancestor.

* *Kshattriya.*

† *Vide infra*, p. 257.

‡ For their names, *vide infra*, p. 255, note 2.

§ Ch. CXII.

|| IX., II., 3—14.

sovereigns of the north.)[1*] The son of Nedishṭha,† named Nábhága, became a Vaiśya:[2]: his son was Bhalan-

---

[1] The Bhágavata§ also places the Kárúshas in the north:||

उत्तरापथगोप्तारो ब्रह्मण्या धर्मवत्सलाः ।

But the country of the Kárúshas is, usually, placed upon the Páripátra or Vindhya mountains. See Vol. II., p. 158, note 2.¶

[2] The Váyu has 'Nábhága, the son of Arishṭa:' नाभागोऽरिष्टपुत्रस्तु ।** The Márkańḍeya†† has 'the son of Dishṭa:' दिष्टपुत्रस्तु नाभागः । The Bhágavata‡‡ also calls him the son of

---

* I do not find this parenthesis in the original; nor is it taken from the commentary.

† One MS. has Dishṭa. *Vide supra*, p. 231, note †.

‡ See *Original Sanskrit Texts*, Part I., pp. 45, 46. § IX., II., 16.

|| By the term *uttarápatha*, used in the original, the regions to the north of the Vindhya mountains are intended. The regions to the south of those mountains are, similarly, denominated *dakshińápatha*. *Vide supra*, p. 237, note *.

¶ But also see Vol. II., p. 129, text and note ||; p. 133, text and note †.

** The verse, as I find it, runs:

नाभागोऽरिष्टपुत्रस्तु विद्वानासीद्भलन्दनः ।

That is to say, Bhalandana is declared to be son of 'Nábhága Arishṭa.' The purport of the verse is, manifestly, to set forth the paternity of Bhalandana. Besides this, not to increase the *Váyu-puráńa*'s tale of the Manu's sons from nine to ten, Nábhága Arishṭa must be taken together, as denoting one person. The sense would not be changed, while the grammar would be amended, by reading नाभागारिष्ट°,—yielding Nábhágárishṭa,—which, as we have seen, occurs elsewhere. *Vide supra*, p. 232, notes ** and ‡‡; also, p. 256, note *, *infra*.

†† CXIII., 2. And so the *Linga-puráńa*, Prior Section, LXVI., 53.

‡‡ IX., II., 23:

नाभागो दिष्टपुत्रोऽन्यः कर्मणा वैश्यतां गतः ।

Śrídhara remarks, on this: दिष्टस्य पुत्रो नाभागो वक्ष्यमाणनाभागादन्य इति धार्मिकपुत्रादाचार्यमनुपादमाणम् ।

The Nábhága from whom this one is thus discriminated is named in IX., IV., 1, 9, 13; also, in VIII., XIII., 2. *Vide supra*, p. 14, note *, and p. 232, note ‡‡.

The commentator on the *Vishńu-puráńa* says: योऽदिष्टस्य पुत्रो नाभागो वैश्यतां गतः ।

dana;[1] * whose son was the celebrated Vatsa-

Dishṭa. According to that authority, he became a Vaiśya by his actions. The other Purāṇas generally agree, that the descendants of this person became Vaiśyas; but the Matsya and Vāyu do not notice it. The Mārkaṇḍeya details a story of Nābhāga's carrying off and marrying the daughter of a Vaiśya; in consequence of which he was degraded, it is said, to the same caste, and deprived of his share of the patrimonial sovereignty, which his son and successor recovered. The Brahma Purāṇa and Hari Vaṁśa † assert, that two sons of Nābhāgārishṭa again became Brahmans: but the duties of royalty imply the Kshattriya caste of his posterity; and the commentator on our text observes,‡ that the son of Nābhāga was born before his father's degradation, and, consequently, the race continued Kshattriya;—an assertion unsupported by any authority: and it must, therefore, appear, that a race of Vaiśya princes was recognized by early traditions.

[1] Bhanandana:§ Bhāgavata.

नाभागो दिष्टपुत्रोऽन्यः कर्मणा वैश्यतां गतः ।

इति शुकोक्तेः । तस्य च पुत्रोत्पत्तेरनन्तरकालमेव वैश्यत्वप्राप्त्या तत्पुत्रस्य भलन्दनस्य क्षत्रियत्वमविरुद्धमेव । अत एव तदन्वयस्य मरुत्तस्य चक्रवर्तित्वं संगच्छते । This imports, that it was not till after the birth of Bhalandana, that Nābhāga was turned into a Vaiśya; and hence it is that his descendants were, like himself in his original dignity of birth, Kshattriyas.

We meet with other Nābhāgas, at pp. 256 and 303, *infra*.

* In two MSS. I find Bhanandana, for which see note §, below.

† नाभागारिष्टपुत्रौ द्वौ वैश्यौ ब्राह्मणतां गतौ ।

So read my best MSS.; the Calcutta edition being defective here. Some MSS. have Nābhāgadishṭa for the name; and, in one, I find Nābhāga:

नाभागस्य तु पुत्रौ द्वौ वैश्यौ ब्राह्मणतां गतौ ।

M. Langlois must have had before him a still different lection, one much like that in the Bombay edition; for he translates: "Les fils de Nābhāgārishṭa, Kchatriyas d'origine, devinrent Vêśyas."

‡ See note ‡‡ in the preceding page.

§ This looks like a Bengal corruption of Bhalandana, the reading in all my best MSS. of the *Bhāgavata*. See note * in the next page.

prí:[1]* his son was Práṁśu;† whose son was Prajáni;[2] whose son was Khanitra;[3] whose son was the very valiant Kshupa;[4]: whose son was Viṁśa;[5]

[1] Vatsapriti: Bhágavata. Vatsaśri: Márkańdeya.§ The latter has a story of the destruction of the Daitya Kujámbha by Vidúratha, the father of Sunandá, the wife of Vatsaśri. The Váyu has Sahasrári.||

[2] Pramati: Bhágavata.¶

[3] According to the Márkańdeya, the priests of the royal family conspired against this prince, and were put to death by his ministers.

[4] Chákshusha: Bhágavata.**

[5] Víra: Márkańdeya.††

* All my best MSS. give Vatsapriti once, or twice, several having both Vatsapriti and Vatsapri; for the name is repeated, in the original, in connexion with Práṁśu. Vatsapri, and as son of Bhalandana, is mentioned several times in the *Anukramańiká* to the *Ṛigveda*.

† Where (for a single instance out of several,) Práṁśu—p. 233, *supra*,—is called one of the "sons" of Manu, are we to understand, by "sons", "descendants"? Or is the Práṁśu here spoken of a second person of that name? He was one of twelve sons of Vatsapri, according to the *Márkańdeya-puráńa*, CXVIII., 1, 2.

According to the *Váyu-puráńa*, Práṁśu was son of Bhalandana:

भलन्दनस्य पुत्रोऽभूत्प्रांशुर्नाम महायशाः ।

: My MSS. read, without exception: ततश्च खनित्रः । तस्माच्च क्षुपः । क्षुपाच्चातिबलपराक्रमो विंशोऽभवत् । Professor Wilson, mistaking the particle *cha*, 'and', for part of the name, printed "Chakshupa", which I have altered as above.

See note § in the next page. That the name is Kshupa is, further, evident from several passages of the *Márkańdeya-puráńa*; as CXX., 1:

क्षुपः खनित्रपुत्रस्तु प्राप राज्यं यथा पिता ।

§ My best MSS. of the *Márkańdeya-puráńa* have, like the Calcutta edition, Vatsapri.

|| In the *Váyu-puráńa*, as known to me, there is no name at all here. See the line quoted in note †, above.

¶ The *Váyu-puráńa* and the *Márkańdeya-puráńa* have Prajáti.

** Pretty certainly, there is, here, a gross mistake in the *Bhágavata-puráńa*. See note :, above.

†† CXX., 12.

whose son was Viviṁśati,[1]* whose son was Khanínetra;† whose son was the powerful, wealthy, and valiant Karandhama;[2] whose son was Avikshi (or Avikshit);[3]‡ whose son was the mighty Marutta,§ of whom this well-known verse‖ is recited:

---

[1] Rambha precedes Viviṁśati: Bhágavata.¶

[2] Baláśwa,** or Balakáśwa, or Subaláśwa, according to the Márkaṇḍeya, which explains his name Karandhama to denote his creation of an army,—when besieged by his revolted tributaries,—by breathing on his hands (कर + धम.).

[3] Both forms occur, as the commentator observes: अविक्षिदेव अविक्षिदित्यपि नाम। The Márkaṇḍeya has a long story of this prince's carrying off the daughter of Viśála, king of Vaidiśa††. Being attacked and captured by his confederated rivals, he was rescued by his father, but was so much mortified by his disgrace, that he vowed never to marry nor reign. The princess, also be-

---

* I find no reading but Viviṁśa, if Viṁśa—which is, of course, a mere clerical inadvertence,—is left out of account. Viviṁśa is, also, the lection of the *Márkaṇḍeya-puráṇa*, CXX., 14, 15; and see note §, below. For this word, as denoting a caste, see Vol. II., p. 193.

† Nearly all my MSS., including every one of the best, here interpose Ativibhúti, or else Vibhúti, as son of Khanínetra and sire of Karandhama.

‡ In the *Váyu-puráṇa* I find Avikshita; and he is named immediately after Khanitra, as if his son. But, almost certainly, there is, here, a hiatus in my MSS.

Avikshita is, also, the reading of the *Márkaṇḍeya-puráṇa*, Ch. CXXIII.

§ In the *Mahábhárata*, *Áśwamedhika-parvan*, Chap. IV., we find the following genealogy, referred to the *Kṛita-yuga*: Manu, Prasandhi, Kshupa, Ikshwáku, Viṁśa (one of a hundred sons, all kings), Viviṁśa, Khanínetra (one of fifteen sons), Karandhama, Avikshit, Marutta.

‖ I find "two stanzas": यत्रेमावत्रापि श्लोकौ गीयेते। And two stanzas are immediately afterwards quoted.

¶ In my MSS., Rambha follows Viviṁśati; and Viṁśa is omitted.

** This appears to be the true reading of the *Márkaṇḍeya-puráṇa*.

†† From the original, वैदिशाधिपतेः, it is safest, pending the production of explicit proof that there is such a name as "Vaidiśa," to infer, in preference, Vaidiśá. *Vide supra*, p. 231, note ‡.

"There never was beheld, on earth, a sacrifice equal to the sacrifice of Marutta. All the implements and utensils* were made of gold. Indra was intoxicated† with the libations of Soma-juice; and the Brahmans were enraptured with the magnificent donations they received. The winds of heaven encompassed the rite, as guards; and the assembled gods attended, to behold it."[1]‡ Marutta was a Chakravartin (or universal

---

coming an ascetic, met with him in the woods; and they were, finally, espoused: but Avikshit kept his other vow, and relinquished his succession in favour of his son, who succeeded to the kingdoms of both Karandhama and Viśála.

[1] Most of our authorities quote the same words, with, or without, addition.§ The Váyu‖ adds, that the sacrifice was conducted by Samvarta, whom the Bhágavata terms a Yogin, the

---

* "Implements and utensils" is to render *vasu*.

† The commentary explains अमाद्यत् by अतितृप्त्या हृष्टो बभूव ।

‡ अमाद्यदिन्द्रः सोमेन दक्षिणाभिर्द्विजातयः ।
मरुतः परिवेष्टारः सदस्याश्च दिवौकसः ॥

According to the scholiast, the Maruts purveyed food, &c., on the occasion: मरुतो देवाः । परिवेष्टार अन्नादिपरिवेषकाः ।

§ Whence the first of these stanzas was derived I am unable to say; but we probably have the prototype of part of the second in the following quotation in the *Aitareya-bráhmańa*, VIII., 21:

मरुतः परिवेष्टारो मरुत्तस्यावसन्गृहे ।
आविक्षितस्य कामप्रेर्विश्वे देवाः सभासदः ॥

See, also, the *Śatapatha-bráhmańa*, XIII., V., IV., 6; and compare the *Bhágavata-puráńa*, IX., II., 27, 28.

‖ Its words are:

संवर्तेन दिवं नीतः ससुहृत्सह बान्धवैः ।
विवादोऽथ महानासीत्संवर्तस्य बृहस्पतेः ॥
ऋद्धिं दृष्ट्वा तु यज्ञस्य कृत्स्नस्य बृहस्पतिः ।
संवर्तेन धृते यज्ञे चुकोप सुभृशं तदा ।
लोकानां च हि नाशाय दैवतैर्हि प्रसादितः ॥

monarch): he had a son named Narishyanta;[1] his son was Dama;[2] his son was Rájyavardhana;[3] his son was Sudhṛiti; his son was Nara; his son was Kevala; his son was Bandhumat; his son was Vegavat; his son was Budha;[4] his son was Tṛinabindu, who had a daughter

---

son of Angiras; and that Bṛihaspati was so jealous of the splendour of the rite, that a great quarrel ensued between him and Saṁvarta. How it involved the king is not told; but, apparently, in consequence, Marutta, with his kindred and friends, was taken, by Saṁvarta, to heaven. According to the Márkaṇḍeya,† Marutta was so named from the paternal benediction, 'May the winds be thine,' or 'be propitious to thee' (मरुत्तव पितावायु). He reigned, agreeably to that record, 85000 years.

[1] Omitted in the Bhágavata.

[2] A rather chivalric and curious story is told of Dama, in the Márkaṇḍeya.‡ His bride, Sumaná, daughter of the king Daśárha,§ was rescued, by him, from his rivals. One of them, Vapushmat, afterwards killed Marutta, who had retired into the woods, after relinquishing his crown to his son. Dama, in retaliation, killed Vapushmat, and made the Piṇḍa (or obsequial offering) to his father, of his flesh: with the remainder he fed the Brahmans of Rákshasa origin: such were the kings of the solar race.

वपुष्मतश्च मांसेन पिण्डदानं चकार सः ।
ब्राह्मणान्भोजयामास रक्षःकुलसमुद्भवान् ।
एवंविधा हि राजानो बभूवुः सूर्यवंशजाः ॥ ||

[4] The Bhágavata has Bandhavat, Oghavat, and Bandha.¶

---

[3] The *Váyu-puráṇa* has Ráshṭravardhana.

† CXXVIII., 33. ‡ Ch. CXXXIV.

§ I find सुता दशार्णाधिपतेः, "daughter of the king of Daśárṇa". See Vol. II., p. 160, note †; p. 176, note *.

|| *Márkaṇḍeya-puráṇa*, Calcutta edition, pp. 657, 658.

¶ I find, in all the MSS. I have examined, Bandhumat and Vegavat; while the prevailing reading of the third name is Bandhu, of which Bandha and Budha are variants. The *Váyu-puráṇa* agrees, as to all three names, with the *Vishṇu-puráṇa*.

named Ilavilá.[1]* The celestial nymph† Alambushá, becoming enamoured of Tríńabindu, bore him a son named Viśála, by whom the city Vaiśálí was founded.[2]

---

[1] The Váyu‡ and Bhágavata both add, that she was the wife of Viśravas, and mother of Kubera.§ In the Linga Puráńa, she is said to have been the wife of Pulastya, and mother of Viśravas. The weight of authority is in favour of the former statement. See Vol. I., p. 154, note 2.

[2] The Bhágavata names three sons, Viśála, Śúnyabandhu, and Dhúmaketu.|| Vaiśálí is a city of considerable renown in Indian tradition; but its site is a subject of some uncertainty. Part of the difficulty arises from confounding it with Viśálá, another name of Ujjayiní:

उज्जयिनी स्याद्विशालावन्ती पुष्पकरण्डिनी ।

Hemachandra.¶ Also, in the Megha Dúta:**

प्राप्यावन्तीमुदयनकथाकोविदग्रामवृद्धा
पूर्वोद्दिष्टामुपसर पुरीं श्रीविशालां विशालाम् ।

'Having arrived at Avanti, • • • proceed to the illustrious city before indicated, Viśálá.' विशालामित्याख्यामुज्जयिनीं पुरीम् । 'To the city Ujjayiní, named Viśálá.' Comment. Vaiśálí††, however, appears to be very differently situated. According to the Buddhists, amongst whom it is celebrated as a chief seat of the labours of Śákya‡‡ and his first disciples, it is the same as Prayága,

---

* Only one of my MSS. has this name; one has Ilirilá; and all the rest have Ilivilá. Also see note ‡, below.

The *Bhágavata-puráńa*, IX., II., 31, represents Idavidá as daughter of Tríńabindu and Alambushá.

† *Apsaras.*

‡ The *Váyu-puráńa* has Ividá, and calls her mother of Viśravas:

कन्या तु तस्य इविडा माता विश्रवसो हि या ।

§ Called Dhanada, in the *Bhágavata-puráńa.*

|| I find Dhúmraketu.

¶ *Abhidhána-chintámańi*, IV., 42.

** *Śl.* 32, Prof. Wilson's second edition.

†† The genuine *Rámáyańa* has Viśálá; the Bengal recension, Vaiśálí. The latter name, Burnouf maintains, is that which was known to the Buddhists. *Introduction à l'Histoire du Buddhisme Indien*, Vol. I., p. 86, note 2.

‡‡ Corrected from "Śákhya."

The son of the first king of Vaiśálí was Hemachandra; his son was Suchandra; his son was Dhúmráśwa; his son was Śrinjaya;[1] his son was Sahadeva;[2] his son was Kriśáśwa; his son was Somadatta, who celebrated, ten times, the sacrifice of a horse; his son was Janamejaya; and his son was Sumati.[3]* These were the

---

or Allahabad;† but the Rámáyańa (I., 45) places it much lower down, on the north bank of the Ganges, nearly opposite to the mouth of the Sone; and it was, therefore, in the modern district of Sáran, as Hamilton (Genealogies of the Hindus‡) conjectured. In the fourth century, it was known, to the Chinese traveller Fa-hian, as Phi-she-li, on the right bank of the Gandak, not far from its confluence with the Ganges.§ Account of the Foe-kúe-ki:|| Journal of the Royal Asiatic Society, Vol. V., p. 128.

[1] Dhúmráksha and Saṁyama: Bhágavata.¶

[2] The text is clear enough; सृञ्जयात्सहदेवः । ततः कृशाश्वः । But, as elsewhere noticed (Hindu Theatre, Vol, II., p. 296), the commentator on the Bhágavata** interprets the parallel passage,

तत्सुतात्संयमादासीत्कृशाश्वः सहदेवजः ।

very differently, or: सहदेवजः । देवजेन सहितः ।†† 'Kriśáśwa with Devaja,' or, as some copies read, Devaka, or Daivata, as if there were two sons of Saṁyama.

[3] The Bhágavata changes the order of these two, making Janamejaya the son of Sumati: or Pramati; Váyu. Sumati, king

---

* Four of my MSS. have Swamati.

† Burnouf, where referred to in note †† in the preceding page, shows this opinion to be groundless. ‡ Pp. 67, 38.

§ General Cunningham, with others, thinks it is now represented by Besáŕh, a village twenty-seven miles nearly north from Patna. *Journal of the Asiatic Society of Bengal*, 1863, Supplementary Number, p. iii.

|| The article referred to was written by Professor Wilson.

¶ The *Bhágavata-puráńa*, IX., II., 34, makes Hemachandra father of Dhúmráksha, father of Saṁyama, father of Kriśáśwa and Devaja.

** IX., II., 34.

†† The commentator adds: पाठान्तरे नामान्तरमात्रम् । अर्थस्तु स एव ।

kings of Vaiśálí;* of whom it it is said:† "By the favour of Trińabindu, all the monarchs of Vaiśálí‡ were long-lived, magnanimous, equitable, and valiant."

Saryáti (the fourth son of the Manu,)§ had a daughter named Sukanyá, who was married to the holy sage Chyavana:[1]‖ he had, also, a righteous son called Ánarta.

---

of Vaiśáli, is made contemporary with Ráma: Rámáyańa, I., 47. 17. The dynasty of Vaiśála kings is found only in our text, the Váyu, and Bhágavata. Hamilton ¶ places them from 1920 to 1240 B. C.; but the latter is incompatible with the date he assigns to Ráma, of 1700 B. C.** The contemporary existence of Sumati and Ráma, however, is rather unintelligible; as, according to our lists, the former is the thirty-fourth, and the latter, the sixtieth, from Vaivaswata Manu.

[1] The circumstance of their marriage, of Chyavana's appropriating a share of offerings to the Aświni Kumáras, and of his quarrel with Indra, in consequence, are told, in detail, in the Bhágavata and Padma Puráńas.

---

* Expressed by *vaiśálaka*.

† श्लोकोऽप्यत्र गीयते । And what follows is a stanza. It occurs in the *Váyu-puráńa*, as well, but not as if a quotation.

‡ *Vaiśálaka*.

§ The *Aitareya-bráhmańa*, IV., 32, and VIII., 21, speaks of Śáryáta, son of Manu. The *Ŕigveda*, also, has Śáryáta. Perhaps this name is here a metronym.

‖ "The Ŕishi Chyavana married his [Vaivaswata's] daughter; and a solemn sacrifice was held on the occasion, at which Indra and the Aświns were present. Chyavana appropriated to himself the share of the oblation intended for the Aświns, at which Indra was very angry; and, to appease him, a fresh offering was prepared. The Scholiast quotes this story from the Kaushítaki Bráhmańa." Professor Wilson's Translation of the *Ŕigveda*, Vol. I., p. 139, note a.

¶ *Genealogies of the Hindus*, &c., p. 38.

** ?

The son of the latter was Revata,[1] who ruled over the country (called, after his father,) Ánarta, and dwelt at the capital, (denominated) Kuśasthalí.[2] The son of this prince was Raivata, or Kakudmin, the eldest of a hundred brethren. He had a very lovely daughter;[*] and (not finding any one worthy of her hand,) he repaired, with her, to the region of Brahmá, to consult the god where a fit bridegroom was to be met with. When he arrived, the quiristers[†] Háhá, Húhú, and others were singing[‡] before Brahmá; and Raivata,[§] waiting till they had finished, imagined the ages that elapsed during their

---

[1] In most of the other Puráńas, Reva, or Raiva.[||] The Linga and Matsya insert a Rochamána before him; and the Bhágavata[¶] adds, to Ánarta, Uttánabarhis and Bhúrisheńa.

[2] The Bhágavata[**] ascribes the foundation of Kuśasthalí to Revata, who built it, it is said, within the sea. The subsequent legend shows, that it was the same, or on the same spot, as Dwáraká; and Ánarta was, therefore, part of Cutch or Gujerat. See Vol. II., p. 171, note 4.[††]

---

[*] The reading of my MSS. is सुता च रैवती नाम कन्या, "and he had a daughter, Revatí."

[†] *Gandharva.* For Háhá and Húhú, see Vol. II., pp. 286, *et seq.*

[‡] अतितानं नाम दिव्यं गान्धर्वमगीयत । The piece of music which they were executing was an *atitána*,—a certain song, according to the commentary. A variant for *gándharvam* is *gándháram*, qualifying *atitánam*. The scholiast takes note of it.

[§] The original has Raivataka, here and below.

[||] My MSS. of the *Váyu-puráńa* have these two readings, and Rava, as well.

[¶] XI., III., 27.

[**] IX., III., 28:

सोऽन्तः समुद्रे नगरीं विनिर्माय कुशस्थलीम् ।

[††] Also see Vol. II., p. 172, note 2.

performance to be but as a moment.* At the end of their singing, Raivata prostrated himself† before Brahmá,‡ and explained his errand. "Whom should you wish for a son-in-law?" demanded Brahmá; and the king mentioned to him various persons with whom he could be well pleased.§ Nodding his head gently, and (graciously) smiling, Brahmá said to him: "Of those whom you have named the third or fourth generation|| no longer survives; for many successions of ages¶ have passed away, whilst you were listening to our songsters.** Now, upon earth, the twenty-eighth great age of the present Manu is nearly finished, and the Kali period is at hand.†† You must, therefore, bestow this virgin gem‡‡ upon some other husband: for you are, now, alone; and your friends, your ministers, ser-

---

* *Muhúrta*. The Sanskrit is: तावच्च त्रिमार्गपरिवर्तैरनेकयुगपरिवृत्ति तिष्ठन्नपि रैवतकः मुहूर्तमिव मेने । *Trimárga* is here a musical technicality.

† *Prańáma*.

‡ Here, and just above, and also below, designated by his epithet of *abjayoni*, 'lotos-born.'

§ And he farther solicited Brahmá's advice as to a choice: क इष्टो भवतोऽभिमतः । कस्मै कन्यामिमां प्रयच्छामीति ।

|| The Sanskrit is चापत्यापत्यसंततिः ।

¶ *Chaturyuga*.

** Literally, 'this music', *etad gándharvam*.

†† साम्प्रतं भूतलेऽष्टाविंशतितमस्य मनोश्चतुर्युगमतीतप्रायम् । आसन्नो हि तत्कलिः । Comment: अत्र रैवतस्य मनोरष्टाविंशतितमं चतुर्युगं गतप्रायम् ।

What is meant is, that, in the meantime, twenty-eight four-*yuga* cycles of the *manwantara* or patriarchate then current had nearly elapsed, &c.

Compare the *Bhágavata-puráńa*, IX., III., 33.

For the length of a *manwantara*, see Vol. I., pp. 50—59.

‡‡ *Kanyá-ratna*.

vants, wife, kinsmen, armies,* and treasures have long since† been swept away by (the hand of) time." Overcome with astonishment and alarm,‡ the Raja then said to Brahmá: "Since I am thus circumstanced, do thou, lord, tell me unto whom the maiden shall be given." And the creator of the world,§ whose throne is the lotos,|| (thus benignantly) replied to the prince, as he stood bowed and humble¶ before him:** "The being of whose commencement, course,†† and termination we are ignorant; the unborn and omnipresent‡‡ essence§§ (of all things); he whose real and infinite|||| nature and essence¶¶ (we do not know), is the supreme Vishńu.*** He is time, made up of moments, and hours, and years;††† whose influence‡‡‡ is the source of (perpetual) change. He is the universal form of all things, from birth to death.§§§ He is eternal, without name or shape. Through the favour of that imperishable|||||| (being) am

* *Bala.*

† *Atyanta*, 'entirely.'

‡ The two substantives are to render *sádhwasa.*

§ *Sapta-loka-guru.*

|| *Abjayoni.*

¶ *Kritánjali-bhúta.*

** All the rest of this chapter is in verse.

†† *Madhya.*

‡‡ *Sarvagata.*

§§ *Dhátu.*

|||| *Para.*

¶¶ *Sára.*

*** "Supreme Vishńu" corresponds to *parameśwara.*

††† *Kálamahirúddhi.*

‡‡‡ *Vibhúti.*

§§§ I find [illegible] According to this, he is said to be 'unborn and indestructible,' &c. &c.

|||||| *Achyuta.* See Vol. I., p. 18, note 3.

I the agent of his power in creation: through his anger is Rudra the destroyer (of the world); and the cause of preservation, Purusha, proceeds, also, from him. The unborn, having assumed my person,* creates (the world); in his own essence,† he provides for its duration; in the form of Rudra, he devours all things; and, with the body of Ananta, he upholds them. Impersonated as Indra‡ and the other gods, he is the guardian of mankind;§ and, as the sun and moon, he disperses darkness. Taking upon himself the nature of fire, he bestows warmth and maturity, and, in the condition of the earth, nourishes all beings.|| As one with air,¶ he gives activity to existence;** and, as one with water, he satisfies (all wants); whilst, in the state of ether, associated with universal aggregation, he furnishes space for all objects.†† He is at once the creator, and that which is created; the preserver, and that which is preserved; the destroyer, and, as one with all things, that which is destroyed: and, as the indestructible,‡‡ he is distinct from these three vicissitudes. In him is the world; he is the world; and he, the primeval self-

---

* *Rúpa.*

† *Purusha-swarúpin.*

‡ Śakra, in the original.

§ *Vidura.*

|| पाकाय यो ऽग्नित्वमुपेत्य लोका-
न्बिभर्ति पृथ्वीवपुरव्ययात्मा ।

¶ *Śwasana*, 'breath.'

** *Loka.*

†† ददाति विश्वस्थितिसंस्थितस्तु
सर्वावकाशं च नभःस्वरूपी ।

‡‡ *Avyayátman.* See Vol. I., p. 17, note *.

born,* is again present in the world.* That (mighty) Vishńu, who is paramount over all beings, is now, in a portion of himself, upon the earth. That (city) Kuśasthalí, which was, formerly, your capital, and rivalled the city of the immortals,† is now (known as) Dwáraká;[1] and there reigns a portion of that divine being,‡ in the person of Baladeva. To him, who appears as a man, present her, as a wife. He is a worthy bridegroom for this excellent damsel; and she is a suitable bride for him."§

Being thus instructed by the lotos-born (divinity), Raivata returned (with his daughter,) to earth, where he found the race of men dwindled in stature, reduced in vigour, and enfeebled in intellect. Repairing to the city of Kuśasthalí, which he found (much) altered,|| the wise monarch bestowed his (unequalled) daughter on the wielder of the ploughshare,¶ whose breast was

---

[1] So called from its many Dwáras, or gateways:

कृतां द्वारवतीं नाम बहुद्वारां मनोरमाम् ।

Váyu.

---

* Compare the *Bhagavad-gítá*, Chapter IX., *passim*.

† The Sanskrit has *amarávatíva*, "like Amarávatí." For this city, see Vol. I., p. 137; and Vol. II., p. 240, text and notes.

‡ Keśava, in the original.

§ तस्मै त्वमेनां तनयां नरेन्द्र
प्रयच्छ मायामनुजाय जायाम् ।
श्लाघ्यो वरोऽसौ तनया तवेयं
स्त्रीरत्नभूता सदृशो हि योगः ॥

|| Because, says the commentator, Kŕishńa had reclaimed from the sea a shire of country measuring twelve *yojanas* in circumference, and, with the aid of Viśwakarman, had renovated the city. For Dwáraká, *vide infra*, Book V., Chapters XXIII. and XXVIII.

¶ *Síra-dhwaja*, 'plough-bannered'.

as fair and radiant as crystal.* Beholding the damsel of excessively lofty height, the chief whose banner is a palm-tree† shortened her with the end of his ploughshare, and she became his wife. Balaráma‡ having espoused, agreeably to the ritual, Revatí, the daughter of Raivata, the king retired to the mountain Himálaya,§ (and ended his days) in devout austerities.[1]

[1] The object of this legend, which is told by most of the authorities, is, obviously, to account for the anachronism of making Balaráma contemporary with Raivata; the one, early in the Tretá age, and the other, at the close of the Dwápara.

* *Sphaťikáchalábha*, "brilliant as a mountain of crystal."

† *Tálaketu.*

‡ Indicated, in the Sanskrit, by his epithet *síráyudha.*

§ Himáchala, in the original.

CHAPTER II.

Dispersion of Revata's descendants: those of Dhrishta: those of Nábhága. Birth of Ikshwáku, the son of Vaivaswata; his sons. Line of Vikukshi. Legend of Kakutstha; of Dhundhumára; of Yuvanáśwa; of Mándhátri: his daughters married to Saubhari.

PARAŚARA.—Whilst Kakudmin, surnamed Raivata, was absent on his visit to the region of Brahmá, the (evil spirits or) Rákshasas named Puńyajanas* destroyed his capital, Kuśasthalí. His hundred brothers, through dread of these foes, fled in different directions; and the Kshattriyas, their descendants, settled in many countries.[1] †

From Dhrishta, the son of the Manu, sprang the Kshattriya race ‡ of Dhárshtaka.[2]

---

[1] According to the Váyu, the brothers of Raivata founded a celebrated race called Śáryáta, from Śaryáti. The Brahma Puráńa says, they took refuge in secret places (gahana); for which the Hari Vaḿśa substitutes (parvata gańa) mountains. The Váyu has neither, and says, merely, that they were renowned in all regions: विख्याता दिक्षु सर्वशः ।

[2] So the Váyu, Linga, Agni, Brahma, and Hari Vaḿśa.§ The Matsya names three sons of Dhrishta,—Dhrishtaketu, Chitranátha, and Rańadhrishta. The Bhágavata|| adds, that the sons of Dhri-

---

* *Puńyajana* is usually considered as synonymous with *yaksha*. For the Yakshas, see Vol. I., p. 83; Vol. II., p. 75.

† सर्वदिक्ष्वभवन् ।

‡ *Kshattra*, in the original.

§ *Śl.* 642. The Calcutta edition has Dhrishńu and Dhárshńaka. Also *vide supra*, p. 232, note ‡.

|| IX., II., 17. Also *vide infra*, p. 280, note 2.

The son of Nabhága* was Nábhága;[1] his son was

---

shis obtained Brahmanhood upon earth, though born Kshattriyas:

धृष्टाद्धार्ष्टमभूत्क्षत्रं ब्रह्मभूयं गतं क्षितौ । †

[1] But who is Nabbága? For, as above observed, (p. 231, note 1,) the son of the Manu is Nabhága-nedishťa;‡ and there is, in that case, no such person as Nabhága.§ On the other hand, if Nabhága and Nedishťha be distinct names, we have ten sons of Vaivaswata, as in the Bhágavata.¶ The descendants of Nedishťha, through his son Nabhága, have been already specified; and, after all, therefore, we must consider the text as intending a distinct

---

* This is the ordinary reading of my MSS., of which three, however, give Nábhága. It will contribute to harmonize the *Vishńu-puráńa* with itself, if we surmise,—*vide supra*, p. 13,—that there is, here, an error for Nabhaga. So Ambarisha's grandfather is called in the *Bhágavata-puráńa*, IX., IV., 1; though the person there meant is, as the context evidences, identified with Nábhánedishťha of the *Aitareya-bráhmańa*. The *Váyu-puráńa*, likewise, in every MS. to which I have access, irregularly derives Nábhága from Nabhaga:

नभगस्य च दायादो नाभागो नाम वीर्यवान् ।

Those Puráńas which speak of Nedishťha (or Dishťa, &c.) preceded by Nábhága, in composition or apart, and also speak of Nabhaga (or Nabhága), recounting, of the latter, the story told in note 1, above, have explicitly misrepresented ancient tradition, inasmuch as this story relates to Nábhánedishťha (नेदिष्ठ preceded by नाभा - नाभि), in whose name we have the source of Nábhágnedishťha and numerous other corruptions previously particularised. There seems to be no authority, older than epic and Pauráńik, for such a person as Nedishťha, or Dishťa, or Arishťa, father of a Nábhága.

† The *Váyu-puráńa* has:

धृष्टस्य धार्ष्टकं क्षत्रं रणधृष्टं बभूव ह ।
त्रिसाहस्रं तु स गणः क्षत्रियाणां महात्मनाम् ॥

‡ This should be Nábhága-nedishťha.

§ See the conjecture ventured in note *, above. Also *vide supra*, p. 232, text and note *; and the Translator's last note on Chapter V. of the present Book. But the *Bhágavata-puráńa*, IX., II., 17, 18, gives an irreconcileable account of the offspring of Nŕiga.

|| Changed, here and just below, from "Nedishťa." Also read Nábhága, and so further on.

¶ *Vide supra*, p. 14, note *; p. 232, note ‡.

Ambarísha;[1] his son was Virúpa;[2]* his son was Pṛi-

person by the name Nabhága; and such a name does occur, in the lists of the Agni, Kúrma, Matsya, and Bhágavata, unquestionably distinct from that with which it is also sometimes compounded. The Bhágavata repeats the legend of the Aitareya Bráhmaṅa,† with some additions, and says, that, Nabhága having protracted his period of study beyond the usual age, his brothers appropriated his share of the patrimony. On his applying for his portion, they consigned their father to him, by whose advice he assisted the descendants of Angiras in a sacrifice, and they presented him with all the wealth that was left at its termination. Rudra claimed it as his; and, Nabhága acquiescing, the god confirmed the gift, by which he became possessed of an equivalent for the loss of territory. Most of the authorities recognise but one name here, variously read either Nabhága or Nábhága, the father of Ambarísha. The Váyu, as well as the Bhágavata, concurs with the text.‡

[1] The Bhágavata§ considers Ambarísha as a king who reigned, apparently, on the banks of the Yamuná. He is more celebrated as a devout worshipper of Vishńu, whose discus protected him from the wrath of Durvásas, and humbled that choleric saint, who was a portion of Śiva:—a legend which, possibly, records a struggle between two sects, in which the votaries of Vishńu, headed by Ambarísha, triumphed.

[2] The Agni, Brahma, and Matsya stop with Ambarísha. The Váyu and Bhágavata proceed as in the text; only the latter‖ adds, to Virúpa, Ketumat and Śambhu.

* See Professor Wilson's Translation of the *Ṛigveda*, Vol. I., p. 122, note a. One MS. of the *Vishńu-puráńa* has Vidwarúpa.

† V., 14. For Nábhánedishṭha, there mentioned, see, further, the *Ṛigveda*, X., LXI. and LXII.; and the *Taittiríya-saṁhitá* of the *Yajurveda*, III., I., IX., 4.

‡ It does not appear so from my MSS. See note * in the preceding page.

§ IX., IV., 13, 30. ‖ IX., VI., 1.

shadaśwa; his son was Rathítara,* of whom it is sung: "These, who were Kshattriyas by birth, the heads of the family of Rathítara, were called Angirasas (or sons of Angiras), and were Brahmans as well as Kshattriyas."[1]†

---

[1] The same verse is cited in the Váyu, and affords an instance of a mixture of character, of which several similar cases occur subsequently.‡ Kshattriyas by birth become Brahmans by profession; and such persons are usually considered as Angirasas, followers or descendants of Angiras, who may have founded a school of warrior-priests. This is the obvious purport of the legend of Nabhága's assisting the sons of Angiras to complete their sacrifice, referred to in a former note;§ although the same authority has devised a different explanation. Rathinara‖ (or Rathítara, as read in some copies, as well as by the Bhágavata¶ and Váyu,) being childless, Angiras begot on his wife sons

---

* The "Rathinara" of the former edition I have altered, here and below, being convinced that it is merely a clerical error of a very few MSS.

† एते क्षत्रप्रसूता वै पुनश्चाङ्गिरसः स्मृताः ।
रथीतराणां प्रवराः क्षत्रोपेता द्विजातयः ॥

"These were born in a Kshattra *or Kshattriya* race, and were subsequently known as Angirasas. *They were* the chief of the Rathítaras,—Bráhmans possessing the rank of Kshattras."

One of my MSS. gives प्रभवाः for प्रवराः.

Commentary: एते रथीतरस्य प्रवरा गोत्रजाः । क्षत्रप्रसूताः क्षत्रियात् क्षत्रस्य रथीतरस्य भार्यायामङ्गिरसा जातत्वात् । तथापि तयोर्योगात्पुनराङ्गिरसो ब्राह्मणाः स्मृताः । अतः क्षत्रोपेता द्विजातयः । इत्यन्वयः । This explanation I have not accepted in full.

See Dr. Muir's remarks on this passage, in *Original Sanskrit Texts*, Part I., pp. 46, 47.

‡ *Vide infra*, p. 260, note 2.

§ Note 1 in p. 256, *supra*. ‖ See note *, above.

¶ IX., VI., 2, 3:

रथीतरस्याप्रजस्य भार्यायां तन्तवेऽर्थितः ।
अङ्गिरा जनयामास ब्रह्मवर्चस्विनः सुतान् ॥

Ikshwáku was born from the nostril of the Manu, as he happened to sneeze.[1] He had a hundred* sons, of whom the three most distinguished† were Vikukshi, Nimi, and Dańda. Fifty (of the rest), under Śakuni,‡ were the protectors of the northern countries. Forty-eight were the princes of the south.[2]

---

radiant with divine glory, who, as the sons of the monarch by his wife, were Kshattriyas, but were Brahmans through their actual father. This, however, is an afterthought, not warranted by the memorial verse cited in our text.

[1] So the Bhágavata:§

क्षुवतस्तु मनोर्जज्ञे इक्ष्वाकुर्घ्राणतः सुतः ।

[2] The Matsya says, that Indra (Devaráj) was born as Vikukshi, and that Ikshwáku had one hundred and fourteen other sons who were kings of the countries south of Meru, and as many who reigned north of that mountain. The Váyu and most of the other authorities agree in the number of one hundred, of whom

---

एते क्षेत्रप्रसूता वै पुनश्चाङ्गिरसाः स्मृताः ।
रथीतराणां प्रवराः क्षत्रोपेता द्विजातयः ॥

These stanzas are thus rendered by Burnouf:

"Rathitara n'eut pas d'enfants; c'est pourquoi il pria Angiras de lui donner des successeurs, et Angiras eut de la femme du prince des fils brillants de l'éclat du Véda.

"Quoique nés de la femme de Rathitara, ces fils d'Angiras n'en sont pas moins reconnus comme Angirasides; ils sont pour les Rathitaras les ancêtres, auteurs de leur race, et ils appartiennent aux deux tribus des Kchattriyas et des Bráhmanes."

* The scholiast considers that 'a hundred' is here used, as a round number, instead of 'a hundred and one.'

† *Pravara*. In the *Váyu-puráńa* and *Bhágavata-puráńa*, the word is *jyeshtha*, 'eldest'.

‡ शकुनिप्रमुखाः । Read, therefore, for "under Śakuni," "Śakuni and others".

§ IX., VI., 4.

Upon one of the days called Ashťaká,[1] Ikshwáku (being desirous of celebrating ancestral obsequies,) ordered Vikukshi to bring him flesh suitable for the offering. The prince, accordingly, went into the forest, and killed many deer and other wild animals,* (for the celebration). Being weary (with the chase), and being hungered, he (sat down and) ate a hare, after which, (being refreshed), he carried the rest of the game to his father. Vasishťha,† the family-priest‡ of the house of Ikshwáku, was summoned to consecrate the food;§

---

fifty, with Śakuni at their head,|| are placed in the north; and forty-eight in the south,—according to the Váyu,—of whom Vimati¶ was the chief. The same authority specifies, also, Nimi and Dańda, as sons of Ikshwáku, as does the Bhágavata,** with the addition of their reigning in the central regions.†† The distribution of the rest, in that work,‡‡ is, twenty-five in the west, as many in the east, and the rest elsewhere,—that is, the commentator adds, north and south. It seems very probable, that, by these sons of Ikshwáku, we are to understand colonies or settlers in various parts of India.

[1] See pp. 163, 169, *supra*.

---

* The original has only *mŕiga*.

† Several of my MSS. omit this name. ‡ *Kuláchárya*.

§ This is expressed by the term *prokshańáya*, 'for aspersion.'

|| The reading is as in note ‡ in the preceding page.

¶ The name appears to be Vimśati; विंशतिप्रमुखाः, "Vimśati and others." Different MSS. of the *Harivaṁśa* give, in ch. 664, Vaśáti, Vasáti, and Śaśáda.

** Vikukshi, Nimi, and Dańdaka. IX., VI., 4.

†† That is to say, between the Himálayas and the Vindhyas. So explains the commentator Śrídhara.

‡‡ IX., VI., 5:

तेषां पुरस्तादभवन्नार्यावर्ते नृपा नृप ।
पञ्चविंशतिः पश्चाच्च त्रयो मध्येऽपरेऽन्यतः ॥

but he declared that it was impure, in consequence of Vikukshi's having eaten a hare from amongst it; (making it, thus, as it were, the residue of his meal). Vikukshi was, in consequence, abandoned by his offended father; and the epithet Śaśáda (hare-eater) was affixed to him by the Guru.* On the death of Ikshwáku, the dominion of the earth descended to Śaśáda,[1] who was succeeded by his son Puranjaya.†

In the Tretá age, a violent war[2] broke out between the gods and the Asuras, in which the former were vanquished. They, consequently, had recourse to

---

[1] The Váyu states, that he was king of Ayodhyá, after the death of Ikshwáku.‡ The story occurs in all the authorities, more or less in detail.

[2] The Váyu§ says, it was in the war of the starling and the stork (आडीबके युद्धे), a conflict between Vasishtha and Viśwámitra, metamorphosed into birds, according to the Bhágavata:‖ but that work assigns it to a different period, or the reign of Hariśchandra. If the tradition have any import, it may refer to the ensigns of the contending parties; for banners with armorial devices were, as we learn from the Mahábhárata, invariably borne by princes and leaders.

---

* आह । शशभक्षणेनाशौचमिति । गुरुणाज्ञातेन ते पुत्रेणैतदाहृतमुपहतं यतोऽनेन शशको भक्षितः । ततश्चासौ विकुक्षिर्गुरुणैवमुक्तः शशादसंज्ञामवाप पित्रापि च परित्यक्तः ।

† Paranjaya is a variant of common occurrence, and the name sanctioned by the scholiast. Vide infra, p. 263, note 1.

‡ इक्ष्वाकौ संस्थिते तस्मिञ्छशादस्तु पृथिवीमिमाम् ॥
प्राप्तः परमधर्मात्मा सोऽयोध्याधिपोऽभवत् ॥

§ And so the *Harivaṁśa*, *ll.* 668.

‖ IX., VII., 6. Also *vide infra*, p. 257, note 1.

Vishńu, for assistance, and propitiated him (by their adorations). The eternal ruler of the universe, Náráyańa, had compassion upon them, and said:* "What you desire is known unto me. Hear how your wishes shall be fulfilled. There is an illustrious prince† named Puranjaya, the son of a royal sage:‡ into his person I will infuse a portion of myself; and, having descended upon earth, I will, in his person, subdue all your enemies. Do you, therefore, endeavour to secure the aid of Puranjaya, for the destruction of your foes."§ Acknowledging, with reverence, the kindness of the deity, the immortals quitted his presence, and repaired to Puranjaya, whom they thus addressed: "Most renowned Kshattriya, we have come to thee, to solicit thy alliance against our enemies: it will not become thee to disappoint our hopes."|| The prince replied: "Let this your Indra, the monarch of the spheres, (the god) of a hundred sacrifices, consent to carry me upon his shoulders, and I will wage battle with your adversaries, as your ally." The gods and Indra readily answered: "So be it"; and, the latter assuming the shape of a bull, the prince mounted upon his shoulder. Being then filled with delight, and invigorated by the power of the eternal¶ ruler of all movable and immovable

---

* प्रसन्नश्च देवानामनादिनिधनः सकलजगत्परायणो नारायणः प्राह ।

† *Kshattriya.*

‡ *Rájarshi.* And the Sanskrit adds 'Śaśáda.'

§ तस्य शरीरेऽहमंशेन स्वयमेवावतीर्य तानशेषानसुरान्निहनिष्यामि । तद्भवद्भिः पुरंजयोऽसुरवधार्थायोद्योगः कार्यः ।

|| *Prasádya.*

¶ *Achyuta.* See Vol. I., p. 15, note 8.

things, he destroyed, in the battle that ensued, all the enemies of the gods; and, because he annihilated the demon-host, whilst seated upon the shoulder (or the hump, Kakud,) of the bull, he, thence, obtained the appellation Kakutstha (seated on the hump).[1]

The son of Kakutstha was Anenas[2] whose son was Prithu, whose son was Viśwagaśwa,[3]* whose son was Árdra,[4]† whose son was Yuvanáśwa,‡ whose son was Śrávasta, by whom the city of Śrávastí[5] was founded.

[1] The Bhágavata adds, that he captured the city of the Asuras,§ situated in the west; whence his name Puranjaya, 'victor of the city.' He is, also, termed Paranjaya, 'vanquisher of foes:' he is, also, called Indraváha, 'borne by Indra.'‖

[2] Suyodhana: Matsya, Agni, Kúrma.¶

[3] Viśwaka: Linga. Viśwagandhi: Bhágavata.** Vishṭaráśwa: Brahma Puráńa and Hari Vaḿśa.††

[4] Ándhra: Váyu. Áyu: Agni. Chandra: Bhágavata.‡‡

[5] Śávasta and Śávastí: Bhágavata.§§ Śravasti:‖‖ Matsya, Linga,¶¶ and Kúrma; which also say, that Śravastí was in the country of Gauda, which is eastern Bengal.*** But it is, more usually,

* One MS. has Viśwaga; another, Viśwagata. The *Váyu-puráńa* seems to give Dŕishadaśwa.

† Two MSS. have Chándra. The *Linga-puráńa*, Prior Section, LXV., 33, has Árdraka.

‡ Yuvanáśwa seems to be the reading of the *Váyu-puráńa*.

§ Daityas, in the original.

‖ IX., VI., 12—16.

¶ And so the *Linga-puráńa*.

** IX., VI., 20.

†† *Śl.* 669.

‡‡ IX., VI., 20.

§§ IX., VI., 21.

‖‖ So reads the *Váyu-puráńa*.

¶¶ Prior Section, LXV., 34. I find Śávastí, also: and the king is there called Śávasti.

*** The term Gauda has not only this signification, but a much wider. See the references and quotations in Messrs. Böhtlingk and Roth's *Sanskrit-Wörterbuch*.

The son of Śrávasta was Bŕihadaśwa,* whose son was Kuvalayáśwa.† This prince, inspired with the spirit of Vishńu, destroyed the Asura Dhundhu, who had harassed the pious sage; Uttanka;§ and he was, thence, entitled Dhundhumára.[1] In his conflict with the demon,

placed in Kośala,' by which a part of Oude is commonly understood. In my Dictionary I have inserted Śrávanti, upon the authority of the Trikáńda Śesha;¶ but it is, no doubt, an error for Śrávasti. It is, there, also called Dharmapattana, being a city of some sanctity, in the estimation of the Buddhists. It is termed, by Fa-Hian, She-wei; by Hwan Tsang, She-lo-va-si-ti; and placed, by both, nearly in the site of Fyzabad in Oude. Account of the Foe-kúe-ki.**

[1] This legend is told, in much more detail, in the Váyu and Brahma Puráńas. Dhundhu hid himself beneath a sea of sand, which Kuvalayáśwa and his sons dug up,—undeterred by the flames which checked their progress,—and finally destroyed most of them. The legend originates, probably, in the occurrence of some physical phenomenon, as an earthquake, or volcano.

* According to the *Váyu-puráńa*, like our text, he had a most numerous family:

बृहदश्वस्य पुत्राणां सहस्राण्येकविंशतिः ।

† The *Váyu-puráńa* has Kuvaláśwa:

बृहदश्वसुतश्चापि कुवलाश्व इति श्रुतिः ।

And from several passages that follow this it is evident that the name is Kuvaláśwa. The *Harivanśa*, *l.* 671, etc., likewise has Kuvaláśwa; and so has the *Linga-puráńa*. ‡ *Maharshi*.

§ In two MSS. I find Utanka, the lection of the *Bhágavata-puráńa*, IX., VI., 22. The *Harivanśa*, *l.* 676, has, in different MSS., Utanka and Uttanka. The *Váyu-puráńa* gives, in my MSS., Uttanka.

|| See Vol. II., p. 172, notes 2, *etc.* ¶ II., I., 13.

** By Professor Wilson; in the *Journal of the Royal Asiatic Society*, Vol. V., pp. 122, 123.

Also see M. Vivien de Saint-Martin's *Mémoire Analytique*, *etc.*, p. 106; and General Cunningham, in the *Journal of the Asiatic Society of Bengal*, 1865, pp. 250—267.

the king was attended by his sons, to the number of twenty-one thousand; and all these, with the exception of only three, perished in the engagement, consumed by the fiery breath of Dhundhu. The three who survived were Dṛiḍháśwa, Chandráśwa,* and Kapiláśwa;† and the son and successor of the elder of these‡ was Haryaśwa:§ his son was Nikumbha; his son was Saṁhatáśwa;|| his son was Kṛiśáśwa; his son was Prasenajit; and his son was (another) Yuvanáśwa.[1]

[1] The series of names agrees very well to Saṁhatáśwa, called Barhaṇáśwa in the Bhágavata.¶ We have, there, some variations, and some details not noticed in our text. The Váyu, Brahma, Agni, Linga, Matsya, and Kúrma ascribe two sons to Saṁhatáśwa, whom the two first name Kṛiśáśwa and Akṛiśáśwa, and the rest, Kṛiśáśwa and Raṇáśwa.** Senajit†† or Prasenajit‡‡ is, generally, though not always, termed the son of the younger brother; but the commentator§§ on the Hari Vaṁśa calls him the son of Saṁhatáśwa, whilst the Matsya, Agni, Linga, and Kúrma omit him, and make Mándhátṛi the son of Raṇáśwa.|||| The mother of Prasenajit and the wife of Akṛiśáśwa or Saṁhatáśwa,—according to the different interpretations,—was the daughter of Himavat,

* In the *Váyu-puráṇa* the name is Bhadráśwa.

† The *Bhágavata-puráṇa*, IX., VI., 24, has Dṛiḍháśwa, Kapiláśwa, and Bhadráśwa.

‡ The original here again names Dṛiḍháśwa, but says nothing of his seniority: [illegible]

§ The *Linga-puráṇa*, Prior Section, LXV., 37, interposes Pramoda between Dṛiḍháśwa and Haryaśwa.

|| One MS. has Hitáśwa; another, Saṁhitáśwa. The latter is the reading of some MSS. of the *Váyu-puráṇa*; others giving Saṁhatáśwa.

¶ IX., VI., 25.

** The *Linga-puráṇa* distinctly calls Yuvanáśwa son of Raṇáśwa.

†† *Bhágavata-puráṇa*, IX., VI., 25.

‡‡ So reads the *Váyu-puráṇa*.

§§ Nílakaṇṭha, on *Sl.* 709. Arjuna Miśra comments to the like effect.

|||| The *Linga-puráṇa* represents Mándhátṛi to be son of Yuvanáśwa.

Yuvanáśwa had no son, at which he was deeply grieved. Whilst residing in the vicinage of the holy Munis, he inspired them with pity (for his childless condition); and they instituted a religious rite, to pro-

known as Drishadwatí, the river so termed"* (Vol. II., p. 142, note 4). The wife of Yuvanáśwa, according to the Váyu, or of Prasenajit, according to the Brahma, was Gaurí, the daughter of Rantinara,† who, incurring the imprecation of her husband, became the Báhudá river (Vol. II., p. 142, note 3). The Brahma and Hari Vaṁśa‡ call Yuvanáśwa her son; but, in another place,§ the Hari Vaṁśa contradicts itself, calling Gaurí the daughter of Matinára,‖ of the race of Puru, the mother of Mándhátṛi; here following, apparently, the Matsya, in which it is so stated. The Brahma Puráńa is not guilty of the inconsistency. The Váyu of course gives the title to Mándhátṛi, with the addition, that he was called Gaurika, after his mother:

तस्मात्तु गौरिकः पुत्रश्चक्रवर्ती बभूव ह ।
मान्धाता यौवनाश्वो वै त्रैलोक्यविजयी नृपः ॥

Mándhátṛi's birth from Gaurí is the more remarkable, as it is incompatible with the usual legend, given in our text and in the Bhágavata, which seems, therefore, to have been of subsequent origin, suggested by the etymology of the name. In the Bhágavata,¶ Mándhátṛi is also named Trasaddasyu, or "the terrifier of thieves."

* The *Váyu-puráńa* states:

कृशाश्वश्चाक्षयाश्वश्च संहताश्वसुतावुभौ ।
तस्य पत्नी हैमवती सती मान्या दृषद्वती ॥

Compare the *Harivaṁśa*, *śl.* 708, 709.

† I have much doubt as to the correctness of this name.

‡ *Śl.* 709.

§ *Śl.* 1715, 1716.

‖ Erroneously printed, in the former edition, "Matimara."

¶ IX., VI., 33:

त्रसद्दस्युरितीन्द्रोऽङ्ग विदधे नाम यस्य वै ।
यस्मात्त्रसन्ति ह्युद्विग्ना दस्यवो रावणादयः ॥

cure him progeny. One night, during its performance, the sages, having placed a vessel of consecrated water upon the altar, had retired to repose. It was past midnight, when the king awoke, exceedingly thirsty; and, unwilling to disturb any of the holy inmates of the dwelling, he looked about for something to drink. In his search, he came to the water in the jar, which had been sanctified and endowed with prolific efficacy* by sacred texts, and he drank it. When the Munis† rose, and found that the water had been drunk, they inquired who had taken it, and said: "The queen[‡] that has drunk this water shall give birth to a mighty and valiant son." "It was I," exclaimed the Raja, "who unwittingly drank the water:" and, accordingly, in the belly of Yuvanáśwa was conceived a child. And it grew; and in, due time, it ripped open the right side of the Raja, and was born: and the Raja did not die. Upon the birth of the child, "Who will be its nurse?" said the Munis; when (Indra,) the king of the gods appeared, and said, "He shall have me for his nurse" (mám ayaṁ dhásyati); and, hence, the boy was named Mándhátri. Indra put his fore-finger into the mouth of the infant, who sucked it, and drew from it (heavenly) nectar.§ And he grew up, and became a mighty monarch,|| and reduced the seven continental zones under his dominion. And here a verse is recited: "From the rising to the going down of the sun, all that is irra-

---

* *Aparimeya-máhátmya.*
† *Rishi*, in the original.
‡ The original has: राज्ञी ऽस्य युवनाश्वस्य पत्नी ।
§ *Amṛita.*
|| *Chakravartin.*

diated by his light is the land of Mándhátri, the son of Yuvanáswa."[1]

Mándhátri married Bindumatí,* the daughter of Śaśabindu,† and had, by her, three sons, Purukutsa,‡ Ambarísha, and Muchukunda:§ he had, also, fifty daughters.[2]

The (devout) sage‖ Saubhari, learned in the Vedas,¶ had spent twelve years immersed in a piece of water; the sovereign of the fish in which, named Sammada,

---

[1] The Váyu cites this same verse, and another, with the remark, that they were uttered by those acquainted with the Puráńas and with genealogies:

अथाप्युदाहरन्तीमौ श्लोकौ पौराणिका द्विजाः ।
यावत्सूर्यस्य उदयो यावदस्तमयं भवेत् ।**
सर्वं तद्यौवनाश्वस्य मान्धातुः क्षेत्रमुच्यते ॥
अथाप्युदाहरन्तीमं श्लोकं वंशविदो जनाः ।
यौवनाश्वं महात्मानं राजानमभितोवदन् ।
मान्धातारं तनुं विष्णोः पुराणज्ञाः प्रचक्षते ॥

[2] The Brahma and Agni omit Ambarísha, for whom the Matsya substitutes Dharmasena. The following legend of Saubhari occurs, elsewhere, only in the Bhágavata,†† and there, less in detail.

---

* A Bindumatí is spoken of, in the *Harshacharita*, as having slain Vidúratha. See my *Vásavadattá*, Preface, p. 53.

† Compare the *Harivamśa*, *sl.* 712.

‡ One MS. has Purushakutsa, a reading of no value; the like of which I often pass by unnoticed. The Purukutsa of the *Rigveda*—see IV., XLII., 8, 9,—is called son of Durgaha, who is again named in the same work, VIII., LIV, 12.

§ The *Linga-puráńa* seems to read Muchakunda.

‖ *Rishi*.

¶ *Bahvricha*. *Vide supra*, p. 50, note ‡.

** In the *Vishńu-puráńa* this verse is read thus:

यावत्सूर्य उदेति स्म यावच्च प्रतितिष्ठति ।

†† IX., VI., 39—55.

of large bulk, had a very numerous progeny. His children and his grandchildren* were wont to frolic around him, in all directions;† and he lived amongst them happily, playing with them night and day. Saubhari, the sage, being disturbed, in his devotions, by their sports, contemplated the patriarchal felicity of the monarch of the lake, and reflected: "How enviable is this creature, who, although born in a degraded state of being, is ever thus sporting cheerfully amongst his offspring and their young! Of a truth, he awakens, in my mind, the wish to taste such pleasure; and I, also, will make merry amidst my children."‡ Having thus resolved, the Muni came up, hastily, from the water, and, desirous of entering upon the condition of a householder, went to Mándhátri, to demand one of his daughters as his wife. As soon as he was informed of the arrival of the sage, the king rose up from his throne, offered him the customary libation,§ and treated him with the most profound respect. Having taken a seat, Saubhari said to the Raja: "I have determined to marry. Do you, king, give me one of your daughters, as a wife. Disappoint not my affection.|| It is not the practice of the princes of the race of Kakutstha to turn away from compliance with the wishes of those who come to them for succour. There are, O monarch, other kings of the

* पौत्रदौहित्राः, "sons' sons and daughters' sons."

† The original says that they "frolicked at his sides, in front of him, on his back, and over his breast, tail, and head": पार्श्वतोऽग्रतः पृष्ठतो वक्षःपुच्छशिरसां चोपरि भ्रमन्तः ।

‡ The translation, hereabouts, is greatly compressed.

§ *Arghya.*

|| *Praṇaya.*

earth to whom daughters have been born; but your family is, above all, renowned for observance of liberality in your donations to those who ask your bounty. You have, O prince, fifty daughters. Give one of them to me; that so I may be relieved from the anxiety I suffer through fear that my suit may be denied."

When Mándhátri heard this request, and looked upon the person of the sage, emaciated by (austerity and) old age, he felt disposed to refuse his consent: but, dreading to incur the anger and imprecation of the holy man, he was much perplexed, and, declining his head, was lost awhile in thought. The Ŕishi, observing his hesitation, said: "On what, O Raja, do you meditate? I have asked for nothing which may not be readily accorded. And what is there that shall be unattainable to you, if my desires be gratified by the damsel whom you must needs give unto me?" To this, the king, apprehensive of his displeasure,* answered and said: "Grave sir, it is the established usage of our house to wed our daughters to such persons only as they shall, themselves, select from suitors of fitting rank; and, since this your request is not yet made known to my maidens, it is impossible to say whether it may be equally agreeable to them as it is to me. This is the occasion of my perplexity; and I am at a loss what to do." This answer of the king was fully understood by the Ŕishi, who said to himself: "This is merely a device of the Raja, to evade compliance with my suit. He has reflected that I am an old man, having no attractions for women, and not likely to be accepted by any of

* *Śápa*, 'curse'.

his daughters.* Even be it so: I will be a match for him." And he then spake aloud, and said: "Since such is the custom, mighty prince, give orders that I be admitted into the interior of the palace.† Should any of the maidens, your daughters, be willing to take me for a bridegroom, I will have her for my bride. If no one be willing, then let the blame attach alone to the years that I have numbered."‡ Having thus spoken, he was silent.

Mándhátri, unwilling to provoke the indignation§ of the Muni, was, accordingly, obliged to command the eunuch to lead the sage into the inner chambers; who, as he entered the apartments, put on a form and features of beauty far exceeding the personal charms of mortals, or even of heavenly spirits.‖ His conductor, addressing the princesses, said to them: "Your father, young ladies, sends you this pious sage,¶ who has demanded of him a bride; and the Raja has promised him, that he will not refuse him any one of you who shall choose him for her husband."** When the damsels heard this, and looked upon the person of the Rishi, they were equally inspired with passion and desire, and, like a troop of female elephants disputing

* वृद्धोऽयमनभिमतः स्त्रीणां किमुत कन्यानामित्यमुना संचिन्त्यैव-मभिहितम् ।

† यद्येवं तदादिश्यतामस्माकं प्रवेशाय कन्यान्तःपुरवर्षधरः ।

‡ अन्यथा चेत्तदलमस्माकमेतेनातीतकालारम्भेण ।

§ *Śápa.*

‖ *Siddha* and *gandharva*, in the original.

¶ *Brahmarshi.*

** मया चास्य प्रतिज्ञातं यद्यस्मत्कन्यकानां काचिद्भगवन्तं वरयति तत्कन्या-च्छन्दस्य नाहं परिपन्थानं करिष्यामि ।

the favours of the master of the herd, they all contended for the choice.* "Away, away, sister!" said each to the other: "this is my election; he is my choice; he is not a meet bridegroom for you; he has been created, by Brahmá, on purpose for me, as I have been created in order to become his wife; he has been chosen, by me, before you; you have no right to prevent his becoming my husband." In this way arose a violent quarrel amongst the daughters of the king, each insisting upon the exclusive election of the Ŕishi; and, as the blameless sage was thus contended for by the rival princesses, the superintendent of the inner apartments, with a downcast look, reported to the king what had occurred.† Perplexed, more than ever, by this information, the Raja exclaimed: "What is all this? And what am I to do now? What is it that I have said? And, at last, although with extreme reluctance, he was obliged to agree that the Ŕishi should marry all his daughters.

Having then wedded, agreeably to law, all the princesses, the sage took them home to his habitation, where he employed the chief of architects, Viśwakarman,—equal, in taste and skill, to Brahmá himself,:—to construct separate palaces for each of his wives: he ordered him to provide each building with elegant couches, and seats, and furniture, and to attach to them gardens and groves, with reservoirs of water, where the wild-duck and the swan should sport amidst beds

* करेणव इवेभयूथपतिं तमृषिमहमहमिकया वरयाम्बभूवुः ।

† Hereabouts the rendering is rather freer than usual.

: विधातारमिवापरम् ।

of lotos-flowers. The divine artist* obeyed his injunctions, and constructed splendid apartments for the wives of the Ṛishi; in which, by command of Saubhari, the inexhaustible† and divine treasure called Nanda[1] took up his permanent abode; and the princesses entertained all their guests and dependants with abundant viands of every description and the choicest quality.§

After some period had elapsed, the heart of King Mándhátṛi yearned for his daughters; and he felt solicitous to know whether they were happily circumstanced. Setting off, therefore, on a visit to the hermitage of Saubhari, he beheld, upon his arrival, a row of beautiful crystal palaces, shining as brilliantly as the rays of the sun, and situated amidst lovely gardens and reservoirs of pellucid water. Entering into one of these magnificent palaces, he found and embraced a daughter, and said to her, as the tears of affection and delight trembled in his eyes: "Dear child, tell me how it is with you. Are you happy here, or not? Does the great sage treat you with tenderness? Or do you revert, with regret, to your early home?" The princess replied: "You behold, my father, how delightful a mansion I inhabit,—surrounded by lovely gardens and lakes,

---

[1] The great Nidhi. A Nidhi is a treasure, of which there are several belonging to Kubera. Each has its guardian spirit, or is personified.

---

* *Twashṭṛi.* † *Anapáyin.*

‡ It is not clear why Professor Wilson here personifies *nanda*, as if this Puráńa were a Tantra. In his *Essays, Analytical, &c.*, Vol. II., pp. 379, 380, there is a valuable note on the nine *nidhis* of Kubera.

§ The translation of this paragraph is not very close; and the same may be said of the remainder of the chapter.

where the lotos blooms, and the wild swans murmur. Here I have delicious viands, fragrant unguents, costly ornaments, splendid raiment,* soft beds, and every enjoyment that affluence can procure. Why, then, should I call to memory the place of my birth?† To your favour am I indebted for all that I possess. I have only one cause of anxiety, which is this: my husband is never absent from my dwelling; solely attached to me, he is always at my side; he never goes near my sisters; and I am concerned to think that they must feel mortified by his neglect: this is the only circumstance that gives me uneasiness."

Proceeding to visit another of his daughters, the king, after embracing her, and sitting down, made the same inquiry, and received the same account of the enjoyments with which the princess was provided. There was, also, the same complaint, that the Rishi was wholly devoted to her, and paid no attention to her sisters. In every palace Mándhátri heard the same story, from each of his daughters, in reply to his questions; and, with a heart overflowing with wonder and delight, he repaired to the wise Saubhari, whom he found alone, and, after paying homage to him, thus addressed him: "Holy sage, I have witnessed this thy marvellous power. The like miraculous faculties I have never known any other to possess. How great is the reward of thy devout austerities!" Having thus saluted the sage, and

* The original here supplies but one epithet, *manonukúla*, to four substantives.

† The question of the princess rather implies, that, in spite of this very luxury, she cannot forget her early home: तथापि किं वा जन्मभूमिर्न स्मर्यते ।

been received, by him, with respect, the Raja resided with him for some time, partaking of the pleasures of the place, and then returned to his capital.

In the course of time, the daughters of Mándhátri bore to Saubhari a hundred and fifty sons; and, day by day, his affection for his children became more intense, and his heart was wholly occupied with the sentiment of self.[1] "These my sons," he loved to think, "will charm me with their infant prattle; then they will learn to walk; they will, then, grow up to youth, and to manhood; I shall see them married, and they will have children; and I may behold the children of those children." By these and similar reflections, however, he perceived that his anticipations every day outstripped the course of time; and, at last, he exclaimed:* "What exceeding folly is mine!† There is no end to my desires. Though all I hope should come to pass for ten thousand or a hundred thousand years, still new wishes would spring up. When I have seen my infants walk; when I have beheld their youth, their manhood, their marriage, their progeny; still my expectations are unsatisfied, and my soul yearns to behold the de-

---

[1] Of Mamatá, 'mineness' (ममता); the notion that wives, children, wealth, belong to an individual, and are essential to his happiness.

---

* एवमादिमनोरथमनुदिनकालसंपत्तिपूर्तिमवेक्ष्य तत्तिचिन्तयामास ।
"Having discovered that some such desire kept pace with the daily increase of time, he took thought as follows."

So the commentary explains this passage, and very naturally: अनुदिनं कालस्य संपत्तिराधिक्यं तया पूर्तिरनुवर्तनं यस्य मनोरथे तमवेक्ष्य ज्ञात्वा अचिन्तयत् । इतद्वक्ष्यमाणम् ।

† The rest of the chapter, from this point, is in verse.

scendants of their descendants. Shall I even see them, some other wish will be engendered; and, when that is accomplished, how is the birth of fresh desires to be prevented? I have, at last, discovered, that there is no end to hope, until it terminates in death; and that the mind which is perpetually engrossed by expectation can never be attached to the supreme spirit. My mental devotions, whilst immersed in water, were interrupted by attachment to my friend the fish. The result of that connexion was my marriage; and insatiable desires are the consequences of my married life. The pain attendant upon the birth of my single body is now augmented by the cares attached to fifty others, and is further multiplied by the numerous children whom the princesses have borne to me.* The sources of affliction will be repeatedly renewed by their children, and by their espousals, and by their progeny, and will be infinitely increased: a married life is a mine of individual anxiety.† My devotions, first disturbed by the fish of the pool, have since been obstructed by temporal indulgence; and I have been beguiled by that desire for progeny which was communicated to me by association with Saṁmada.‡ Separation from the world

---

* दुःखं यदैवैकशरीरजन्म
शतार्धसंख्यं तदिदं प्रसूतम्।
परिग्रहेण क्षितिपात्मजानां
सुतैरनेकैर्बहुलीकृतं तत्॥

† "Individual anxiety" is to render *mamatá*, for which see the Translator's note in the preceding page.

‡ चीर्णं तपो यत्तु जलाश्रयेण
तस्यर्द्धिरेषा तपसोऽन्तरायः।
मत्स्यस्य सङ्गादभवच्च यो मे
सुतादिरागो मुषितोऽस्मि तेन॥

is the only path of the sage to final liberation: from commerce with mankind innumerable errors proceed. The ascetic who has accomplished a course of self-denial falls from perfection, by contracting worldly attachments. How much more likely should one so fall, whose observances are incomplete![*] My intellect has been a prey to the desire of married happiness: but I will, now, so exert myself, for the salvation of my soul, that, exempt from human imperfections, I may be exonerated from human sufferings.[†] To that end, I will propitiate, by arduous penance, Vishńu, the creator of the universe, whose form is inscrutable, who is smaller than the smallest, larger than the largest, the source of darkness and of light, the sovereign god of gods.[‡] On his everlasting body, which is both discrete and indiscrete substance, illimitably mighty, and identical with the universe, may my mind, wholly free from sin, be ever steadily intent, so that I may be born no more! To him I fly for refuge; to that Vishńu who is the teacher of teachers, who is one with all beings, the

---

* निःसंगता मुक्तिपदं यतीनां
संगादशेषाः प्रभवन्ति दोषाः ।
आरूढयोगोऽपि निपात्यतेऽधः
संगेन योगी किमुताल्पसिद्धिः ॥

† अहं चरिष्यामि तथात्मनोऽर्थे
परिग्रहग्राहगृहीतबुद्धिः ।
यथा हि भूयः परिहीनदोषो
जनस्य दुःखैर्भविता न दुःखी ॥

‡ सर्वस्य धातारमचिन्त्यरूप-
मणोरणीयांसमतिप्रमाणम् ।
सितासितं चेश्वरमीश्वराणा-
माराधयिष्ये तपसैव विष्णुम् ॥

pure eternal lord of all, without beginning, middle, or end, and besides whom is nothing."*

---

* तस्मिन्नशेषौजसि सर्वरूपि-
ण्यव्यक्तविस्पष्टतनावनन्ते ।
ममाचलं चित्तमपेतदोषं
सदास्तु विष्णावभवाय भूयः ॥
समस्तभूतादमलादनन्ता-
त्सर्वेश्वरादन्यदनादिमध्यात् ।
यस्मान्न किंचित्तमहं गुरूणां
परं गुरुं संश्रयमेमि विष्णुम् ॥

CHAPTER III.

Saubhari and his wives adopt an ascetic life. Descendants of Mándhátri. Legend of Narmadá and Purukutsa. Legend of Triśanku. Báhu driven from his kingdom by the Haihayas and Tálajanghas. Birth of Sagara: he conquers the barbarians, imposes upon them distinguishing usages, and excludes them from offerings to fire and the study of the Vedas.

HAVING thus communed with himself, Saubhari abandoned his children, his home, and all his splendour, and, accompanied by his wives, entered the forest, where he daily practised the observances followed by the ascetics termed Vaikhánasas* (or anchorets having families), until he had cleansed himself from all sin. When his intellect had attained maturity, he concentrated in his spirit the (sacramental) fires,[1] and became a religious mendicant.† Then, having consigned all his acts to the supreme,‡ he obtained the condition of Achyuta, which knows no change, and is not subject to the vicissitudes of birth, transmigration,§ or death. Whoever reads, or hears, or remembers, or understands‖ this legend of Saubhari and his espousal of the daugh-

---

[1] So Manu; "Having reposited, as the law directs, the holy fires in his breast," &c. VI., 25.¶

---

* The *vaikhánasa* is the same as the *vánaprastha*, for a detail of whose duties, and of those of the *bhikshu*, *vide supra*, pp. 94—97.

† *Bhikshu*. ‡ *Bhagavat*. § *Avikára*.

‖ *Avadháryati*.

¶ अग्नीनात्मनि वैतानान्समारोप्य यथाविधि ।
अनग्निरनिकेतः स्यान्मुनिर्मूलफलाशनः ॥

ters of Mándhátri shall never, for eight successive births, be addicted to evil thoughts; nor shall he act unrighteously, nor shall his mind dwell upon improper objects, nor shall he be influenced by selfish attachments. The line of Mándhátri is now resumed.

The son of Ambarísha, the son of Mándhátri, was Yuvanáswa:* his son was Harita,[1]† from whom the Angirasa Háritas‡ were descended.[2]

---

[1] The Váyu, Linga, Kúrma, and Bhágavata§ agree in this series: the others omit it.

[2] The words of the text are: तस्माद्धरितो यतोऽङ्गिरसो हारिताः। And the commentator explains the phrase: 'The Angirasa Brahmans, of whom the Hárita family was the chief.'|| The Linga¶ reads:

हरितो युवनाश्वस्य हारिता यत आत्मजाः।
एते ह्यङ्गिरसः पक्षे क्षत्रोपेता द्विजातयः॥

'Harita was the son of Yuvanáswa, whose sons were the Háritas. They were on the part (or followers) of Angiras, and were Brahmans with the properties of Kshattriyas.' The Váyu has:

हरितो युवनाश्वस्य हारीता भूरयः सुताः।
एते ह्यङ्गिरसः पुत्राः क्षत्रोपेता द्विजातयः॥**

'Harita was the son of Yuvanáswa, from whom were many

---

* The *Bhágavata-puráńa*, IX., VII., 1, has Yauvanáswa. See the next page, note ‡.

† Some MSS. have Hárita, like the *Bhágavata*.

‡ All my best MSS., supported by the commentary, yield 'Háritas'.

§ But see note ‡ in the page next following.

|| I find: अम्बरीषस्य युवनाश्वः प्रपितामहसनामा यतो हरिता- हारीता आङ्गिरसो द्विजा हरितगोत्रप्रवराः। अत्र हरितानामादिवंशा आङ्गिरसाम्बरीषयौवनाश्वेति प्रवरपाठात्।

¶ Prior Section, LXV., 40, 41.

** My MSS. differ, as to this stanza, from those followed by Professor Wilson. *Vide infra*, p. 263, note ¶.

In the regions below the earth,* the Gandharvas called Mauneyas † (or, sons of the Muni Kaśyapa), who

---

called Háritas. They were sons of Angiras, and Brahmans with the properties of Kshattriyas.' The Bhágavata ‡ has only: मान्धातृप्रवरा इमे । These (Ambarisha, Purukutsa, and Harita,) were, according to Śrídhara Swámin's comment, the chiefs of Mándhátri's descendants; being founders of three several branches: or it may mean, he says, merely that they had Mándhátri for their progenitor; Mándhátri being, by some, also named Angiras, according to Áśwaláyana.§ It may be questioned if the compilers of the Puráńas, or their annotators, knew exactly what to make of this and similar phrases,|| although they were, probably, intended to intimate, that some persons of Kshattriya origin became the disciples of certain Brahmans, particularly of Angiras, and, afterwards, founders of schools of religious instruction, themselves. Mándhátri himself is the author of a hymn in the Ṙig-veda. Asiatic Researches, Vol. VIII., p. 385.¶ Hárita is the name of an individual

---

* *Rasátala*. See Vol. II., p. 209, note 1.

† The commentator says they were Chitrasena and others: see Vol. II., p. 285, note †. The term seems to be a general epithet of the Gandharvas, derived from their mother, Muni: see the *Mahábhárata*, *Ádi-parvan*, *śl.* 2552; *Harivaḿśa*, *śl.* 11553. In Vol. II., p. 75, it is the Apsarases that spring from Kaśyapa and Muni; the Gandharvas being the offspring of Kaśyapa and Arishṫá.

‡ IX., VII., 1. Subjoined are the original and Burnouf's translation:

मांधातुः पुत्रप्रवरो योऽम्बरीषः प्रकीर्तितः ।
पितामहेन प्रवृतो यौवनाश्वश्च तत्सुतः ।
हारीतस्तस्य पुत्रोऽभून्मांधातृप्रवरा इमे ॥

"Le fils aîné de Mândhâtri qui est célèbre sous le nom d'Ambaricha, fut adopté par son grand-père Yuvanâçva; c'est pourquoi le fils d'Ambaricha est nommé Yâuvanâçva. Ce dernier prince eut pour fils Hârita; ces [trois] personnages (Ambaricha, Yâuvanâçva et Hârita) ont pour auteur commun Mândhâtri."

§ ? See Professor Max Müller's *History of Ancient Sanskrit Literature*, p. 383.

|| *Vide supra*, p. 255, note 2; p. 268, note 1.

¶ Or Colebrooke's *Miscellaneous Essays*, Vol. I., p. 25.

were sixty millions in number, had defeated the tribes of the Nágas (or snake-gods), and seized upon their most precious jewels, and usurped their dominion. Deprived of their power by the Gandharvas, the serpent-chiefs addressed the god of the gods, as he awoke from his slumbers; and the blossoms of his lotos-eyes opened, while listening to their hymns.* They said: "Lord, how shall we be delivered from this great fear?" Then replied the first of males,† who is without beginning: "I will enter into the person of Purukutsa, the son of Mándhátri, the son of Yuvanáśwa; and in him will I quiet these iniquitous Gandharvas." On hearing these words, the snake-gods bowed and withdrew, and, returning to their country, despatched Narmadá, to solicit the aid of Purukutsa.[1].

Narmadá accordingly went to Purukutsa, and conducted him to the regions below the earth,‡ where, being filled with the might of the deity, he destroyed the Gandharvas. He then returned to his own palace; and the snake-gods, in acknowledgement of Narmadá's services, conferred upon her, as a blessing, that, who-

---

sage, considered as the son of Chyavana, and to whom a work on law is attributed. It is, probably, rather that of a school, however, than of an individual.

[1] Narmadá, the personified Nerbudda river, was, according to the Bhágavata,§ the sister of the Nágas.||

---

* The rendering here is somewhat lax.

† *Purushottama*. See Vol. I., p. 16, note ‡.

‡ *Rasátala*.

§ IX., VII., 2.

|| For another origin of her, *vide supra*, p. 162, note ||; p. 185, note ‡.

soever should think of her, and invoke her name, should never have any dread of the venom of snakes.* This is the invocation: "Salutation be to Narmadá in the morning; salutation be to Narmadá at night; salutation be to thee, O Narmadá! Defend me from the serpent's poison."† Whoever repeats this, day and night, shall never be bitten by a snake, in the dark, or in entering a chamber; nor shall he who calls it to mind, when he eats, suffer any injury from poison, though it be mixed with his food. To Purukutsa, also, the snake-gods announced, that the series of his descendants should never be cut off.

Purukutsa had a son, by Narmadá, named Trasadasyu,‡ whose son was Sambhúta,[1]§ whose son was

---

[1] We have some varieties here. Instead of Trasadasyu, the Matsya has Dussaha, whom it makes the husband of Narmadá, and father of Sambhúti, the father of Tridhanwan. The Bhágavata|| omits Sambhúti; the Linga¶ makes him the brother of Trasadasyu; and the Agni has, in his place, Sudhanwan.

---

* For सर्पविषभयं there is a variant, सर्वविषभयं, "dread of any poison."

† नर्मदायै नमः प्रातर्नर्मदायै नमो निशि ।
नमोऽस्तु नर्मदे तुभ्यं त्राहि मां विषसर्पतः ॥

‡ Some MSS. read, like the *Bhágavata-puráńa*, Trasaddasyu. *Vide supra*, p. 266, note ¶, for this word as an epithet.

§ The *Váyu-puráńa* reads, in my MSS.,

नर्मदायां समुत्पन्नः संभूतस्तस्य चात्मजः ।

It seems, then,—*vide supra*, p. 165, Sanskrit extract in note †,—that Trasadasyu and Sambhúta are one, unless they are brothers.

|| IX., VII., 3. It says that Anaranya was son of Trasaddasyu.

¶ Prior Section, LXV., 41, 42. Then follows:

विष्णुवृद्धः सुतस्तस्य विष्णुवृद्धा यतः स्मृताः ।
इति हारितकः पश्चात् ब्रह्मोपेताः समाश्रिताः ।
संभूतिरपरं पुत्रमनरण्यमजीजनत् ॥

Anarańya, who was slain by Rávańa, in his triumphant progress through the nations.* The son of Anarańya was Prishadaśwa;† his son was Haryaśwa; his son was Sumanas;[1] his son was Tridhanwan; his son was Trayyáruńa:‡ and his son was Satyavrata, who obtained the appellation of Triśanku,§ and was degraded to the

---

[1] Bŕishadaśwa: Váyu.|| The Matsya, Agni, and Brahma omit all between Sambhúta and Tridhanwan.¶ The Bhágavata** has a rather different series, or, Anarańya, Haryaśwa, Arińa, Tribandhana, Triśanku. As Anarańya is famous in Hindu story,†† and Trayyáruńa‡‡ is a contributor to the Ŕig-veda, their omission shows careless compilation.

Sambhúti is, thus, provided with two sons, Vishńuvŕiddha—founder of the Vishńuvŕiddhas,—and Anarańya.

The first two of these lines—only with the substitution of सुता: for सुते—occur in the Váyu-puráńa, likewise. *Vide supra*, p. 280, note * *.

* The *Váyu-puráńa* distinctly says, in my MSS., that he slew Rávańa:

रावणो निहतो येन त्रिलोकविजये पुरा ।

† Bŕihadaśwa. *Linga-puráńa*. And so, I think, the *Váyu-puráńa* is intended to read.

‡ One MS. has Trayyárańí.

§ *Vide infra*, p. 286, note †.

|| There, as in the *Linga-puráńa*, Prior Section, LXV., 45, I find Vasumanas, with Dŕishadwatí—which name seems to have been misread Bŕishadaśwa—for his mother:

हर्यश्वाद्दृषद्वत्यां जज्ञे वसुमना नृपः ।

Vasumanas, son of Rohidaśwa, is mentioned in the *Anukramańiká* to the *Ŕigveda*, X., 179.

¶ The *Harivanśa*, *ll.* 715, 716, has, also, Sambhúta, Sudhanwan, Tridhanwan.

** IX., VII., 4.

†† Particularly in the *Rámáyańa*.

‡‡ Read "Tryaruńa." *Vide supra*, p. 36, note †. In the *Ŕigveda*, V., XXVII., 3, Tryaruńa and Trasadasyu are mentioned as if contemporaries.

condition of a Cháńdála (or outcaste).[1]* During a twelve years' famine,† Triśanku provided the flesh of deer, for the nourishment of the wife and children of Viśwámitra; suspending it upon a (spreading) fig-tree:‡ on the borders of the Ganges,§ that he might not subject them to the indignity of receiving presents from an outcaste.|| On this account, Viśwámitra, being highly

---

[1] The Váyu states, he was banished, by his father, for his wickedness (Adharma). The Brahma Puráńa and Hari Vaḿśa¶ detail his iniquity at length; and it is told more concisely in the Linga. He carried off the betrothed wife of another man;—one of the citizens, according to the two former; of Vidarbha, according to the latter. For this, his father, by the advice of Vasishtha, banished him; and he took refuge with Śwapákas. The Rámáyańa** has a different story, and ascribes Triśanku's degradation to the curse of the sons of Vasishtha, to whom the king had applied to conduct his sacrifice, after their father had refused to do so. Before that, he is described†† as a pious prince (सत्य-वादी जितेन्द्रियः); and the object of his sacrifice was to ascend to heaven.

---

* For Triśanku, a Cháńdála king known to Buddhist tradition, and probably the same person, see Burnouf's *Introduction à l'Histoire du Buddhisme Indien*, Vol. I., pp. 207, *et seq.*

† Literally, 'drought,' *anávrishti*.

‡ *Nyagrodha*.

§ Jáhnaví, in the original.

|| An expansion of चण्डालप्रतिग्रहपरिहाराय।

¶ *St.* 717, *et seq.*

** *Bála-káńda*, LVIII.

†† *Ibid.*, LVII., 10.

pleased with him, elevated him, in his living body, to heaven.[1]

---

[1] The occurrence of the famine, and Satyavrata's care of the wife and family of Viśwámitra, are told, with some variations, in the Váyu, which has been followed by the Brahma and Hari Vaḿśa.* During the famine, when game fails, he kills the cow of Vasishṭha; and, for the three crimes of displeasing his father, killing a cow, and eating flesh not previously consecrated, he acquires the name of Triśanku (tri, 'three', śanku, 'sin').† Vasishṭha refusing to perform his regal inauguration, Viśwámitra celebrates the rites, and, on his death, elevates the king, in his mortal body, to heaven. The Rámáyańa relates the same circumstance, but assigns to it a different motive,—Viśwámitra's resentment of the refusal of the gods to attend Triśanku's sacrifice. That work also describes the attempt of the gods to cast the king down upon earth, and the compromise between them and Viśwámitra, by which Triśanku was left suspended, head downwards, in mid-air, forming a constellation in the southern hemisphere, along with other new planets and stars formed by Viśwámitra. The Bhágavata‡ has an allusion to this legend, saying that Triśanku is still visible in heaven.

---

* *Sl.* 724, *et seq.* See *Original Sanskrit Texts*, Part I., pp. 86—88.

† *Triśanku*—"he of three delinquencies,"—was so called, according to the commentator on the *Vishńu-puráńa*, because he ate what was unhallowed, slew his spiritual teacher's cow, and disobeyed his father's commands: अप्रोक्षितभक्षणगुरुधेनुवधपितृवाक्यलङ्घनरूपैस्त्रिभिः शङ्कुभिरिव हृदि व्यथाहेतुभिस्त्रिशङ्कुसंज्ञामवाप। Then follows a quotation of the *Harivaḿśa*, *sl.* 748, 749:

पितुश्चापरितोषेण गुरोर्दोग्ध्रीवधेन च।
अप्रोक्षितोपयोगाच्च त्रिविधस्ते व्यतिक्रमः॥
एवं त्रीण्यस्य शङ्कूनि तानि दृष्ट्वा महातपाः।
त्रिशङ्कुरिति होवाच त्रिशङ्कुस्तेन स स्मृतः॥

Also see Śrídhara on the *Bhágavata-puráńa*, IX., VII., 5.

‡ IX., VII., 5.

The son of Triśanku was Hariśchandra;[1]* his son

सशरीरो गतः स्वर्गमद्यापि दिवि दृश्यते ।

The Váyu furnishes some farther information, from an older source:

अत्राप्युदाहरन्तीमौ श्लोकौ पौराणिका जनाः ।
विश्वामित्रप्रसादेन त्रिशङ्कुर्दिवि राजते ।
देवैः सार्धं महातेजा अनुग्रहात्तस्य धीमतः ॥
शनैर्यात्ति —— रम्या हेमन्ते चन्द्रमण्डिता ।†
अलंकृता त्रिभिर्यामैस्त्रिशङ्कुग्रहभूषिता ॥

Both my copies leave a blank, where it is marked; and a similar passage does not elsewhere occur: but the word should, probably, be स्त्रिया; and the whole may be thus rendered: "Men acquainted with the Puráńas recite these two stanzas: 'By the favour of Viśwámitra, the illustrious Triśanku shines in heaven, along with the gods, through the kindness of that sage. Slowly passes the lovely night in winter, embellished by the moon, decorated with three watches, and ornamented with the constellation Triśanku.'" This legend is, therefore, clearly astronomical, and alludes, possibly, to some reformation of the sphere by Viśwámitra, under the patronage of Triśanku, and in opposition to a more ancient system advocated by the school of Vasishtha. It might be no very rash conjecture, perhaps, to identify Triśanku with Orion, the three bright stars of whose belt may have suggested the three Śankus (stakes or pins) which form his name.‡

[1] The Pauráńik lists generally dismiss Hariśchandra very summarily; but he makes a conspicuous figure in legends of an apparently later date. In the Mahábhárata, Sabhá Parvan,§ it is

---

* According to the *Harivaḿśa*, *śl.* 754, he married Satyarathá, of the Kaikaya family. And so says the *Váyu-puráńa*.

† The MSS. of the *Váyu-puráńa* used by me, and to which the Translator had access, read this line thus:

शनैर्यात्यबला रम्या हेमन्ते चन्द्रमण्डिता ।

The missing word is, then, अबला, 'a woman.' In the next verse, my MSS. have भावैः, instead of यामैः.

‡ The reading of the *Váyu-puráńa*, as now restored, militates against this conjecture.

§ Chapter XII.

was Rohitáśwa;[1] his son was Harita;[2] his son was

stated, that he resides in the court of Indra, to which he was elevated for his performance of the Rájasúya sacrifice, and for his unbounded liberality. This seems to have served as the groundwork of the tale told in the Márkańdeya* and Padma Puráńas, of his having given his whole country, his wife and son, and, finally, himself, to Viśwámitra, in satisfaction of his demands for Dakshińá. In consequence, he was elevated, with his subjects, to heaven, from whence, having been insidiously led, by Nárada, to boast of his merits, he was again precipitated. His repentance of his pride, however, arrested his downward descent; and he and his train paused in mid-air. The city of Hariśchandra is popularly believed to be, at times, still visible in the skies. The indignation of Vasishtha at Viśwámitra's insatiableness produced a quarrel, in which their mutual imprecations changed them to two birds, the Śaráli (a sort of Turdus,) and the Baka (or crane). In these forms they fought for a considerable term, until Brahmá interposed, and reconciled them. The Bhágavata alludes to this story, in its notice of Hariśchandra; but the Váyu refers the conflict to the reign of a different prince: *vide supra*, p. 261, note 2. According to the Śiva Puráńa, Hariśchandra was an especial worshipper of that deity; and his wife Satyavatí was a form of Jayá, one of Durgá's handmaids.

[1] Also read Rohita.† Traces of his name appear in the strongholds of Rotas, in Behar‡ and in the Punjab. The Bhágavata has a legend of his having been devoted to Varuńa, before his birth, by his father, who, having, on various pleas, deferred

* Chapter VIII.

† In the *Váyu-puráńa*; in the *Bhágavata-puráńa*, IX., VIII., 8; in the *Linga-puráńa*, Prior Section, LXVI., 11, 12; and in the *Harivaṁśa*, *l*. 758.

‡ The *Harivaṁśa* states that he founded Rohitapura.

"Harischandra was a very great conqueror; and his son Rohita or Rohitáśwa founded, and is said to have resided at, the fortress which, from him, is called Rohitás, a name corrupted, in our maps, to Rotás." Hamilton's *Genealogies of the Hindus*, &c., p. 32.

Chunchu,[1] * who had two sons, named Vijaya and Sudeva.† Ruruka[2] was the son of Vijaya, and his own son was Vŕika,‡ whose son was Báhu (or Báhuka§). This prince was vanquished by the tribes of Haihayas and Tálajanghas,[3] || and his country was overrun by them;

offering his son, as promised, was afflicted by a dropsy. Rohita, at last, purchased Śunahśepha,¶ who was offered, as a victim, in his stead: see hereafter, note on Śunahśepha.**

[1] Omitted: Agni, Linga,†† and Matsya.

[2] Omitted: Agni. Dhundhu: Linga‡‡ and Kúrma. Champa, founder of Champamálini: §§ Bhágavata.|||| But all other authorities make Champa a different person, a descendant of Anga: see family of Anu, of the lunar race.¶¶

[3] Karuka: Linga*** and Kúrma. Bharuka: Bhágavata.†††

[4] Descendants of Yadu. The first springs from a prince who

---

* Several MSS. give Chanchu; and other Puráńas, and also the *Harivaḿśa*, exhibit the same variety.

† Vijaya was son of Sudeva, according to the *Bhágavata-puráńa*, IX., VIII., 1. Instead of Sudeva, the *Linga-puráńa*, Prior Section, LXVI., 12, has Satejas.

‡ One MS. has Vrisha. The *Váyu-puráńa* reads, in different MSS., Vŕitaka and Dhŕitaka.

§ I find this, the longer, form only in the *Bhágavata-puráńa*, IX., VIII., 2.

|| These are said to be a branch of the Haihayas. See the Translator's last note on Chapter XI. of this Book.

¶ Corrected, here and just below, from "Śunahśephas." See the *Bhágavata-puráńa*, IX., VII., 19, 22.

** Chapter VII. of this Book.

†† I find Harita, followed by Dhundhu, in the *Linga-puráńa*, Prior Section, LXVI., 12:

हरितो रोहितस्याथ धुन्धुर्हारित उच्यते ।

‡‡ See the preceding note.

§§ I find Champápuri.

|||| IX., VIII., 1.

¶¶ Chapter XVIII. of this Book.

*** This Puráńa has Ruchaka, in some MSS.

††† IX., VIII., 2.

in consequence of which, he fled into the forests, with his wives. One of these was pregnant; and, being an object of jealousy* to a rival queen, the latter gave her poison, to prevent her delivery. The poison had the effect of confining the child in the womb for seven years. Báhu, having waxed old, died in the neighbourhood of the residence† of (the Muni) Aurva. His queen, having constructed his pile, ascended it, with the determination of accompanying him in death; but the sage‡ Aurva, who knew all things, past, present, and to come, issued forth from his hermitage, and forbade her, saying: "Hold! hold! This is unrighteous. A valiant prince, the monarch of many realms,§ the offerer of many sacrifices, the destroyer of his foes, a universal emperor,|| is in thy womb. Think not of committing so desperate an act!" Accordingly, in obedience to his injunctions, she relinquished her intention. The sage then conducted her to his abode, and, after some time, a very splendid boy was there born. Along with

---

is the twelfth, and the second, from one who is the eighteenth, in the lunar line; and both are, thus, contemporary with a prince who is the thirty-fifth of the solar dynasty. The Váyu adds, that they were assisted by Śakas, Yavanas, Kámbojas, Páradas,¶ and Pahlavas.

---

* This is an inference. The original runs: तस्याश्च सपत्न्या गर्भस्तम्भनाय गरो दत्तः ।

† *Áśrama.*

‡ *Bhagavat.*

§ अखिलभूमण्डलपतिरतिवीर्यपराक्रमः ।

|| *Chakravartin.*

¶ Corrected from "Páravas,"—a typographical error, presumably.

him, the poison that had been given to his mother was expelled; and Aurva, after performing the ceremonies required at birth,* gave him (on that account) the name of Sagara (from Sa, 'with', and Gara, 'poison'). The same holy sage celebrated his investure with the cord of his class, instructed him (fully) in the Vedas,† and taught him the use of arms, especially those of fire, called after Bhárgava.‡

When the boy (had grown up, and) was capable of reflection, he said to his mother, (one day): "Why are we dwelling in this hermitage? Where is my father? And who is he?" His mother, in reply, related to him all (that had happened); upon hearing which, he was highly incensed, and vowed to recover his patrimonial kingdom, and exterminate the Haihayas and Tálajanghas,§ by whom it had been overrun. Accordingly, (when he became a man), he put nearly the whole of the Haihayas to death, and would have, also, destroyed the Śakas, the Yavanas, Kámbojas, Páradas, and Pahlavas,[1] but that they applied to Vasisht́ha, the family-

[1] The Haihayas|| we shall have further occasion to notice. The

* जातकर्मादिकाः क्रियाः निवर्त्य । The *játa-karman* is described as "a ceremony ordained on the birth of a male, before the section of the navel-string, and which consists in making him taste clarified butter out of a golden spoon." Colebrooke's *Digest*, &c., Vol. III., p. 104, note †.

† Insert '*and* all sciences', शास्त्राण्यशेषाणि ।

‡ Read "called after Bhṛigu": अस्त्रं चाग्नेयं भार्गवाख्यम् । The *Váyu-puráńa* alleges that Sagara's instructor in the use of such arms was Bhṛigu himself. For Hindu fiery weapons, *vide supra*, p. 81, note *.

§ Add "and others," *ádi*.

|| For mention of this race in a mediæval inscription, see the *Journal of the Asiatic Society of Bengal*, 1862, p. 117, line 1.

priest* (of Sagara), for protection. Vasishtha, regarding them as annihilated (or deprived of power), though

Śakas † are, no doubt, the Sacæ or Sakai of the classical geographers,—Scythians and Indo-Scythians, Turk or Tartar tribes, who established themselves, about a century and a half before our era, along the western districts of India, and who are, not improbably, connected with our Saxon forefathers. The Yavanas ‡ are the Ionians or Greeks. The Kámbojas § were a people on the northwest of India, of whom it is said, that they were remarkable for a capital breed of horses. There is an apparent trace of their name in the Caumojees of Kaferistán, who may have retreated to the mountains before the advance of the Turk tribes. (Elphinstone's Account of the Kingdom of Caubul, &c., 1st ed., p. 619: see, also, Vol. II., p. 182, note I). The Páradas ‖ and Pahlavas ¶ or Pahnavas may designate other bordering tribes in the same direction, or on the confines of Persia. Along with these, in the legend that follows, the Bhágavata ** enumerates Barbaras. †† The Váyu adds Máhishikas, ‡‡ Dárvas, §§ Chaulas, ‖‖ and Khaśas; ¶¶ the two former

* *Kula-guru*. † See Vol. II., p. 165, note 8.

‡ See Vol. II., p. 181, note 6.

§ See Vol. II., p. 182, notes 1, *etc.*; p. 183, note 3, and annotations thereon.

‖ See Vol. II., p. 182, note 4; p. 183, note ‡.

¶ This, undoubtedly, is the right word: and, on the authority of all my best MSS., I have amended the text accordingly, in the preceding page, and in p 294, *infra*. See Vol. II., p. 167, note §. At p. 339 of that volume, I have silently corrected the statement previously made at p. 166, note ‖, that the Pahlavas are not named in the genuine *Rámáyańa*.

** IX., VIII., 5. Along with the Barbaras are there named only the Tálajanghas, Yavanas, Śakas, and Haihayas.

†† See Vol. II., p. 176, notes 8 and **; p. 178, note §.

‡‡ See Vol. II., p. 166, notes 8, *etc.*

§§ See Vol. II., p. 178, text and notes † and ††.

‖‖ Identified, here, with the Cholas, for whom see Vol. II., p. 178, note 13. The *Harivańśa*, in the corresponding passage, has Cholas.

¶¶ See Vol. II., p. 186, note 6.

living,* thus spake to Sagara: "Enough, enough, my

---

of which are people on the Malabar and Coromandel coasts; the two latter are, usually, placed amongst the mountaineers of the Hindu Kush. The Brahma Puráṇa lengthens the list with the Kolas (the forest races of eastern Gondwana), the Sarpas,† and the Keralas,‡ (who are the people of Malabar). The Hari Vaṁśa§ still further extends the enumeration with the Tushâras or Tokhâras|| (the Turks of Tokharestán), the Chinas¶ (Chinese), the Madras** (people in the Punjab), the Kishkindhas [††] (in Mysore), Kauntalas‡‡ (along the Nerbudda), Bangas§§ (Bengalis), Śâlwas|||| (people in western India), and the Konkaṇas [¶¶] (or inhabitants of the Concan). It is evident, from the locality of most of the additions of the last authority, that its compiler, or corrupter, has been a native of the Dekhin.

---

* *Jívanmṛitaka.* The scholiast hereupon quotes the following stanza from some unnamed *Smṛiti*:

यः स्वधर्मात्परिभ्रष्टो विप्रैश्च बहिष्कृतः ।
स जीवन्नेव लोकेऽस्मिन्मृत इत्यभिधीयते ॥

"He who *has* fallen away from his duty, and *is* cast out by Brâhmans, though living in this world, is declared *to be* dead."

† In the corresponding passage of the *Harivaṁśa*,—namely, at *śl.* 787,—I find, much more frequently than कोलसर्पाः,—yielding Kolas and Sarpas, or else Kolasarpas,—कोलिसर्पाः, कोलिसर्शाः, &c. All these, I strongly suspect, are corruptions of कलिस्पर्शाः, an epithet which the *Vâyu-purâṇa*—see a few lines before, in Professor Wilson's foot-note,—applies to the Mâhishikas.

‡ See Vol. II., p. 175, notes 1 and §.

§ *Śl.* 783—784.

|| See Vol. II., p. 186, notes 5, *etc.*

¶ See Vol. II., p. 181, note 7.

** See Vol. II., p. 163, notes 11, *etc.*

†† Tradition places the Kishkindhas in Odra, or Orissa. See the *Śabdakalpadruma*, *sub voce*; also, Vol. II., p. 177, note 3.

‡‡ Some MSS. have Kontalas. And see Vol. II., p. 157, notes 9, *etc.* I know not on what authority M. Langlois asserts, that these people, "aux longs cheveux étaient près des Tchinas."

§§ "Vangas", in Vol. II., p. 166.

|||| See Vol. II., pp. 133—135; p. 156, note *.

¶¶ See Vol. II., p. 178, notes 14 and ‡.

son! Pursue no further these objects of your wrath, whom you may look upon as no more.* In order to fulfil your vow,† I have separated them from affinity to the regenerate tribes, and from the duties of their castes." Sagara, in compliance with the injunctions of his spiritual guide, contented himself, therefore, with imposing upon the vanquished nations peculiar distinguishing marks.‡ He made the Yavanas[1] shave their heads entirely;§ the Śakas he compelled to shave (the upper) half of their heads; the Páradas wore their hair long; and the Pahlavas let their beards grow; in obedience to his commands.[2] Them, also, and other

---

[1] And Kámbojas: Váyu.

[2] The Asiatic nations generally shave the head, either wholly, or in part. Amongst the Greeks, it was common to shave the fore part of the head; a custom introduced, according to Plutarch, by the Abantes,—whom Homer|| calls ὄπιθεν κομόωντες,—and followed, according to Xenophon, by the Lacedæmonians. It may be doubted, however, if the Greeks or Ionians ever shaved the head completely. The practice prevails amongst the Mohammedans; but it is not universal. The Śakas (Scythians, or Tartars) shave the fore part of the head, gathering the hair at the back into a long tail, as do the Chinese. The mountaineers of the Himálaya shave the crown of the head, as do the people of Kaferistán, with exception of a single tuft. What oriental people wore their hair long, except at the back of the head, is questionable; and the usage would be characteristic rather of the Teutonic and Gothic nations. The ancient Persians had long bushy

---

* अलमेभिरतिजीवमृतैरनुसृतैः।

† *Pratijná.*

‡ *Vedáyatwa.*

§ *Muńd́ita-śiras.*

|| *Iliad*, II., 542.

Kshattriya races, he deprived of the established usages of oblations to fire* and the study of the Vedas; and, thus separated from religious rites,† and abandoned by the Brahmans, these different tribes became Mlechchhas. Sagara, after the recovery of his kingdom, reigned over the seven-zoned earth, with undisputed dominion.[1] ‡

---

beards, as the Persepolitan sculptures demonstrate. In Chardin's time, they were out of fashion; but they were again in vogue, in that country, in the reign of the last king, Fath Sháh.

[1] So the Váyu, &c.; and a similar statement is given in Manu, X., 44, where,§ to the Śakas, Yavanas, Kámbojas, Páradas, and Pahlavas,|| are added the Paunḿdrakas¶ (people of western Bengal), Odras** (those of Orissa), Dravidas†† (of the Coromandel coast), Chinas (Chinese), Kirátas (mountaineers), and Daradas‡‡ (Durds of the Hindu Kush). From this passage, and a similar one in the Rámáyańa, in which the Chinas§§ are mentioned, the late Mr. Klaproth inferred those works to be not older than the third century B. C., when the reigning dynasty of Thsin first gave that

---

* *Vashaṭkára.* See Vol. II., p. 29, note §.

† *Dharma.*

‡ सगरोऽपि स्वमधिष्ठानमागम्यास्खलितचक्रः सप्तद्वीपवतीमिमामुर्वीं प्रशशास ।

§ See Vol. II., p. 183, note 3, and annotations thereon.

|| Corrected from "Pahnavas." The Translator has Pahlavas in Vol. II., p. 183, note 3. *Vide supra*, p. 292, note ¶.

¶ Professor Wilson had "Paunḿdras," which I do not find in the original. For the Paunḿdrikas, see Vol. II., p. 177, note ††.

** This is, perhaps, to be altered. See Vol. II., p. 184, note †; p. 177, notes 3 and **.

†† Elsewhere read Drávidas. See Vol. II., p. 177, text and note 5.

‡‡ See Vol. II., p. 185, notes 3, *etc.*

§§ It is only in the Bengal recension of the *Rámáyańa* that the Chinas are mentioned. See Vol. II., p. 176, note **.

name to China (see, also, Vol. II., p. 181, note 7). It was probable, he supposed, that the Hindus became acquainted with the Chinese only about 200 B. C., when their arms extended to the Oxus: but it is difficult to reconcile this date with the difference of style between the Rámáyańa, particularly, and the works of the era of Vikramáditya. It would seem more likely, that the later appellations were interpolated. It must have been a period of some antiquity, when all the nations from Bengal to the Coromandel coast were considered as Mlechchhas and outcasts.

CHAPTER IV.

The progeny of Sagara: their wickedness: he performs an Aśwamedha: the horse stolen by Kapila: found by Sagara's sons, who are all destroyed by the sage: the horse recovered by Aṁśumat: his descendants. Legend of Mitrasaha or Kalmáshapáda, the son of Sudása. Legend of Khaṭwánga. Birth of Ráma and the other sons of Daśaratha. Epitome of the history of Ráma: his descendants, and those of his brothers. Line of Kuśa. Bṛihadbala, the last, killed in the Great War.

SUMATI, the daughter of Kaśyapa, and Keśiní,* the daughter of Raja Vidarbha,† were the two wives of Sagara.[1]: Being without progeny, the king solicited

---

[1] So the Rámáyaṅa.§ Sumati is called the daughter of Arishṭanemi:|| the Mahábhárata¶ calls her Śaibyá. The story of Sa-

---

* This was the elder wife, the Váyu-puráṅa alleges.

† In the *Váyu-puráṅa* and *Harivaṁśa*, he is called simply Vidarbha.

‡ The following genealogy is given in the *Rámáyaṅa*, *Bála-káṅḍa*, LXX., 19—37: Brahmá, Maríchi, Kaśyapa, Vivaswat, Manu, Ikshwáku (first king of Ayodhyá), Kukshi, Vikukshi, Báṅa, Anaraṅya, Pṛithu, Triśanku, Dhundhumára, Yavanáśwa, Mándhátṛi, Susandhi, Dhruvasandhi (with Prasenajit), Bharata, Asita, Sagara. The same detail is found in the *Ayodhyá-káṅḍa*, CX., 5—24.

In the Bengal recension of the *Rámáyaṅa*, *Ádi-káṅḍa*, LXXII., Angiras and Prachetas intervene between Kaśyapa and Manu, Vivaswat being omitted; as is Kukshi, also.

The *Ayodhyá-káṅḍa*, CXIX., in the same recension, names, somewhat discrepantly: Brahmá, Maríchi, Kaśyapa,—and then, a break being announced,—Vivaswat, Manu, Ikshwáku, Kukshi, Vikukshi, Beṅu, Pushya, Anaraṅya, Pṛithu, Triśanku, Dhundhumára, Yuvanáśwa, Mándhátṛi, Susandhi, Dhṛitasandhi (with Prasenajit), Bharata, Asita, Sagara.

Most of this is very different from what we meet with in the Puráṅas.

§ *Bála-káṅḍa*, XXXVIII., 3, 4.

|| This is another name of Kaśyapa. See Vol. II., p. 28, note 2. For the stanza there cited from the *Mahábhárata*, see the *Śánti-parvan*, *śl.* 7574.

¶ *Vana-parvan*, *śl.* 8833.

the aid of the sage Aurva, with great earnestness;* and the Muni pronounced this boon, that one wife should bear one son, the upholder of his race, and the other should give birth to sixty thousand sons; and he left it to them to make their election. Keśiní chose to have the single son; Sumati, the multitude: and† it came to pass, in a short time, that the former bore Asamanjas,[1] a prince through whom the dynasty continued; and the daughter of Vinatá,‡ Sumati, had sixty thousand sons. The son of Asamanjas was Aḿśumat.

Asamanjas was, from his boyhood, of very irregular conduct.§ His father hoped, that, as he grew up to manhood, he would reform; but, finding that he continued guilty of the same immorality, Sagara abandoned him. The sixty thousand sons of Sagara followed the example of their brother Asamanjas. The path of virtue and piety being obstructed, in the world, by the sons of Sagara,‖ the gods repaired to the Muni¶

---

gara and his descendants is told at length in the Rámáyańa, First Book; and in the Mahábhárata, Vana Parvan, III., 106, et seq.; as well as in most of the Puráńas.

[1] Or Panchajana:** Brahma.††

---

* *Samádhi*, = *chittaikágrya*, the scholiast says.

† Insert "the Ŕishi having pronounced 'So be it'": तथेति च व्याभि-व्याहिते।

‡ See Vol. II., pp. 26 and 73. § *Apavritta.*

‖ बालादेवप्रभृत्यसद्वृत्तो भवति।

¶ Substituted for Ŕishi.

** This is an epithet of Asamanjas, in the *Harivaḿśa*, *l.* 802, *et seq.*

†† Asamanja: *Rámáyańa*, *Váyu-puráńa*, and *Linga-puráńa*. Asamanjasa: *Bhágavata-puráńa*, IX., VIII., 14.

Kapila, who was a portion of Vishńu,* free from fault, and endowed with all (true) wisdom. Having approached him with respect, they said: "O lord, what will become of the world, if these sons of Sagara are permitted to go on in the evil ways which they have learned from Asamanjas! Do thou, then, assume a visible form,† for the protection of the afflicted universe." "Be satisfied", replied the sage: "in a brief time, the sons of Sagara shall be, all, destroyed."

At that period, Sagara commenced the (performance of the solemn) sacrifice of a horse, who was guarded by his own sons: nevertheless, some one stole the animal, and carried it off into a chasm in the earth. Sagara commanded his sons to search for the steed; and they, tracing him by the impressions of his hoofs, followed his course, with perseverance, until, coming to the chasm where he had entered, they proceeded to enlarge it, and dug downwards, each, for a league.‡ Coming to Pátála, they beheld the horse wandering freely about; and, at no great distance from him, they saw the Rishi Kapila sitting, with his head declined in meditation,§ and illuminating the surrounding space with radiance as bright as the splendours of the autumnal sun shining in an unclouded sky.|| Exclaiming "This

* Purushottama, in the original.

† "Visible form" is to render *śaríra*, 'body'.

‡ तत्खातमेकैको योजनं योजनमवनेश्चखान ।

§ This specification does not appear in the original. See the next note.

|| भगवन्तमपघने शरत्कालेऽर्कमिव तेजोभिरनवरतमूर्ध्वमधश्चाशेषा दिशश्चोद्भासयमानं कपिलर्षिमपश्यन् । Commentary: अपघने । अपगतमेघे ।

is the villain who has maliciously interrupted our sacrifice, and stolen the horse: kill him! kill him!" they ran towards him, with uplifted weapons. The Muni slowly raised his eyes,* and, for an instant, looked upon them; and they were reduced to ashes by the (sacred) flame that darted from his person.[1]

---

[1] The Bhágavata † has, for a Puráńa, some curious remarks on this part of the story, flatly denying its truth:

न साधुवादो मुनिकोपभर्जिता
नृपेन्द्रपुत्रा इति सत्त्वधामनि ।
कथं तमो रोषमयं विभाव्यते
जगत्पवित्रात्मनि खे रजो भुवः ॥
यस्येरिता सांख्यमयी दृढेह नौ-
र्यया मुमुक्षुस्तरते दुरत्ययम् ।
भवार्णवं मृत्युपथं विपश्चितः
परात्मभूतस्य कथं पृथङ्मतिः ॥

"The report is not true, that the sons of the king were scorched by the wrath of the sage. For how can the quality of darkness, made up of anger, exist in a world-purifying nature, consisting of the quality of goodness;—the dust of earth, as it were, in the sky? How should mental perturbation distract that sage, who was one with the Supreme, and who has promulgated that Sánkhya philosophy which is a strong vessel by which he who is desirous of liberation passes over the dangerous ocean of the world, by the path of death?" ‡

---

* The original, परिवर्तितलोचनेन, implies that he cast his eyes about.

† IX., VIII., 12, 13.

‡ Burnouf's more exact translation of this passage is as follows:

"Elle n'est pas vraie la tradition qui prétend que les fils du roi furent détruits par la colère du sage; comment en effet les Ténèbres que produit la colère auraient-elles pu exister chez un sage, dont la Bonté était le corps, et qui purifiait le monde? c'est comme si l'on voulait attribuer au ciel la poussière née de la terre.

"Comment eût-il pu croire à des distinctions (comme celles d'ami et

When Sagara learned that his sons whom he had sent in pursuit of the (sacrificial) steed had been destroyed by the might of the great Ṛishi Kapila, he despatched Aḿśumat, the son of Asamanjas, to effect the animal's recovery. The youth, proceeding by the (deep) path which the princes had dug, arrived where Kapila was, and, bowing respectfully,* prayed† to him, (and so propitiated him), that the saint said: "Go, (my son), deliver the horse to your grandfather; and demand a boon. Thy grandson shall bring down the river of heaven‡ (on the earth)." Aḿśumat requested, as a boon, that his uncles§ who had perished through the sage's displeasure‖ might, although unworthy of it, be raised to heaven, through his favour. "I have told you," replied Kapila, "that your grandson shall bring down upon earth the Ganges (of the gods); and, when her waters shall wash the bones and ashes of thy grand-

---

d'ennemis], ce sage identifié avec l'Esprit suprême, qui dirigea ici-bas le solide vaisseau de la doctrine Sánkhya, à l'aide duquel l'homme désireux de se sauver traverse le redoutable océan de l'existence, ce chemin de la mort?"

A tolerably full account of Kapila will be found in my edition of the *Sánkhya-sára*, Preface, pp. 13—21. Several things, however, are to be corrected there; as the work was sent out, by the Asiatic Society of Bengal, without my authority, and while I was known to be still employed on what would have made ten or twelve pages of additional matter, including various readings of MSS. collated since I left India, besides minute indexes and numerous emendations. The copies of the *Daśa-rúpa* in circulation are similarly unamended and imperfect.

* *Bhakti-namra.* † *Tushṭáva*, 'lauded'.

‡ "River of heaven" is for Gangá, the word in the Sanskrit.

§ Aḿśumat rather strangely calls them *pitṛi*, 'fathers'. The scholiast explains that the term is used for *pitṛivya*.

‖ The original has ब्रह्मदण्डहतानाम्, "smitten by the punishment of a Bráhman."

father's sons,* they shall be raised to Swarga. Such is the efficacy of the stream that flows from the toe of Vishńu, that it confers heaven upon all who bathe in it designedly, or who even become accidentally immersed in it: those, even, shall obtain Swarga, whose bones, skin, fibres, hair, or any other part, shall be left, after death, upon the earth which is contiguous to the Ganges." Having acknowledged, reverentially, the kindness of the sage, Aḿśumat returned to his grandfather, and delivered to him the horse.† Sagara, on recovering the steed, completed his sacrifice, and, in affectionate memory of his sons, denominated Ságara the chasm which they had dug.[1]:

---

[1] Ságara is still the name of the ocean, and, especially, of the Bay of Bengal, at the mouth of the Ganges. On the shore of the island called by the same name, tradition places a Kapiláśrama, or hermitage of Kapila, which is still the scene of an annual pilgrimage. Other legends assign a very different situation for the abode of the ascetic, or, the foot of the Himálaya, where the Ganges descends to the plains.§ There would be no incompatibility, however, in the two sites, could we imagine the tra-

---

* "Thy grandfather's sons" is an expansion of the word for 'them'.

† अश्वमादाय पितामहयज्ञमाजगाम ।

: सागरं चात्मजप्रीत्या पुत्रत्वे कल्पयामास; "and, from love of his sons, he set up the ocean as a son."

Ságara, the word here used for 'ocean', is, in form, patronymic of Sagara. The commentator says: सागरं सगरसुतैः खननाद्वर्धितम् । तत्र सगर-आत्मजप्रीत्या पुत्रत्वे कल्पयामास स्थापयामास । तस्मिन्पुत्रबुद्धिं कृतवानित्यर्थः ।

§ In the *Padma-puráńa*, Kapila is said to have dwelt in the village of Indraprastha.

The son of Aṁśumat was Dilípa;[1] his son was Bhagíratha, who brought Gangá down to earth; whence she is called Bhágírathí.* The son of Bhagíratha was Śruta;[2]† his son was Nábhága;[3] his son was Ambarísha; his son was Sindhudwípa;‡ his son was Ayutáśwa;[4]§ his son was Ṛituparṇa,|| the friend¶ of Nala, skilled profoundly in dice.[5] The son of Ṛituparṇa was

---

dition referred to a period when the ocean washed, as it appears once to have done, the base of the Himálaya, and Saugor (Ságara) was at Haridwára.

[1] Or Khaṭwánga: Brahma and Hari Vaṁśa:** but this is, apparently, an error. *Vide infra*, p. 311, note 1.

[2] Omitted: Matsya and Agni. Vièruta:†† Linga.

[3] Nábha:‡‡ Bhágavata.

[4] Ayutáyus:§§ Váyu, Linga, and Kúrma. Śrutáyus: Agni. Ayutájit:||| Brahma.

[5] अक्षहृदयज्ञः, 'knowing the heart of the dice.' The same epi-

---

* The *Váyu-puráṇa* hereupon gives the following quotation:

अथाप्युदाहरन्तीमौ श्लोकौ पौराणिका जनाः ।
भगीरथस्तु तां गंगामानयामास कर्मभिः ।
तस्माद्भागीरथी गंगा कथ्यते वंशवित्तमैः ॥

Two stanzas are here promised; but only one is cited.

† A single MS. has Suhotra.

‡ According to the *Bhágavata-puráṇa*, IX., IX., 16, he was son of Nábha; Ambarísha being there omitted.

§ In two MSS. the name is Ayutáyus.

|| The *Harivaṁśa* has Ṛitaparṇa, and gives the patronym Ártaparṇi to Sudása.

¶ *Sakhya*.

** *Śl.* 808. *Khaṭwánga* is given there as Dilípa's surname. Khaṭwánga, as the name of a royal sage, appears in the *Bhágavata-puráṇa*, II., I., 13.

†† I find Śruta.

‡‡ Corrected from "Nábhin".

§§ So, too, reads the *Bhágavata-puráṇa*.

||| This is the reading of the *Harivaṁśa*, also.

Sarvakáma;[1]* his son was Sudása; his son was Sau-

---

that, as well as that of 'friend of Nala,' is given him in the Váyu, Bhágavata, and Brahma Puráńas, and in the Hari Vaḿśa, and leaves no doubt of their referring to the hero of the story told in the Mahábhárata. Nala, however, as we shall hereafter see, is some twenty generations later than Ŕituparńa, in the same family; and the Váyu, therefore, thinks it necessary to observe, that two Nalas are noticed in the Puráńas, and the one here adverted to is the son of Virasena:

नलौ द्वाविति विख्यातौ पुराणेषु दृढव्रतौ ।
वीरसेनात्मजश्चैव यश्चेक्ष्वाकुकुलोद्वहः ॥

whilst the other belongs to the family of Ikshwáku. The same passage occurs in the Brahma Puráńa and Hari Vaḿśa;† and the commentator‡ on the latter observes: निषधात्मजो नलो वीरसेनसुतान्नलादन्यः । 'Nala the son of Nishadha is different from Nala the son of Virasena.' It is, also, to be observed, that the Nala of the tale is king of Nishadha, and his friend Ŕituparńa is king of Ayodhyá. The Nala of the race of Ikshwáku is king of Ayodhyá; he is the son of Nishadha, however; and there is, evidently, some confusion between the two. We do not find Virasena, or his son, in any of the lists. *Vide infra*, p. 320, note 1.

[1] There is considerable variety in this part of the lists; but the Vayu and Bhágavata agree with our text. The Matsya and others make Kalmáshapáda the son or grandson of Ŕituparńa,

---

* Sárvabhauma: *Linga-puráńa.*

† *Śl.* 831, 832:

नलौ द्वावेव विख्यातौ पुराणे भरतर्षभ ।
वीरसेनात्मजश्चैव यश्चेक्ष्वाकुकुलोद्वहः ॥

We read, too, in the *Linga-puráńa*, Prior Section, LXVI., 24, 25:

नलौ द्वावेव विख्यातौ पुराणेषु दृढव्रतौ ।
वीरसेनसुतस्तद्वद्यश्चेक्ष्वाकुकुलोद्भवः ॥

‡ Nilakańtha.

dása, named, also, Mitrasaha.[1]*

---

and place Sarvakáma, or Sarvakarman, after him.† See further on.‡

[1] The Váyu, Agni, Brahma, and Hari Vaṁśa read Amitrasaha, 'foe-enduring;'§ but the commentator on our text explains it Mitra, a name of Vasishṭha, Saha, 'able to bear' the imprecation of;|| as in the following legend, which is similarly related in the Bhágavata.¶ It is not detailed in the Váyu. A full account occurs

---

* The *Bhágavata-puráṇa*, IX., IX., 18, says that he was called Kalmáshánghri, also. This is a synonym of Kalmáshapáda, for which epithet *vide infra*, p. 308.

† In the *Harivaṁśa*, *śl.* 817, Sarvakarman appears as son of Mitrasaha. In the next two stanzas, the names of his successors are: Anaraṇya, Nighna, Anamitra (and Raghu, his brother), Dulidaha, Dilípa.

‡ *Vide infra*, p. 313, note 1.

§ The first and fourth works named have—as has, also, the *Linga-puráṇa*, Prior Section, LXVI., 27,—नाम्ना मित्रसहः; the second and third, राजा मित्रसहः. The words of our text are सौदासो मित्रसहनामा; and here, but for the commentary, there is just as good reason as there is in the other instances, to infer that the name is Amitrasaha. The momentary indignation of Saudása against Vasishṭha justifies but ill the supposition that the term *amitra*, 'enemy', was applied to the latter. The *Bhágavata-puráṇa*, IX., IX., 18, in its आहुर्मित्रसहं च, reads Mitrasaha, unmistakeably; and so does the *Mahábhárata*, *Ádi-parvan*, *śl.* 6720; *Áśwamedhika-parvan*, *śl.* 1690.

In Dr. Goldstücker's *Sanskrit Dictionary* there is, however, an article अमित्रसह, which word there points to our king, "also called Saudása: according to the *Váyu-*, *Agni-*, *Brahma-Pur.* and the *Harivaṁśa*; the *Vishṇu-Pur.* calls him Mitrasaha." Were not these particulars taken from the note under annotation? Even a reference to so accessible a work as the *Harivaṁśa* would have suggested a doubt of there being such a name as Amitrasaha.

|| The commentator's words are: मित्रं वसिष्ठं प्रतिशप्तुं समर्थोऽपि सहते स्म। तेन मित्रसहनामा। This imports, that Mitrasaha was so called, because, though he had it in his power to retaliate, in kind, the curse of his friend (*mitra*), namely, Vasishṭha, he forbore (*sahate sma*, from *sah*).

¶ IX., IX., 19—39.

The son of Sudása, having gone into the woods to hunt, fell in with a couple of tigers, by whom the forest had been cleared of the deer.* The king slew one of these tigers with an arrow. At the moment of expiring, the form of the animal was changed, and it became that of a fiend† of fearful figure and hideous aspect.

in the Mahábhárata, Ádi Parvan, s. 176, but with many and important variations. Kalmáshapáda, whilst hunting, encountered Śaktri,‡ the son of Vasishíha, in the woods, and, on his refusing to make way, struck the sage with his whip. Śaktri cursed the king to become a cannibal; and Viśwámitra, who had a quarrel with Vasishíha, seized the opportunity to direct a Rákshasa to take possession of the king, that he might become the instrument of destroying the family of the rival saint. Whilst thus influenced, Mitrasaha, a Brahman, applied to Kalmáshapáda for food; and the king commanded his cook to dress human flesh, and give it to the Brahman, who, knowing what it was, repeated the curse of Śaktri, that the king should become a cannibal; which taking effect with double force, Kalmáshapáda began to eat men. One of his first victims was Śaktri, whom he slew and ate, and then killed and devoured, under the secret impulse of Viśwámitra's demon, all the other sons of Vasishíha. Vasishíha, however, liberated him from the Rákshasa who possessed him, and restored him to his natural character. The imprecation of the Brahman's wife, and its consequences, are told, in the Mahábhárata, as in the text; but the story of the water falling on his feet appears to have grown out of the etymology of his name, which might have referred to some disease of the lower extremities; the prince's designation being, at length, Mitrasaha Saudása Kalmáshapáda, or, 'Mitrasaha, son of Sudása, with the swelled feet.'

* *Apamŕiga.*

† *Rákshasa.*

‡ On the correct name, Śakti, *vide supra*, p. 35, note ‡.

Its companion, threatening the prince with its vengeance, disappeared.

After some interval, Saudása celebrated a sacrifice, (which was conducted by Vasishṫha). At the close of the rite, Vasishṫha went out; when the Rákshasa, the fellow of the one that had been killed in the figure of a tiger, assumed the semblance of Vasishṫha, and (came and) said (to the king): "Now that the sacrifice is ended, you must give me flesh to eat. Let it be cooked; and I will presently return." Having said this, he withdrew, and, transforming himself into the shape of the cook, dressed some human flesh, which he brought to the king, who, receiving it on a plate of gold, awaited the reappearance of Vasishṫha. As soon as the Muni returned, the king offered to him the dish. Vasishṫha, surprised at such want of propriety* in the king, as his offering him meat to eat, considered what it should be that was so presented, and, by the efficacy of his meditations, discovered that it was human flesh. His mind being agitated with wrath, he denounced a curse upon the Raja, saying: "Inasmuch as you have insulted all such holy men† as we are, by giving me what is not to be eaten, your appetite shall, henceforth, be excited by similar food."

"It was yourself," replied the Raja to the (indignant) sage, "who commanded (this food to be prepared)." "By me!" exclaimed Vasishṫha. "How could that have been?" And, again having recourse to meditation,‡

* *Dauhśílya.*

† *Tapaswin.*

‡ *Samádhi.*

he detected the whole truth. Foregoing, then, all displeasure towards the king,* he said: "The food (to which I have sentenced you) shall not be your sustenance for ever: it shall (only) be so for twelve years." The king, who had taken up water in the palms of his hands, and was prepared to curse the Muni, now considered that Vasishtha was his spiritual guide,† and, being reminded,‡ by Madayantí, his queen, that it ill became him to denounce an imprecation upon a holy teacher who was the guardian divinity of his race,§ abandoned his intention.|| Unwilling to cast the water upon the earth, lest it should wither up the grain,—for it was impregnated with his malediction,—and equally reluctant to throw it up into the air, lest it should blast the clouds, and dry up their contents, he threw it upon his own feet.¶ Scalded by the heat which the water had derived from his angry imprecation, the feet of the Raja became spotted black and white;** and he, thence, obtained the name of Kalmáshapáda, or he with the spotted (kalmásha) feet (páda).††

---

* अनुग्रहं चकार।

† In the original, this consideration is suggested by Madayantí.

‡ *Prasádita*, 'appeased.'

§ कुलदेवताभूतमाचार्यम्।

|| This, though implied, is not expressed in the Sanskrit.

¶ सस्याम्बुदरक्षार्थं तच्छापाम्बु नोर्व्यां नाकाशे चिक्षेप किन्तु स्वपादौ सिषेच। "That water for cursing he threw neither on the earth nor into the air, for sustenance of the grain or of the clouds; *but* he sprinkled his own feet with it."

** This is borrowed from the scholiast, who says: कल्माषतां कृष्णपाण्डुताम्।

†† तेन क्रोधयुतेनाम्बुना दग्धच्छायौ तत्पादौ कल्माषतामुपगतौ। ततश्च स कल्माषपादसंज्ञामवाप।

In consequence of the curse of Vasishṭha, the Raja became a cannibal * every sixth watch of the day, † (for twelve years), and, in that state, wandered through the forests, and devoured multitudes of men. On one occasion, he beheld a holy person ‡ engaged in dalliance with his wife. As soon as they saw his terrific form, they were frightened, and endeavoured to escape; but the (regal) Rákshasa (overtook and) seized the husband. The wife of the Brahman, then, also desisted from flight, and earnestly entreated the savage § (to spare her lord), exclaiming: "Thou, Mitrasaha, art the pride ‖ of the (royal) house of Ikshwáku,—not a (malignant) fiend. ¶ It is not in thy nature, who knowest the characters of women, to carry off and devour my husband." ** But all was in vain; and, regardless of her reiterated supplications, he ate the Brahman, as a tiger devours a deer. †† The Brahman's wife, furious with wrath, then addressed the Raja, and said: "Since you have barbarously disturbed the joys of a wedded pair, and killed my husband, your death shall be the conse-

---

* राक्षसभावमुपेत्य।

† Read "every sixth meal-time;" *i. e.*, at the close of every third day. The original is षष्ठे काले, on which the comment is: षष्ठे षष्ठे काले तृतीयदिवसान्ते।

‡ *Muni.*

§ *Bahu-lasta.*

‖ *Tilaka.*

¶ *Rákshasa.*

** नार्हसि स्त्रीधर्मसुखाभिज्ञो ह्यकृतार्थायामिमं मद्भर्तारमत्तुम्। Comment: स्त्रीधर्मो मैथुनं तत्सुखाभिज्ञः।

†† I find *pala.*

quence of your associating with your queen."* So saying, she entered the flames.

At the expiration of the period of his curse, Saudása returned home. Being reminded of the imprecation of the Brahmani, by his wife, Madayantí, he abstained from conjugal intercourse, and was, in consequence, childless; but, having solicited the interposition of Vasishtha, Madayantí became pregnant.† The child, however, was not born for seven years, when the queen, (becoming impatient), divided the womb with a (sharp) stone, and was thereby delivered. The child was, thence, called Aśmaka (from Aśman, 'a stone'). The son of Aśmaka was Múlaka, who, when the warrior tribe was extirpated upon earth, was surrounded and concealed by a number of females;‡ whence he was denominated Nárikavacha (having women for armour).[1] The son of Múlaka was Daśaratha; his son

---

[1] His name, Múlaka, or 'the root', refers, also, to his being the stem whence the Kshattriya races again proceeded.§ It may be doubted if the purport of his title Nárikavacha is accurately explained by the text.||

---

* यस्मादेवं मय्यतृप्तायां त्वयायं मत्पतिर्भक्षितस्तस्मात्त्वमप्यन्तकामोपभोगप्रवृत्तो मरिष्यसि ।

† Hereabouts the rendering is free.

‡ Rather, "surrounded and guarded by garmentless women:" स्त्रीभिर्विवस्त्राभिः परिवार्य रक्षितः । I find no other reading than this.

§ See the *Bhágavata-puráńa*, IX., IX., 40, and Śrídhara's supplementation thereof.

|| The *Váyu-puráńa* reports, as follows, on the origin of Múlaka's epithet:

was Ilavila;* his son was Viśwasaha;† his son was Khatwánga,‡ (called, also,) Dilípa,[1] who, in a battle between the gods and the Asuras, being called, by the former, to their succour, killed (a number of) the latter. Having, thus, acquired the friendship of the deities in heaven, they desired him to demand a boon. He said to them: "If a boon is to be accepted by me, then tell me, as a favour, what is the duration of my life." "The length of your life is but an hour,"§ the gods replied. On which, Khatwánga, who was swift of motion,|| de-

---

[1] This prince is confounded with an earlier Dilípa by the Brahma Puráńa and Hari Vamśa.¶

यथाबुद्धाहरन्तोर्वं मूलकं वै नृपं प्रति ।
स हि रामभयाद्गुप्ता स्त्रीभिः परिवृतोऽवसत् ।
विवस्त्रस्त्रीभिरावृत्य नारीकवचमीश्वरः ॥

Paraśuráma is here intended, according to Śrídhara, in his comment on the parallel passage in the *Bhágavata-puráńa*,—IX., IX., 40. Two verses, which, it may be conjectured, closely correspond, in a correct reading, to the stanza quoted in the preceding extract, appear in the *Linga-puráńa*, Prior Section, LXVI, 29.

* Not one of my MSS. has this name. Four give Ilivila; others, Ilavila and Allavila. The *Váyu-puráńa* reads, in different MSS., Iłavida, Iđivida, and Aidivida; the *Linga-puráńa*, Ilavila; the *Bhágavata-puráńa*, Aiđavida. Compare the variants noticed in p. 346, note *, *supra*.

† The *Linga-puráńa* interpolates Vŕiddhaśarman before Viśwasaha.

‡ This name is frequently and variously corrupted, especially into Katwánga and Khatwanga. It does not seem necessary to dwell on these depravations.

§ *Muhúrta*.

|| *Laghima-guńa*, "endowed with lightness." *Laghiman* is "the faculty of assuming levity," illustrated by "rising along a sunbeam, to the solar orb." It must be equally easy to the adept to travel a ray downwards. See Colebrooke's *Miscellaneous Essays*, Vol. I., p. 250.

¶ *Vide supra*, p. 303, note 1; p. 305, note †.

scended, in his easy-gliding chariot, to the world of mortals. Arrived there, he prayed, and said: "If my own soul has never been dearer to me than (the sacred) Brahmans; if I have never deviated from (the discharge of) my duty; if I have never regarded gods, men, animals, vegetables, all created things,* as different from the imperishable;† then may I, with unswerving step, attain to that divine being on whom holy sages meditate!" Having thus spoken, he was united with that supreme being,‡ who is Vásudeva; with that elder§ of all the gods, who is abstract existence,|| and whose form cannot be described. Thus he obtained absorption, according to this stanza, which was repeated, formerly, by the seven Ŕishis: "Like unto Khaťwánga will be no one upon earth, who, having come from heaven, and dwelt an hour amongst men, became united with the three worlds, by his liberality and knowledge of truth."[1] ¶

[1] The term for his obtaining final liberation is rather unusual; त्रयोऽभिसंहिता लोकाः, 'By whom the three worlds were affected,

* *Vŕikshádika.*

† *Achyuta.*

‡ *Paramátman.*

§ *Guru.*

|| *Sattá-mátrátman.*

¶ खट्वाङ्गेन समो नान्यः कश्चिदुर्व्यां भविष्यति ।
येन स्वर्गादिहागम्य मुहूर्तं प्राप्य जीवितम् ।
त्रयोऽभिसंहिता लोका बुद्ध्या दानेन चैव हि ॥

Comment: मुहूर्तं जीवितं प्राप्य ज्ञात्वा । बुद्ध्या वासुदेवः सर्वमिति ज्ञानेन । यद्वार्थं समर्पयं सत्यज्ञानमिति वा प्रविलाप्यमिति वाक्यै-नाभिसंहिता विषयीकृतास्त्रयो लोकाः । त्रिलोकी प्रविलापिता इत्यर्थः ।

According to this, partially accepted, the last two lines may be ren-

The son of Khaṫwánga was Dírghabáhu; his son was Raghu; his son was Aja;[*] his son was Daśaratha.[1]

---

or beloved:'† विचक्षिताः,‡ the three worlds being identified with their source, or the Supreme. The text says, of this stanza, श्रूयते; and the Váyu, citing§ it, says, इति श्रुतिः.|| The legend is, therefore, from the Vedas.

[1] The lists here differ very materially, as the following comparison will best show:

Vishńu.	Matsya.¶	Rámáyańa.**
Kalmáshapáda	Kalmáshapáda	Kalmáshapáda

---

dered: "by whom, arrived here *below* from paradise, having obtained an hour's *prolongation of* life, the three worlds were mastered through wisdom and self-surrender."

The scholiast puts much more of Vedántism into these verses than it is likely they were intended to convey.

Compare the *Harivańśa*, *sl.* 809. The ordinary reading, there, in the last line, is अनुसंधिता..

* The *Bhágavata-puráńa*, IX., X., 1, has Raghu, Prithuśravas, Aja.

† अभिसंधित can scarcely bear either of these meanings. Its most probable signification, here, is 'contemplate thoroughly'.

‡ This means 'experienced', *i. e.*, recognized as vanity.'

§ The *Váyu-puráńa* has only the last two verses, and does not call them a citation. It reads सत्येन for ज्ञानेन.

|| The *Váyu-puráńa* uses this expression in connexion with something else:

दिलीपस्तस्य पुत्रोऽभूत्खट्वाङ्गद इति श्रुतिः ।

Khaṫwángada is, moreover, the form here presented.

¶ Whether the names particularised here, as in many other lists throughout this work, are correctly represented, or not, I do not pretend to pronounce. To this point I have already adverted; giving the reason why we must, at present, look with distrust, in most cases, upon any express or implied claim to punctual accuracy as regards Pauráńik minutiæ: see Vol. I., p. 153, note ‡. In annotating these volumes, all that, as a rule, I have undertaken to do, touching the numerous works referred to in the Translator's commentary, has been, to restrict myself to the most important and most accessible of them, and to collate these, in such manuscripts as are within my reach, and in the printed editions, with my best diligence.

** *Bála-káńḋa*, LXX., 40—43; *Ayodhyá-káńḋa*, CX., 29—34.

The god from whose navel the lotos springs became fourfold, as the four sons of Daśaratha,—Ráma, Laksh-

Vishńu.	Matsya.	Rámáyańa.
Aśmaka	Sarvakarman	Śankhańa *
Múlaka	Anarańya	Sudarśana
Daśaratha	Nighna	Agnivarńa
Ilavila	Anamitra	Śighraga
Viśwasaha	Raghu	Maru
Dilípa	Dilípa	Praśuśruka †
Dírghabáhu	Aja	Ambarísha
Raghu	Dírghabáhu	Nahusha
Aja	Ajapála	Yayáti ‡
Daśaratha	Daśaratha	Nábhága
		Aja
		Daśaratha.

The Váyu, Bhágavata,§ Kúrma, and Linga agree with our text, except in the reading of a few names: as, Śataratha,|| for Daśaratha the first; Vairivira, for Ilavila; and Kritaśarman, Vriddhaśarman, or Vriddhakarman, for Viśwasaha.¶ The Agni and Brahma and Hari Vaḿśa agree with the second series, with similar occasional exceptions;** showing that the Puráńas admit two series, differing in name, but agreeing in number. The Rámáyańa, however, differs from both, in a very extraordinary manner; and the variation is not limited to the cases specified; as it begins with Bhagíratha, as follows:

* Corrected from "Śankana." The Bengal recension of the *Rámáyańa* has, in the *Ádi-káńda*, Śankhana; in the *Ayodhyá-káńda*, Khanitra.

† For the Pauráńik son of Maru, *vide infra*, p. 325, l. 6.

‡ Both the genuine *Rámáyańa* and the Bengal recension omit Yayáti in the *Ayodhyá-káńda*.

§ The readings of this Puráńa I have detailed, as will have been seen.

|| So read the *Váyu-puráńa* and the *Linga-puráńa*.

¶ *Vide supra*, p. 311, note †.

** All these, so far as the *Harivaḿśa* is concerned, have been specified in my annotations.

mańa, Bharata, and Śatrughna,*—for the protection† of the world. Ráma, whilst yet a boy, accompanied Viśwámitra, to protect his sacrifice, and slew Táďaká. He afterwards killed Márícha with his resistless shafts;‡

Puráńas.	Rámáyańa.§
Bhagíratha	Bhagíratha
Śruta	Kakutstha‖
Nábhága	Raghu
Ambarísha	Kalmáshapáda
Sindhudwípa	
Ayutáswa ¶	
Ŕituparńa	
Sarvakáma	
Sudása	
Kalmáshapáda	

The entire Pauráńik series comprises twenty descents; and that of the Rámáyańa, sixteen. Some of the last names of the poem

* Insert 'as parts of himself,' आत्मांशेन.

† *Sthiti*, 'stability'.

‡ यज्ञे च मारीचमिषुपाताहतं दूरं चिक्षेप । "And, at the sacrifice, he hurled to a distance Márícha, struck by the blast of *his* shaft."

We read, in the *Rámáyańa*, *Bála-káńda*, XXX., 16—18:

इत्युक्त्वा वचनं रामश्चापे संधाय वेगवान् ।
मानवं परमोदारमस्त्रं परमभास्वरम् ।
चिक्षेप परमक्रुद्धो मारीचोरसि राघवः ॥
स तेन परमास्त्रेण मानवेन समाहतः ।
संपूर्णं योजनशतं क्षिप्तः सागरसंप्लवे ॥

It appears, from this, that Márícha, struck, in the breast, by the weapon Mánava, discharged from Ráma's bow, was projected, by the impact, a hundred *yojanas*, into the sea.

The story of the death of Márícha, in the guise of a golden deer, at the hands of Ráma, is told in the same poem, *Áranya-káńda*, XLIV.

§ *Bála-káńda*, LXX., 39, 40; *Ayodhyá-káńda*, CX., 28, 29.

‖ Corrected from the impossible "Kakutshtha."

¶ *Vide supra*, p. 303, notes 4, §, ‡‡, and ‖‖.

and Subáhu and others fell by his arms. He removed the guilt of Ahalyá, by merely looking upon her. In the palace of Janaka, he broke, with ease, the mighty bow of Maheśwara, and received the hand of Sítá, the daughter of the king, self-born from the earth,* as the prize of his prowess.† He humbled the pride of Paraśuráma, who vaunted his triumphs over the race of Haihaya,‡ and his repeated slaughters of the Kshattriya tribe. Obedient to the commands of his father, and cherishing no regret for the loss of sovereignty,§ he entered the forest, accompanied by his brother (Lakshmańa) and by his wife, where he killed, in conflict, Virádha, Khara, Dúshańa,‖ and other Rákshasas, (the headless giant) Kabandha, and Bálin ¶ (the monkey monarch).

---

occur amongst the first of those of the Puráńas; but there is an irreconcilable difference in much of the nomenclature. The Agni, under the particular account of the descent of Ráma, has, for his immediate predecessors, Raghu, Aja, Daśaratha, as in our text; and the author of the Raghu Vamśa agrees with the Puráńas,** from Dilípa downwards.

---

* *Agonijá.*

† *Vírya-śulká.*

‡ यशोवीर्यहैहयकुलकेतुभूतम् ।

§ अनभिमतराज्याभिलाषः ।

‖ Corrected from "Kharadúshana". The original is विराधखरदूष-णादीन् । For Khara and Dúshańa, see the *Rámáyańa*, I., I., 47; the *Raghuvamśa*, XII., 42, 46; the *Bhágavata-puráńa*; IX., X., 9: &c. &c.

¶ कबन्धबालिनौ । Hence I have altered "Bali", which, however, is a form that occurs elsewhere.

** With which of them, except the *Agni-puráńa*? In the *Raghuvamśa*, VI., 74—78, we find Dilípa, Raghu, Aja, and then, in VIII., 29, Daśaratha.

Having built a bridge across the ocean,[*] and destroyed the whole Rákshasa nation, he recovered (his bride,) Sítá, whom their ten-headed (king, Rávańa,) had carried off, and returned to Ayodhyá, with her, after she had been purified, by the fiery ordeal, from the soil contracted (by her captivity), and had been honoured by the assembled gods, (who bore witness to her virtue).[1]

---

[1] This is an epitome of the Rámáyańa, the heroic poem of Válmíki, on the subject of Ráma's exploits. A part of the Rámáyańa was published, with a translation, by Messrs. Carey and Marshman, several years since; but a much more correct edition of the text of the two first books, with a Latin translation of the first and part of the second, have been more recently published by Professor Schlegel,—a work worthy of his illustrious name.† A summary of the story may be found in Sir William Jones's Works, Maurice's Hindustan, Moor's Pantheon, &c. It is, also, the subject of the Uttara Ráma Charitra, in the Hindu Theatre; in the introduction to which an outline of the whole is given. The story is, therefore, no doubt, sufficiently familiar, even to English readers. It seems to be founded on historical fact; and the traditions of the south of India uniformly ascribe its civilization,

---

* बद्ध्वा चाम्भोनिधिम् ।

† For Signor Gorresio's edition of the spurious *Rámáyańa*, see Vol. II., p. 190, note *. The genuine *Rámáyańa*—which Professor Wilson does not seem to have known, save in Schlegel's composite edition of the first two books,—has been lithographed at Calcutta and Bombay. For some idea of the difference between the two, the reader is referred to the *Journal of the Royal Asiatic Society*, Vol. XIX., pp. 303—306, and to Dr. Muir's *Original Sanskrit Texts*, Part IV., pp. 377—418. I have seen, in India, no less than seven different commentaries on the real *Rámáyańa*; a copy of one of which, accompanying the text, was transcribed nearly five hundred years ago.

Bharata made himself master of the country of the Gandharvas, after destroying vast numbers of them;* and Śatrughna, having killed the Rákshasa chief, Lavańa, the son of Madhu, took possession of his capital, Mathurá.†

Having, thus, by their unequalled valour and might, rescued the whole world from the dominion of malignant fiends, Ráma, Lakshmańa, Bharata, and Śatrughna reascended to heaven, and were followed by those of the people of Kośala:‡ who were fervently devoted to these incarnate portions of the supreme (Vishńu).§

Ráma (and his brothers) had (each,) two sons. Kuśa and Lava were the sons of Ráma; those of Lakshmańa were Angada and Chandraketu;‖ the sons of Bharata

---

the subjugation or dispersion of its forest tribes of barbarians, and the settlement of civilized Hindus, to the conquest of Lanká by Ráma.

---

* The original says that he destroyed thirty millions of terrible *gandharvas*: घोरगन्धर्वकोटीस्तिस्रो जघान ।

† Rather, "founded Mathurá"; the Sanskrit being *niveśitá*. Moreover, the original has nothing corresponding to "his capital".

The *Váyu-puráńa* reads:

माधवं लवणं हत्वा गत्वा मधुवनं च तत् ।
शत्रुघ्नेन पुरी तत्र मथुरा संनिवेशिता ॥

And the *Bhágavata-puráńa* says, at IX., XI., 14:

शत्रुघ्नश्च मधोः पुत्रं लवणं नाम राक्षसम् ।
हत्वा मधुवने चक्रे मथुरां नाम वै पुरीम् ॥

Three of my copies of the *Vishńu-puráńa*, and two of the *Váyu*, have Madhurá, instead of Mathurá. It is not altogether certain that Madhurá was not the original name, and even that heard by Hiouen Thsang.

‡ Strictly, "people of the city of Kośala," कोशलनगरजानपदाः ।

§ This sentence is very freely rendered.

‖ A Chandraketu, prince of the city of Chakora, who was killed by an emissary of King Śúdraka, is mentioned in the *Harshacharita*. See my edition of the *Vásavadattá*, Preface, p. 53.

were Taksha* and Pushkara;† and Subáhu and Śúrasena‡: were the sons of Śatrughna.

[1] The Váyu specifies the countries or cities over which they reigned. Angada and Chitraketu§—as the Váyu terms the latter,—governed countries near the Himálaya, the capitals of which were Ángadí and Chandravaktrá.|| Taksha and Pushkara were sovereigns of Gandhára, residing at Takshaśilá¶ and Pushkarávatí.** Subáhu and Śúrasena reigned at Mathurá; and, in the latter, we might be satisfied to find the Suraseni†† of Arrian, but that there is a subsequent origin, of perhaps greater authenticity, in the family of Yadu, as we shall hereafter see.‡‡ Kuśa built Kuśasthalí on the brow of the Vindhya, the capital of Kośalá; and Lava reigned at Śrávastí (*vide supra*, pp. 249, 263) in Uttara

* Two MSS. have the elongated form, Takshaka.

† One of my MSS. has Pushkala; and so has the *Bhágavata-puráńa*.

‡ All my MSS., and most of those of the *Váyu-puráńa*, have Śúra-sena. Śrutasena: *Bhágavata-puráńa*, IX., XI., 13.

§ My MSS. have Chandraketu,—the reading of the *Raghuvaḿśa*, XV., 90, also. But Chitraketu is the name in the *Bhágavata-puráńa*, IX., XI., 12.

|| हिमवत्पर्वताभ्याशे स्फीतौ जनपदौ तयोः ।
अङ्गदस्याङ्गदी नाम देशे कारपथे पुरी ॥

Ángadí is, here, located in Kárapatha; as I find the name spelled. In the line following this stanza, the country *seems* to be named, of which Chandraketu's Chandravaktrá was the capital; but, unfortunately, it is illegible in all my MSS.

The *Raghuvaḿśa*, XV., 90, places both the brothers in Kárápatha.

¶ A large number of useful references bearing on this city will be found in Messrs. Boehtlingk and Roth's *Sanskrit-Wörterbuch*, *sub voce*.

** गन्धारविषये सिद्धे तयोः पुर्यौ महात्मनोः ।
तक्षस्य दिक्षु विख्याता रम्या तक्षशिला पुरी ।
पुष्करस्यापि वीरस्य विख्याता पुष्करावती ॥

Takshaśilá and Pushkarávatí have been identified with the *Taxila* of Ptolemy and the *Πευκελαῶτις* of Arrian. For the people of Gandhára, see Vol. II., p. 174, note 2.

†† See Vol. II., p. 156, note 2.

‡‡ In Chapter XI. of this Book.

The son of Kuśa was Atithi; his son was Nishadha; his son was Nala;[1] his son was Nabhas;* his son was Puńdaríka; his son was Kshemadhanwan; his son was Deváníka; his son was Ahínagu;[2]† his son was Pári-

---

(northern) Kośala:‡

कुशस्य कोशलाः राज्यं पुरी चापि कुशस्थली ।
रम्या निवेशिता तेन विन्ध्यपर्वतसानुषु ॥
उत्तरकोशले राज्यं लवस्य च महात्मनः ।
श्रावस्ती लोकविख्याता कुशवंशं निबोधत ॥ §

The Raghu Vaḿśa|| describes Kuśa as returning from Kuśávatí to Ayodhyá, after his father's death; but it seems not unlikely, that the extending power of the princes of the Doab, of the lunar family, compelled Ráma's posterity to retire more to the west and south.

[1] The Bhágavata is the only Puráńa that omits this name; as if the author had been induced to correct the reading, ¶ in order to avoid the necessity of recognizing two Nalas. *Vide supra*, p. 303, note 5.

[2] Here, again, we have two distinct series of princes, inde-

---

* Nabha, in a few MSS.

† Ruru has here been omitted by the Translator. One of my MSS., —that which, I believe, Professor Wilson generally, and all but exclusively, used,—here exhibits the mutilation सुतो रुरुस्य च. There is no Ruru, however, in the *Váyu-puráńa*.

‡ Query, कोशले, in 'Kosála'?

§ This extract is from a somewhat long quotation in the *Váyu-puráńa*. In a verse a little before these, we are told that Ráma established a rule of ten thousand years:

दश वर्षसहस्राणि रामो राज्यमकारयत् ।

With this compare the *Linga-puráńa*, Prior Section, LXVI., 37.

|| XVI., 25. From the same work, XV., 97, it appears on what ground the Translator identified one of the Kuśasthalís with Kuśávatí. See Vol. II., p. 172, note ‡.

¶ He reads—IX., XII., 1,—Nabha, in its stead:

कुशस्य चातिथिस्तस्मान्निषधस्तत्सुतो नभः ।

And Nabha's son is Puńdaríka.

pátra;* his son was Dala;[1]† his son was Chhala;[2]‡ his son was Uktha;[3]§ his son was Vajranábha; his son

pendently of variations of individual names. Instead of the list of the text, with which the Váyu and Bhágavata nearly, and the Brahma and Hari Vaméa indifferently, conform, we have, in the Matysa, Linga, Kúrma, and Agni, the following: Ahinagu,|| Sahasráśwa (Sahásráya, or Sahasrabala),¶ Chandrávaloka, Tárápíḍa (or Táráḍhíśa), Chandragiri, Bhánuratha (or Bhánumitra),** and Srutáyus, with whom the list ends, except in the Linga, which adds Báhula,†† killed by Abhimanyu: enumerating, therefore, from Devánika, but seven or eight princes, to the Great War, instead of twenty-three, as in the other series. The Raghu Vaméa gives much the same list as our text, ending with Agnivarńa.‡‡

[1] Bala: Bhágavata. Nala: Hari Vaméa.

[2] Sthala: Bhágavata. Śala:§§ Váyu and Brahma. Śila: Raghu Vaméa.||||

[3] Omitted: Bhágavata.¶¶

* My MSS. leave it very dubious whether the name is Páripátra or Páriyátra. There are two mountain-ranges, one imaginary, and the other real, regarding which there is, likewise, uncertainty as to the name being Páripátra or Páriyátra. See Vol. II., p. 123, note ‡; p. 128, notes, 1. 6.

† A single MS. gives Bala.

‡ I find Śala in one MS.

§ The *Harivamśa*, *sl.* 825, 826, has Ahinagu, Sudhanwan, Śala, Uktha. For Śala I find Nala and Gaya, in some MSS.

|| In some MSS. of the *Linga-puráńa* the name is Ahinara.

¶ Here, I believe, the *Linga-puráńa* inserts Śubha.

** Bhánuchandra seems to be the reading of the *Linga-puráńa*.

†† I find Bŕihadbala.

‡‡ *Vide infra*, p. 384, note ||.

§§ My MSS. of the *Váyu-puráńa* have Bala.

|||| Not so. The *Raghuvamśa*, XVIII., 17, make Śila son of Páriyátra, and mentions no one corresponding to Chhala.

¶¶ The *Raghuvamśa* has Unnábha, son of Śila. The *Váyu-puráńa* seems to exhibit Anka.

was Śankhanábha;[1]* his son was Dhyushitáśwa;[2]† his

[1] Śankha: Brahma.‡ Khagaṅa: Bhágavata.§

[2] Dúshitáśwa: Váyu. Adhyúshitáśwa:‖ Brahma. Vidhṛiti: Bhágavata.

* One MS. gives Śankhaṅa; one, Chhampaṅa.

† By the kindness of Professor Monier Williams, of Oxford, I am enabled to state, that one of the MSS. of the text of the *Vishńu-puráńa* which formerly belonged to Professor Wilson has तस्माद्ध्युषिताश्वः, *i. e.*, Adhyushitáśwa; another, ततो ध्युषिताश्वः, the same name, or else Dhyushitáśwa; another, ततो व्युत्थिताश्वः, *i. e.*, Vyutthitáśwa, or Avyutthitáśwa. Again, all Professor Wilson's and all my own MSS. that contain both the text and the commentary here read ततो व्युत्थिताश्वः; while my other MSS.—except one which has ततो ध्युषिताश्वः,—give तस्माद्ध्युषिताश्वः or शङ्खणाद्व्युषिताश्वः, *i. e.*, Dhyushitáśwa and Vyushitáśwa. Dhyushitáśwa is the name—corrupted, in some copies, into Vyushitáśwa,—in the *Váyu-puráńa*, where we read:

शङ्खणस्य सुतो विद्वान्ध्युषिताश्व इति श्रुतः ।
ध्युषिताश्वसुतश्चापि राजा विश्वसहः किल ॥

In the *Harivaṃśa*, likewise, the true reading, as shown by my best MSS., is, undoubtedly, Dhyushitáśwa. This has been corrupted into Vyushitáśwa, and regularized into Adhyushitáśwa. Vyutthitáśwa looks like a heedless and uninquiring venture at emendation, on the part of the commentator on the *Vishńu-puráńa*.

Conclusively, we find, in the *Raghuvaṃśa*, XVIII., 23:

तस्यावसाने हरिदश्वधामा
पित्र्यं प्रपेदे पदमश्विरूपः ।
वेलातटेषूषितसैनिकाश्वं
पुराविदो यं ध्युषिताश्वमाहुः ॥

"On his [Śankhaṅa's] death, one endued with the effulgence of the sun, handsome as the Aświns, *and* whom those conversant with antiquity call Dhyushitáśwa,—the horses *of his* troops having encamped on the declivity of the sea-shore,—acceded to the dignity of *his* fathers."

My best MSS. of the *Raghuvaṃśa* read as above; and the best MSS. of Mallinátha's commentary that I have access to give, likewise, Dhyushitáśwa. Moreover, from a grammatical point of view, Kálidása's very etymology, and, similarly, Mallinátha's gloss, unquestionably favour this name, as against Vyushitáśwa.

The strange, but not unjustifiable, name Dhyushitáśwa would naturally

son was Viśwasaha;[1]* his son was Hirańyanábha,† who was a pupil of the mighty Yogin Jaimini, and communicated the knowledge of spiritual exercises‡ to Yájnavalkya.[2] The son of this saintly king was

---

[1] Omitted: Brahma and Bhágavata.

[2] Omitted: Brahma and Hari Vaḿśa; but included, with similar particulars, by the Váyu,§ Bhágavata, and Raghu Vaḿśa.

---

provoke, to a careless scholar, a surmise of mistake; and the close resemblance between ध्यु and व्यु, hastily written, may have seemed to support such a surmise. We thus see how, in all likelihood, Vyushitáśwa originated.

"Abhyutthitáśwa", the name in the former edition of the work under annotation, is in none of the MSS. that were used by Professor Wilson; and I have dismissed it for Dhyushitáśwa. It may be added, that Vyutthitáśwa is the name in the translation of the *Vishńu-puráńa* that was prepared for the Professor in Bengal.

Messrs. Boehtlingk and Roth, in their *Sanskrit-Wörterbuch*, referring to Professor Lassen,—who confessedly copies from Professor Wilson,—insert Adhyushitáśwa, an unavowed alteration of Adhyúshitáśwa.

Turning, for comparison, to the *Sanskrit Dictionary* of Dr. Goldstücker, we here find that very critical work not only scrupulously holding with Professor Wilson, even to his long and short vowels, but doing so in silence, and, manifestly, without any care of verification. Abhyutthitáśwa is registered; and equally is Adhyúshitáśwa,—a name I have found nowhere,—for the constituent participle of which, rendered "very diseased," recourse is had to the verb *úsh*, *aegrotare*, a mere invention, there is reason to suspect, of the grammarians. At the same time, Kálidása's word should seem to have escaped the observation of the learned and researchful lexicographer.

‡ And *Harivaḿśa*. § Śankhana: *Váyu-puráńa* and *Raghuvaḿśa*.

‖ On this and "Dushitáśwa", see note † in the preceding page and the present.

* And so reads the *Váyu-puráńa*.

† In one view, the *Bhágavata-puráńa*, IX., XII., 2, 3, has, instead of Ahinagu, &c., Aniha, Páriyátra, Bala, Sthala, Vajranábha, Khagańa, Vidhŕiti, Hirańyanábha.

‡ The expression "knowledge of spiritual exercises" is to render *yoga*.

§ Premising the name of Viśwasaha, the *Váyu-puráńa* states:

हिरण्यनाभः कौसल्यो वसिष्ठस्तत्सुतोऽभवत् ।

Hirańyanábha seems, thus, to be called the Vasishtha of Kośala. But

Pushya;* his son was Dhruvasandhi;¹ his son was

See, also, p. 58, *supra*, where Kauśalya is, likewise, given as the synonym of Hiraṇyanábha;† being, as the commentator observes, his Viśeshaṇam, his epithet or attribute,—born in, or king of, Kośala. The Váyu, accordingly, terms him हिरण्यनाभः कौशल्यः; but, in the Bhágavata,‡ the epithet Kauśalya is referred, by the commentator,§ to Yájnavalkya, the pupil of Hiraṇyanábha: यतः सकाशाद्याज्ञवल्क्यो याज्ञवल्क्य ऋषिर्हिरण्यनाभाद् योगमध्यगात् । The author of the Raghu Vaṁśa, not understanding the meaning of the term, has converted Kauśalya into the son of Hiraṇyanábha.‖ Raghu Vaṁśa, XVIII., 27. The Bhágavata, like our text, calls the prince the pupil of Jaimini; the Váyu, more correctly, जैमिनेः पौत्रस्य शिष्यः, 'the pupil of the sage's grandson'. There seems to be, however, something unusual in the account given of the relation, borne by the individuals named, to each other. As a pupil of Jaimini, Hiraṇyanábha is a teacher of the Sáma-veda (*vide supra*, p. 58); but Yájnavalkya is the teacher of the Vájasaneyi branch of the Yajus (*vide supra*, p. 57). Neither of them

---

some MSS. have Kauśilya, not Kauśalya. *Vide supra*, p. 58, note †.

Then follows the stanza:

पौत्रस्य जैमिनेः शिष्यः स्मृतः सर्वेषु धर्मसु ।
शतानि संहितानां तु पञ्च योऽधीतवांस्ततः ॥

Here, as before, Hiraṇyanábha is associated with five hundred *Saṁhitás*.

* In the *Harivaṁśa*, *ll*. 827, 828, we find Dhyushitáśwa, and then Pushya.

† Corrected from "Hiraṇyagarbha", a mere slip of the pen.

‡ IX., XII., 4:

शिष्यः कौशल्य अध्यात्मं याज्ञवल्क्योऽध्यगाद्यतः ।
योगं महोदयमृषिर्हृदयग्रन्थिभेदकम् ॥

"C'est de ce maître que le Richi Yâdjnavalkya, qui était né dans le Kôçala, apprit le Yôga de l'Esprit suprême, ce Yôga qui donne des facultés si puissantes, et qui tranche le lien du cœur."

§ Śrídhara.

‖ The *Raghuvaṁśa*, proceeding, makes Kauśalya father of Brahmishṭha; him, father of Putra; and him, father of Pushya.

Sudarśana; his son was Agnivarńa; his son was Śighra; his son was Maru,[2] who, through the power of devotion (Yoga), is still living in the village called Kalápa,* and, in a future age, will be the restorer of the Kshattriya race in the solar dynasty.† Maru had a son named Prasuśruta; his son was Susandhi;‡ his son was Amarsha;§ his son was Mahaswat;[3] his son was Viśrutavat;[4]|| and his son was Bŕihadbala,¶ who was killed, in the

---

is specified, by Mr. Colebrooke, amongst the authorities of the Pátanjala or Yoga philosophy; nor does either appear as a disciple of Jaimini, in his character of founder of the Mimáńsá school. Transactions of the Royal Asiatic Society, Vol. I.**

[1] Arthasiddhi: Brahma Puráńa and Hari Vańśa.

[2] Maruta: Brahma Puráńa and Hari Vańśa. These authorities†† omit the succeeding four names.

[3] Sahaswat: Váyu.

[4] Viśwasáhwan:‡‡ Bhágavata.

---

* The *Harivańśa* has Kalápadwípa; some MSS. reading Káliyadwípa. For the situation of the village of Kalápa, *vide supra*, p. 197, note §.

† आगामियुगे सूर्यवंशक्षत्रप्रवर्तयिता भविष्यति। The *Váyu-puráńa* seems to declare, that he will reestablish the Kshattras in the nineteenth coming *yuga*:

एकोनविंशयुगे क्षत्रप्रवर्तकः प्रभुः।

Some MSS. read एकोनत्रिंश, 'twenty-ninth.'

‡ All my MSS. but two—showing Sasandhi,—have Sugavi. Sandhi is the reading of the *Bhágavata-puráńa*, IX., XII., 7. The *Váyu-puráńa* has Susandhi, distinctly.

§ Amarshańa: *Bhágavata-puráńa*.

|| One MS. has Viśwaváha.

¶ The *Bhágavata-puráńa*, IX., XII., 7, 8, names Viśwasáhwan, Prasenajit, Takshaka, Bŕihadbala.

** Or Colebrooke's *Miscellaneous Essays*, Vol. I., pp. 230—238, 206.

†† *Harivańśa*, *ll*. 829, 830.

‡‡ Corrected from "Viśwasaha."

Great War,* by Abhimanyu, the son of Arjuna.† These are the most distinguished princes in the family of Ikshwáku. Whoever listens to the account of them will be purified from all his sins.[1]:

---

[1] The list closes here; as the author of the Puráṇas, Vyása, is contemporary with the Great War. The line of Ikshwáku is resumed, prophetically, in the twenty-second chapter.

---

* *Bhárata-yuddha.*

† The former edition had "Anjuna", by error of the press.

: एते हीक्ष्वाकुभूपालाः प्राधान्येन मयोदिताः ।
एतेषां चरितं शृण्वन्सर्वपापैः प्रमुच्यते ॥

CHAPTER V.

Kings of Mithilá. Legend of Nimi, the son of Ikshwáku. Birth of Janaka. Sacrifice of Síradhwaja. Origin of Sítá. Descendants of Kuśadhwaja. Kriti the last of the Maithila princes.

THE son of Ikshwáku, who was named Nimi,[1] instituted a sacrifice that was to endure for a thousand years, and applied to Vasisht́ha to offer the oblations.* Vasisht́ha, in answer, said, that he had been preengaged, by Indra, for five hundred years, but that, if the Raja would wait for some time, he would come and officiate as superintending priest.† The king made no answer; and Vasisht́ha went away, supposing that he had assented.‡ When the sage had completed the performance of the ceremonies he had conducted for Indra, he returned, with all speed, to Nimi, purposing to render him the like office. When he arrived, however, and found that Nimi had retained Gautama and other priests to minister at his sacrifice, he was much displeased, and pronounced upon the king, who was then asleep, a curse, to this effect, that, since he had not intimated his intention, but transferred to Gautama the duty he had first entrusted to himself, Vasisht́ha, Nimi

---

[1] None of the authorities, except the Váyu and Bhágavata, contain the series of kings noticed in this chapter.

---

* "Chose Vasisht́ha as the *hotri*," literally.

† *Ritwij.*

‡ Here the scholiast quotes a proverb, मौनं संमतिलक्षणम्, which may be translated, almost word for word, "Silence implies consent."

should, thenceforth, cease to exist in a corporeal form. When Nimi woke, and knew what had happened, he, in return, denounced, as an imprecation upon his unjust preceptor, that he, also, should lose his bodily existence, as the punishment of uttering a curse upon him, without previously communicating with him. Nimi then abandoned his bodily condition. The spirit of Vasishtha, also, leaving his body, was united with the spirits of Mitra and Varuńa, for a season, until, through their passion for the nymph Urvaśí, the sage was born again, in a different shape.* The corpse of Nimi was preserved from decay, by being embalmed with fragrant oils and resins; and it remained as entire as if it were immortal.[1]† When the sacrifice was concluded,

---

[1] This shows that the Hindus were not unacquainted with the Egyptian art of embalming dead bodies. In the Káśí Khańda, s. 30, an account is given of a Brahman who carries his mother's bones, or, rather, her corpse, from Setubandha (or Rámeśwara) to Káśí. For this purpose, he first washes it with the five excretions‡ of a cow, and the five pure fluids, (or, milk, curds, ghee, honey, and sugar).§ He then embalms it with Yakshakardama||

---

* For a more literal rendering of this sentence, see *Original Sanskrit Texts*, Part I., pp. 73, 74. The notes in the latter page may, also, be consulted to advantage.

† निमेरपि तच्छरीरमतिमनोहरगन्धतैलादिभिरुपसंस्क्रियमाणं नैव क्लेदादिकं दोषमवाप । सद्यो मृतमिव तस्थौ । The whole of this paragraph would admit of being much more closely Englished.

‡ They can hardly be generalized as "excretions". For particulars, see note ** to p. 193, *supra*.

§ So says Raghunandana, in the *Jyotistattwa*.

|| According to Colebrooke, in his edition of the *Amara-kosha*, it consists of "camphor, agallochum, musk, and bdellium (or else the three first, with saffron and sandal-wood), in equal proportions."

the priests applied to the gods, who had come to receive their portions, that they would confer a blessing upon the author of the sacrifice. The gods were willing to restore him to bodily life; but Nimi declined its acceptance, saying: "O deities, who are the alleviators of all worldly suffering, there is not, in the world, a deeper cause of distress than the separation of soul and body. It is, therefore, my wish to dwell in the eyes of all beings, but never more to resume a corporeal shape." To this desire the gods assented; and Nimi was placed, by them, in the eyes of all living creatures; in consequence of which, their eyelids are ever opening and shutting.*

(a composition of agallochum, camphor, musk, saffron, sandal, and a resin called Kakkola), and envelopes it, severally, with Netra vastra (flowered muslin), Paṭṭámbara (silk), Surasa vastra (coarse cotton), Mánjishṭhavásas † (cloth dyed with madder), and Nepála Kambala (Nepal blanketing). He then covers it with pure clay, and puts the whole into a coffin of copper (Támra sampuṭaka).‡ These practices are not only unknown, but would be thought impure, in the present day.

---

* ततो भूतान्युन्मेषनिमेषं चक्रुः । This legend would connect the word nimisha, 'wink', with the name of Nimi.

† Corrected from "Mánjishṭha", which means only "dyed with madder".

‡ धर्मज्ञोऽपि धर्मात्मा मातृभक्तिपरायणः ।
चाहृत्याक्षीण्यथो मातुर्भक्त्या मार्गितोऽभवत् ॥
पञ्चगव्येन संस्नाप्य ततः पञ्चामृतेन वै ।
यक्षकर्दमलेपेन लिप्त्वा पुष्पैः प्रपूज्य च ॥
वासेभ्य नेत्रवस्त्रेण ततो माञ्जिष्ठवाससा ।
नेपालकम्बलेनाथ मृदा चाथ विशुद्धया ।
ताम्रसंपुटके कृत्वा मातुरङ्गान्यसौ पचेत् ॥

In the text of my MS., paṭṭámbara and surasavastra do not appear; but the latter is given as a gloss on netravastra.

As Nimi left no successor, the Munis, apprehensive of the consequences of the earth being without a ruler, agitated the body of the prince,* and produced, from it, a prince, who was called Janaka, from being born without a progenitor.† In consequence of his father being without a body (videha), he was termed, also, Vaideha (the son of the bodiless); and (he, further, received the name of) Mithi, from (having been produced by) agitation (mathana).[1] The son of Janaka was Udá-

---

[1] These legends are intended to explain, and were, probably, suggested by, the terms Videha‡ and Mithilá, applied to the country upon the Gunduk and Coosy§ rivers, the modern Tirhoot. The Rámáyańa‖ places a prince named Mithi between Nimi and

---

* अपुत्रस्य तस्य भूभुजः शरीरमराजकभीरवस्ते मुनयोऽरण्यां ममन्थुः ।
All my MSS. have अरण्यां, by which we are to understand the nether piece of timber used to produce fire, by attrition, at sacrifices,—the *arańi* containing a socket, into which the king's body was introduced, by way of upper *arańi*. On the reading अरण्या, things would be reversed, and a socket for the upper *arańi* would be furnished in the royal corpse.

The *Váyu-puráńa* says:

तस्य पुत्रो मिथिर्नाम जनितः पर्वभिस्त्रिभिः ।
अरण्यां मथ्यमानायां प्रादुर्भूतो महायशाः ।
नाम्ना मिथिरिति ख्यातो जननाज्जनकोऽभवत् ॥

A very complete dissertation on the *arańi* will be found in Dr. Goldstücker's *Sanskrit Dictionary*, *sub voce*.

† तत्र च कुमारो जज्ञे । जननाज्जनकसंज्ञां चावाप । It was by reason of the peculiar way in which he was engendered, that he was called Janaka.

The *Bhágavata-puráńa*, IX., XIII., 13, says:

जन्मना जनकः सोऽभूद्वैदेहस्तु विदेहजः ।

"On l'appela Djanaka à cause de la manière dont il était né", *etc.*

‡ Corrected from "Vaideha". See Vol. II., p. 165.

§ For these two rivers, see Vol. II., p. 146, note 3.

‖ *Bála-káńda*, LXX., 4.

vasu;* his son was Nandivardhana; his son was Suketu;† his son was Devaráta; his son was Bŕihadukṭha;‡ his son was Mahávírya;§ his son was Satyadhŕiti;|| his son was Dhŕishṭaketu; his son was Haryaśwa; his son was Maru; his son was Pratibandhaka;¶ his son was Kŕitaratha;** his son was Kŕita;†† his son was Vi-

Janaka, whence comes the name Mithilá. In other respects, the list of kings of Mithilá agrees, except in a few names. Janaka, the successor of Nimi, is different from Janaka who is celebrated as the father of Sítá. One of them—which, does not appear,—is, also, renowned as a philosopher, and patron of philosophical teachers. Mahábhárata, Moksha Dharma. According to the Váyu Puráńa, Nimi founded a city called Jayanta, near the Áśrama of Gautama.:: The remains of a city called Janakpur, on the northern skirts of the district, are supposed to indicate the site of a city founded by one of the princes so named.

* Two of my MSS. have Udáravasu.

† The majority of my MSS. have Swaketu. But Suketu is the accepted reading, as in the *Rámáyańa*, *Bála-káńḍa*, LXXI., 5, 6; &c. &c.

‡ Bŕihadratha: *Rámáyańa*.

§ Mahávíra: *Rámáyańa*.

|| Two MSS. give Sudhŕiti, the reading of the *Rámáyańa* and *Váyu-puráńa*. The *Bhágavata-puráńa* exhibits Sudhŕiti and Sudhŕit in one and the same stanza.

¶ In one copy I find Pratíka. Pratindhaka is read in the *Rámáyańa* and *Váyu-puráńa*, and is, almost certainly, the correct name. Pratipaka is the *Bhágavata's* ordinary corruption. The Bengal *Rámáyańa* has, according to Signor Gorresio, Prasiddhaka.

** One MS. has Kŕitiratha; another, Śrutiratha. Kírttiratha is the reading of the *Rámáyańa* and *Váyu-puráńa*. The Bengal *Rámáyańa* has Kŕittiratha, in Signor Gorresio's edition.

†† I find Kŕiti. The *Rámáyańa*, the *Váyu-puráńa*, and the *Bhágavata* have Devamíḍha.

:: सोऽसौ निमिश्चकाराथ पुरं देवपुरोपमम् ।
जयन्तमिति विख्यातं गौतमस्याश्रमाभितः ॥

budha;* his son was Mahádhriti;† his son was Kritiráta;‡ his son was Mahároman;§ his son was Suvarńaroman;|| his son was Hraswaroman; his son was Síradhwaja.

Síradhwaja ploughing the ground, to prepare it for a sacrifice (which he instituted), in order to obtain progeny, there sprung up, in the furrow,¶ a damsel, who became his daughter, Sítá.[1]** The brother of Síradhwaja

---

[1] This identifies Síradhwaja with the second Janaka, the father-in-law of Ráma. The story of Sítá's birth, or, rather, discovery, is narrated in the Árańya Káńda of the Rámáyańa, the Vana Parvan of the Mahábhárata, and in the Váyu, Brahma Vaivarta, Káliká, and other Puráńas.

---

* Vidrata is the name in the *Bhágavata-puráńa*.

† The *Váyu-puráńa* shows both this and Dhriti. One of them is, perhaps, for the sake of metre. *Vide infra*, p. 335, note †. The *Rámáyańa* seems to have Mahídhraka, corrupted, in some copies, into Mahíndhraka; while the Bengal recension has Andhaka.

‡ Kraturáta occurs in one MS. Kírttiráta: *Rámáyańa* and *Váyu-puráńa*.

§ The inferior character of the Bengal recension of the *Rámáyańa* is evidenced by the fact that it here reads, at variance with all authority, Kritiroman.

|| A single copy has Swarńaroman, the synonymous reading of the *Rámáyańa*, of the *Váyu-puráńa*, and of the *Bhágavata*.

¶ *Sîre*, 'on *his* ploughshare'; for which the word for 'plough' seems to be here used by synecdoche. In the *Bhágavata-puráńa*, IX., 13, 18, we read as follows:

सीता सीराग्रतो जाता तस्मात्सीरध्वजः स्मृतः ।

** The *Váyu-puráńa*, having named Síradhwaja, says:

सन्निधा कृषतो येन सीता राज्ञा यशस्विनी ।

Śáńśapáyana interrupts with questions, which the other interlocutor, Súta, answers as follows:

वर्षिचैवे क्षत्रमार्गे यज्ञमेधे महात्मनः ।

विधिना शुभक्षेत्रेण तस्मात्तामुपसुत्थिता ॥

was Kuśadhwaja, who was king of Káśí:[1]* he† had a son, also, named Bhánumat.[2] The son of Bhánumat was Śatadyumna;‡ his son was Śuchi;§ his son was Úrjaváha;|| his son was Satyadhwaja;¶ his son was

---

[1] The Rámáyańa** says, 'of Sánkáśyá',†† which is, no doubt, the correct reading.‡‡ Fa Hian found the kingdom of Sang-kia-shi in the Doab, about Mainpooree.§§ Account of the Foe-kúe-ki.|||| The Bhágavata makes Kuśadhwaja the son of Síradhwaja.¶¶

[2] The Bhágavata differs from our authority, here, considerably, by inserting several princes between Kuśadhwaja and Bhánumat; or, Dharmadhwaja, who has two sons, Kritadhwaja and Khándikya: the former is the father of Keśidhwaja; the latter, of Bhánumat.*** See the last Book of the Vishńu.

---

* The text of all my MSS. but two has साङ्काश्याधिपतिः, 'king of Sánkáśyá'. And herewith agrees the *Váyu-puráńa*. See the quotation in note ***, below. I have corrected the Translator's "Sankaśya".

† Namely, Síradhwaja.

‡ One MS. gives Sudyumna. Pradyumna: *Váyu-puráńa*.

§ In the *Váyu-puráńa* the name is Muni.

|| Or the equivalent Úrjavaha, in some copies; as in the *Váyu*. One MS. has Úrja.

¶ Variants, each in one MS.: Śatadhwaja and Bharadwája.

** *Bála-káńda*, LXXI., 19. Just before, the *Rámáyańa* states that Kuśadhwaja conquered Sánkáśyá from Sudhanwan.

†† And so reads the *Váyu-puráńa*. See note ***, below.

‡‡ See the note next following.

§§ For Sánkáśyá, its site, &c., see the *Journal of the Asiatic Society of Bengal*, 1865, Part I., pp. 195—203.

|||| See the *Journal of the Royal Asiatic Society*, Vol. V., p. 121.

¶¶ See the next note.

*** This requires correcting. According to the *Bhágavata-puráńa*, IX., XIII., 19—21, Síradhwaja begot Kuśadhwaja; he, Dharmadhwaja; he, Kritadhwaja and Mitadhwaja; Kritadhwaja, Keśidhwaja; Mitadhwaja, Khándikya; Keśidhwaja, Bhánumat.

But the *Vishńu-puráńa* has the support of the *Váyu-puráńa*, with regard to the relationship between Síradhwaja, Kuśadhwaja, and Bhánumat:

सीरध्वजात्तु जातस्तु भानुमान्नाम मैथिलः ।
भ्राता कुशध्वजस्तस्य साङ्काश्याधिपतिर्नृपः ॥

Kuńi;[1]* his son was Anjana;† his son was Ritujit;‡ his son was Arishṭanemi;[2] his son was Śrutáyus;§ his son was Supárśwa;|| his son was Sanjaya;[3] his son was Kshemári;[4]¶ his son was Anenas;[5] his son was Mínaratha;[6]** his son was Satyaratha; his son was Sátyarathi;[7] his son was Upagu;[8]†† his son was Śruta;[9] his son was Śáśwata;[10] his son was Sudhanwan;‡‡ his son was Subhása;§§ his son was Suśruta;[11] his son was

---

[1] Śakuni; and the last of the series, according to the Váyu.||

[2] Between this prince and Śuchi the series of the Bhágavata is: Sanadhwaja, Úrdhwaketu, Aja, Purajit.¶¶ The following variations are from the same authority.

[3] Chitraratha.

[4] Kshemádhi.***

[5] Omitted.

[6] Samaratha.

[7] Omitted.

[8] Upaguru.

[9] Upagupta.

[10] Vaswananta.

[11] Yuyodhan,††† Subháshańa, Śruta.

---

* The *Váyu-puráńa* has Śakuni; and then follow Swágata, Suvarchas, Sutoya, Suśruta, Jaya, &c.

† In one copy, Arjuna.

‡ Kratujit, in two MSS.; Kuntijit, in one.

§ A single MS. gives Śatáyus.

|| Supárśwaka, the longer form, in the *Bhágavata-puráńa*.

¶ One MS. has Kshemádhi; another has Kshemavat, followed by Váramatha, after whom comes Sátyarathi.

** One copy has Mánaratha. Also see the last note.

†† In one MS. the name is Upagupta. In another MS., which I purchased at Ajmere, occur Upagu, Upagupta, Upayuta, Swága (Swágata?), Suvarchas, Supárśwa, Suśruta, Jaya, &c. Compare note *, above.

‡‡ Vasuvarchas, in one copy.

§§ One MS. gives Subhávya.

|| See note *, above.

¶¶ Corrected from "Purujit".

*** Corrected from "Kshemadhi".

††† Corrected from "Yuyudhána".

Jaya; his son was Vijaya; his son was Ŕita;* his son was Sunaya;[1] his son was Vítahavya; his son was Dhŕiti;† his son was Bahuláśwa; his son was Kŕiti,‡ with whom terminated the family of Janaka. These are the kings of Mithilá, who, for the most part,§ will be|| proficient in spiritual knowledge.[3]

---

[1] Śunaka.

[2] आत्मविद्याश्रयिणो भविष्यन्ति । is the reading of all the copies; but why the future verb, 'will be', is used does not appear.

[3] Descendants of two of the other sons of the Manu are noticed in the Bhágavata. From Nŕiga, it is said, proceeded Sumati, Bhútajyotis, Vasu, Pratíka, Oghavat, and his sister Oghavatí, married to Sudarśana.¶ The Linga** gives three sons to Nŕiga,—Vŕisha, Dhŕishtaka, and Rańadhŕishta,†† and alludes to a legend of his having been changed to a lizard, by the curse of a Brahman. Narishyanta's descendants‡‡ were Chitrasena, Daksha, Madhwat,§§ Púrva, Indrasena, Vítihotra, Satyaśravas, Uruśravas,

---

* Kŕita seems to be the name in the *Váyu-puráńa*.

† The *Váyu-puráńa* seems to place, here, Manodhŕiti, whom it forthwith calls Dhŕiti. Perhaps the first name is a lengthening of the second, to fill out the line. *Vide supra*, p. 332, note †. One of my MSS. of the *Vishńu-puráńa*, which I procured from Arrah, gives, instead of Vítahavya, Dhŕitahavya, followed by Sanjaya, Jhasáśwa, Dhŕiti.

‡ The *Bhágavata-puráńa* gives him a son, Vaśin.

§ *Práchuryeńa*, 'abundantly'.

|| One of my MSS. has the present, भवन्ति; and this tense is implied in the parallel passage of the *Bhágavata-puráńa*.

¶ *Bhágavata-puráńa*, IX., II., 17, 18.

** Prior Section, LXVI., 48; where, however, I find Dhŕishta, Dhŕishtaketu, and Rańadhŕishta.

†† It looks as if there were some confusion between these persons and the *Matsya-puráńa*'s sons of Dhŕishta and their father. *Vide supra*, p. 255, note 3.

‡‡ *Bhágavata-puráńa*, IX., II., 19—22.

§§ I find Mídhwas. Professor Wilson's "Madhwat" is, almost certainly, wrong. Pauráńik names that are restrictively so, are, with rare exceptions,

Devadatta, Agnivesya (also called Játukarńa*), a form of Agni, and progenitor of the Ágnivesya Brahmans.† In the Brahma Puráńa and Hari Vaḿśa, the sons of Narishyat—whom the commentator on the latter considers as the same with Narishyanta,‡—are termed Śakas (Sacæ or Scythians); whilst, again, it is said, that the son of Narishyanta was Dama, or, as differently read, Yama. As this latter affiliation is stated in the authorities, it would appear as if this Narishyanta was one of the sons of the Manu: but this is only a proof of the carelessness of the compilation; for, in the Vishńu,§ Váyu, and Márkańdeya Puráńas, Narishyanta, the father of Dama, is the son of Marutta, the fourteenth of the posterity of Dishía or Nedishíha.||

significant. In the generality of instances, it is only when we recede into rather remote antiquity, that there is a difficulty in making Hindu proper names amenable to etymological investigation.

* Likewise called Kánina.

† The Ágniveśyáyanas.

‡ We have, here, only two forms of one name.

§ *Vide supra*, p. 353.

|| Corrected from "Nedishía."

CORRIGENDA, &c.

P. 3, note *. See Vol. II., p. 26, note 2.

P. 4, l. 1. *Read* Úrja.

P. 11, note ‡. See Vol. II., p. 100, note 1. We read, in the *Bhágavata-puráńa*, V., I, 28: अन्यस्यामपि जायायां त्रयः पुत्रा आसन्नुत्त-मस्तामसो रैवत इति मन्वन्तराधिपतयः ।

P. 13, l. 1. *Read* Úru.

P. 13, note §. For the Manu's wife, Śraddhá, see p. 233, note §. The Manu's correct epithet, as Dr. Muir reminds me, is Śráddhadeva, of which Śraddhadeva is a corruption. Śraddhadeva is, however, appropriate to Yama. See *Original Sanskrit Texts*, Part I., p 209, note 66 (2nd ed.). Also see the *Mahábhárata*, *Śánti-parvan*, *ll.* 9449.

P. 13, note ‡‡. *For* Dhrishńu *read* Dhrishnu. See p. 232, note ‡‡, foot of the page.

P. 13, note §§. Burnouf, in his *Bhágavata-puráńa*, Vol. III., Preface, p. CVI., takes the printer's error "Sanyati", in the former edition, for a real reading.

P. 14, note *, end. The commentary there spoken of as ampler than the other is so, I am now convinced, only by interpolations; and these are comparatively rare, after the first few chapters of Book III.

P. 16, note *. Its last sentence may be a misstatement. See note below, on p. 24, note 1.

P. 16, note †. See p. 80, note †.

P. 23, l. 2 *ab infra.* I owe to Dr. Muir the indication of *sávarńya* and *sávarńi* in the *Ŕigveda*, X., LXII., 8—11; and of the Muni Sávarńi, in the same Veda, *Válakhilya*, III., 1. See, further, *Original Sanskrit Texts*, Part I., p. 217, note 71 (2nd ed.).

P. 24, note 1. I am unable to decipher, in any of my MSS. of the *Váyu-puráńa*, the passage there abstracted in translation.

P. 24, l. 3. The ninth Manu and the eleventh are called Dakshaputra and Dharmaputra, in a Pauráńik extract already referred to: see Vol. II., p. 339, supplement to p. 131, note ¶.

P. 26, l. 1. *Read* Ŕishis.

P. 26, l. 6. "Dharma-sávarńi." See supplementary note, just above, on p. 24, l. 3.

P. 28, l. 6. Many particulars regarding the Manus, which I have not incorporated in my annotations, may be found in Messrs. Boehtlingk and Roth's *Sanskrit-Wörterbuch*, *sub voce* मनु.

P. 29, notes, l. 2 *ab infra.* Read *Śánti-parvan.*

P. 34, notes, l. 7. *For* यथा *read* यया.

P. 34, note §. For Vamra, son of Vikhanas, see Professor Wilson's Translation of the *Ŕigveda*, Vol. I., p. 293, note a.

P. 34, notes, last line. *For* Traijáruńi *read* Traiyáruńi.

P. 37, notes, l. 11 *ab infra.* See p. 221, note ‡.

P. 40, notes, l. 11 *ab infra.* *Read* वृषविषस्वम्.

P. 40, notes, l. 9 *ab infra.* Read *paribandha.*

P. 44, notes † and ‡. The commentator on the *Vishńu-puráńa* says: वाचक एव वाचकिः स्वार्थे इञ् ।

P. 52, note †, line 1. *Read* यजुर्वेद्.

P. 56, note †. See p. 323, note §.

P. 63, l. 3. For the technicality *caitána*, see Dr. Stenzler's edition of Áśwaláyana's *Gṛihyasútra*, Part II., p. 1, note 1.

P. 66, note §. See, in explanation of *gáthá*, the same work, Part II., p. 90, III., 1, note 2.

P. 67, l. 1. *Read* Ágneya.

P. 68, l. 3. For the *artha-śástra*, see the *Mitákshará* on the *Yájnavalkya-smṛiti*, II., 21.

P. 84, note †. In the *Matsya-puráńa*, Chapter CXXVIII., the *brahmástra* is represented as shot from a bow.

For Bhṛigu, in connexion with fiery weapons, see p. 291, text and note ‡.

P. 86, l. 4. *Read* Śúdra.

P. 88, notes, l. 6. *Read* ब्राह्मो ऽग्नि.

P. 89, note ‡. In the *Nirńayasindhu*, the passage cited is attributed to Gautama.

P. 90, notes, ll. 6—11. Compare the *Nirńayasindhu*, Bombay edition of 1857, III., B, *fol.* 10 r.

P. 90, notes, l. 2 *ab infra*. *Read* चार्यं.

P. 93, note 2. Sáyańa Áchárya, however, commenting on the *Aitareya-bráhmańa*, VII., IX., cites the following *śruti*: यज देवानधीष्व वेदान्प्रजामुत्पादय । "Sacrifice to the gods, read the Vedas, beget offspring."

See, further, the *Kaushítaki-bráhmańa Upanishad*, and the *Bṛihad-áraṇyaka Upanishad*, VI., IV.

P. 94, note †. See p. 123, note ‖.

P. 98, l. 7 *ab infra*. Compare pp. 146, 147, text and notes.

P. 103, notes, ll. 5, 6. *Read* III., A, *fol.* 30 *v*.

P. 104, notes, last line. See p. 197, note ¶.

P. 107, note ‡. The *Mitákshará*, commenting on the *Yájnavalkya-smṛiti*, I., 7, has: सदाचारः । सतां शिष्टानामाचारो ऽनुष्ठानम् ।

P. 109, note *. For Mitra, &c., see, further, the *Laws of the Mánavas*, XII., 121.

P. 118, ll. 5, *et seq.* See p. 171, note §.

P. 123, notes, l. 9. For *swadhá*, see Professor Wilson's Translation of the *Rigveda*, Vol. I., p. 34, note a.

P. 139, l. 3 *ab infra*. The double asterisks should be attached to the word "towel".

P. 141, note *, l. 12 *ab infra*. *Read* एकमन्यत्र.

P. 146, ll. 1—4. The original is as follows:

सचैलस्य पितुः स्नानं जाते पुत्रे विधीयते ।
जातकर्म तथा कुर्याच्छ्राद्धमभ्युदये च यत् ॥

"When a son is born, the bathing of the father, in his clothes, is enjoined. Let him perform the *játa-karman*, also, and the *śráddha* for joyous occasions."

Compare p. 98, ll. 7—4 *ab infra*, the original of which is as follows:

जातस्य जातकर्मादि क्रियाकाण्डमशेषतः ।
पुत्रस्य कुर्वीत पिता श्राद्धं चाभ्युदयात्मकम् ॥

P. 146, note *. See p. 291, note *.

P. 151, notes, l. 4 *ab infra*. *Read* निवर्तेत चतुर्दशात्.

P. 153, note ‖. Compare the following stanza, referred to the *Kúrma-puráńa*, quoted in the *Nirńayasindhu*, Bombay edition, III., C, *fol.* 15 *v.*:

आपाद्येव चाज्ञानं स्वयमग्न्युदकादिभिः ।
विहितं तस्य नाशौचं नापि कार्योदकक्रिया ॥

P. 156, note ‡‡. See p. 221, note ‡.

P. 159, notes, l. 12 *ab infra*. For विश्रुता: read विश्रुताः.

P. 160, note ‡. See p. 147, notes, l. 1.

P. 161, notes, l. 3. *Read* Attáñ.

P. 162, note ‡, l. 1. *Read* बर्हिषदां.

P. 166, note ‡. Hemádri's quotations from the *Nandi-puráńa* are, I find, too incorrect to be transcribed. They recognize five classes of *pitris*: Agnishwáttas, Barhishads, Kávyas, Sukálins, and Vyámas. The *Nágara-khańda* of the *Skanda-puráńa* names six classes: Agnishwáttas, Barhishads, Ájyapas, Somapas, Raśmipas, and Upahútas. In the *Vishńudharmottara* we find seven classes, in two groups: Subháswaras, Barhishads, Agnishwáttas, without form; Kravyádas, Upahútas, Ájyapas, Sukálins, possessing forms. The *Śráddhakalpa*, from which these particulars are taken, is very full on the subject of the *pitris*.

The *Vahni-puráńa* reckons seven classes of *pitris*, entitled Subháswaras, Barhishads, Agnishwáttas, Ájyapas, Upahútas, Kravyádas, and Sukálins. It agrees, thus, precisely, with the *Vishńudharmottara*, as just above referred to.

In the *Mahábhárata*, *Sabhá-parvan*, *ll.* 341, the names are given of classes of *pitris* called, agreeably to the best MSS. within my reach, Phenapas, Ushmapas, and Sudhávats. In *ll.* 461—463, seven classes are enumerated: Vairájas, Agnishwáttas, Gárhapatyas, Somapas, Ekaśŕingas, Chaturvedas, and Kalas:

पितॄणां च गणान्विद्धि सप्तैव पुरुषर्षभ ।
मूर्तिमन्तो हि चत्वारस्त्रयश्चाप्यशरीरिणः ॥
वैराजाश्च महाभागा अग्निष्वात्ताश्च भारत ।
गार्हपत्या नाकचराः पितरो लोकविश्रुताः ॥
सोमपा एकशृङ्गाश्च चतुर्वेदाः कलास्तथा ।
एते चतुर्षु वर्णेषु पूज्यन्ते पितरो नृप ॥

The last-named classes are said to be honoured among the four castes. Compare p. 163, note †.

In the *Rigveda*, X., XIV. and XV., we read of the Kavyas, Barhishads, Agnishwáttas, Upahútas, &c. &c.; and—compare p. 166, note *,—the distinction is, thus early, made of *pitris* into the divisions of Agnidagdhas and Anagnidagdhas.

To exhaust the subject of these demigods, or even to collect all the more ancient passages in which they figure, would require considerable research.

In the *Váyu-puráña*, the origin of the *pitris* is stated as follows:

पितृवन्मन्यमानस्तान्पुत्रान्प्राध्यायत प्रभुः ।
पितरो ह्युपपक्षाभ्यां रात्र्यह्नोरन्तरासृजत् ॥
तस्मात्ते पितरो देवाः पुत्रत्वं तेन तेषु तत् ।
यया सृष्टास्तु पितरस्तां तनुं स व्यपोहत ॥

"Regarding himself as a father, he [Prajápati] thought upon these sons: he created Fathers (*Pitris*) from his armpits, in the interval between day and night. Hence these Fathers are gods: therefore that sonship belongs to them. He cast aside the body with which the Fathers were created." *Original Sanskrit Texts*, Part I., pp. 78, 79. (2nd ed.).

P. 170, note ||. In p. 66, note §, the *Pitri-gítá* is instanced as a specimen of a *gáthá*.

P. 175, note §. For further information regarding the sacrificial fires, see Śankara Áchárya's commentary on the fourth chapter of the *Praśna Upanishad*.

P. 184, notes, last line. *For* त सुख *read* तं सुखं.

P. 188, l. 2 *Read* Śráddha.

P. 190, l. 15. The work there named seems to be entitled, in preference, *Vahni-puráña*.

P. 190, l. 18. *Read* दोषकषाद्वादिव.

P. 194, note **, l. 1. Read *priyangu*.

P. 196, note ||. Compare p. 130, note *.

P. 198, notes, l. 9. *Read* vague sense.

P. 205, ll. 6 *et seq. ab infra*. The original is as follows:

नैवोक्तं यज्ञभागाश्च दैविध्याद्पुरोगमैः ।
इति नो मन्मथोऽप्याज्ञानुगश्च परमेश्वर ॥
यज्ञस्यैकभूतस्य यथं ते च तथांशकाः ।
तथाप्यविद्याभेदेन भिन्नं पश्यामहे जगत् ॥

P. 209, note 1. Were the Sáptatantavas a sect of Jainas? They are named, as are the Jainas, in the *Harshacharita*. See my edition of the *Vásavadattá*, Preface, p. 53.

P. 215, notes, l. 2 *ab infra*. Triśanku, the Buddhist, uses the following language regarding Bráhmans: "Quand ils veulent manger de la viande, voici le moyen qu'ils emploient: ils tuent les animaux en prononçant des Mantras, parce que, disent-ils, les brebis ainsi immolées vont droit au ciel. Mais si c'est là le chemin du ciel, pourquoi donc ces Bráhmanes n'immolent-ils pas aussi avec des Mantras eux et leurs femmes, leur père et leur mère, leurs frères et leurs sœurs, leurs fils et leurs filles? * * * Non, il n'est pas vrai que l'eau lustrale et que les Mantras fassent monter au ciel les chèvres et les brebis; toutes ces inventions sont des moyens employés par ces méchants Bráhmanes pour satisfaire leur désir de manger de la viande." Burnouf's *Introduction à l'Histoire du Buddhisme Indien*, Vol. I., p. 209.

P. 221, notes, l. 6. *Read* स भोगान् and संभोगान्.

P. 221, notes, l. 6 *ab infra*. *Read* Triyáraṅi.

P. 230, note ||. See, further, Vol. II., p. 27.

P. 231, note *. The legend of the *Aitareya-bráhmaña*, there referred to, is translated, by Dr. Muir, as follows: "The brothers of Nábhánedishṭha disinherited him, whilst he was living in the state of a Brahmachárin. Coming (to them), he said: 'What share have you given to me?' They replied: '(We have given thee) this judge and divider, (as thy share).' In consequence, sons, even now, speak of their father as the 'judge and divider.' He came to his father, and said: 'Father, they have given thee to me, as my share.' His father answered: 'Do not, my son, care about that. These Angirases are performing a sacrifice, in order to (secure) the heavenly world; but, as often as they come to the sixth day (of the ceremony), they become bewildered. Make them recite these two hymns (R. V., x., 61 and 62) on the sixth day; and, when they are going to heaven, they will give thee that provision of a thousand which has been made for the sacrifice.' He said: 'So be it.' He approached them, saying: 'Receive me, the son of Manu, ye sages.' They replied: 'With what object dost thou speak?' He said: 'Let me make known to you this sixth day: and then you shall give me this sacrificial provision of a thousand, when ye are going to heaven.' 'Let it be so,' they answered. He made them repeat these two hymns on the sixth day. They then knew the sacrifice and the heavenly world. Hence, when any one repeats these two hymns on the sixth day, it is with a view to a knowledge of the sacrifice, and to the revelation of the heavenly world. When they were going to the heavenly world, they said to him: 'This thousand, O Bráhman, is thine.' As he was collecting (the thousand), a man in dark clothing rose up before him, from the north, and said: 'This is mine; what remains on the spot is mine.' Nábhánedishṭha replied: 'But they have given it to me.' (The man) rejoined: 'It belongs to (one of) us; let thy father be asked.' He went to his father, who asked: 'Have they not given thee (the thousand), my son?' 'They did give it to me,' he replied; 'but a man in dark clothes rose up before me, from the north, and took it from me, saying, 'This is mine; what remains on the spot is mine.'' His father said: 'It is his; but he will give it to thee.' He returned, and said (to the man): 'This is thine, reverend sir; so my father says.' (The man) replied: 'I will give it to thee, who hast spoken the truth.' Wherefore one who has this knowledge should speak only truth. That is a hymn which bestows a thousand,—that Nábhánedishṭha hymn. A thousand falls to his lot, he knows the heavenly world on the sixth day—the man who knows this." *Original Sanskrit Texts*, Part I., pp. 192, 193, (2nd ed.).

A relative passage, referred to in p. 257, note †, is then given, from the *Taittiríya-sanhitá* of the *Yajurveda*: "Manu divided his property to his sons. He disinherited his son Nábhánedishṭha, who was living as a Brahmachárin. He came and said: 'How hast thou disinherited me?' 'I have not disinherited thee,' replied (his father); 'these Angirases are celebrating a sacrifice. They do not know the heavenly world. Declare to them this *Bráhmaṇa*; and, when they are going to heaven, they will give thee the cattle they have.' He declared the *Bráhmaṇa* to them; and, when they were going to heaven, they gave him the cattle they had. Rudra came to him, as he was on the place of sacrifice, employed with the cattle, and said: 'These are my cattle.' 'But,' replied Nábhánedishṭha, 'they have given them to me.' 'They have not power to do so: that which is left on the place of sacrifice is mine,' answered Rudra. Hence, the place of sacrifice must not be approached. (Rudra farther) said: 'Give me a share in the sacrifice, and I shall not injure thy cattle.' He offered him this libation of *soma* and flour. Then Rudra did not injure his cattle. Whenever any one knows this libation of *soma* and flour, and offers it up, Rudra does not injure his cattle."

P. 232, notes, l. 6 *ab infra*. According to the *Linga-puráńa*, the Manu's sons were nine; and their names are as in the *Márkańd́eya-puráńa*, saving that Dhrishńu and Arishńa take the places of Dhrishńa and Dishńa. Except for Arishńa instead of Dishńa, the nine names, in the *Brahma-puráńa*, are the same as those in the *Márkańd́eya-puráńa*. The *Váyu-puráńa* gives Manu ten sons, with appellations altogether peculiar, as a whole; and the same may be said of the *Matsya-puráńa*, my MSS. of which here present, for the rest, a good number of various readings.

P. 234, notes, l. 13. *Read* Rámáyańa.

P. 240, notes, last line. *Read* [illegible].

P. 246, note *. See p. 311, note *.

P. 248, note ||. The ensuing legend is taken from the *Śatapatha-bráhmańa*, IV., V., 1, *etc.*: Chyavana of the race of Bhŕigu, or Chyavana of the race of Angiras, having magically assumed a shrivelled form, was abandoned. Śaryáta, the descendant of Manu, wandered over this [world], with his tribe. He sat down in the neighbourhood [of Chyavana]. His youths, while playing, fancied this shrivelled magical body to be worthless, and pounded it with clods. Chyavana was incensed at the sons of Śaryáta. He created discord among them, so that father fought with son, and brother with brother. Śaryáta bethought him, 'what have I done, in consequence of which this calamity has befallen us?' He ordered the cowherds and shepherds to be called, and said, 'which of you has seen anything here to day?' They replied, 'this shrivelled magical body which lies there is a man. Fancying it was something worthless, the youths pounded it with clods.' Śaryáta knew, then, that it was Chyavana. He yoked his chariot, and, taking his daughter Sukanyá, drove off, and arrived at the place where the Ŕishi was. He said, 'Reverence to thee, Ŕishi! I injured thee, because I did not know. This is Sukanyá: with her I appease thee. Let my tribe be reconciled.' His tribe was, in consequence, reconciled; and Śaryáta, of the race of Manu, strove that he might never again do injury to any one. Now, the Aświns used to wander over this world, performing cures. They approached Sukanyá, and wished to seduce her; but she would not come at. They said to her: 'Sukanyá, what shrivelled magical body is this by which thou liest? Follow us.' She replied: 'I will not abandon, while he lives, the man to whom my father gave me.' The Ŕishi became aware of this. He said, 'Sukanyá, what was this that they said to thee?' She told it to him. When informed, he said, 'If they address thee thus again, say to them, 'ye are neither complete nor perfect, and yet ye speak contemptuously of my husband;' and, if they ask 'In what respect are we incomplete and imperfect?' then reply, 'make my husband young again, and I will tell you.' Accordingly, they came again to her, and said the same thing. She answered, 'Ye are neither complete nor perfect, and yet ye talk contemptuously of my husband.' They inquired, 'In what respect are we incomplete and imperfect?' She rejoined, 'make my husband young again, and I will tell you.' They replied, 'take him to this pond, and he shall come forth with any age which he shall desire. She took him to the pond; and he came forth with the age that he desired. The Aświns then asked, 'Sukanyá, in what respect are we incomplete and imperfect?' To this the Ṛishi replied: 'The other gods celebrate a sacrifice in Kurukshetra, and exclude you two from it. That is the respect in which ye are incomplete and imperfect.' The Aświns then departed, and came to the gods who were celebrating a sacrifice, when the *Bahishpavamána* text had been recited. They said, 'Invite us to join you.' The gods replied, 'We will not invite you; for ye have wandered about very familiarly among men, performing cures.' The Aświns rejoined, 'Ye worship with a headless sacrifice.' They asked, 'How [do we worship] with a headless [sacrifice]?' The Aświns answered, 'Invite us to join you, and we will tell you.' The gods consented, and invited them. They offered this Áświna draught (*graha*) to the Aświns, who became the two *adhwaryu* priests of the sacrifice, and restored the head of the sacrifice. It is related, in the Bráhmańa of the Divákírttyas, in what manner they restored the head of the sacrifice," *etc.*, *etc.* Dr. Muir, in the *Journal of the Royal Asiatic Society*, New Series, Vol. II., pp. 11—13.

P. 259, l. 1. The proper name Ikshwáku occurs in the *Ṛigveda*, X., LX., 4., on which Professor Max Müller remarks: "This is the first mention of Ikshwáku, and the only one in the *Ṛigveda*. I take it not as the name of a king, but as the name of a people,—probably, the people who inhabited Bhájeratha, the country washed by the northern Gangá or the Bhágírathí." *Journal of the Royal Asiatic Society*, New Series, Vol. II., p. 462, note 1.

P. 264, note †. *Read* बृहद्वसुनवाणि.

P. 264, note ‡. See p. 319, note 1.

P. 269, note †. *Pṛishṭhatas* rather means, there, 'behind *him*.'

P. 283, notes, l. 7 *ab infra*. *For* note † *read* note ‡. There must be an omission, in the *Váyu-puráńa*, before the verse there quoted from it.

P. 297, note ‡. Another inconsistency of the *Rámáyańa* may be mentioned. In the *Araṅya-káńḍa*, XIV., 8, 9, Maríchi, Kaśyapa, and Vivaswat are spoken of as sons of Brahmá. Elsewhere in the same poem, as we have seen, they are represented as being, respectively, grandfather, father, and son.

P. 308, note ¶. A better rendering is as follows: "With a view to the preservation *from injury* of the grain and the clouds, he threw that water for coming neither on the earth nor into the air," &c.

P. 311, notes, l. 4 *ab infra*. *Read* चीरिवां.

P. 313, note ¶. A special reason for my having declined to enter into particulars as to what is found in the *Matsya-puráńa* is, that the copies of it accessible to me are, for the most part, exceedingly incorrect, and, in the matter of proper names, exhibit the widest discrepancy. I may add, that my MSS. seem to support the list of names to which this note is appended.

P. 315, notes, l. 5 *ab infra*. *Read* Bali.

Berlin, printed by Unger brothers (C. Unger), Printers to the King.

www.ingramcontent.com/pod-product-compliance
Lightning Source LLC
Chambersburg PA
CBHW032048220426
43664CB00008B/913
* 9 7 8 3 7 4 1 1 8 2 7 6 1 *